RENEWALS 458-4574

DATE DUE

APR 7	9·25	DEC 22 2008	
DEC 14	11·23		
~~MAY 10~~			
MAY 10	829		
JUN 24			
	2n		
~~DEC 13~~	400		
FEB 25	3.50		
6·50	MAR 2 0		
6·08	DEC 13		
8·50	AUG 1 2		
4·18	NOV 1 2		
6·51		PRINTED IN U.S.A.	
GAYLORD	DEC 0 9		

Teaching Composition

Teaching Composition

Twelve Bibliographical Essays

Edited by GARY TATE

REVISED AND ENLARGED EDITION

TEXAS CHRISTIAN UNIVERSITY PRESS
Fort Worth

WITHDRAWN
UTSA LIBRARIES

Copyright © 1987 by *Texas Christian University Press*
All rights reserved

Library of Congress Cataloging-in-Publication Data
Teaching composition.

Includes index.
1. English language—Rhetoric—Study and teaching.
2. English language—Rhetoric—Bibliography.
I. Tate, Gary.
PE1404.T39   1987   808'.042'07   86-40376
ISBN 0-87565-069-4 (pbk.)

Design by WHITEHEAD & WHITEHEAD

LIBRARY
The University of Texas
at San Antonio

Contents

Preface

NOWHERE IS THE IMMATURITY OF COMPOSI-
tion studies more evident than in its bibliographical efforts.
When I wrote the Preface to the first edition of this book ten
years ago, I expressed my belief that better bibliographies would
appear in the future. Yet we have seen in the past decade only one
major bibliographical effort come to fruition: Michael G. Moran
and Ronald Lunsford (eds.), *Research in Composition and Rhetoric*
(Westport, Conn.: Greenwood Press, 1984). Excellent as the
Moran and Lunsford collection is, it shares with this revision certain significant weaknesses. Both books are unsystematic and incomplete. They serve the newcomer better than the seasoned
researcher; they are introductions rather than sophisticated research tools. (For an excellent discussion of bibliographical problems in composition studies, see Patrick Scott, "Bibliographical
Problems in Research on Composition," *CCC,* 37 [May
1986], 167–77.)

There have been glimmers of hope in recent years that one of
our professional organizations would initiate and support a systematic annual bibliography in composition studies, but at the
moment there seems to be no movement in that direction. I suspect that one of the major reasons nothing has happened is that
we are not yet convinced of the absolute necessity of the bibliographical search as a prelude to research and writing. As long as
we feel that our speculations, reflections, case studies, protocol
analyses, ethnographic studies, and historical forays are without
precedent, then the cause of systematic bibliographical work will
not be furthered. It is typical of both the adolescent human and

the adolescent discipline to assume that nothing in the past is of value. Only as we grow and mature—better metaphors than "paradigm shift"—do we realize that the past can be ignored only at great risk.

Our best current hope for something approaching a systematic annual bibliography is the work of Erika Lindemann, who is supervising approximately 180 contributing bibliographers in the preparation of the first volume of a projected annual bibliography. To be published by Longman, the first volume of the *Longman Bibliography of Composition and Rhetoric* will cover the years 1984 and 1985. It will contain approximately 3,800 annotated entries covering scholarly books, textbooks, journals (some 300), dissertations, and ERIC documents. It is scheduled for publication in early 1987. A second volume will cover 1986.

The Lindemann project should be applauded and supported in every possible way, but I fear that such efforts on the part of a single scholar and a commercial publisher will not serve as an answer for the long run. Ultimately, I believe, only a professional organization can sustain a systematic annual bibliographical effort that will continue in operation in spite of changes in personnel and changes in the interests and priorities of publishers. But while we wait, there is work to do: courses to teach, students to educate, research to conduct.

The second edition of this book differs from the first in several significant ways. Three new authors have been added to the original ten: Richard Lloyd-Jones has written about evaluation, a topic that many readers missed finding in the first edition; Hugh Burns helps us understand something of the history of computers as they relate to composition studies; and Andrea Lunsford has appended to Mina Shaughnessy's original essay a survey of the most significant work in basic writing during the past decade.

Two of the original authors have written on new topics: James Kinneavy looks at writing across the curriculum, and Joseph Comprone examines some of what has been written about literary theory as it relates to composition studies. Edward P. J. Corbett has chosen to let his original essay on style stand. To it he has added a substantial "Update" to cover the years since his original survey. The remaining essays represent not only major revisions and updatings, but often new conceptions of the topics. Finally, an index is provided to help readers searching for topics, authors, and titles. The failure to provide an index in the first edition was a major editorial error on my part, and I would like to take this opportunity to apologize to all users of the book for the needless inconvenience caused by my oversight.

Many people contributed to the making of this book and deserve my thanks: the twelve authors, several of whom wrote their essays under the most difficult personal and professional circumstances; D. F. Shaughnessy, for permission to reprint Mina Shaughnessy's essay; Keith Gregory, formerly of TCU Press, whose relaxed and good-natured intelligence made the tense moments seem somehow not so bad; Matthew Abbate, who edited the manuscript with quiet care and efficiency; and finally, of course, Priscilla.

Gary Tate
July 7, 1986

Abbreviations

ASHA	*American Speech and Hearing Association* (the journal)
ADE	Association of Departments of English
CCC	*College Composition and Communication*
CCCC	Conference on College Composition and Communication
CE	*College English*
CEA	College English Association
EE	*Elementary English*
EJ	*English Journal*
ERIC	Educational Resources Information Center (Documents can be ordered by using the number listed by citations in this book. Order from: Document Reproduction Service, P.O. Box 190, Arlington, VA 22210.)
FEN	*Freshman English News*
JAC	*Journal of Advanced Composition*
JBW	*Journal of Basic Writing*
JEGP	*Journal of English and Germanic Philology*
JEL	*Journal of English Linguistics*
JL	*Journal of Linguistics*
LCHC	*Laboratory of Comparative Human Cognition Quarterly Newsletter*
LL	*Language Learning*
MLA	Modern Language Association of America
NCTE	National Council of Teachers of English
P and R	*Philosophy and Rhetoric*

PMLA	*Publications of the Modern Language Association*
QJS	*Quarterly Journal of Speech*
RR	*Rhetoric Review*
RSQ	*Rhetoric Society Quarterly*
RTE	*Research in the Teaching of English*
ST	*Speech Teacher*
TESOL	Teachers of English to Speakers of Other Languages

Teaching Composition

Recent Developments in Rhetorical Invention

RICHARD YOUNG, Carnegie-Mellon University

THIS ESSAY IS INTENDED AS AN EXTENSION OF an earlier bibliographical study on invention that surveyed developments from the late 1950s—which marked the reemergence in English departments of interest in invention as a formal rhetorical art—to approximately 1973 ("Invention: A Topographical Survey," in *Teaching Composition: 10 Bibliographical Essays,* ed. Gary Tate [Fort Worth: Texas Christian University Press, 1976], pp. 1–43). The present essay, which covers the interval from 1973 to the present, was written with the earlier one in mind and is probably best read that way.

Basic to the developments that have been taking place in rhetoric during the last twenty years is the notion of process; rhetoric is being reconceptualized as an activity. The older rhetoric, the "rhetoric of the finished word," as Gordon Rohman once described it, is being supplanted or treated as a limited case. Even textbooks that are in their essential features traditional, i.e., that focus attention by and large on the analysis and emendation of compositions, often use vocabulary and techniques drawn from the newer rhetoric—a symptom of the growing influence of the change. In place of traditional "comp" is a conception of rhetoric as a special kind of behavior—a linguistic activity carried on within a social context, and furthermore, an activity that makes meaning as well as transmits it. For discussions of this change, see

Richard Young, "Paradigms and Problems: Needed Research in Rhetorical Invention," in *Research on Composing: Points of Departure,* ed. Charles Cooper and Lee Odell (Urbana, Ill.: NCTE, 1978), pp. 29–47, and Maxine Hairston, "Winds of Change: Thomas Kuhn and the Revolution in the Teaching of Writing," *CCC,* 33 (Feb. 1982), 76–88. Both argue that rhetoric is undergoing a paradigm shift—a repudiation of what has come to be known as "current-traditional rhetoric" and an affirmation of an emerging rhetoric in which invention is the dominant art.

The essay that follows is an effort to examine developments in invention as part of this trend. It is divided into six sections that reflect what seem to me to have been the major areas of inquiry in recent scholarly work on invention: the Composing Process, Rhetoric as an Epistemic Activity, Situational Context, Heuristics, Pedagogy and Methods of Invention, and the History of Invention. It is of necessity a highly selective bibliography, sometimes distressingly so. But there are many more people publishing on rhetoric today than there were a dozen years ago and much of what is being published now falls within the domain of invention.

THE COMPOSING PROCESS

It is no accident that interest in the process of composing emerged at the same time as the interest in invention. All arts of invention present either explicitly or implicitly a conception of the composing process, and conceptions of the process influence the design of arts of invention and the teacher's choice of which art, if any, to teach. For a discussion of the relationship between conceptions of composing, invention, and pedagogy, see Richard E. Young, "Concepts of Art and the Teaching of Writing," in *The Rhetorical Tradition and Modern Writing,* ed. James J. Murphy (New York: MLA, 1982), pp. 130–41.

A review of recent research and theory on the composing process can be found in John Warnock's "The Writing Process," in *Research in Composition and Rhetoric,* ed. Michael G. Moran and

Ronald Lunsford (Westport, Conn.: Greenwood Press, 1984), pp. 3–26; Warnock surveys work in this relatively new area of rhetorical research and discusses a number of problems that remain to be addressed. A more detailed account of research on composing can be found in Ann Hume's "Research on the Composing Process," in *Writing: Policies, Problems, and Possibilities,* ed. Bruce Cronnell and Joan Michael (Los Alamitos, Cal.: Southwest Regional Laboratory of Educational Research and Development, 1982). Marlene Scardamalia and Carl Bereiter's "Written Composition" is a thorough survey of current research on writing, including the composing process and invention (in *Handbook of Research on Teaching,* Third Edition, ed. Merlin C. Wittrock, New York: Macmillan, 1985).

Conceptions of Composing

Richard C. Gebhardt ("Initial Plans and Spontaneous Composition: Toward a Comprehensive Theory of the Writing Process," *CE,* 44 [Oct. 1982], 620–27) notes basic differences between two general conceptions of the composing process that frequently appear in our professional literature, i.e., conceptions that emphasize linear, deliberate, rational features of the process and those that emphasize the recursive, spontaneous, and intuitive features. He suggests that in the work of James Britton, Sondra Perl, Nancy Sommers, Linda Flower and John Hayes we find a more detailed and adequate conception of the composing process, one that is capable of accommodating the truths in the other conceptions. Gebhardt's "Writing Processes, Revision, and Rhetorical Problems: A Note on Three Recent Articles," *CCC,* 34 (Oct. 1983), 294–96, summarizes a number of distinctive features of the new conception of composing taking shape, namely its insistence that audience and purpose are integral to the process; that revision, like composing as a whole, is a complex, recursive activity in which rhetorical considerations are central; and that it must account for all acts of composing, i.e., that it must not ignore one kind of writing while valorizing another.

3

The sharp dichotomies noted by Gebhart that characterize so much of present-day thinking on composing (organic/ mechanical, reason/imagination, deliberate/spontaneous, etc.) are put in historical perspective in Jacqueline de Romilly's *Magic and Rhetoric in Ancient Greece* (Cambridge, Mass.: Harvard University Press, 1975). Although it is a critical analysis of opposing conceptions of the creative process in all the arts, D. N. Perkins's *The Mind's Best Work* (Cambridge, Mass.: Harvard University Press, 1981) is clearly useful in understanding the conceptions of original composing that have dominated the teaching of writing in this country. The following works exemplify but certainly do not exhaust the trend toward a more detailed and adequate conception of the composing process: James Britton, "The Process of Writing," in *The Development of Writing Abilities (11-18)* (London: Macmillan Education, 1975), pp. 19–49; Sondra Perl, "Understanding Composing," *CCC*, 31 (Dec. 1980), 363–69, and with Arthur Egendorf, "The Process of Creative Discovery: Theory, Research, and Implications for Teaching," in *Linguistics, Stylistics, and the Teaching of Composition,* ed. Donald McQuade (Akron, Ohio: L&S Books and the Department of English, University of Akron, 1979), pp. 118–34; Sharon Pianko, "Reflection: A Critical Component of the Composing Process," *CCC,* 30 (Oct. 1979), 275–78; Nancy Sommers, "Revision Strategies of Student Writers and Experienced Adult Writers," *CCC,* 31 (Dec. 1980), 378–88; and Linda Flower and John R. Hayes, "A Cognitive Process Theory of Writing," *CCC,* 32 (Dec. 1981), 363–87.

Variations

Substantial variations in the way people carry out the composing process are becoming increasingly evident in the research—a sign that we are looking more closely at the process than we used to. On the other hand, the existence of significant differences among instances of the composing process raises the question of whether it is possible to generalize about composing in a useful way. Variation is not in itself problematic, since everything we can conceive of has a range of variation. Nor does wide variation across instances necessarily preclude useful generalization. But it does mean that we must be cautious when we draw conclusions from research results and when we try to help students compose more effectively.

The issue of variation in composing and something of the difficulty it presents to both teacher and researcher is apparent in the following articles. Mimi Schwartz tracks the composing processes of an accomplished poet and an eleven-year-old novice and generalizes about the preconditions for successful composing and the effective teaching of writing: "Two Journeys Through the Writing Process," CCC, 34 (May 1983), 188–201. However, Schwartz's description of what happens in the composing process is quite different from the description given by Jack Selzer in "The Composing Process of an Engineer," CCC, 34 (May 1983), 178–87; Selzer concludes from his case study that there may be more diversity in the way writers compose than many have assumed and that more research is needed before teachers will know how best to prepare students for the sort of writing they do in their vocations. Selzer's conclusion about the diversity of composing processes is consistent with survey findings reported by Lester Faigley and Thomas P. Miller in "What We Learn from Writing on the Job," CE, 44 (Oct. 1982), 557–69. More generally, Arthur N. Applebee argues that in both our research and teaching we have not distinguished between writing for which we have well-established routines and for which no pre-writing and revision are required, and writing which is in one way or another new to us and which, therefore, calls for a more elaborated and creative response ("Musings . . . Writing Processes, Revisited," RTE, 19 [Oct. 1985], 213–15).

Carol Berkenkotter's study of Donald Murray's writing reveals the diversity that has made generalizing about the process so risky, yet at the same time the study tends to confirm a general conception of the process that is emerging in research ("Deci-

5

sions and Revisions: The Planning Strategies of a Publishing Writer," *CCC*, 34 [May 1983], 156–69). Murray, in his response to Berkenkotter, notes the different effects on revision and planning of working with familiar as opposed to unfamiliar genres ("Response of a Laboratory Rat—or, Being Protocoled," *CCC*, 34 [May 1983], 169–72). No matter what the source, diversity in composing is to be expected, just as it is in other areas of human performance. But it presents substantial problems for the teacher, who may be tempted, as Jack Selzer suggests, to prescribe a single model for composing rather than develop ways of expanding the student's repertoire of composing strategies ("Exploring Options in Composing," *CCC*, 35 [Oct. 1984], 276–84).

Shaping at the Point of Utterance

In his article entitled "Shaping at the Point of Utterance," James Britton argues that "a better understanding of how a writer shapes at the point of utterance might make a major contribution to our understanding of invention in rhetoric" (in *Reinventing the Rhetorical Tradition,* ed. Aviva Freedman and Ian Pringle [Conway, Ark.: L&S Books for the Canadian Council of Teachers of English, 1980], pp. 61–65). The phenomenon and implications for the teacher are discussed by Donald M. Murray in "The Feel of Writing—and Teaching Writing" (in *Reinventing the Rhetorical Tradition,* pp. 67–73), Barrett J. Mandel in "Losing One's Mind: Learning to Write and Edit," *CCC*, 29 (Dec. 1978), 362–68, and Mike Rose in "Rigid Rules, Inflexible Plans, and the Stifling of Language: A Cognitivist Analysis of Writer's Block," *CCC*, 31 (1980), 389–400. In an experimental study, Marlene Scardamalia, Carl Bereiter, and Hillel Goelman examine children writing under conditions designed to test a series of hypotheses (e.g., that attention to low-level matters interferes with attention to higher-level ones) and relate shaping at the point of utterance to other activities of the writing process, such as planning ("The Role of Production Factors in Writing Ability," in *What Writers Know: The Language, Process, and Structure of Written Discourse,* ed.

Martin Nystrand [New York: Academic Press, 1982], pp. 173–210). Another discussion of the phenomenon can be found in Linda Flower and John R. Hayes's "Images, Plans, Prose: The Representation of Meaning in Writing," *Written Communication,* 1 (Jan. 1984), 120–60, where it is approached in terms of their model of the composing process.

RHETORIC AS AN EPISTEMIC ACTIVITY

In a sense, rhetoric has been epistemic from its beginning, that is, it has been concerned with issues of coming to know something and with how others can be brought to know. As St. Augustine put it when speaking of his own rhetoric over 1500 years ago, "There are two things necessary . . . a way of discovering those things that are to be understood, and a way of teaching what we have learned." But the emphasis in rhetorical studies since the eighteenth century has been on communication alone. For historical discussions of this reduction of rhetoric to the study of communication and the proprieties of writing, see James Berlin, "The Triumph of Eighteenth-Century Rhetoric," in *Writing Instruction in Nineteenth-Century American Colleges* (Carbondale: Southern Illinois University Press, 1984), pp. 19–34, and Sharon Crowley, "The Evolution of Invention in Current-Traditional Rhetoric: 1850–1970," *RR,* 3 (Jan. 1985), 146–62.

Since the 1960s, however, a new appreciation of the relation of rhetoric and knowledge has been emerging. Michael Leff identifies at least four different reasons that rhetoric can be said to be epistemic: 1) rhetoric is concerned with the relation and adjustment of abstract principles to particular situations, and hence can be said to be epistemic; 2) it is concerned with the creation of social knowledge and its use as a criterion for evaluating new knowledge; 3) it can have a "meta-logical" function in assessing and resolving conflicts between competing philosophic and scientific paradigms; and 4) since it assumes that we deal with symbolic realities rather than actualities, knowing is a symbolic, evaluative, and argumentative process, i.e., essentially a rhetorical process ("In Search of Ariadne's Thread: A Review of the Recent Literature on Rhetorical Theory," *Central States Speech Journal,* 29 [1978], 73–91). A bibliographical essay, Leff's work is a good source for additional citations, the majority of which are in Speech Communication, where the idea of epistemic rhetoric has been more widely discussed than it has in English.

Leff's argument is developed further in a second article, with Margaret Organ Procario, "Rhetorical Theory in Speech Communication," in *Speech Communication in the 20th Century,* ed. Thomas W. Benson (Carbondale: Southern Illinois University press, 1985), pp. 3–27. Richard Fulkerson offers another survey of the ways in which rhetoric can be said to be epistemic and raises a number of significant questions about the positions now being advocated in both Speech Communication and English ("On Theories of Rhetoric as Epistemic: A Bi-Disciplinary View," in *Oldspeak/Newspeak: Rhetorical Transformations,* ed. Charles W. Kneupper [Arlington, Texas: Rhetoric Society of America, 1985], pp. 194–207). A useful collection of articles on language and epistemology can be found in Martin Nystrand's *Language as a Way of Knowing: A Book of Readings* (Toronto: The Ontario Institute for Studies in Education, 1977). As Leff and Fulkerson point out, "epistemic rhetoric" is a term that encompasses a wide range of positions, not all of which are wholly consistent with each other.

Of the four reasons noted by Leff for considering rhetoric to have an epistemological function, it is the last, language as symbolic action, that has captured the interest of those in English studies, particularly as it involves writing. Indeed, the concern in English for the epistemological implications of writing may be adding a fifth reason for considering rhetoric to be epistemic: i.e., the activity of writing can function as an aid to learning and discovery. There is a growing body of literature devoted to writing as a means of engaging in complex linear thought, of coming to understanding during that act of writing, and to composing as the making of meaning. For example, Walter J. Ong, S. J., dis-

8

cusses social, cultural, and psychological consequences of literacy in his *Interfaces of the Word: Studies in the Evolution of Consciousness and Culture* (Ithaca, N.Y.: Cornell University Press, 1977) and *Orality and Literacy: The Technologizing of the Word* (London: Methuen, 1982). Richard Young and Patricia Sullivan pursue Ong's argument that writing enables a certain kind of thinking that is otherwise difficult or impossible in "Why Write? A Reconsideration," in *Essays on Classical Rhetoric and Modern Discourse,* ed. Robert J. Connors, Lisa S. Ede, and Andrea A. Lunsford (Carbondale: Southern Illinois University Press, 1984), pp. 215–25.

Arguing for an expanded notion of literacy that includes social and cognitive factors as well as linguistic ones, Anne Ruggles Gere maintains that the writing teacher's role requires helping students use the knowledge and oral facility they have to move from a simpler conception of the world to a more complex one ("A Cultural Perspective on Talking and Writing," in *Exploring Speaking-Writing Relationships: Connections and Contrasts,* ed. Barry M. Kroll and Roberta J. Vann [Urbana, Ill.: NCTE, 1981], pp. 111–23). Janet Emig argues that writing is a unique mode of learning because it possesses attributes that correspond to powerful learning strategies ("Writing as a Mode of Learning," *CCC,* 28 [May 1977], 122–27). Ann E. Bertoff's collection of articles, *The Making of Meaning: Metaphors, Models, and Maxims for Writing Teachers,* develops various aspects of the idea that teaching writing is or should be teaching the making of meaning (Montclair, N.J.: Boynton/Cook, 1981). Emphasizing the pedagogy of this approach for unskilled writers, James L. Collins develops an extended contrast between teaching for meaning and teaching for error avoidance ("Speaking, Writing and Teaching for Meaning," in *Exploring Speaking-Writing Relationships: Connections and Contrasts,* pp. 198–214). James Britton argues that if the epistemic potential of writing is to be exploited, we must give more attention to shaping at the point of utterance and not inhibit discovery by insisting that children know exactly what they are going to say before they come to say it ("Writing to Learn and Learning to Write," in *Prospect and Retrospect: Selected Essays of James Britton,* ed. Gordon M. Pradl [Montclair, N.J.: Boynton/Cook, 1982], pp. 94–111).

Responding to the debate over whether core curricula should emphasize the acquisition of knowledge or development of mental powers, Janice Lauer argues that composition, already a requirement in most curricula, can be used to develop the student's power of inquiry; using composition for this purpose requires a pedagogy that centers on methods of invention and writing as an epistemic activity ("Writing as Inquiry: Some Questions for Teachers," *CCC,* 33 [Feb. 1982], 89–93). Several pedagogical applications of the principles associated with epistemic rhetoric can be found in *Eight Approaches to Teaching Composition,* ed. Timothy R. Donovan and Ben W. McClelland (Urbana, Ill.: NCTE, 1980), especially in Donald M. Murray's "Writing as Process: How Writing Finds Its Own Meaning" (pp. 3–20); Stephen Judy's "The Experiential Approach: Inner Worlds to Outer Worlds" (pp. 37–51); Janice M. Lauer's "The Rhetorical Approach: Stages of Writing and Strategies for Writers" (pp. 53–64); and Kenneth Dowst's "The Epistemic Approach: Writing, Knowing, and Learning" (pp. 65–85).

John Gage discusses the relation of epistemology and rhetoric generally; how concepts and methods used in both classical and modern rhetoric are rooted in epistemological assumptions; and how composition teaching might benefit from more attention to assumptions about language and knowing that are passed on to students, often implicitly and inadvertently ("An Adequate Epistemology for Composition: Classical and Modern Perspectives," in *Essays on Classical Rhetoric and Modern Discourse,* pp. 152–69).

Assumptions about the epistemic potential of rhetoric, if acted on, could substantially change rhetorical studies in English departments. Three significant changes are already apparent: 1) the effort in many departments to integrate the activities of reading and writing on the grounds that both are essentially involved with the making of meaning; 2) the writing-across-the-curriculum movement with its insistence that the activity of writing is in itself a powerful means of acquiring knowledge and that writing is strongly influenced by situation, so much so that it makes sense to speak of the ethnolects of various disciplinary communities; and 3) the reconceptualizing of technical writing to include rhetorical invention. Because recent efforts to integrate writing and reading and to teach writing across the curriculum are discussed in detail elsewhere in this book, it is unnecessary to do more here than observe that they both depend heavily on work in modern invention. However, technical and scientific writing is not treated separately. Because the assumption that invention plays a significant role in such writing runs contrary to long-established tradition and because acting on it would substantially change the teaching and practice of the art, recent developments in technical writing should get more than passing mention here.

Over the years "tech writing" has been for the most part characterized by a sharp split between form and meaning, along with equally sharp distinctions between convention and originality, objective and subjective knowledge, personal and impersonal style. The technical writer is to be concerned only with issues of linguistic form and convention, accuracy of statement about objective reality, and an impersonal style; the scientist and engineer address issues of meaning. The teaching and practice of technical writing has been by and large an ahistorical, atheoretical enterprise with only the weakest of ties to rhetorical studies.

However, a recent reconceptualization of technical writing as essentially rhetorical is producing some startling changes. This reorientation in thinking about technical discourse is exemplified in Merrill D. Whitburn's "The Ideal Orator and Literary Critic as Technical Communicators: An Emerging Revolution in English Departments" (in *Essays on Classical Rhetoric and Modern Discourse*, pp. 226–47); Carolyn Miller's "A Humanistic Rationale for

11

Technical Writing," *CE,* 40 (Feb. 1979), 610–17; and Walter B. Weimer's "Beyond Philosophical Reconstruction," Chapter 8 in *Notes on the Methodology of Scientific Research* (Hillsdale, N.J.: Erlbaum, 1979), pp. 72–92, and "Science as a Rhetorical Transaction: Toward a Nonjustificational Conception of Rhetoric," *P and R,* 10 (Winter 1977), 1–29. In her fine bibliographic study of technical discourse, "Invention in Technical and Scientific Discourse: A Prospective Survey" (in *Research in Technical Communication,* ed. Michael G. Moran and Debra Journet [Westport, Conn.: Greenwood Press, 1985], pp. 117–62), Carolyn Miller remarks that "without a theory of technical and scientific discourse as argument, asking about invention in such discourse is an irrelevant—or foolish—undertaking. But with the beginning attempts to examine technical and scientific discourse as rhetoric, work that had seemed fragmented and unrelated acquires a new orientation, as though magnetized."

SITUATIONAL CONTEXT

In a recent bibliographic study James L. Kinneavy calls situational context "one of the most overpowering concepts in contemporary rhetoric" ("Contemporary Rhetoric," in *The Present State of Scholarship in Historical and Contemporary Rhetoric,* ed. Winifred Bryan Horner [Columbia: University of Missouri Press, 1983], p. 174). First formulated as the ancient Greek concept of *kairos,* the importance of situation for the speaker and writer is not new in rhetoric, though it has been largely ignored in current-traditional composition. Recently, however, as Kinneavy points out, its value is being reaffirmed in a wide range of disciplines that study language. Kinneavy's "The Relation of the Whole to the Part in Interpretation Theory and in the Composing Process" is a thorough introduction to situational context, from *kairos* on, as it bears on composing and criticism (in *Linguistics, Stylistics, and the Teaching of Composition,* ed. Donald McQuade [Akron, Ohio: L&S Books and the Department of English, University of Akron, 1979], pp. 1–23).

Two Variations

Perhaps the best-known effort in English studies to articulate the situational nature of the rhetorical act is Wayne Booth's "The Rhetorical Stance," *CCC*, 14 (Oct. 1963), 139–45, an article which helped at the time to stimulate interest in rhetoric in departments of English. The rhetorical stance is the balance the writer strikes among the components of the writing situation, i.e., the available arguments on the subject, the voice or implied character of the writer, and the relevant features of the audience. Recently R. D. Walshe criticized Booth for his failure to discuss how the writer actually develops and maintains a stance in the act of writing and argued that a process view requires that technique be added to the three components Booth discusses ("A Model of the Writing Situation," *CCC*, 28 [Dec. 1977], 384–86). Booth's design of a course that combines instruction in both literature and composition appears to be based on the concept of rhetorical stance ("'LITCOMP': Some Rhetoric Addressed to Crypto-rhetoricians about a Rhetorical Solution to a Rhetorical Problem," in *Composition and Literature: Bridging the Gap,* ed. Winifred Bryan Horner [Chicago: University of Chicago Press, 1983], pp. 57–80).

In what has been an extremely influential and controversial article, Lloyd Bitzer remarks, "When I ask, What is a rhetorical situation?, I want to know the nature of those contexts in which speakers or writers create rhetorical discourse" ("The Rhetorical Situation," *P and R,* 1 [Jan. 1966], 1–14). His answer is that a rhetorical situation has three components: an exigency marked by a sense of urgency in the mind of the would-be speaker or writer, which initiates the rhetorical process; an appropriate audience, i.e., an audience that has the ability to eliminate or mitigate the exigency; and a set of constraints that affect the choices of writer or speaker and audience, e.g., the constraints imposed by working within a particular rhetorical genre. But the guiding principles of the discussion are the notions of fitness and situation: a rhetorical act is precipitated by a certain kind of situation that calls for a certain kind of response. For a discussion of the role of genre in the rhetorical situation, see Kathleen M. Hall Jamieson's "Generic Constraints and the Rhetorical Situation," *P and R*, 6 (Summer 1973), 162–70. Linda Flower and John R. Hayes incorporate Bitzer's concept into their theory of the composing process as a partial explanation of the choices the writer makes while composing ("A Cognitive Process Theory of Writing," *CCC*, 32 [Dec. 1981], 365–87).

Much of the controversy has centered on the epistemological status of the rhetorical situation. As Alan Brinton puts the issue in his effort at clarifying the concept, "To what extent are the constituents of the rhetorical situation objective matters of fact?" ("Situation in the Theory of Rhetoric," *P and R*, 14 [Fall 1981], 234–48). The answers have varied to extremes. Bitzer's view is that the rhetorical situation has an objective status independent of the writer or speaker and that it controls the response of the rhetor who enters it. Among the alternatives is Richard Vatz's answer that the rhetorical situation has no nature independent of the perception of the rhetor and the rhetoric with which he chooses to characterize it and that what constitutes a fitting response is determined by the rhetor ("The Myth of the Rhetorical Situation," *P and R*, 6 [Summer 1973], 154–61). In "Rhetoric and Its Situations," *P and R*, 7 (Summer 1974), 175–86, Scott Consigny replies that "the real question for rhetorical theory will become not whether the rhetor or situation is dominant, but how, in each case, the rhetor can become engaged in the novel and indeterminant situation and yet have a means of making sense of it," the means for Consigny being an art of topics. Bitzer continues what is becoming a complicated dialogue in his "Functional Communication: A Situational Perspective" (in *Rhetoric in Transition: Studies in the Nature and Uses of Rhetoric,* ed. Eugene E. White [University Park: Pennsylvania State University Press, 1980], pp. 21–38).

14

Audience

One of the most notable developments in rhetorical theory and pedagogy in English studies over the last several years is the still growing interest in the nature and role of the audience in written discourse. However, the concept of audience, not to mention the role of audience in writing and the teaching of writing, is proving to be surprisingly elusive; even so, empirical and theoretical work over the last several years has disabused us of earlier, easy views of the subject and has substantially enriched both our theory and our pedagogy. For a bibliographic study of past and present thinking on audience to about 1980, see Lisa Ede's "Audience: An Introduction to Research," *CCC,* 35 (May 1984), 140–54. A more specialized resource, *Teaching Technical Writing: Audience Analysis and Adaptation,* edited by Paul V. Anderson, contains several articles on audience as an issue in technical writing, including an annotated bibliography on resources for teaching analysis and adaptation (ATTW Anthology No. 1; Morehead, Ky.: ATTW, 1980).

Seeking a more adequate view of the nature and role of the writer's audience, Lisa Ede and Andrea Lunsford ("Audience Addressed/Audience Invoked: The Role of Audience in Composition Theory and Pedagogy," *CCC,* 35 [May 1984], 155–171) develop a position that mediates between the widely-shared view of the audience as a discovered entity that is subsequently addressed by the writer and the more recent view of the audience as a creation of the writer, i.e., the audience as a kind of fiction. (For the latter view, see Walter J. Ong, S. J., "The Writer's Audience Is Always a Fiction," *PMLA,* 90 [Jan. 1975], 9–21.) Barry M. Kroll discusses what he regards as at present the three basic approaches to the relationship of writer and reader and the strengths and weaknesses of each approach ("Writing for Readers: Three Perspectives on Audience," *CCC,* 35 [May 1984], 172–85).

Chaim Perelman's *Realm of Rhetoric* (Notre Dame, Ind.: University of Notre Dame Press, 1982), which treats the entire realm of argumentative discourse, is a discussion of the methods used in probabilistic arguments addressed to and contingent on audiences of any sort; it is an audience-centered rhetoric. Among Perelman's contributions to our thinking about audience, the most discussed is his concept of "universal audience," an original and important concept in both this book and the earlier *New Rhetoric* (with Olbrechts-Tyteca [Notre Dame, Ind.: University of Notre Dame Press, 1969]). It is, Perelman argues, the audience of philosophic discourse. The concept implies that the quality of an argument is to be judged by the qualifications of the audience and its willingness to adhere to it. Henry W. Johnstone, Jr., criticizes the concept as unnecessary and ambiguous in "The Idea of a Universal Audience" (in *Validity and Rhetoric in Philosophical Argument: An Outlook in Transition* [University Park, Pa.: Dialogue Press of Man and World, 1978], pp. 101–06).

James E. Porter argues that post-structuralist literary theories provide a framework for discussing the influence of social context on the writer as well as the reader; Porter's discussion of the audience as discourse community is particularly interesting when compared with Perelman's audience, Booth's rhetorical stance, and Bitzer's rhetorical situation ("Reading Presences in Texts: Audience as Discourse Community," in *Oldspeak/Newspeak: Rhetorical Transformations,* ed. Charles W. Kneupper [Arlington, Texas: Rhetoric Society of America, 1985], pp. 241–56). Martin Nystrand discusses the relation of audience to another analogous concept, that of "speech community," in "Rhetoric's 'Audience' and Linguistics' 'Speech Community': Implications for Understanding Writing, Reading, and Text" (in *What Writers Know: The Language, Process, and Structure of Written Discourse,* ed. Martin Nystrand [New York: Academic Press, 1982], pp. 1–28).

Something of the complexity of the notion of audience is also apparent in Donald M. Murray's comment that "we command our students to write for others, but writers report they write for themselves" ("Teaching the Other Self: The Writer's

First Reader," *CCC*, 33 [May 1982], 140–47). Murray's article exemplifies an important feature of modern rhetoric, i.e., the scope of invention has been extended to include explicit interest in the self as our first and sometimes only audience. But Murray has something quite different in mind than Linda Flower has in "Writer-Based Prose: A Cognitive Basis for Problems in Writing," *CE*, 41 (Sept. 1979), 19–37. Flower remarks that writer-based prose is natural and adequate for those writing for themselves, but it is the source of some of the most common and pervasive problems in academic and professional writing.

After studying the way skilled writers address audience, Carol Berkenkotter notes the difficulty in cultivating comparable expertise in novice writers because conventional classroom assignments fail to confront the student with a variety of rhetorical situations and audiences with differing needs ("Understanding a Writer's Awareness of Audience," *CCC,* 32 [Dec. 1981], 388–99). As instances of alternatives, she suggests the rhetorical case method; audience-based heuristics (such as Fred R. Pfister and Joanne F. Petrick's "A Heuristic Model for Creating a Writer's Audience," *CCC,* 31 [May 1980], 213–20); and Peter Elbow's transactional approach, which helps writers cope with affective problems presented by the audience ("Audience," in *Writing with Power: Techniques for Mastering the Writing Process* [New York: Oxford University Press, 1981], pp. 177–235).

Perhaps because our thinking about rhetoric continues to be centered so exclusively on the classroom, we have tended to ignore the audience, at least certain audiences, as a source of public knowledge and as a truth test. (Wayne Booth's *Modern Dogma and the Rhetoric of Assent* [Chicago: University of Chicago Press, 1974] is a notable exception.) Theorists in speech communication, however, have approached the issue with considerable sophistication: see, for example, Lloyd F. Bitzer's "Rhetoric and Public Knowledge," in *Rhetoric, Philosophy, and Literature,* ed. Don M. Burks (West Lafayette, Ind.: Purdue University Press, 1976), pp. 67–93.

Concluding a discussion of the various meanings of "audience," Douglas Park remarks that the concept of "audience is elusive in much teaching of writing not only because the concept itself is difficult. A fully serious art of rhetoric and a concomitant sophistication with audience . . . must grow from a clear understanding of the kinds of discourse to be served and their purpose in society. Our composition courses do not operate with such an understanding" ("The Meanings of Audience," *CE,* 44 [March 1982], 247–57).

The Ethos of the Writer

When we speak of *ethos,* we are concerned not with the individual as an isolated being but with the individual in a social context. Concepts usually associated with ethos—credibility, authenticity, sincerity, voice, tone, persona—all imply a relationship between the writer or speaker and an other. We are credible to someone, our voice is heard by someone, we play a role in a particular situation for someone. As Aristotle pointed out, ethos is a special sort of appeal (*Rhetoric,* 1356A).

S. M. Halloran observes that there is no set of beliefs the modern writer can assume is widely shared and little that can be taken for granted, including an effective rhetoric. Rhetoric today, he remarks, is distinguished by "its emphasis on the responsibility of the speaker (or author) to articulate his own world, and thereby his own self. The seriousness with which he undertakes this task, hence the rigor and passion with which he discloses his world to the audience, is his *ethos,*" ("On the End of Rhetoric, Classical and Modern," *CE,* 36 [Feb. 1975], 621–31). This deprivation of a sense of certainty and of community may be one reason for what appears to be a renewed interest in the concept of *ethos.*

What has been a central concept in rhetorical invention from its inception is acquiring a new richness. For example, Jim W. Corder points out that the Aristotelian view of *ethos* fails to account for the variety we find in experience; as a way of demonstrating the complexity of the concept, he identifies a number of variants and suggests ways in which they can be exploited in both composition and criticism ("Varieties of Ethical Argument, with Some Account of the Significance of *Ethos* in the Teaching of Composition," *FEN,* 6 [Winter 1978], 1–23). Drawing on Mina Shaughnessy's call for research on teaching advanced skills of literacy to young adults who have not yet acquired them ("Some Needed Research on Writing," *CCC,* 28 [Dec. 1977], 317–20), Patricia L. Bizzell argues that we need to develop ways of making the *ethos* of academic discourse more accessible to students ("The Ethos of Academic Discourse," *CCC,* 29 [Dec. 1978], 351–55). Nan Johnson's "Ethos and the Aims of Rhetoric" (in *Essays on Classical Rhetoric and Modern Discourse,* ed. Robert Connors, Lisa Ede, and Andrea A. Lunsford [Carbondale: Southern Illinois University Press, 1984], pp. 98–114), argues that the twin conceptions of *ethos* articulated in Plato's *Gorgias* and *Phaedrus* and in Aristotle's *Rhetoric*—i.e., *ethos* as the moral intention of the speaker and ethos as a pragmatic intention—vary with the historical context. In theoretical discussions our approach to *ethos* tends to be Platonic; in discussions of rhetorical practice, pragmatic. However, our texts tend to be morally neutral.

The position one takes on the nature and function of *ethos* has strong implications for what one considers to be the proper scope of rhetoric. Consideration of *ethos* draws one into ethical, philosophic, and psychological issues that surround the rhetorical act. For example, S. Michael Halloran criticizes the work of E. D. Hirsch and Louis Milic for their reduction of rhetoric to technical matters of stylistic choice; he argues that rhetorical choices define the character of the speaker and the world and in so doing help to shape them both, a view that considerably enlarges the scope of the discipline ("Aristotle's Concept of Ethos, or If Not His Somebody Else's," *RR,* 1 [Sept. 1982], 58–63).

Preoccupation with one or another feature of the situational context to the exclusion of others produces unfitting discourse. Uneasy with the rapid growth of interest in audience, Gary Tate cautions that making the intended response of the audience the test of rhetorical effectiveness, without introducing concomitant tests, can lead to manipulation ("Searching for a Romantic Rhetoric," in *A Symposium in Rhetoric,* ed. J. Dean Bishop, Turner S. Kobler, and William E. Tanner [Denton: Texas Woman's University, 1975], pp. 5–10). S. Michael Halloran argues that the ethos the writer establishes by the choices he makes must be responsive to the claims of the individual and his vision as well as the claims of the audience and established values, or else the notion of appropriateness degenerates into correctness ("On Making Choices, Sartorial and Rhetorical," *CCC,* 29 [Dec. 1978], 369–71).

HEURISTICS

With the possible exception of research methodologies, heuristics has been the most controversial subject in rhetorical studies for the last several years. One reason for the continuing controversy is that consideration of heuristics moves us beyond broad areas of agreement about composing and the teaching of composition (e.g., the value to research and teaching of a process view of writing, the function of writing as an epistemic as well as a communicative activity) to particular conceptions of the composing process and teaching; here we find deep disagreements over the nature of the creative act and the contingent issues of whether writing can be taught and, if so, how it should be taught. For an elaboration of this argument see Richard Young, "Arts, Crafts, Gifts, and Knacks: Some Disharmonies in the New Rhetoric," in *Reinventing the Rhetorical Tradition,* ed. Aviva Freedman and Ian Pringle (Conway, Ark.: L&S Books for the Canadian Council of Teachers of English, 1980), pp. 53–60. For an extensive bibliography on heuristics in rhetoric covering the period from 1970 to 1980, see Richard Leo Enos, Barry M. Jereb, Paul L. Kravits, and Honora Mary Rockar, "Heuristic Procedures and the Composing Process: A Selected Bibliography," *RSQ* Special Issue, No. 1, 1982.

The Nature of Heuristic Procedures

The nature of heuristic procedures has itself been a major point of contention. Although the argument between Janice Lauer and Ann Bertoff falls a bit outside the period we are examining, it is a good place to begin the discussion since it was one of the earliest, certainly the best known, of the exchanges on the subject and lays out many of the motifs that run through subsequent discussions. (Janice Lauer, "Heuristics and Composition," *CCC*, 21 [Dec. 1970], 396–404; Ann E. Bertoff, "The Problem of Problem Solving," *CCC*, 22 [Oct. 1971], 237–42; Janice Lauer, "Response to Ann E. Bertoff, 'The Problem of Problem Solving,'" *CCC*, 23 [May 1972], 208–10; Ann E. Bertoff, "Response to Janice Lauer, 'Counterstatement,'" *CCC*, 23 [Dec. 1972], 414–16). The articles are conveniently collected in W. Ross Winterowd's *Contemporary Rhetoric: A Conceptual Background with Readings* (New York: Harcourt Brace Jovanovich, 1975), pp. 79–103.

Since many of those working in rhetoric frequently cross disciplinary boundaries, it happens that they sometimes import other concepts and terminologies that seem in some way to be useful in addressing our problems. "Heuristics" is one of these terms, "problem solving" another, both coming to us principally from work in cognitive psychology and artificial intelligence, though George Polya's efforts in the mid-1940s to revive heuristics as a part of mathematical education was probably the source of the recent revival of interest in that art. (For exemplary readings see G. Polya, *How to Solve It* [Princeton, N.J.: Princeton University Press, 1945]; Herbert A. Simon, *The Sciences of the Artificial* [Cambridge, Mass.: MIT Press, 1969]). Discussions of the current state of knowledge about problem solving, heuristics and their educational implications can be found in *Problem Solving and Education: Issues in Teaching and Research,* ed. D. T. Tuma and F. Reif (Hillsdale, N.J.: Erlbaum, 1980).

But before "heuristics" was used in these disciplines, it was used in logic to refer to methods concerned with inquiry and discovery. And before that, it was used in Greek rhetoric to refer to what the Romans later called "invention." For discussions of early uses of the term see Richard Leo Enos's "Emerging Notions of Heuristic, Eristic, and Proleptic Rhetoric in Homeric Discourse: Proto-Literate Conniving, Wrangling and Reasoning" (in *Selected Papers from the 1981 Texas Writing Research Conference*, ed. Maxine C. Hairston and Cynthia L. Selfe [Austin: Texas Writing Research Group, University of Texas, 1981], pp. 44–64); and George A. Kennedy's "Later Greek Philosophy and Rhetoric" (*P and R*, 13 [Summer 1980], 181–97). "Problem solving" is a more recent name for a range of psychological activities, centering on original inquiry, that are as old as man. For a study that views composing as problem solving and suggests the range of heuristics normally used in composing, see Linda Flower and John R. Hayes's "Plans That Guide the Composing Process" (in *Writing: Process, Development, and Communication*, ed. Carl H. Fredericksen and Joseph F. Dominic, Vol. 2 of *Writing: The Nature, Development and Teaching of Written Communication* [Hillsdale, N.J.: Erlbaum, 1981], pp. 39–58).

A "heuristic," as the term is used in this essay, is a codification of a particular sort of cognitive skill; it is a plan designed to help one in carrying out complex, non-routine activities for which trial and error is undesirable or unmanageable, and for which we lack a rule-governed plan (even though it might be usefully developed) or for which a rule-governed plan would be impractical or impossible. It helps us translate knowledge about something into knowledgeable practice. More specifically, it helps us initiate and to some extent guide promising lines of inquiry—to pose good questions, for example, better questions than we might otherwise pose; it does not, however, guarantee good answers, as do rule-governed procedures. For discussions of this conception see George A. Miller, Eugene Galanter, and Karl H. Pribram, *Plans and the Structure of Behavior* (New York: Holt, Rinehart and Winston, 1960); and D. N. Perkins, *The*

Mind's Best Work (Cambridge: Harvard University Press, 1981), especially Chapter 7.

That this definition is but one of several possibilities can be seen from several recent articles that raise questions about the nature of heuristics. Many of the definitions rely on classification schemes drawn from particular psychologies and philosophies, often simple dichotomies, often highly value laden (artificial vs. natural, reason vs. imagination, rationalist vs. empiricist, conscious vs. unconscious, scientific vs. humanist, etc.). For example: Susan Wells classifies heuristics by their ethos and epistemology ("Classroom Heuristics and Empiricism," *CE,* 39 [Dec. 1977], 467–76); James Kinney's "Classifying Heuristics" groups them according to three traditional ways of knowing: empiricism, rationalism, and intuitionism (*CCC,* 30 [Dec. 1979], 351–56); Sabina Thorne Johnson classifies them as either intellectual or intuitional ("The Ant and the Grasshopper: Some Reflections on Prewriting," *CE,* 43 [March 1981], 232–41).

Such classifications are no doubt useful, but they do not carry us very far toward an understanding of heuristics. Other kinds of inquiry are necessary. Responding to an argument by James Kinney ("Tagmemic Rhetoric: A Reconsideration," *CCC,* 29 [May 1978], 141–45), Lee Odell discusses kinds of research that appear to be required if we are going to develop a fuller understanding ("Another Look at Tagmemic Theory: A Response to James Kinney," *CCC,* 29 [May 1978], 146–52). Richard E. Young attempts to develop an agenda for research in "Paradigms and Problems: Needed Research in Rhetorical Invention" (in *Research on Composing: Points of Departure,* ed. Charles R. Cooper and Lee Odell [Urbana, Ill.: NCTE, 1978], pp. 29–47).

The Utility of Heuristics

Another controversy centers on the utility of heuristics. For example, are they a substitute for subject-matter knowledge? If not, what do they contribute to learning? Sabina Thorne Johnson sees all methods of invention as emergency responses to the present-day students' lack of intellectual preparation ("The Ant and the Grasshopper," *CE,* 43 [March 1981], 232–41). Such a view sets up sharp dichotomies—skill vs. knowledge, methods of invention, i.e., heuristics of various sorts, vs. subject-matter knowledge. Johnson attacks the assumption that heuristic knowledge can substitute for knowledge of a field. For an alternative argument that presents a procedural knowledge and subject-matter knowledge as phases of a continuum rather than a dichotomy, see James G. Greeno, "Trends in the Theory of Knowledge for Problem Solving," in *Problem Solving and Education,* pp. 9–23. Consistent with Greeno's position is D. N. Perkins's view that knowledge, experience, and the specific heuristics associated with a field, i.e., the procedural knowledge we might refer to as "know-how," are necessary for competent performance (*The Mind's Best Work,* especially pp. 207–214).

When Janice Lauer proposes "transcendency" as a criterion for evaluating heuristic procedures, she is implicitly arguing that general heuristics (those not limited to particular disciplines or kinds of data) not only have utility but on the whole are to be preferred to heuristics with a more limited range of applicability ("Toward a Metatheory of Heuristic Procedures," *CCC,* 30 [Oct. 1979], 268–69). On the other hand, Lee Odell and Dixie Goswami's study of non-academic writers suggests that writers in different jobs use different kinds of reasoning, which may indicate that in the world out there general heuristics and for that matter "general" rhetorics are less useful than those tailored to specific kinds of tasks ("Writing in a Non-Academic Setting," *RTE,* 16 [Oct. 1982], 201–23). For a discussion of the relationship and relative power of general heuristics and discipline-specific heuristics, see Chapter 7 in D. N. Perkins, *The Mind's Best Work.* Since most of the heuristics in the various arts of invention are general heuristics, the issue is clearly an important one for both the teacher and the theorist.

A closely related issue has to do with the transferability of knowledge and skill. If we believe that they transfer readily from one disciplinary area to another, we are less likely to insist on covering the topics and skills associated with those areas and more likely to focus on training the mind as an instrument of inquiry and on methods of inquiry. If we believe that there is little transfer, we are likely to be concerned with predicting what our students need to know, with covering the subject, and with rigid curricular requirements. The enormous expansion of knowledge and the rapidity of change in nearly every aspect of our lives make the issue a crucial one, not just in rhetorical invention but in education as a whole. For a general discussion of the issue see Herbert A. Simon's "Problem Solving and Education" (in *Problem Solving and Education*, pp. 81–96). Janice Lauer discusses the issue in terms of rhetorical education in "Writing as Inquiry: Some Questions for Teachers," *CCC,* 33 (Feb. 1982), 89–93. The writing-across-the-curriculum movement and changes in our conception and teaching of technical writing will test the range of applicability of our arts of invention and the adequacy of our assumptions about the transfer of rhetorical knowledge and skill.

PEDAGOGY AND METHODS OF INVENTION

A method of invention, as I am using the term, is composed of a set of heuristic procedures along with their theoretical rationale. They can be seen as arguments for promising paths through the large number of choices open to the writer during processes of origination; the teacher of methods of invention is concerned primarily with cultivating the student's ability to find such paths. In "Invention: A Topographical Survey" I said that recent work on methods of invention has been done, by and large, within the context of four theoretical positions: that of classical rhetoric, of what can be characterized as romantic rhetoric, of Kenneth Burke's rhetoric, and of tagmemic rhetoric. By and large, the situation is unchanged, although attention appears to have shifted from explications of the methods themselves to their use and evaluation. For a discussion of textbooks rooted in these positions, see David V. Harrington et al., "A Critical Survey of Resources for Teaching Rhetorical Invention: A Review-Essay," *CE*, 40 (Feb. 1979), 641–61. It is worth noting that the four theoretical positions share some assumptions and that the inventional methods and teaching strategies developed in the context of one position may well be useful to those working in another; the paths converge from time to time.

Classical Invention

For the teacher new to classical rhetoric, a useful and informed introduction to classical invention as a method of thinking can be found in Eugene Garver's "Demystifying Classical Rhetoric," *RSQ*, 10 (Spring 1980), 75–82.

Logic has been receiving considerable attention in rhetorical studies as a result of influential theorists such as Henry Johnstone, Chaim Perelman, and Stephen Toulmin; in addition, problem-solving rhetorics necessarily raise issues of validity and evidence in the verification of proposed solutions and thus must incorporate logic in one form or another as part of the art. David S. Kaufer and Christine M. Neuwirth argue that formal logic has more to contribute to argumentation than recent criticism suggests, and propose a heuristic that encourages inquiry that is flexible, multiperspectived, and creative ("Integrating Formal Logic and the New Rhetoric: A Four-Stage Heuristic," *CE*, 45 [April 1983], 380–89). In "Teaching Argument: A Theory of Types," Jeanne Fahnestock and Marie Secor propose a way of teaching argument that avoids extensive use of formal logic while maintaining the principles of sound reasoning (*CCC*, 34 [Feb. 1983], 20–30).

Fahnestock and Secor suggest that stasis, the ancient heuristic for discovering and formulating questions to be argued in courts of law, can become a major component of a field-independent theory of invention ("Toward a Modern Version of Stasis," in *Oldspeak/Newspeak: Rhetorical Transformations,* ed.

Charles Kneupper [Arlington, Texas: Rhetoric Society of America, 1985], pp. 217–26). John C. Adams extends the concept of stasis to non-public discourse, interpersonal conflict in particular, and lays a theoretical foundation for a program of research in "An Explication and Presentation of an Expanded Typology of Forensic Stases for Use in the Study and Practice of Interpersonal Conflict" (in *Oldspeak/Newspeak,* pp. 227–37). Richard A. Katula and Richard W. Roth's "A Stock Issues Approach to Writing Arguments" provides a detailed discussion of the use of a heuristic based on the concept of stasis that aids in the analysis and composition of deliberative arguments, i.e., arguments of policy (*CCC,* 31 [May 1980], 183–96).

As Michael D. Hood indicates in "The Enthymeme: A Brief Bibliography of Modern Sources," the enthymeme, or rhetorical syllogism, is becoming a major subject of investigation in composition studies (*RSQ,* 14 [Summer and Fall 1984], 159–62). Frank J. D'Angelo discusses the relation between topoi, enthymemes, and structural principles in paragraphs and entire discourses in "Topoi, Paradigms, and Rhetorical Enthymemes" (in *Oldspeak/Newspeak,* pp. 208–16). In a somewhat related discussion, Lawrence D. Green argues that structural enthymemes provide a powerful guide to invention by enabling the writer to foresee strategic necessities in the act of composing ("Enthymemic Invention and Structural Prediction," *CE* [Feb. 1980], 623–34).

The writing of dialogues, Socratic and otherwise, has been proposed as a means of encouraging student sensitivity to voice, the need for elaboration of generalizations, the disposition of arguments, and other features of discourse that are, or should be, shaped by ethical and situational considerations. David S. Kaufer and Christine M. Neuwirth propose a heuristic for helping the student engage in responsible refutation of an opponent's position in "The Irony Game: Assessing a Writer's Adaptation to an Opponent," *JAC,* 2 (1982), 89–101. The following articles treat dialogue as part of an integrated series of language tasks that make up a course of study, a kind of *progymnasmata:* Alan J. Chaffee,

"The Ghostly Paradigm in Composition," *CE,* 39 (Dec. 1977), 477–83; Frank J. D'Angelo, "The Dialogue," *RR,* 1 (Sept. 1982), 72–80.

One of the reasons that persuasion has for years been pushed to the periphery of composition studies is that it raises difficult questions about not only the possibility but the propriety of trying to change the ways other people think; exposition, which merely adds information to someone's knowledge of the world, has proven to be a more comfortable kind of discourse. As argument and persuasion begin to recapture our attention, articles on the ethics of persuasion have begun to appear more frequently. For example: Alan Chaffee discusses the "toto principle" (one's ethical obligation to the opposition) in "The Ghostly Paradigm of Composition" cited earlier. I. Hashimoto discusses the complexity of ethical persuasion and questions the effectiveness of conventional approaches to teaching it ("Persuasion as Ethical Argument," *RR,* 4 [Sept. 1985], 46–53). Jim W. Corder questions the efficacy of traditional as well as Rogerian argument in situations where conflict is extreme and suggests an alternative that stretches our moral as well as our intellectual capacities; in doing so he reopens *ethos* as a subject for research ("Argument as Emergence, Rhetoric as Love," *RR,* 4 [Sept. 1985], 16–32). In "The Ethics of Rhetoric: A Bibliography," Frederick J. Antczak and Alan Brinton provide a list heavily weighted with citations from Speech Communication, which is where most of the work on the subject has been done (*RSQ,* 11 [Summer 1981], 187–90).

Romantic Invention

In contrast to the other theoretical positions discussed in this section, romantic rhetoric has no formal method of invention in the sense in which the term is being used here, though it has a theory of invention. Tenets of the theory discourage explicit methods. (For a general account and critique of romantic assumptions about creativity in all the arts, see D. N. Perkins, *The Mind's Best Work* [Cambridge: Harvard University Press, 1981]).

Taking the work of D. Gordon Rohman as the exemplar of romantic invention, as I did in my earlier bibliographic study, masked this feature of romantic invention, since Rohman was experimenting with specific heuristics that were subsequently treated by many as a coherent method (i.e., the "pre-writing" method). If romantic rhetoric has developed no characteristic method of invention, it has nevertheless encouraged development of pedagogical practices designed to foster the ability to invent, and it has clearly contributed to a critical self-consciousness in the discipline that has encouraged theoretical work and research on the processes that concern us here. (For an elaboration of this line of argument, see Richard Young, "Concepts of Art and the Teaching of Writing," in *The Rhetorical Tradition and Modern Writing,* ed. James J. Murphy [New York: MLA, 1982], pp. 130–41.)

The romantic's traditional insistence on the value of the non-conscious and non-rational powers of the mind is apparent in, for example, James E. Miller's "Rediscovering the Rhetoric of Imagination," *CCC,* 25 (Dec. 1974), 360–67; Robert Baden's "Pre-writing: The Relation Between Thinking and Feeling," *CCC,* 26 (Dec. 1975), 368–70; and Barrett J. Mandel's "Losing One's Mind: Learning to Write and to Edit," *CCC,* 29 (Dec. 1978), 362–68. The most elaborate recent discussion of romantic assumptions as they manifest themselves in the teaching of writing is Ann E. Bertoff's *The Making of Meaning: Metaphors, Models, and Maxims for Writing Teachers* (Montclair, N.J.: Boynton/Cook, 1981). What emerges from such discussions is a conception of composing as organic, essentially mysterious, and hence inaccessible to analysis and resistant to deliberate control. This conception of composing coupled with a desire to help students learn to carry out the process is, I think, what has stimulated the romantic rhetorician to experiment so widely with pedagogical methods. Trying to teach a mystery stretches our ingenuity.

James Britton's "Shaping at the Point of Utterance," discussed earlier, should be mentioned here as well because the concept it presents, i.e., spontaneous inventiveness at the moment of utterance, is one of the principal alternatives proposed by the romantics to the formal methods of invention so prominent in the other schools of rhetoric (in *Reinventing the Rhetorical Tradition,* ed. Aviva Freedman and Ian Pringle [Conway, Arkansas: L&S Books for the Canadian Council of Teachers of English, 1980], pp. 61–65). Though not intended as such, Barrett Mandel's "Losing One's Mind" and Donald M. Murray's "The Feel of Writing—and Teaching Writing" (in *Reinventing the Rhetorical Tradition,* pp. 67–73) can be read as elaborations of Britton's discussion.

A number of discussions of romantic pedagogy center on expressive discourse, a genre or aim often associated with this rhetorical position in much the same way as persuasive discourse is associated with classical rhetoric. A rather slippery term, "expressive discourse" is variously defined, meaning anything from uncritical effusion about the self, for those who are critical of romantic theory and pedagogy, to, for the more sympathetic, an aim of discourse prerequisite to all other aims of discourse. But always, as James Britton says, it is language close to speech, close to the self. Two discussions of expressive discourse that have shaped current thinking are James Britton's "Writing to Learn and Learning to Write" (in *Prospect and Retrospect: Selected Essays of James Britton,* ed. Gordon M. Pradl [Montclair, N.J.: Boynton/ Cook, 1982], pp. 94–111) and James L. Kinneavy's "Expressive Discourse" in *A Theory of Discourse* (New York: Norton, 1971), pp. 393–449.

Kenneth Burke's Dramatism

Given the richness of Kenneth Burke's work, its range of applicability, and its potential usefulness to writers, surprisingly little has been done to develop it into a full-fledged method of invention that could be used in the teaching of writing. One reason for this inertia may well be Burke's own lack of interest in rhetorical composition in contrast to his intense interest in rhetorical analysis. In "Questions and Answers about the Pentad,"

CCC, 29 (Dec. 1978), 330–35, Burke comments on efforts to use the pentad as a heuristic strategy in composing, as opposed to its intended use in the analysis of discourse. (In doing so he provides a convenient introduction to dramatism and the pentad.)

We do seem to be slowly moving toward a method of invention based on Burke's work that can serve as both an art of reading and an art of writing. For example, in "Dramatistic Invention: The Pentad as Heuristic Procedure," Charles Kneupper seeks to isolate the components of dramatistic theory that could form the basis of a method that aids in generating discourse (*RSQ,* 9 [Summer 1979], 130–36). Joseph Comprone argues that writing can be seen as "a dramatic attempt to complete an action that begins with a linguistic struggle with the world out there and closes with a recreation of that struggle for readers"; from such a perspective Burke's theories, particularly dramatism, offer a method for teaching writing as a process ("Kenneth Burke and the Teaching of Writing," *CCC,* 29 [Dec. 1978], 336–40).

Comprone elaborates this argument in "Burke's Dramatism as a Means of Using Literature to Teach Composition," *RSQ,* 9 (Summer 1979), 142–55; the article contains detailed suggestions for using Burke's theories in teaching the critical essay. Philip Keith uses a set of terms from Burke's *Grammar of Motives* for a series of dialectical exercises designed to help students develop arguments while avoiding the simplifications encouraged by conventional textbooks ("Burke for the Composition Class," *CCC,* 28 [Dec. 1977], 348–51). He continues the discussion, suggesting use of a number of Burke's concepts in pre-writing and revision processes ("Burkean Invention, from Pentad to Dialectic," *RSQ,* 9 [Summer 1979], 137–41). Clayton W. Lewis argues that efforts to make use of Burke's dramatism in the teaching of writing have suppressed the importance of act while emphasizing agent and agency; the student writer, he maintains, needs to re-experience language as act addressed to a situation in an effort to transform it, as an effort to make a difference ("Burke's Act in *A Rhetoric of Motives,*" *CE,* 46 [April 1984], 368–76).

Chris Anderson argues that Burke's conception of dramatism offers the basis for an alternative kind of deliberative discourse that recreates the experience of the event rather than demonstrating a thesis logically ("Dramatism and Deliberation," *RR*, 3 [Sept. 1985], 34–43). In a related article, W. Ross Winterowd discusses the dramatism of language and its implications for the teaching of composition, focusing on the use of Burke's notion of the "representative anecdote" as a rhetorical alternative to the enthymeme ("Dramatism in Themes and Poems," *CE*, 45 [Oct. 1983], 581–88).

Tagmemic Invention

Two components of tagmemic invention—problem formulation and systematic exploration—are discussed in the following articles: Richard Young argues that problematic situations initiate the composing process and that our conception of rhetorical invention should be expanded to address this kind of experience ("Problems and the Composing Process," in *Writing: Process, Development and Communication,* ed. Carl H. Fredericksen and Joseph F. Dominic, Vol. 2 of *Writing: The Nature, Development and Teaching of Written Communication* [Hillside, N.J: Erlbaum, 1981], pp. 59–66). He discusses and exemplifies the process of formulating problems using a heuristic in "Richard Young's Assignment," in *What Makes Writing Good,* ed. William E. Coles, Jr., and James Vopat (Lexington, Mass.: Heath, 1985), pp. 314–20. Both articles can be related to the concept of exigency in rhetorical situations, discussed earlier in "Situational Context."

In "Methodizing Nature: The Tagmemic Discovery Procedure," Young illustrates the use of the tagmemic exploratory procedure with a student's efforts to understand a poem (in *Rhetoric and Change,* ed. William E. Tanner and J. Dean Bishop [Mesquite, Texas: Ide House, 1982], pp. 126–37). And in "Theme in Fictional Literature: A Way into Complexity," he suggests the use of field perspective in thematic analysis (in *Linguistics, Stylistics, and the Teaching of Composition,* ed. Donald McQuade [Akron, Ohio:

L&S Books and the Department of English, University of Akron, 1979], pp. 61–71). A more general discussion of field perspective in literary analysis can be found in William Holtz's "Spatial Form in Modern Literature: A Reconsideration," *Critical Inquiry,* 4 (Winter 1977), 271–83.

Several studies argue that though the theory is essentially sound, the theoretical presentation and the pedagogy are too complex and demanding, especially in the case of the exploratory procedure. Responding to the difficulty, Charles W. Kneupper proposes alterations in the discovery procedure in the interest of simplicity, comprehensibility, and ease of teaching ("Revising the Tagmemic Heuristic: Theoretical and Pedagogical Considerations," *CCC,* 31 [May 1980], 160–68). After summarizing a number of controlled studies of efforts to teach tagmemic invention, George Hillocks, Jr., argues that the ambivalent results (some studies report significant change in student abilities, others no change) may be the result of the complexity of the exploratory heuristic and the cognitive demands it places on the student; his response to the difficulty with the tagmemic procedure is a simpler set of strategies designed to develop cognitive abilities that tagmemicists assume already exist in the student ("Inquiry and the Composing Process: Theory and Research," *CE,* 44 [Nov. 1982], 659–73). Hillocks's alternative strategies are drawn from his *Observing and Writing* (Urbana, Ill.: ERIC and NCTE, 1975). Quite another sort of response to the difficulty is Sandra Katz's *Teaching the Tagmemic Discovery Procedure: A Case Study of a Writing Course* (unpublished doctoral dissertation, Carnegie-Mellon University, 1983); using various ethnographic methods Katz seeks to identify the problems students have with the exploratory procedure and to develop hypotheses for subsequent research aimed at improving instruction.

A comprehensive and informed commentary on tagmemic rhetoric, particularly tagmemic invention, can be found in Bruce Edwards, Jr.'s "The Tagmemic Contribution to Composition Teaching," (*Occasional Papers in Composition History and Theory,* ed. Donald C. Stewart [Manhattan, Kansas: Kansas State University, 1979]). Useful introductions written for the non-specialist are John Algeo's "Tagmemics: A Brief Overview" (in *Advances in Tagmemics,* ed. Ruth M. Brend [Amsterdam: North-Holland Publishing, 1974], pp. 1–9) and Kenneth L. Pike's *Linguistic Concepts: An Introduction to Tagmemics* (Lincoln: University of Nebraska Press, 1982). More demanding are Kenneth L. Pike and Evelyn G. Pike's *Grammatical Analysis* (Dallas: Summer Institute of Linguistics and University of Texas, Arlington, 1977) and their *Text and Tagmeme* (Norwood, N.J: Ablex, 1983), both of which offer extended discussions of tagmemic analytical methods; the latter work in particular illustrates the strong tendency of tagmemic linguistics to move into problems traditionally associated with rhetoric and literary criticism.

We began this section noting that the various theories and methods share significant features. It might be well to end by noting that there are significant differences. The various methods of invention available to the teacher do not all imply the same conception of the composing process or of the function and scope of rhetorical invention; assuming that they do and hence are basically interchangeable can create conceptual and pedagogical problems. A method of invention is embedded in a larger body of theoretical assumptions that are essential to understanding it; it is not wholly intelligible out of context. Janice Lauer offers some help in sorting out what can be a confusing situation in her "Issues in Rhetorical Invention," where she discriminates among methods on the basis of differing views about the genesis of writing, the function of topoi and comparable heuristics, and the province of invention (in *Essays on Classical Rhetoric and Modern Discourse,* ed. Robert J. Connors, Lisa Ede, and Andrea A. Lunsford [Carbondale: Southern Illinois University Press, 1984], pp. 127–39).

THE HISTORY OF INVENTION

Though they encompass considerably more than issues of invention, the following bibliographic studies are particularly helpful for those working on the history of invention. First and foremost is Winifred Bryan Horner's collection of annotated bibliographies, both primary and secondary sources, covering the entire history of rhetoric in the West (*Historical Rhetoric: An Annotated Bibliography of Selected Sources in English,* [Boston: G. K. Hall, 1980]); while the bibliographies are not comprehensive, they are extensive and authoritative. A subsequent collection of bibliographic essays edited by Horner, *The Present State of Scholarship in Historical and Contemporary Rhetoric* (Columbia: University of Missouri Press, 1983) is a useful companion to the earlier work. The *Rhetoric Society Quarterly* has regularly published substantial bibliographies on topics of current interest in the discipline; Volume XI (Fall 1981) contains a list of the bibliographies published in *RSQ* from 1968 through 1981. Ronald Mantlon's *Index to Journals in Communication Studies Through 1979* is a convenient means of accessing articles on invention in Speech Communication journals (Annandale, Va.: Speech Communication Assoc., 1980). A comprehensive overview of historical research on rhetoric in Speech Communication, a much richer tradition than we find in English studies, can be found in Richard Leo Enos's "The History of Rhetoric: The Reconstruction of Progress," in *Speech Communication in the 20th Century,* ed. Thomas W. Benson (Carbondale: Southern Illinois University Press, 1985), pp. 28–40.

During the last ten years several major studies of rhetoric have appeared in which invention receives significant treatment: George A. Kennedy's *Classical Rhetoric and Its Christian and Secular Tradition from Ancient to Modern Times* is a substantial introduction to classical rhetoric from its beginning to its decline in the latter part of the eighteenth century (Chapel Hill: University of North

Carolina Press, 1980). Jacqueline de Romilly's *Magic and Rhetoric in Ancient Greece* examines the language act as a mysterious power and efforts to understand and control it by means of reason in the discipline of rhetoric; she suggests that speculation about language use throughout our history has swung between these two positions (Cambridge: Harvard University Press, 1975). Wilbur Samuel Howell's *Poetics, Rhetoric, and Logic: Studies in the Basic Disciplines of Criticism* is a collection of essays on the relation of these three disciplines at various times in our literary history; the book reminds us that invention served throughout much of our history as an art for analyzing discourse as well as an art for producing discourse (Ithaca, N.Y.: Cornell University Press, 1975). Invention is located in an exceedingly rich context of cultural history in Walter Ong's *Interfaces of the Word: Studies in the Evolution of Consciousness and Culture* (Ithaca, N.Y.: Cornell University Press, 1977) and *Orality and Literacy: The Technologizing of the Word* (London: Methuen, 1982). However, what seems to me the most notable development in historical scholarship over the last dozen years is not the appearance of such scholarly works, impressive as they are, but our profession's growing interest in rhetorical history. Only a few years ago historical work in rhetoric was left almost exclusively to our colleagues in Speech Communication. Now we are beginning to write our own history, and in a way that addresses our own theoretical and pedagogical needs.

The growing awareness of other rhetorics, rhetorics that are alternatives to current-traditional rhetoric, encourages the self-consciousness about the discipline that is necessary for historical research. It is not surprising to find that most of the historical studies that are appearing with increasing frequency in English publications focus on the last two centuries, the period during which both current-traditional and Romantic rhetoric developed. An integral part of that history is the virtual disappearance of rhetorical invention—one reason for this change being that the theoretical assumptions of both rhetorics are inhospitable to any formal art of invention, ancient or modern.

Much of our recent historical research is devoted to explaining not only what happened to rhetoric during this period but why it happened, which has tended to produce a strong theoretical bias in the accounts. The following exemplify what is a surprisingly large and growing body of scholarly works: In "Rhetoric in the American College Curriculum: The Decline of Public Discourse," S. Michael Halloran asks how we got from the rhetorical tradition to current-traditional rhetoric (*Pre/ Text*, 3 [Fall 1982], 245–69). James A. Berlin poses a similar question in *Writing Instruction in Nineteenth-Century American Colleges* (Carbondale: Southern Illinois University Press, 1984). Berlin's "Richard Whately and Current Traditional Rhetoric" discusses the historical context that shaped Whately's thinking and his influence on late nineteenth-century textbooks (*CE*, 42 [Sept. 1980], 10–17). Robert J. Connors examines some of the forces that produced our national obsession with mechanical correctness ("Mechanical Correctness as a Focus in Composition Instruction," *CCC*, 36 [Feb. 1985], 61–72). In "Invention in Nineteenth-Century Rhetoric," *CCC*, 36 (Feb. 1985), 51–60, Sharon Crowley discusses the efforts of some nineteenth-century rhetoricians to develop a pedagogy based on eighteenth-century assumptions about the nature of the process of invention. In his account of the social and economic forces that shaped what came to be known as current-traditional rhetoric, or "composition," Gene L. Piché offers at least a partial explanation for the disappearance of a formal art of invention in the English curriculum after the turn of the century ("Class and Culture in the Development of the High School English Curriculum, 1880–1900," *RTE*, 11 [Spring 1977], 17–27).

Robert J. Connors argues that we have no histories of classroom practice to match our histories of theory; we are, however, beginning to get them. By examining the first seven editions of James McCrimmon's *Writing with a Purpose*, Connors tracks variations in current-traditional rhetoric over the last thirty years as it responds to changes in rhetorical theory and social context (*RSQ*, 11 [Fall 1981], 208–21). His "Handbooks: History of a

Genre" is a companion to this article (*RSQ*, 13 [Spring 1983], 87–98). In order to understand analogous efforts today, Kenneth J. Kantor considers earlier efforts during this century to introduce instruction in creative expression ("Creative Expression in the English Classroom: An Historical Study," *RTE*, 9 [Spring 1975], 5–29). Kantor's account of nearly a century of effort at pedagogical innovation bears out the truth of Douglas Ehninger's observation that "in the absence of history, we always have to be starting afresh."

Patrick Scott's "Jonathan Maxcy and the Aims of Early Nineteenth-Century Rhetorical Teaching," *CE*, 45 (Jan. 1983), 21–30, examines the use of popular Scottish texts by an American teacher at a time much like our own, when the relation between the theoretical and the practical sides of rhetoric and between rhetoric and literary criticism were being worked out again. Nan Johnson in her "Three Nineteenth-Century Rhetoricians: The Humanist Alternative to Rhetoric as Skills Management" (in *The Rhetorical Tradition and Modern Writing*, ed. James J. Murphy [New York: MLA, 1982], pp. 105–117) discusses the humanist tradition in rhetoric as it manifests itself in the texts of Franz Theremin, Henry Day, and Matthew Hope, whose work provided an alternative to the more narrowly conceived, skills-oriented rhetoric that came to dominate composition teaching in this country. In their work she identifies a problem facing the modern teacher: the reconciliation of the need for practical language skills with the humanist's insistence that writing must be related to a larger culture.

As the history of current-traditional rhetoric becomes clearer we also begin to see that if we do not know our history we do not, cannot, in some important sense know our pedagogy either. When we knew nothing else but traditional composition, we did not even know that; as Einstein once remarked, "What does a fish know about water?"

Structure and Form
in Non-Narrative Prose

RICHARD L. LARSON, Herbert H. Lehman College
of The City University of New York

ALTHOUGH THERE IS A LARGE BODY OF LITERA-
ture about invention in composing, and an even larger body of
literature about syntax and the rhetoric of the sentence, structure
and form in non-narrative prose beyond the sentence have only
recently become the subject of serious, many-sided theoretical
investigation, even though the paragraph has received a good deal
of attention from teachers who look upon the paragraph as the
fundamental unit of composition (and from those who resist that
view of the paragraph) and want to be sure that students are suita-
bly guided in the construction, or discovery, of paragraphs. In
this essay I begin by reviewing briefly some major reflections on
structure and form that appeared before (roughly) 1975, then examine in more detail approaches to the study of structure that
have flourished since then. I then review some rhetorical approaches to the teaching of structure. Finally, moving from the
perspective of a whole text to focus on smaller units and how
they are held together, I consider recent approaches to the coherence and cohesion of a text, and try to describe where the theory
and analysis of the paragraph are now moving.

I

Some classic essays on form, such as Kenneth Burke's discussion in *Counter-Statement* (Los Altos, California: Hermes Publi-

cations, 1953, pp. 124–49; reprinted in W. Ross Winterowd, *Contemporary Rhetoric: A Conceptual Background with Readings* [New York: Harcourt Brace Jovanovich, 1975], pp. 183–98), focus more on form in literary writing than on form in expository or argumentative composition. Burke's general definition of form as "an arousing and fulfillment of desires . . . one part of [a work] . . . lead[ing] a reader to anticipate another part, to be gratified by the sequence" (Winterowd, p. 183) is useful, of course, for the discussion of writing in whatever mode, but the kinds of form that Burke enumerates—syllogistic progression, repetitive form, conventional form, etc.—are illustrated in his essay mostly from literary texts. Burke does cite syntactic, semantic, and rhythmic structures of nonfictive prose, but he says little about the overall design or structure of such prose.

A few theorists have commented on possible definitions of form. W. Ross Winterowd, for example, has defined form as *"the internal set of consistent relationships perceived in any stretch of discourse, whether poem, play, essay, oration, or whatever"* ("Dispositio: The Concept of Form in Discourse," *CCC,* 22 [February 1971], 41; the essay is reprinted with some changes in his *Contemporary Rhetoric,* pp. 163–70, and the quoted passage is on p. 165 of the book). Winterowd goes on to elaborate the view that perception of form includes recognition of the "deep structure" of an utterance, the surface structure in which it appears, and the other alternatives available for setting forth the substance of what is to be said (*Contemporary Rhetoric,* p. 166). But Winterowd's discussion focuses more on the language of literature and on connections between sentences than on form in complete pieces of discourse.

Others do not so much look into fundamental characteristics of form in composition as advance their preferences concerning the forms that should be taught. Keith Fort, in "Form, Authority, and the Critical Essay," *CE,* 32 (March 1971), 629–39 (reprinted in Winterowd, *Contemporary Rhetoric,* pp. 172–83), suggests that form "comprises those elements in an expression that reflect the attitude of the speaker and that tend to control the audience's relation to the expression's subject matter and the speaker." Thus defined, form to Fort reveals what we might characterize as a set of wishes about how the reader should view the writer and a set of assumptions about how the reader will and should want to respond. Fort does not, however, initiate a full investigation of form; instead, he deplores the usual demand for customary kinds of logic and argument in the writing (and teaching) of critical essays on literature. The insistence that writers of critical essays establish their authority over their texts by arguments structured in traditional patterns is, according to Fort, unduly restrictive; our tastes in critical essays—by professionals and students alike—on literary texts should accommodate greater variety in structure and in relationship among writer, subject, and audience.

Making a somewhat similar appeal (though not only for essays in literary criticism), Walt Stevens, in "A Proposal for Non-Linear Disposition," *Western Speech,* 37 (Spring 1973), 118–28, cites writers of poems and novels as well as theorists of rhetoric, well-known speechmakers, and social scientists to establish that failure of a work or a process to conform to familiar patterns of linear organization need not be damaging, but can lead to "individuality, novelty, variety, invention, or creativity." He is, like Fort, arguing in support of a particular outlook on form more than he is investigating principles of form.

Howard Brashers, however, does attempt the discovery of formal principles mainly for their value in illuminating non-narrative prose. In his "Aesthetic Form in Familiar Essays," *CCC,* 22 (May 1971), 147–55, Brashers identifies several techniques of design: contrast, gradation, theme and variation, restraint (and climax), and several typical patterns that bring such devices into unity: linear patterns, radial-circular patterns, and mytho-literary patterns (sequences of experiences "recognizable as a unit in a culture"). In discussing these techniques, Brashers explores how connections are made between parts of works, and how unity is achieved within variety of detail. But Brashers applies his analysis only to what he calls the "familiar essay" (other kinds of essays, he says, have other principles of form), and he has carried his analysis no further.

Willis Pitkin, Jr., has attempted to offer a more general theory of the structure of discourse. In his most accessible article, "Discourse Blocs," *CCC,* 20 (May 1969), 138–48, Pitkin argues that discourse may be usefully viewed not simply as a collection of sentences and paragraphs, but as a hierarchical arrangement of "blocs" of thought, most of which can be subdivided into smaller blocs, and combined with other blocs to form larger blocs. The blocs are discovered, not by how long they are or by how they are punctuated, or by their appearance on the page, but by the function each serves in the discourse. At the top of the hierarchy, a bloc can presumably include several sentences (or paragraphs); near the bottom of the hierarchy, it may consist of a small part of a sentence.

Most blocs come in pairs; the blocs in each pair are related in one of four ways: by simple coordination (since it is possible to coordinate more than two items, there can be more than two blocs in a coordinate series); by complementation, in which one bloc starts a unit of thought and a second bloc completes the unit (e.g., question/answer, assertion/reassertion, cause/effect, negative/positive, premise/conclusion, etc.); by subordination, in which the first bloc mentions genus, the second mentions species; and by superordination, in which the first bloc mentions species, the second genus.

II

In the past decade, the most conspicuous and influential developments in the theoretical study of structure in non-literary prose have come, I believe, in the work of psycholinguists and students of cognitive psychology: scholars investigating the operations of the minds of writers and of readers, insofar as they can make those operations available for examination and generalization. Such scholars explore as much how readers read as how writers write: they try to identify how readers understand, and retain in memory, texts that they have just read, and they try to derive structural concepts from observing what features make the substance of a passage enter with reasonable clarity into readers' memories, and remain there for periods of time. In doing so they respond as scholars, in effect, to the findings of James Coomber ("Perceiving the Structure of Written Materials," *RTE*, 9 [Winter 1975], 263–66) that many students do not grasp the structure of the main ideas in texts that they read, and that inability may partly explain the weaknesses in the organization of what they write.

Although they are not primarily psycholinguists, Brent Davis and Ellen Nold, in "The Discourse Matrix," *CCC*, 31 (May 1980), 141–52, cite the studies of such psycholinguists as Walter Kintsch and Herbert Clark while advancing a theory about how discourse can be described. Suggesting that the three principal relationships of units within a discourse are coordination (successive units are at the same level of abstraction), subordination (the succeeding unit is at a lower level of abstraction than the preceding unit), and superordination (the succeeding unit is at a higher level of abstraction than the immediately preceding unit), they analyze (and diagram) several texts to show how the relationships are exemplified. Further, they describe constraints on the movement of thought within a text—constraints that a writer must observe if the text is to appear to the reader to be well-formed. What they offer, then, is a theoretical model for the structure of a text *and* a test for clarity of structure. This work of Davis and Nold has not, to my knowledge, been tested empirically, but its claims may deserve further exploration.

Surely one of the leaders in the study of how form in prose affects the reader's ability to understand and retain what has been read is Bonnie J. F. Meyer, who in order to study the effects of prose structures on readers has been led to elaborate descriptions of ways to describe those structures. In *The Organization of Prose and Its Effects on Memory* (Amsterdam: North Holland, 1975), she introduced a technique for representing diagrammatically in great detail the structure of a complex prose text as a hierarchy of concepts and assertions. She also began the presentation of her view that a text can be viewed as an assembling of five different elements: collections (ideas grouped together on the basis of shared properties, or because a subject shares them), causation (including covariance), response (including problem and solution), comparison, and description. She argued, further, that when signals of structure are present in a text, the load upon the reader in inferring the structure of a text is diminished, so that the energy saved can be reallocated to improved recollection.

In "Identification of the Structure of Prose and Its Implications for the Study of Reading and Memory," *Journal of Reading Behavior,* 7 (Spring 1975), 7–47, she explored the concepts further, distinguishing between "lexical predicates" and "rhetorical predicates." The former establish the role that an item plays in an assertion (e.g., "agent," "instrument," "patient," and so on); the latter are "explicit organizing relations in prose": paratactic (relations between equally weighted items: alternatives, or responses, as in question–answer), hypotactic (relations involving main and subordinated items, such as attribution, equivalence or restatement, specification, and so on), and "neutral" (items that can be either paratactic or hypotactic, e.g., "collection"). In the same article, she reported further on the readability of passages organized in different ways. Two years later, she reported that the "height" of a unit in the structure of a passage—as analyzed according to her procedures—was related to the likelihood of its being remembered, and noted that signaling the importance of information helps insure recall of "less obviously important" material ("What Is Remembered from Prose: A Function of Passage Structure," in *Discourse Production and Comprehension,* ed. Roy O. Freedle [Norwood, N.J.: Ablex, 1977], pp. 306–36). I might add that readers interested in an alternative, and more recent, source in which to locate a list of Meyer's terms for sentence "roles"—which derive from J. E. Grimes, *The Thread of Discourse* (The Hague: Mouton, 1975)—may consult Charles R. Cooper, "Procedures for Describing Written Texts," in *Research on Writing: Principles and Methods,* ed. Peter Mosenthal, Lynne Tamor, and Sean A. Walmsley (New York: Longman, 1983), pp. 300–301.

Later, in an essay written with M. Elizabeth Rice, "The Interaction of Reader Strategies and the Organization of Text" (*Text,* 2 [Nos. 1–3, 1982], 155–92), she observed that perception of different structural plans affects readers' expectations about a text differently, and suggested, not surprisingly, that a writer might facilitate the reader's work by making explicit statements of structural relations, offering preview and summary statements, and using "pointer" devices along the way. Professor Meyer's investigations of the elements and relationships that make up texts continued in two essays on "Prose Analysis: Purposes, Procedures, and Problems" in Bruce Bitton and John Black, eds., *Understanding Expository Text* (Hillsdale, N.J.: Lawrence Erlbaum, 1985), where she reasserted the seminal importance of the basic plans she had previously identified and broke "comparison" down into three and "description" into a dozen individual elements or relationships, partly as a guide to others in their analytical research.

Professor Meyer's research is most accessible to teachers of writing through her "Reading Research and the Composition Teacher: The Importance of Plans," *CCC,* 33 (February 1982), 37–50, where she describes her research procedures, identifies important plans in prose texts, illustrates her hierarchical analyses of texts, and in effect advocates the use by writers and the teaching of specific plans as well as the use of signals to clarify the plan being followed in a given text. The notes to her essay identify several of her other writings on the subject of structure and readers' recall of texts.

Bonnie Meyer may be the best known, but she is by no means the only important scholar studying how the shaping and styling of prose affects readers' comprehension and response. In the volume just mentioned, *Understanding Expository Text,* Bruce Bitton, Shawn Gwynn, and Jeffrey Smith ("Cognitive Demands

of Processing Expository Text: A Cognitive Workbench Model,"
pp. 227–47) urge writers to increase the "predictability" of their
texts and reduce the burden on readers by activating in the readers' minds interpretive "schemas" for understanding the text: ab-
stracting and summarizing regularly, describing the structure of
their texts, foreshadowing, providing headings, using appropriate redundancy, using cataphoric (forward-looking) cohesive devices, increasing "locality" of reference, and signaling transitions.
Still in the same volume, Richard Mayer, in "Structural Analysis
of Scientific Prose: Can We Increase Problem-Solving Performance?" suggests that "advance organizers" help readers focus
their attention on explanative information and assist them in
using the texts in problem-solving (pp. 82–83). In "Thematic
Processes in the Comprehension of Technical Prose" (in the same
volume), David Kieras, a well-known investigator of the features
in prose that promote readability, reports that if the main idea of a
text is stated at the beginning or at the end, readers will be more
likely to recognize its importance. He finds that readers recognize
and grasp more easily passages of explicit generalization than
they do passages that simply offer an account of causes and consequences. In another study, also concerned with preferable ways
for arranging information in a text but less directly related to
research on readability, Rachel Giora observes that "final position" in a segment or paragraph—before the announcement of the
topic of the next segment—is a natural and preferable position
"for dominant/ foreground information," and indeed gives "foreground status" to the information so placed ("Segmentation and
Segment Cohesion," *Text,* 3 [No. 2, 1983], 155–81). We will discuss other investigations of the linkage between structure and
comprehension (as established *and signaled*) in our examination of
theories about the paragraph and about coherence and cohesion,
below.

It may be well at this point to differentiate the work of cognitive pyschologists such as Meyer and Kieras from that of other
cognitive psychologists, very well known to scholars of rhetoric

and writing, like Linda Flower. Meyer, Kieras, and other such scholars are concerned with plans discovered in texts, with the desirability of making clear use of different kinds of plans, and with the desirability of signaling those plans. They are interpreting the texts in order to observe why the texts have different impacts on readers. Flower, though concerned, as in "A Cognitive Process Theory of Writing" (*CCC*, 32 [December 1981], 365–87), with the role of planning in composing and with the kinds of planning that different writers do (or do not do), looks less frequently at plans as they emerge in finished texts. A broad distinction might be that Meyer and Kieras are concerned with the cognition of interpreting a text, Flower with the cognition of discovering and creating it.

The work of psycholinguistic researchers, though conspicuous, has not been greeted with unanimous acclaim by scholars interested in reading and writing. An audibly skeptical judgment of some of their efforts has come, for example, from George Dillon, whose *Constructing Texts* (Bloomington: Indiana University Press, 1981), includes psycholinguistic research among the many approaches to the study of texts that oversimplify, even demean, the experiences of readers and writers. Reading is not just the decoding of propositional content, Dillon suggests in his first two chapters, any more than writing is simply the encoding of propositional content. And one does not learn much that is significant about reading by focusing exclusively on the limitations of the "channel" through which a reader receives ideas. In many respects psycholinguistic research fails to take account of the complexities of language and of reading. But Dillon's criticisms, though trenchant, have not reverberated widely; psycholinguistic studies remain influential on the thinking of scholars concerned with structure in prose.

But it is not only the psycholinguists who have looked in the last decade at characteristics of form in expository texts; linguists themselves have begun examining them. Indeed a branch of linguistics that deals with the structure of texts beyond the sentence has come into being: text linguistics. A full review of the literature reporting these studies, many of them conducted, or heavily influenced, by European linguists, would require vastly more space than is available here, but some major scholars in this field deserve mention. For our purposes in this discussion, a representative and important investigator, a European whose work is often discussed in American scholarship, is Teun A. Van Dijk, whose *Text and Context: Explorations in the Semantics and Pragmatics of Discourse* (London: Longman, 1977) lays out the foundations of a concept that is proving of much interest to investigators of the structure of prose: that of *macrostructures*. A macrostructure, says Van Dijk, is characterized "in terms of SETS of propositions, whole sequences and certain operations on sets and sequences of propositions of a discourse" (p. 95)—that is, it permits the central idea to be derived from several individual propositions as logically (and, usually, hierarchically) related. Later on, Van Dijk is more specific about the definition of a macrostructure (which closely resembles, he says, the "topic" of a discourse): "a proposition entailed by the sequence of propositions underlying the discourse (or part of it)" (p. 137), where the concept of "entailment" has the force that a logician would accord it. He adds that there can be "levels" of macrostructure: "any proposition entailed by a subset of a sequence is a macro-structure for that subsequence. At the next level these macro-structural propositions may again be subject to integration into a larger frame, i.e., jointly, a more general macro-structure. . . . when we speak of THE macro-structure of a sequence we refer to the most general macro-structure, entailed by the other macro-structures, 'dominating' the whole sequence" (p. 137). For Van Dijk, another term for the concept of macrostructure is "topic of conversation," so that "topic" becomes for him the proposition entailed, strictly, by the sub-propositions, taken as a whole, in a sequence of text. From these definitions, and this line of reasoning, can follow an interest in the units of thought nested, hierarchically, in any stretch of text—an interest that implies a particular view of what constitutes a text.

Readers may suspect that some of the psycholinguists whose work was discussed a couple of paragraphs above have found much to interest them in the concept of macrostructure, and those readers are correct. Witness David Kieras's "The Role of Major Referents and Sentence Topics in the Construction of Passage Macrostructure," *Discourse Processes,* 4 (January–March 1981), 1–15, especially p. 14. It is a short step from having the concept of macrostructure to suggesting that readers will grasp a text better and remember it longer if the macrostructure is announced and signaled, not allowed to remain implicit.

Those wishing to familiarize themselves further with essential concepts in text linguistics may want to examine the references in the notes to William VandeKopple, "Functional Sentence Perspective," *CCC,* 33 (February 1982), 50–63, which applies insights from text linguistics to the construction and arrangement of sentences (focusing on the readability of a text), and Stephen P. Witte, "Topical Structure and Revision," *CCC,* 34 (October 1983), 313–41. In "Defining Thematic Progressions and Their Relationship to Reader Comprehension," Barbara Glatt elaborates the theory behind "thematic progressions" and behind advocating that "given" information precede "new" information within sentences to assure effective communication (*What Writers Know: The Language, Process, and Structure of Written Discourse,* ed. Martin Nystrand [New York: Academic Press, 1982], pp. 87–103). Van Dijk, a highly productive linguist, has elaborated his notion of macrostructures in a book with that term as its title (Hillsdale, N.J.: Erlbaum, 1979). With Walter Kintsch, he produced in 1983 *Strategies of Discourse Comprehension* (Orlando, Florida: Academic Press), in which he reviews and proposes strategies that readers use or might use to understand different lengths of text. He offers advice about how readers infer macropropositions to construct the macrostructure of a text (Chapter

6), and discusses the role of schemata, which he calls "superstructures": recurrent plans for the organization of texts that the reader is familiar with and can recognize as part of the process of interpretation (Chapter 7). (The discussion of schemata wins much more favor from Dillon—who finds in *Constructing Texts,* Chapter 3, that schemata can organize, integrate, and help predict content—than does the text linguists' advocacy of "topical progression" based on the "given-new" contract, which Dillon believes oversimplifies the richness of relationships among successive sentences in skillfully written texts.)

Finally, a reader interested in a compact account of essential principles (going well beyond the concept of macrostructures) and applications (to reading and to the construction of discourse) of text linguistics might examine Robert de Beaugrande and Wolfgang Dressler, *Introduction to Text Linguistics* (London and New York: Longman, 1981).

Linguists, and not only text linguists, share many concerns with philosophers; the last group of investigators I discuss whose studies have been applied to illuminating the structures of complete texts are the "speech act" theorists, whose approach takes its inspiration from the writings of the philosopher J. L. Austin (notably *How to Do Things with Words* [Cambridge, Mass.: Harvard University Press, 1962]) and is probably best exemplified today in the writings of J. R. Searle: *Speech Acts: An Essay in the Philosophy of Language* (Cambridge, England: Cambridge University Press, 1969) and "A Taxonomy of Illocutionary Acts," in K. Gunderson, ed., *Language, Mind, and Society* (Minneapolis: University of Minnesota Press, 1975). Briefly, a speech act theorist looks upon a verbal utterance in a social context (including the act of writing to readers) as an action performed in reference to an audience; one can judge actions on whether or not they are "felicitous." One can label and enumerate the various actions (e.g., to state, claim, request, beg, promise, congratulate) and one can group the actions into categories (e.g., directives [acts that order, beg, invite, advise], commissives [acts that promise or vow], expressives [acts that apologize, congratulate, and the like], declarations [acts that nominate, appoint, define and the like]), as R. G. D'Andrade and M. Wish, summarizing Searle, do in "Speech Act Theory in Quantitative Research on Interpersonal Behavior," in *Discourse Processes,* 8 (April–June 1985), 229–59, especially pp. 234–37. An investigator of the structure of prose can then note the acts that make up a text, discover patterns in the occurrence of those acts, and even argue that particular acts effectively obligate the writer to accomplish other specific acts elsewhere in the text if that text is to be successful. See, for example, Marilyn Cooper, "The Pragmatics of Form: How Do Writers Discover What to Do When?" in Richard Beach and Lillian Bridwell, eds., *New Directions in Composition Research* (New York: Guilford Press, 1984), pp. 109–29. A rather full discussion of speech act theory and its implications for reading can be found in Martin Steinmann, Jr., "Speech-Act Theory and Writing," in Nystrand, ed., *What Writers Know,* pp. 291–323. An outline of "sentence roles" in writing, blending notions derived from speech act theory and from other linguistic studies, can be found in Charles Cooper, "Procedures for Describing Written Texts," pages 302–3. The full implications of speech act theory for studies of the structure of non-narrative prose and for the establishment of criteria with which to judge such prose remain to be explored; Marilyn Cooper herself is working on these subjects.

From investigations conducted essentially by scholars outside of rhetoric, composition, and literary criticism, then, we have learned much in the last decade about how to look at the structure of non-narrative texts: how to describe the parts of such texts, how to depict the interrelationships of those parts, how to judge the structures thus identified, and how to begin to study their effects on readers. Such investigations will no doubt continue; readers interested in the concept of structure may want to follow them carefully—in order, among other reasons, to see whether those investigations capture readers' own experiences with the texts.

Meanwhile, another scholar, looking for a way to describe *students'* texts so that he can trace developmental trends in students' writing (including differences between the styles of younger and older students) and offer suggestions about cognitive-logical operations that might be deliberately taught, has arrived inductively at a plan for describing students' writings. His plan might be developed into an approach to describing structural patterns— patterns that connect sentences into groups, then connect groups of sentences with other groups—in much non-narrative prose.

Writing for the December 1986 issue of *CCC* ("The Organization of Impromptu Essays," 402–15) Richard Haswell looks for patterns in the arrangement of units in the students' "impromptu" (in-class) essays, and attempts to classify the principles of arrangement. He identifies two *kinds* of principles: *Unchained Patterns* and *Chained Patterns*. Under Unchained Patterns, those composed entirely of a single logical unit, he includes symmetrical patterns (all parts of which are categories of a single class), and asymmetrical patterns, whose parts need not be categories of the same class. Chained Patterns link two or more Unchained Patterns, each unchained pattern playing a role in two larger patterns. Unchained symmetrical patterns include partition, seriation, development (division into chronological stages), and others. Unchained asymmetrical patterns include consequence, causation, process, inference, and others. Chained patterns include causal chains, sorites (where the conclusion of one inference acts as the premise of a second inference), sequence (e.g., from cause to effect to problem to solution). Haswell then examines the impromptu essays of a number of students of varying ages, noting (among other trends) the inclination among older students toward using the more complex patterns, and the extent to which students and adults enlarge (by added words) the density of the more complex patterns. He finds in students "an intuitive sense of logical coherence," and suggests the deliberate teaching of organizational patterns, especially those patterns used by older students and adults. Haswell's is the only study of form in student writing I have encountered that is based upon a conceptual model for analyzing patterns in that writing, and on research into students' use of the cognitive procedures identified in that model. For study of the structure of non-narrative prose, Haswell's model could prove highly informative. At this moment, his approach is unique, and its application has only begun.

III

Despite the substantial recent increase in research on ways to talk about form in non-narrative prose (some of it a by-product of other kinds of inquiries), the weight of scholarship about the teaching of order and arrangement in discourse is still largely where it lay ten years ago. Such scholarship is largely concerned with enumerating plans for the presentation of ideas, and with describing ways for a writer to make connections between major ideas once that author has chosen an overall pattern for the essay. (Rarely, still, do writers dealing with order and form consider incisively the possible connections between the arrangement of ideas and the discovery of ideas to be arranged.) Most discussions of form that are available to teachers of writing, then, are enumerations of plans and stock formulas from which writers can choose; when it comes to guidance in making the choices, the writer is pretty much left to his intuitive guesses.

The classic plan for organizing a piece of discourse—"classic" in the dual sense of being derived from theorists in classical antiquity and of being cited frequently in contemporary texts—is still the pattern of the formal oration, or persuasive speech. The plan is most accessibly discussed by Edward P. J. Corbett in *Classical Rhetoric for the Modern Student* (second edition, New York: Oxford University Press, 1971), Chapter 3.

Summarizing the views of Cicero (*De Oratore*) and Quintilian (*Institutio Oratoria*) on structure, Corbett notes that the typical plan for a discourse included five parts: an introduction; a statement of the facts or circumstances that a reader of the discourse needs to know; the points that tend to support the writer's arguments; the points that tend to refute opposition to the writer's arguments; and a conclusion that brings together and re-states, amplifies, or shows the significance of what has been ar-gued. Elaboration of ideas under these headings can be based, Corbett points out, on the application of topoi: for instance, defi-nition, comparison, relationship (cause and effect, antecedent and consequent, for example), and testimony—which in this century convert themselves easily into "methods of development."

Possibly anticipating criticisms such as those voiced by Richard Young and Alton Becker in their article, "Toward a Mod-ern Theory of Rhetoric: A Tagmemic Contribution," *Harvard Educational Review,* 35 (Fall 1965), 450–68 (reprinted in Martin Steinmann, Jr., ed., *New Rhetorics* [New York: Charles Scribner's Sons, 1967], pp. 78–107), that this view of arrangement divorces form from content, "failing to consider the importance of the act of discovery in the shaping of form," Corbett cites the experi-ences of Ronald Crane (in *The Languages of Criticism and the Struc-ture of Poetry* [Toronto: University of Toronto Press, 1952]). Crane asserts that he had never been able to write anything that seemed to him unified, organically whole, "except in response to . . . a synthesizing idea," the perception of a "subsuming form," for his materials (Corbett, p. 301). From Crane's experience, Corbett in-fers the need for the writer to exercise a good deal of judgment and discretion in adapting the standard pattern to his or her pur-poses in addressing a particular audience on a particular occasion; Corbett insists on the need for adjusting form to ideas and cir-cumstances, even as he offers extended and useful advice about the management of each part in the standard pattern.

That the arrangement of parts envisaged by classical theo-rists reflects a powerful insight into effective ways of putting ar-guments, however, is revealed in the advocacy by Young and Becker themselves of a structure different in name from but simi-lar in essentials to that of the classical oration. In their original and fresh view of rhetoric, set forth in *Rhetoric: Discovery and Change* (co-authored with Kenneth Pike; New York: Harcourt,

Brace, and World, 1970), they identify as one strategy for reconstructing the reader's "image" of a subject this arrangement of parts:

> Introduction
> Background
> Argument
>> (major premise
>> minor premise
>> conclusion
>> superiority of argument offered to alternative
>>> positions)
> Conclusion
>> (summary of argument and statement of its
>>> implications)

(pp. 234–35)

Young and Becker are careful to discuss ways for a writer to vary the basic strategy depending on what the reader knows and what the reader thinks of the writer and/or of the writer's views on the subject. But their discussion of form, quite brief in comparison to their discussion of heuristic techniques for invention and of ways for analyzing the reader's ideas and attitudes, in effect supports the views of Corbett about the usefulness of the classical paradigm.

There are eighteenth- and nineteenth-century antecedents for the pattern of oratorical discourse discussed by Corbett, in case the teacher wishes to consult "early modern" treatments of the standard oration. One of the best known is by Hugh Blair, Professor at the University of Edinburgh, whose *Lectures on Rhetoric and Belles Lettres* were widely read in the half-century after 1780; the *Lectures* have been reprinted (ed. Harold Harding; Carbondale: Southern Illinois University Press, 1965), and are excerpted in James Golden and Edward P. J. Corbett, eds., *The Rhetoric of Blair, Campbell, and Whately* (New York: Holt, Rinehart, and Winston, 1968). Blair's entire discussion of order (Lectures 31

55

and 32) is an elaboration of how the different parts of the oration might be handled, together with an admonition to restraint in the appeal to a listener's feelings—which Blair identifies as an optional, separate part of the discourse (coming between one's refutation of the opponent's views and one's conclusion). In his comments on the rationale for different sequences of arguments, Blair gets little beyond discouraging long, impassioned introductions and suggesting that a proposition likely to be resisted by the hearer should be approached gradually, while a proposition likely not to evoke disagreement may be asserted early and defended in the rest of the discourse.

One other "modern" source for the discussions in Corbett is the work of Richard Whately, a clergyman, whose *Elements of Rhetoric* flourished in the early nineteenth century. The *Elements,* like Blair's *Lectures,* have been reprinted (ed. Douglas Ehninger; Carbondale: Southern Illinois University Press, 1963)—parts of it also appear in the volume by Golden and Corbett cited above— and may also be worth the attention of those interested in the antecedents of current treatments of organization. Whately's remarks on arrangement of topics are few, and are tied in to a discussion of how a speaker accepts (or transfers) the "burden of proof" of his argument and of how one refutes an opponent, but he introduces the two patterns (general to particular, and particular to general) that are highlighted in many texts on writing to this day. And, perhaps his most important contribution, he enumerates several kinds of introductions (inquisitive, paradoxical, corrective, preparatory, narrative) that a discourse can have—introductions that survive, with slightly different names, in current texts (including Corbett, who on pages 304–8 names and illustrates each of Whately's principal types of introduction).

Oral rhetoric, as distinguished from written, is the source of many concepts set forth by Blair and Whately and summarized by Corbett. But recently scholars of oral rhetoric have proposed additional contributions to the field of written discourse: several have suggested the value that students of writing might find in plans for argument as taught in the field of speech communication. In "A Stock Issues Approach to Writing Arguments," *CCC*, 31 (May 1980), 183–96, Richard Katula and Richard Roth suggested the advantages of organizational plans that traverse the "stock issues": Is there a problem? What is the essence of the problem? How serious is the problem? Will the solution address the problem? Can the solution accomplish what it promises? and so on. Though the questions are heuristic, the sequence of questions furnishes a structure. Almost three years later, Theodore F. Sheckels, Jr., in "Three Strategies for Deliberative Discourse: A Lesson from Competitive Debating," *CCC*, 34 (February 1983), 31–42, reviewed the issues identified by Katula and Roth and discussed other strategies taught in competitive debate: what he calls the "Needs Case," the "Comparative Advantages Case," and the "Goals Case," suggesting how the strategies differ and how they might apply to different kinds of issues. Again the strategy for inquiry furnishes a structure. The following year, noting the interest in stock issues, David Kaufer proposed "A Plan for Teaching the Development of Original Policy Arguments" (*CCC*, 35 [February 1984], 57–70): a sequence of steps that a writer can take in approaching policy questions to locate the sources of disagreement, define differences in values, and work toward mutually acceptable resolutions of the conflict. Less visibly a structural plan, Kaufer's proposal nonetheless can suggest one.

Corbett, recently, and Blair, Whately, and the investigators of "stock issues" offer their patterns, they would admit, largely for "argumentative" or "persuasive" discourse (though one might argue that most discourse has its "argumentative" or "persuasive" edge). Persuasion is only one of the possible "aims" of discourse identified by James L. Kinneavy in *A Theory of Discourse* (Englewood Cliffs, N.J.: Prentice-Hall, 1971)—a theory compactly summarized two years earlier in his "The Basic Aims of Discourse," *CCC*, 20 (December 1969), 297–304. Kinneavy identifies four kinds of discourse, differentiated by aim: persuasive discourse; referential discourse (for giving information, recording scientific research, or exploring problems); literary discourse; and expressive discourse (for recording the feelings of an individual or the aspirations and convictions of a group). He asserts that discourse serving each one of these aims tends to have its distinctive pattern of organization. In persuasive discourse, Kinneavy finds essentially the pattern discussed by Corbett. And in the various forms of referential discourse he discerns a number of different patterns, e.g., "inverted induction"—giving the generalization first, followed by the details that lead to it—in "scientific" discourse, and problem-solving in "exploratory" discourse. (See pp. 151–66, *passim.*) Yet Kinneavy himself acknowledges that the effort to connect particular forms with particular aims of discourse can lead to oversimplification. Though informative or factual discourse, for instance, is organized to achieve accuracy, comprehensiveness, and surprise in the reader, different examples of such discourse may follow different organizational plans (including narration, description, classification, evaluation—which Kinneavy calls the "modes" of discourse), and may even be ordered according to "literary" *or* "expressive" *or* "persuasive" principles. Kinneavy discusses the organization of "literary" discourse mainly with concepts taken from linguistics and semantics, rather than with concepts customarily employed to describe organization. And he does not discern any typical patterns in what he calls "expressive" discourse. His suggestion of a correspondence, then, between "aim" of discourse and organizational plan remains unconvincing. And indeed some questions have recently been raised about the basic classification of aims, notably by Richard Fulkerson in "Kinneavy on Referential and Persuasive Discourse: A Critique," *CCC,* 34 (February 1984), 43–56.

Among modern theorists of rhetoric, one of the more emphatic in resisting theoretical reliance on generalized patterns (patterns advocated irrespective of subject and audience) and more subtle in recognizing the possible consequences of different ways to arrange ideas is Chaim Perelman, whose *The New Rhetoric: A*

Treatise on Argument (trans. John Wilkinson and Purcell Weaver; Notre Dame: University of Notre Dame Press, 1969) concludes with some reflection on how the arrangement of arguments affects readers. Perelman lists some "points of view" to be taken in the development of a plan for a persuasive discourse and in the analysis of the values in any plan: "the argumentative situation itself, by which is meant the influence of the earlier stages of the discussion on the argumentative possibilities open to the speaker"; the "conditioning of the audience, which comprises changes of attitude brought about by the speech" as it progresses; and "the reactions occasioned in the audience by its perception of the order or arrangement adopted in the speech" (p. 491). Perelman examines briefly, as Corbett does, some of the effects on audiences that can be achieved in an introduction, and he explores some of the values of different ways for sequencing arguments. But his discussion is, like those of most rhetoricians, primarily concerned with persuasive argument, and it offers more of theoretical considerations and possibilities than it does of direct guidance in the selection and working out of plans for arrangement. Perelman's major value for the teacher of writing is in his insistence upon the interaction of audience and arrangement—an insight that will apply to virtually any composed piece.

But for specific, empirically based guidance in the *selection* of *order* in arrangement, as distinguished from theoretical discussions based upon classical oratory or research on readability and on ways of describing the structure of a text, there are few studies to recommend. Among those few are two volumes by Carl I. Hovland, Irving Janis, and Harold H. Kelley, psychologists working at Yale. One of their books, *The Order of Presentation in Persuasion* (New Haven: Yale University Press, 1957), reports the results of particular experiments in the arrangement of persuasive arguments with audiences that had different orientations toward the subject of the argument. Hovland's more general discussion of the subject is an earlier volume, *Communication and Persuasion: Psychological Studies of Opinion Change* (New Haven: Yale University Press, 1957; pages 1–18 are reprinted in Steinmann, ed., *New Rhetorics*, pp. 35–57). This volume details the interdisciplinary foundations of studies on persuasion and opinion change, describes the difficulties confronting those who undertake research on opinion change—the number of variables to be dealt with other than the content and structure of the communication, for example—and examines the various elements in persuasive communication. The elements Hovland and his colleagues list are familiar: the communicator; the stimuli transmitted in the communication (content and organization of ideas); the audience (including predispositions and individual personality features); and the responses of that audience (how far the responses are overt, how far opinion change is retained for periods of time). Those interested in observing directly the interdisciplinary dimensions of empirical studies in rhetorical form may find the work of Hovland and his colleagues revealing. Such readers might also wish to note, however, the criticisms of "scientific" studies of persuasion in Charles Larson and Robert Sanders, "Faith, Mystery, and Data: An Analysis of 'Scientific' Studies of Persuasion," in *QJS*, 61 (April 1975), 178–94.

Not much of the scholarship on readability, the structure of texts, or "stock issues" has, in fact, affected instruction or the scholarship on instruction in writing. Linda Flower and her colleagues, as well as some other psycholinguists, study the importance of plan*ning,* but the discussion of alternate plans or approaches to planning has not yet made its way deeply, or even superficially, into teaching. As a result, what is taught these days under the rubric of organization and planning—apart from discussions of the paragraph, to which I turn later—is a combination of long-held views about "modes" of discourse and standard patterns of organization. Studies that I am now undertaking of college curricula in writing suggest that in many institutions, however humane the teaching *techniques,* the views of structure in non-narrative prose taught reflect little serious examination of fresh ideas about structure. A reader interested in an overview of the history of the teaching of writing that focuses on this subject might want to consult Robert Connors's "The Rise and Fall of the Modes of Discourse," *CCC*, 32 (December 1981), 444–55, though Connors is, on the evidence I have seen, much too optimistic in asserting that the modes as categories for organizing instruction have faded away.

IV

The discussions of form at which we have looked in Sections II and III sometimes appear to view the composed piece as a succession of discrete units, each more or less self-contained, open to being arranged in different orders and not necessarily disclosing a progressive sequence of thought that follows a movement begun in the opening sentences of the piece. (Some of the reports of research on readability and some discussions of "stock issues" are exceptions to this tendency.) Some discussions in modern rhetorical theory, however, now suggest ways in which an essay, looked at as a total unit, may be said to exhibit a plan that evolves, or develops, from commitments made by the writer at the outset. Perception of how that plan unfolds can enable a reader to see the essay as an organic unit, beginning with the introduction of an idea and working through a describable plan toward completion of the statement of that idea.

In a major attempt to see a text as a planned total unit, Frank D'Angelo, in *A Conceptual Theory of Rhetoric* (Cambridge, Mass.: Winthrop Publishing Company, 1975) argues (pp. 56ff.) that such moves in a text as definition, description, classification, and so on derive from classical "topics for invention"; they are plans for thinking. Arguing that steps in arrangement connect with procedures for thinking—and eventually with ways of putting sentences together, i.e., with expression—D'Angelo tries to bring out the unity of rhetorical theory and the dangers of separating arrangement from invention and style. Despite D'Angelo's efforts, the acts of inquiry and exposition that he discusses retain their status as separate acts; he does not show how these acts assemble into structural patterns along which a text moves from its inception to its conclusion.

D'Angelo (who notes, but does not discuss extensively, the possibility that teachers should heed such "nonlogical" patterns of arrangement as fantasy, dream reverie, etc.) contributes useful suggestions about ways of looking at the total movement of discourse. One, drawn from scholars of myth and fairy tale, D'Angelo identifies as the analysis of "paradigmatic" structure— the search for paradigms of form in similar kinds of discourse. D'Angelo illustrates the kinds of paradigms that can sometimes be found in narrative pieces, and then locates other kinds of paradigms, for instance the enumeration of instances of a generalization, in so-called expository discourse. The paradigms that D'Angelo locates are rather familiar, but his comments on paradigmatic form obviously assist our search for ways of seeing the evolving shape of total units of discourse.

D'Angelo's other suggestion about viewing the structure of discourse draws heavily upon the work of Francis Christensen, about whose work we shall have more to say in discussions of theories of the paragraph. D'Angelo notes the applications of Christensen's work to the whole essay that have been attempted by people such as Michael Grady ("A Conceptual Rhetoric of the Composition," CCC, 22 [December 1971], 348–54), who argues that essays can be conceived as sequences of structurally related paragraphs, each paragraph functioning in relation to the whole discourse much as a sentence functions as part of a paragraph. D'Angelo prefers to look at a total discourse as a sequence of structurally related sentences bound to each other, and to the lead sentence of the discourse, through coordination or subordination, and he offers an extended analysis of a political commentary from a newspaper to illustrate this "syntagmatic" view of structure. While the detailed discriminating of coordinate and subordinate sentences in a complete essay may seem to obscure the development of a discourse more than D'Angelo's paradigmatic analysis does, his presentation of both approaches to the study of form may help readers to understand some issues currently being raised in analyses of form. (See also D'Angelo's article, "A Generative Rhetoric of the Essay," *CCC*, 25 [December 1974], 388–96.)

I have myself proposed that readers observe the paradigms created by the progress of writers' thought in their essays, in my "Invention Once More: A Role for Rhetorical Analysis," *CE*, 32 (March 1971), 668–72. Although the article is intended to direct students toward a way of discovering ideas, its focus is on the form in which ideas appear in the work of professional writers. In effect, the article substantiates D'Angelo's contention that plans of organization are tightly related to procedures and habits in thinking; it asserts that patterns followed in thinking can themselves be discovered inferentially from the plans that organize professional writers' work. Calling these plans "movements of mind," I argue that most successful pieces of discourse will exhibit discernible "movements," that these movements are not necessarily identifiable from the short list of organizational plans presented to writers in most textbooks, and that attempting to duplicate the movements of mind followed by professional writers is, for the student writer, a useful procedure in learning how to develop ideas.

One paradigm that I believe to be worth a student's attention I have discussed in "Problem-Solving, Composing, and Liberal Education," *CE*, 33 (March 1972), 628–35. Through an analysis of Swift's *A Modest Proposal*, I try to identify the elements of the problem-solving process and to show how this process informs and organizes Swift's essay. Arguing that the problem-solving process underlies the structure of much writing by intellectual, social, and political theorists (as indeed investigators of "stock issues" have directly asserted), I encourage teachers to introduce students to the process as both a way of finding their ideas about a topic and a way of giving rough structure to those ideas while composing a first draft. My discussion works with a somewhat narrower model of problem-solving than Young, Becker, and

Pike advance in *Rhetoric: Discovery and Change,* but the narrower model may be a useful paradigm for students to observe and practice while learning how to advance deliberative discourse.

In a subsequent essay, "Toward a Linear Rhetoric of the Essay," *CCC,* 22 (May 1971), 140–46, I elaborate the proposition that professional essays reveal typical movements of mind, arguing that any essay may be perceived as a sequence of steps taken in order to reach a particular goal, and that the individual steps in the sequence can be described in such a way that a student of organization can almost diagram the action of the piece. (This suggestion is partly influenced by the approach to discourse taken by "speech act" theory; see pages 50–51, above.) I suggest that the successive acts performed by the successive sentences in a discourse can be identified, and the pattern established by the successive acts can quite possibly be described. I call this pattern the "linear plan" for the discourse, distinguishing this plan from the kind of hierarchical "outline" advocated in many texts on composing by insisting that the "linear plan" identifies and clarifies the principle, the force if you will, that drives the forward motion in the essay. This is the dynamic process by which an essay reaches, through successive steps, the particular argumentative or persuasive goal sought by the writer. If the steps are well ordered and well taken, the result of their having come in their particular succession will be a feeling in the reader of satisfaction or conviction of the rightness of the conclusion—or at least a feeling of respect for the writer's argument. The planning of any piece of writing thus involves much more than the replication of a previously discerned general pattern of discourse. It requires the choice of an order specially tailored to the subject, to the writer's view of that subject, to the goal sought by the writer, to the reader(s), and to the situation within which the writing will be perceived.

Implicit in this discussion of inferring plans from pieces of professional writing are the generalizations that for the working writer the process of writing is partly the process of choosing an appropriate plan, and that the available plans, while perhaps not infinite in number, are quite varied. How, then, does the working writer stay on the track? Particularly if she is working out her plan as she devises material (the task of inventing and the task of arranging, as we have suggested, are not separable), how does she determine whether she is carrying her reader along and satisfying her that the promised job is being done? Guidance in testing one's discourse is not widely available in the literature on form, but one essay that offers help is Robert Gorrell's "Not by Nature: Approaches to Rhetoric," *EJ*, 55 (April 1966), 409–16, 449. In this essay, Gorrell observes that when a writer sets pen to paper and begins writing, she limits the options that are available for continuing the essay, and establishes a commitment to the reader concerning the subject to be discussed, the comment to be made about that subject, and the manner in which the comment will be developed. In the rest of the essay, the writer must carry out, or discharge, that commitment, and the reader must be able to observe how the commitment is being carried out; otherwise the reader will experience puzzlement and (by implication) the writer will fail of her purpose. Gorrell enumerates the ways—when identified at a high level of abstraction, the ways are few—by which a writer can move in carrying out her commitment; he identifies in general terms the kinds of steps that the writer can take, besides offering that writer some advice on how to test the effectiveness with which the successive steps are taken. Like most of the articles discussed in this section, this piece offers an analysis of some professional writing to illustrate both the commitments made by a writer and the procedures employed by the writer in discharging those commitments. Gorrell's is one of the essays a teacher might turn to for help in analyzing—and teaching—an approach to structure that even inexperienced writers should be able to adopt with profit.

V

The preservation of form, of course, is not simply a matter of choosing a recognized pattern or working out, while inventing one's material, a plan for its presentation. The writer also has the task of welding the sections of the piece, however neatly progressive, into a reasonably seamless whole. The standard texts, not to mention studies of readability in non-narrative prose, are full of advice about achieving coherence: build one of the key ideas from the conclusion of one part of the paper into the opening of the next part; employ recognized transitional connectives; occasionally sum up, in a short transitional paragraph, where the essay has been, and indicate where it will next go; and so on.

This advice may well come to seem simplistic, however, if and as the fruits of scholarship about coherence during the last decade are gradually drawn upon by teachers. For if attention to any element of structure in non-narrative (as well as narrative) prose has burgeoned in scholarly inquiry recently, it is attention to the concepts of coherence and cohesion, as these concepts apply to both shorter and longer units of a text. In this essay I can do no more than begin to tap the range of inquiries that have been applied to this subject and the insights that have emerged about it.

An early, brief, and (in effect) preliminary essay on how writers create coherent text is W. Ross Winterowd's "The Grammar of Coherence," *CE,* 31 (May 1970), 828–35, reprinted in his *Contemporary Rhetoric,* pp. 225–33. Winterowd proposes, by analogy with the relationships that can be used to combine shorter sentences to form longer sentences, a suggested set of seven relationships that may obtain between sentences within paragraphs and—for our purposes more important—by which paragraphs and sections can be combined into essays, or chapters combined into books. The seven relationships, which Winterowd evidently considers an exhaustive list and which he illustrates with many examples, are coordinate, observative, causative, conclusive, alternative, inclusive, and sequential. (In an essay entitled "Transitions: Relationships Among T-Units," *CCC,* 34 [December 1983], 447–53, Gary Sloan argued that Winterowd's list was seriously incomplete and that some of his examples did not make their point. Winterowd replied to Sloan's comment in the February 1985 issue.) Implied in Winterowd's essay is the suggestion that the relationships employed in a given text—the paths of inquiry followed—need to be reasonably visible to the alert observer, and that by making the relationships visible a writer can control the perceived movement and improve the impact of her whole discourse.

In the discussions of coherence over the last ten years, these questions have emerged as investigators' central concerns: What *are* cohesion and coherence? What features of a text create them? Where are they likely to break down? How important are they to the quality of writing as perceived by readers? And what is the role of the reader in finding and establishing the coherence of a text? I will glance at studies that address each question.

The impetus for most of these inquiries, and the reference point to which subsequent writers return over and over again even when they disagree with its assertions, is M. A. K. Halliday and Ruqaiya Hasan, *Cohesion in English* (London: Longman, 1976). Viewing cohesion as one of the qualities that give "texture"—status as text—to a connected stretch of discourse, Halliday and Hasan offer a detailed enumeration (with analysis of numerous examples) of several kinds of cohesive ties: reference, substitution (replacement of one item by another), ellipsis (omission of an item, in such a way that it is understood), conjunction, and some kinds of lexical cohesion (reiteration of a word or idea; collocation of words that tend to appear frequently together). In their list, and in the insistent focus on "cohesion," Halliday and Hasan activate the issue of whether there is a difference between "coherence" and "cohesion" (a distinction on which subsequent investigators seem not to agree).

In one response ("Semantic and Lexical Coherence," *CCC*, 34 [December 1983], 400–16), Jeanne Fahnestock notes Winterowd's and Halliday and Hasan's enumerations (she divides Halliday and Hasan's "conjunction" into four categories of transitions: additive, adversative, causative, and temporal), and then offers her own enumeration of the semantic relationships between items in a text, dividing them into "continuative" and "discontinuative" relationships. Continuative relationships include such steps as sequence, restatement, exemplification, and similarity; discontinuative relationships include replacement (a second point is more correct than the first), concession, contrast, and anomalous sequence (a sequence other than immediate succession of events). Fahnestock demonstrates that her list of relationships can describe the successive relationships in a paragraph; she implies that it can also describe relationships between longer units in a text. But Sandra Stotsky, in "Types of Lexical Cohesion in Expository Writing: Implications for Developing the Vocabulary of Academic Discourse," *CCC*, 34 (December 1983), 430–46, finds inadequate the analysis of "lexical" cohesion offered in Halliday and Hasan's discussion: it fails to clarify adequately the kinds of lexical linkages often found in expository texts. Stotsky proposes a revised division of items in lexical cohesion: semantically related words (related by repetition, synonymy or near-synonymy, opposition or contrast, inclusion as members of a set, derivation from the same word) and collocationally related words (where the relationship is through "frequent co-occurrence in similar contexts"). The revised division, Stotsky suggests, can furnish guidance to those who would assist students in developing an academic vocabulary by encouraging them to read widely and attend to the contexts in which words appear.

Other studies, varying in approach, illustrate the slipperiness of the terms "cohesion" and "coherence" in discussions of the features that bind texts together. Raoul Smith and William Frawley, for example, explore the kinds of "conjunction" found in prose texts from different fields: the conjunctions used in fiction resemble those used in religion more than those used in journalism and science, though the conjunctions in science emphasize additive words and hypotheticals, postulating causes in "possible worlds," and highlighting "logical and necessary" succession in preference to the "physical" succession reported by the journalist ("Conjunctive Cohesion in Four Discourse Types," *Text*, 3

[No. 4, 1983], 347–74). John B. Black looks at what he calls the "coherence relations" in expository texts, and enumerates them as "referential, causal, and motivational," as well as "property" (interconnecting descriptive details) and "support" (as in evidence for an argument) ("An Exposition on Understanding Expository Text," in *Understanding Expository Text,* pp. 249–267).

Finally, and perhaps most visibly within recent investigations, Robin Markels, in a short essay and in a longer monograph, uses the term "cohesion" to include "coherence" (defined as semantic and syntactic relations among links in a chain of unified thought) and "unity" (manifested as the "recurrence" of dominating items in a "chain" and the pattern or totality thus created). See "Cohesion Paradigms in Paragraphs," *CE,* 45 (September 1983), 450–64, and *A New Perspective on Cohesion in Expository Paragraphs* (Carbondale: Southern Illinois University Press, 1984)—in both of which Markels is talking specifically about paragraphs but may be trying to contribute to the theoretical exploration of cohesion and coherence. Markels attempts to establish the existence of several different kinds of lexical chains within sequences of thought (her examples come from paragraphs): chains with a single term dominant, semantically and syntactically, in the sequence; chains with two terms dominant, with the successive connections expressed; chains with two or more terms, where the reader must draw on world knowledge to infer and interpret connections; mixed chains without "topic sentences," having characteristics of both of the last two kinds; and mixed chains with topic sentences—in which terms are compactly introduced through single words and phrases within the topic sentence. Markels's analyses appear to be thoughtful, and they may describe the reader's experience of the passages studied. Still, the analyses are not highly accessible to an interested reader, and Markels's assumption that students can be taught to produce paragraphs on the various models is offered without any supporting evidence and without much effort to make the classroom applications of her theory clear or plausible.

While these scholars have looked at features of texts that create cohesion—or coherence—others have looked to see where texts, particularly student texts, break down. In "Discourse Analysis and the Art of Coherence," *CE,* 44 (January 1982), 57–63, George Goodin and Kyle Perkins trace the breakdown to writers' failure to embed effectively material that ought to have been part of other sentences—thereby producing sentences that seem to be afterthoughts and digressions—along with their failure to establish a clear sense of purpose and plan for the development of a sequence. Generalizing from her reading of essays written for the National Assessment of Educational Progress, Betty Bamberg, in "What Makes a Text Coherent?" (*CCC,* 34 [December 1983], 417–30), suggests that failure of coherence in students' essays results from their incomplete announcement of their topic, from their failure to establish a context for their writing, and from failure to select an adequate organizational plan, but she implies that all these difficulties are due to students' inability to revise their drafts into "reader-based" as distinguished from writer-based prose; what they produce as the finished draft is still writer-based prose. It is not the presence or absence of cohesive ties that affects coherence; it is these more fundamental inadequacies.

Does the use of linguistic features such as those discussed by Halliday and Hasan (and by Fahnestock and Stotsky, though their models are too recent to have been subjected to empirical investigation) affect the quality of students' writing as perceived by readers? Opinions and findings differ. Robert J. Tierney and James Mosenthal, in "Cohesion and Textual Coherence," *RTE,* 17 (October 1983), 215–29, find in student essays "no causal relationship between proportional measures of cohesive ties within topic and coherence rankings within topic," and caution against counting cohesive ties as a way of discovering the coherence of a text. But George McCulley, in "Writing Quality, Coherence, and Cohesion," *RTE,* 19 (October 1985), 269–82, concludes that the presence of synonyms, hyponyms, and lexical collocations in

NAEP essays was closely related to judgments of coherence and of writing quality; he takes issue with Tierney and Mosenthal. And Stephen Witte and Lester Faigley, in "Coherence, Cohesion, and Writing Quality," *CCC,* 32 (May 1981), 189–204, using Halliday and Hasan's classification of cohesive ties, but also differentiating between immediate ties (in adjacent T-units), remote ties (separated by one or more T-units), mediated ties (where a word is repeated, to make a bridge between two T-units on either side), and mediated-remote ties, conclude that cohesive ties, particularly lexical collocations, are closely connected to perceptions of coherence and to the judged quality of writing. But coherence, for them, embraces the "fit" of a text to its context—the writer's purpose, the medium of discourse, the audience, i.e., a "real world" setting—and "quality" includes invention and the development of ideas as well.

And still other scholars have asserted that the judgment of "coherence" about a text reflects the reader's knowledge and approach to the text as much as it does any properties in the text. In "Coherence and Connectedness in the Development of Discourse Production," *Text,* 2 (Nos. 1–3, 1982), 113–39, Deborah McCutchen and Charles Perfetti note that knowledge of the topic and of "text-form constraints" goes along with the "underlying semantic integrity" of the topic and instances of local connectedness to create a sense of coherence. M. Charolles, in "Coherence as a Principle in the Interpretation of Discourse," *Text,* 3 (No. 1, 1983), 71–97, is quite explicit: "No text is inherently coherent or incoherent. In the end, it all depends on the receiver, and his ability to interpret the indications present in the discourse so that, finally, he manages to understand it . . . in a way which corresponds with his idea of what it is that makes a series of actions into an integrated whole." This *may* be the essential point (I cannot be sure) that Louise Phelps was trying to make in a long and in some ways impenetrable essay worth mentioning because it appeared in a journal more likely than *Text* to be available to readers interested in this issue: "Dialectics of Coherence: Toward an Integrative Theory," *CE,* 47 (January 1985), 12–29. Studying cohesion, says Phelps, relies "on readers' instincts and experience to pick out points in the text and features that are salient and significant in their ability to integrate coherent meanings" (p. 28).

From all these studies one must draw the reminder that however imaginative one may be in identifying features of language that contribute to cohesion (and coherence), however indefatigable one may be in counting those features, however artful one may be in designing research on reading, the determination of coherence is fundamentally an interpretation by a reader. It is part of a transaction between text and reader—between the reader's world and the writer's language.

VI

Our discussion of coherence, particularly of the observations by Markels, leads us easily to an examination of scholarship and theories about the formation of paragraphs. It is to the paragraph, far more than to the total essay, that textbooks and writers on the teaching of composition usually give most attention.

The paragraph, over the last twenty years, has been approached for the most part from three distinct perspectives. It has been approached as, in effect, an expanded sentence: a unit of discourse about which one can talk usefully in language comparable to that used about sentences. It has been approached as a self-contained unit of writing, with distinctive principles of structure that need to be understood and observed by all writers. And it has been approached as a subdivision in a total discourse—a unit whose length and form depend on the strategies of the writer in managing an entire piece, rather than on some rules governing what may appear in the space between one indentation and the next. We will examine briefly here the work of some proponents of these varied ways of viewing the paragraph.

This plan has the virtue of allowing us to begin with the work of Francis Christensen, whose "A Generative Rhetoric of the Paragraph," *CCC,* 16 (October 1965), 144–56, following by exactly two years his "A Generative Rhetoric of the Sentence," initiated the flow of discussions on the paragraph two decades ago. In his earlier essay on the sentence, Christensen had said that the sentence modifiers which create what he called the "cumulative sentence" are related to structures preceding them either by coordination or by subordination, and he had developed a scheme for numbering these modifiers to reveal whether they are coordinate or subordinate, and to what. In discussing the paragraph, Christensen applies the same procedures, calling the paragraph a "sequence of structurally related sentences," most of them related to a topic sentence or to each other by coordination or subordination, just as sentence modifiers are related to base clauses. Christensen identifies three principal kinds of paragraphs: coordinate sequences, subordinate sequences, and mixed sequences (sequences having some coordinate and some subordinate sentences), and, by numbering the sentences in sample paragraphs to show their level of subordination, he illustrates how these sequences work. It is Christensen's contention that awareness of whether a sentence is coordinate with, or subordinate to, a sentence preceding it will enable a writer to see when, if at all, his paragraph is losing coherence. Such analysis, Christensen claims, also can show when, if at all, additional sentences— coordinate or subordinate—are needed for the adequate development of the paragraph.

Christensen's numbering of the levels of coordination and subordination in successive sentences is sometimes mysterious, and analyzing paragraphs by his method may do no more to generate thought on the part of a writer than the admonitions of older writers about the need for "adequate development" in a paragraph. Still, Christensen's impact upon other theorists of the paragraph—inspiring followers and stimulating alternative views—has probably been as great as that of any theorist of composition in this generation. See, in particular, the "Symposium on the Paragraph," to which Christensen and others contributed, in *CCC*, 17 (May 1966), 60–87.

Two followers of Christensen deserve notice. One is Willis Pitkin, whose work on the structure of discourse (work illustrated by the analysis of paragraphs) we noted earlier. The other is David Karrfalt, a contributor to the "Symposium on the Paragraph" and author of a later essay entitled "The Generation of Paragraphs and Larger Units," *CCC,* 19 (October 1968), 211–17. Karrfalt anticipated some of Pitkin's ideas by identifying paragraphs in which some sentences complete, or extend to a higher level of abstraction, the ideas in previous sentences (rather than being subordinate to—i.e., more specific and particular than—or coordinate with those sentences). Karrfalt calls this relationship of completion a "horizontal" relationship, and he also notes passages in which other sorts of sentences appear that cannot be accounted for neatly by Christensen's theories.

If Christensen and his followers have tried to extend their conceptual framework for the study of sentences so that it will illuminate paragraphs, other theorists, traditional and modern, treat the paragraph as a self-contained unit of composition without reference to the structure of sentences. Much of this work draws on writing about the paragraph that dates back to the time of Alexander Bain, who devised six influential rules for the construction of paragraphs. (See Paul Rodgers, Jr., "Alexander Bain and the Rise of the Organic Paragraph," *QJS,* 51 [December 1965], 399–408, and, for an analysis of antecedents of Bain's thought, Ned A. Shearer, "Alexander Bain and the Genesis of Paragraph Theory," *QJS,* 58 [December 1972], 408–17.) Some of the older theorists are excerpted in Virginia Burke's anthology, *The Paragraph in Context* (Indianapolis: Bobbs-Merrill, 1969), to which Burke has contributed a brief introduction sketching the history of paragraphs in English and tracing the concept of the paragraph as "a prose structure capable of organic internal arrangement." A particularly well known exposition of these traditional views, one that has survived through several editions of his book, has been a feature of James McCrimmon's *Writing with a Purpose.* McCrimmon has argued that successful paragraphs should be characterized by unity, completeness, coherence, and adequacy of development; he reviews the obvious techniques for assuring cohesion in a paragraph that has the desired characteristics. He has insisted, as have most theorists, on the importance of the writer's including and developing a topic sentence as a way of helping to organize his ideas. (Even Christensen views the "topic sentence" as the first step in a well-ordered paragraph. But Christensen's "topic sentence" is simply the top of a sequence of related sentences—usually a more general or abstract sentence than those that follow, which are coordinate with or subordinate to the topic sentence.)

While McCrimmon's views of the characteristics needed in a paragraph have a superficial plausibility, they tell the writer not much about how to attain these characteristics. Moreover, in an important piece of scholarship written just before his death, Richard Braddock analyzes the use of topic sentences in the writing of several professional writers and finds that the topic sentence is far less prominent in their work than standard texts would lead us to suppose. Braddock concludes: "Teachers and textbook writers should exercise caution in making statements about the frequency with which contemporary professional writers use simple or even explicit topic sentences in expository paragraphs. It is abundantly clear that students should not be told that professional writers usually begin their paragraphs with topic sentences. . . . While helping students use clear topic sentences in their writing and identify variously presented topical ideas in their reading, the teacher should not pretend that professional writers largely follow the practices he is advocating" ("The Frequency and Placement of Topic Sentences in Expository Prose," *RTE,* 8 [Winter 1974], 287–302). And comparable findings about the ways in which professional writers develop paragraphs had been advanced earlier, but less visibly (because the researchers were less prominent), by Richard A. Meade and W. Geiger Ellis in "Paragraph Development in the Modern Age of Rhetoric," *EJ,* 59 (February 1970), 219–26.

But although Braddock's report (which concluded by noting that the work of some professional writers might have been more effective if they *had* made larger use of topic sentences) has caused some teachers—perhaps by no means the majority—to reconsider their demand for topic sentences in students' paragraphs, the topic sentence has by no means been shrugged off among scholars in rhetoric. And some scholars try overtly to reassert the value of topic sentences, as does Frank D'Angelo in "The Topic Sentence Revisited" (*CCC* [December 1986], 431–41). D'Angelo cites the work of several psycholinguists (including some referred to earlier in this essay), who find that placing topic sentences first in a writer's paragraph improves the readability of the paragraph, and increases the ease with which the content of the paragraph can be remembered as well as the length of time it can be retained. Besides Meyer's work, D'Angelo cites in particular a study by David Kieras, "Good and Bad Structure in Simple Paragraphs: Effects on Apparent Theme, Reading Time, and Recall," *Journal of Verbal Learning and Verbal Behavior,* 17 (February 1978), 13–28, in which Kieras finds that paragraphs containing an initial announcement of "theme" or "main idea" and continuing with sentences that clearly tie to previous ideas are faster to read and easier to recall. D'Angelo draws on the writings not only of researchers on reading but also of proponents of "schema" theory to argue that a clear statement of the "macrostructure" of a text, which may well be a topic sentence, enhances retention. That professional writers often do not use identifiable topic sentences, says D'Angelo, is no reason at all not to teach them.

Instead of sketching a profile of a well-constructed organic paragraph, Richard Young and Alton Becker at the University of Michigan, following out some of the implications of their tagmemic approaches to description of sentences, attempt through analysis of professional writing to discern recurrent patterns in the arranging of sentences into paragraphs that might be noted by writers interested in assuring that the structure of their paragraphs is regularly clear. Young and Becker identify a number of such patterns, among the most prominent being what they call TRI (Topic-Restriction-Illustration). (See Alton Becker, "A Tagmemic Approach to Paragraph Analysis," *CCC,* 16 [December 1965], 237–42, or Young and Becker's essay, "Toward a Modern Theory of Rhetoric," previously cited. For a useful, brief introduction to tagmemic theory that may help toward an understanding of the conceptual background of these articles, see Kenneth L. Pike, "A Linguistic Contribution to Composition," *CCC,* 15 [May 1964], 82–88.)

An early essay of my own discusses the paragraph as a succession of sentences each of which performs an identifiable and separate action for the writer ("Sentences in Action: A Technique for Analyzing Paragraphs," *CCC,* 18 [February 1967], 16–22). Arguing that an utterance is not only a locution conforming to rules of grammar, but an action performed in the service of some purpose, I list a number of actions that a sentence can perform within a paragraph, and analyze a number of paragraphs to reveal the successive actions performed by individual sentences. This procedure does not yield a heuristic for composing a paragraph, any more than the identification of possible linear plans yields a heuristic for designing an essay. What such analysis can do is disclose the options open to the writer as she moves sentence by sentence, and encourage the writer to think about which of these possible actions she wishes to perform at each step in the paragraph, and why. This method of analysis is also useful for the evaluation of paragraphs, since the role played by each sentence in the paragraph must be evident to the reader if that paragraph is to be fully understood. If the role of a given sentence is unclear, the paragraph loses force and coherence at that point, just as in Christensen's method of analysis a sentence that is not clearly coordinate or subordinate to a sentence above it signals a break in coherence and a failure of design in the paragraph.

What of the view that the paragraph should be treated as a subdivision of the total discourse of which it is a part? Except for isolated early glances (such as that by E. H. Lewis—p. 17 in Virginia Burke's collection) and modern suggestions (such as those of Young and Becker), discussions of the paragraph from the perspective of the complete essay have been infrequent. The most important analysis is that by Paul Rodgers, Jr.: "A Discourse-Centered Rhetoric of the Paragraph," *CCC,* 17 (February 1966), 2–11. Rodgers argues that to view the paragraph as a self-contained unit leads to incomplete vision, because many considerations—of tone, of emphasis, of appearance on the printed page, to name a few—affect the length and shape of professional writers' paragraphs. He further argues that in fact professional writers punctuate their discourse into paragraphs as part of their efforts to achieve the desired total effect in their pieces, not in conformity to predetermined rules for the construction of paragraphs.

> Paragraph structure is part and parcel of the structure of the discourse as a whole; a given [unit of discourse] becomes a paragraph not by virtue of its structure but because the writer elects to indent, his indentation functioning, as does all punctuation, as a gloss upon the overall literary process under way at that point. Paragraphs are not composed; they are discovered. To compose is to create, to indent is to interpret. (p. 6)

Rodgers supports his contentions with an analysis of an essay ("Style") by Walter Pater, showing that ordinary observations about paragraphing will not explain how Pater paragraphed his essay, because Pater sought special effects of tone and emphasis in the division of his essay.

Rodgers's study is distinctive and important; if heeded, it might discourage teachers from assigning paragraphs as if they were self-contained units of writing, and encourage them instead to help students plan and compose complete pieces of writing, in that process deciding how they want to divide their essays in order to achieve a desired effect. Paragraphs collaborate, Rodgers argues; for the practicing writer what is done in one paragraph may depend significantly on what happens on either side of that paragraph, or elsewhere in the complete piece. For further discussion of Rodgers's views, see his contribution—pp. 72–80—to the "Symposium on the Paragraph," previously cited, and his article, "The Stadium of Discourse," *CCC,* 18 (October 1967), 178–85.

A similar perspective is implied by Van Dijk and Kintsch in *Strategies of Discourse Comprehension;* they view paragraphs as roughly equivalent to "episodes" (sequences of sentences dominated by a macroproposition) and see the indentation of a paragraph as a mark of the surface structure of the whole text: a signal of episode change (p. 204).

In this connection we can note a bit of research by Young and Becker (cited briefly in "Toward a Modern Theory of Rhetoric," Steinmann, p. 100). It must be, suggest Young and Becker, that there are in any discourse semantic clues that a reader can pick up to identify when one sequence of thought has been terminated and another begun, because in experimental tests readers have shown that they could agree on the placing of most paragraph breaks in passages typed without paragraph indentations.

Rodgers has not written accessibly for nearly twenty years, and his "discourse-centered" approach to the paragraph has not been taken up by many scholars until quite recently, when Rick Eden and Ruth Mitchell developed their essay, "Paragraphing for the Reader" (*CCC* [December 1986], 416–30). Eden and Mitchell bring together ideas drawn from Rodgers, from the reading theorists, and from their own analyses of the rhetoric of illustrative paragraphs to argue that paragraphing is best viewed not as a part of composing but as a part of editing—as a visual signaling system by which the writer lets the reader know how the writer wishes the text as a whole to be read. Deployment of paragraphs will differ depending on the response the writer wishes to evoke in the reader. They retain the concept of the "topic sentence," referring to it, however, as an "orienting sentence" or an "umbrella sentence" that, as the psycholinguists insist, gives the reader a sense of direction. Eden and Mitchell propose that students be encouraged to conduct rhetorical, not just formal, analyses of professional paragraphs, be encouraged to imitate skillfully written paragraphs, and be asked to write, as compositions, not paragraphs but short essays.

Lately there are signs that the three approaches to the paragraph that I have been describing are proving insufficient. Several scholars have begun looking at paragraphs from fresh perspectives, asking, in effect, what fundamentally is this structure, this phenomenon, that we have agreed to call by the name of "paragraph," and how does it work in different settings? This sort of "conceptual blockbusting"—to borrow a term from the literature on creativity—is perhaps not yet widespread, but it is conspicuous. I conclude this essay by citing two cases in point.

One is proposed, in passing, by Stephen Witte as he discusses ("Topical Structure and Revision: An Exploratory Study" *CCC*, 34 [October 1983], 313–41) his research on the moves that student writers make in revising a passage of serious academic text (Witte's research focused primarily on these moves made in revision). As a basis for describing what the student writers accomplished, and how, Witte draws from European theorists of "topic" in discourse the concepts of "topical depth," "topical progression," and "topical structure analysis." In analyzing a paragraph, one determines which "topic" is discussed in the greatest number of sentences, counts the number of sentences in which it appears, identifies the topics of other sentences, counts the number of different sentence topics, and counts the number of sentences with different topics that intervene between any two of those sentences that develop the topic most frequently mentioned. From this analysis one can infer the "discourse topic" (the principal topic of the text), and, looking at the principal verbs, can construct the "gist" or "macroproposition" that summarizes the point of the text. Witte applies this technique of analysis to a study of revision by noting, among other phenomena, how well the revisers appear to have understood the gist and structure of the text they were revising. He does not in this essay, and has not yet to my knowledge, applied this technique of analysis to studies focused on discovering how paragraphs work. But one suspects that he could. One wonders what findings might emerge if a researcher combined Haswell's interest in patterns and structures with Witte's interest in the topical "depth" of a paragraph (the number of sentences with different subjects between sentences built around the "discourse topic"). And one wonders what other perspectives researchers might identify for describing the structure of a paragraph.

A second perspective worth noting on the structure of the paragraph is adopted by Rochelle Smith in "Paragraphing for Coherence: Writing as Implied Dialogue," *CE,* 46 (January 1984), 8–21, where she urges, as her title implies, that successive paragraphs (and sentences within paragraphs) be viewed as portions of a dialogue between writer and reader. Drawing from the suggestions of the sociolinguist Eliot Mishler, Smith suggests that paragraphs can usefully be viewed as successive steps in a dialogue: a speaker's question, an answer from a respondent, and a confirmation of some sort from the speaker, which may contain or be in the form of another question. Or the respondent's answer may itself be a question, and the original questioner may become a respondent. The conclusion of a paragraph, Smith suggests, may be thought of as the conclusion of a unit of dialogue. She supports her suggested view of the paragraph by analyzing a stretch of text from Jacob Bronowski, and a stretch from a student in a liberal arts college which did not use the pattern of dialogue effectively over its full length.

VII

Witte and Smith have offered suggestions about new ways of approaching studies of the paragraph. The profession could benefit from more such studies. For despite the advances achieved over the last decade in studying the structural characteristics of paragraphs and whole texts, only a few of the useful questions have been addressed, and the explorations of these few questions have not, by and large, reached the profession as a whole. A compressed essay of this sort cannot, perhaps, whet readers' appetites for further reading in the books and articles discussed here (which are often not aimed at applications to practice), but it can remind readers of subjects that deserve their reflection. In 1975 I wrote that "the reasons for the effectiveness of different [structural] patterns, the ways in which their parts interact [to influence how a reader makes meaning from a text], the most useful techniques of deciding upon particular sequences of steps in [a composition]— in short, many of the fundamental topics one has to address in choosing forms [for one's writings]—have been dealt with slightly, hesitantly, or not at all." After ten years, that generalization remains more true than not.

Confronting the present state of scholarship about form (despite its recent enrichment), the teacher today, as in 1975, might wisely exercise caution. Instead of talking about "good organization" in the abstract, or advocating one plan of organization (or one framework for describing organization) in preference to all others, the teacher should regularly ask students to recognize the interconnections of form and content, and help students quietly in the subtle task—one that each student as an individual must undertake—of creating a form that suits well their ideas and emphases. Since a heuristic for such choosing is not available, flexibility and sensitivity to the values of different structures are attitudes for students and teachers to cultivate. Students and teachers need to acquire the habit of pondering, as they read, the form that a text has taken and the way that form is working. Form may not *be* substance, but it interprets substance while relaying it: it signals to the reader how substance is to be understood. We all need, basing our best judgment on sensitive, practiced reading of our drafts and our finished essays, to take account of how our thought is communicated and interpreted through its form.

Approaches to the Study of Style

EDWARD P. J. CORBETT, Ohio State University

1976

STYLE HAS BEEN A CONCERN OF RHETORICIANS from the beginning of rhetoric in fifth-century Athens. During the long history of rhetoric, the concern for style has had its ups and downs. There were rhetoric texts preoccupied almost exclusively with style; there were periods, on the other hand, when the emphasis shifted so heavily toward *res* that the study of *verba* was neglected and even deplored. But the fascination with the stylistic aspects of discourse never really died; it faded at times, but it invariably revived. Today, stylistic study is the most advanced and flourishing area of the so-called "new rhetoric." Evidence of the prosperous state of stylistic study is everywhere to be found. In addition to the growing number of articles on style in our professional journals, we now have two journals devoted exclusively to articles on style: *Style,* founded in 1967, and *Language and Style,* founded in 1968. Evidence of the sheer volume of work on style can be found in the Annual Bibliography on Style appearing each year in *Style.* The Annual Bibliography for 1972, for instance, covered 153 pages in the Winter 1974 issue of *Style.* [This had become 125 pages in the 1981 Bibliography, *Style,* Summer 1983.] A peek at recent issues of *Dissertation Abstracts* reveals the great number of graduate students who have turned, for the subjects of their dissertations, to the many unplowed fields of style.

Two factors that have contributed significantly to the flourishing stylistic scene are the computer and linguistics. It took a long time for us humanists to overcome our antipathy for electronic hardware and to recognize it as a helpful tool for literary studies. The production of computer–assisted concordances and word–lists probably first led humanists to recognize that what the computer had to offer was relief from the tedium of manual tabulating and the means of achieving accuracy, objectivity, and completeness of data. For many years what hampered the development of descriptive studies of style, comparable to descriptive studies of grammar, was simply that, aside from the statistical information about sentence length and paragraph length compiled by such assiduous counters as Edwin Lewis and Lucius Sherman in the last decade of the nineteenth century, there was a dearth of raw data about stylistic features available to scholars. But thanks to the help of the computer, we now have valuable banks of information about the style of literary texts, such as Sally Sedelow's work on Milton's *Paradise Lost,* and about the style of workaday prose, like the corpus of over a million words that Henry Kucera and W. Nelson Francis drew from 500 samples of pedestrian American prose in 1967 (see their *Computational Analysis of Present-Day American English* [Providence, R.I.: Brown University Press, 1970]).

The computer will continue to facilitate the production of additional concordances and of attribution studies, like those of Alvar Ellegard on the Junius letters of Frederick Mostellar and Davis L. Wallace on the Federalist Papers, and of further stylistic studies of literary prose, like Louis Milic's *A Quantitative Approach to the Style of Jonathan Swift* (The Hague: Mouton, 1967). Fortunately, we humanists do not have to be computer experts to be able to make use of the computer. We have to gain just enough elementary knowledge about computers to be aware of the kinds of information a computer can spit out and to be able to explain fully and clearly to a programmer what kind of information we want to gather. As a good basic article on the capabilities of the computer for stylistic studies, I would recommend Robert S. Wachal's "On Using a Computer" in *The Computer and Literary Style,* ed. Jacob Leed (Kent, Ohio: Kent State University Press, 1966), pp. 14–37.

If the contribution of modern linguistics to stylistics is not obvious to you, it will be obvious before this bibliographical survey reaches its conclusion. A convenient summary of the contributions that various linguistic schools have made to stylistic studies can be found in Nils Erik Enkvist's "On the Place of Style in Some Linguistic Theories" in *Literary Style: A Symposium,* ed. Seymour Chatman (New York: Oxford University Press, 1971) and in Julie Carson's article "Proper Stylistics" in the Spring of 1974 issue of *Style.* Carson regards Archibald Hill, Samuel R. Levin, and Richard Ohmann as the most representative of the linguist-analysts in America. As she says, "Hill came to stylistics as a structuralist; Ohmann, as a tranformationalist. And Levin got caught in the crossfire." Enkvist maintains that although traditional grammar was "amorphous and flexible enough to swallow stylistic considerations *ad libitum,*" the study of style was "on the whole, a marginal, rather than a central pursuit" of both structural and transformational grammarians. Nevertheless, Enkvist recognizes some valuable contributions to stylistic studies in the works of such structuralists as Zellig Harris, Bernard Bloch, Kenneth Pike, Martin Joos, and Archibald Hill, and, largely because of the work of Richard Ohmann, he is disposed to regard transformational grammar as the most promising of the linguistic systems for stylistic studies. "If style is choice," says Enkvist, "then transformational grammar is, I take it, the grammatical model that so far most fully maps out the system and range of this choice."

This essay will also discuss some of the contributions that speech-act theory is making to stylistic studies and that various theories of conceptual rhetoric are likely to make to the analysis of linguistic units larger than the sentence. What we are witnessing in the studies of inter-sentence relationships and of larger units than the sentence is a movement toward holistic criticism, a truly rhetorical kind of criticism that relates the syntagmatic and paradigmatic features of a text not only to the dynamics of the whole text but also to the author, the audience, and the universe of discourse. If this movement toward a holistic kind of analysis continues, the apprehensions that some literary critics have about the limitations of purely linguistic analysis may be allayed. Those apprehensions were well summarized by Elias Schwartz in "Notes on Linguistics and Literature," *CE,* 32 (November 1970), 190:

> What distinguishes the language of literature is not some inherent feature, but its function in relation to the whole of which it is a part. This function is not marked in the language so used; it inheres rather in the relation of that language to the total structure of the poem, a structure which is aesthetic, not linguistic. There is no such thing as a distinctive literary language. And if this is true, though linguists tell us a great deal about language, they can tell us nothing about literature.

The linguist is equipped by training to describe and analyze the linguistic structures in a text and to classify the patterns of those structures, but he is not especially equipped by his training to utilize the data that he discovers and identifies in the critical interpretation of the whole text. For that reason, the current feeling is that the student of style will have to combine the expertise of the linguist, the rhetorician, and the literary critic.

Given the current state and the great volume of stylistic studies, I despaired of being able to adequately survey, in a relatively short essay, the literature on style. Even to touch on the most important books and articles on style is too vast a project. Clearly, I would have to carve out an even smaller section than that from the vast acreage. What might be manageable would be for me to concentrate on those books and articles that would, in my judgment, be most useful and usable to teachers of composition who might want to engage their students in a stylistic study of English prose on a fairly elementary level. That focus would exclude from the survey the highly technical literature in stylistics and most of the stylistic studies of belletristic texts. Even within those limits, my choices of the books and articles to talk about would have to be arbitrary, and I suspect that ten minutes after this essay has been finally locked into print, I will think of half a dozen books or articles that should have been mentioned. But who of us is not liable to fallibility of judgment and myopia of vision?

I have grouped my selections under the headings Collections, Bibliography, History, Theory, and Methodology and Application. I sometimes had difficulty settling on a category for a particular entry. A basically theoretical article, for instance, sometimes slid over into methodology and application. I finally had to adopt the joint category of Methodology and Application, rather than a separate section for each, because most of the authors who started out by talking about methodology eventually exemplified the method by applying it to an analysis of a particular text. The numbers enclosed in brackets after some of the items mentioned in the essay indicate that the item is reprinted in one or more of the collections that will be discussed in the next section (see the apppendix for the numbers assigned to these collections).

Collections

The available anthologies of articles on style fall into two general classes: those that reprint papers delivered at a single conference and those that reprint pieces that were previously published in journals or books. Some of the latter kind are not given over wholly to articles on style; only a section of the anthology presents articles on style.

There are two anthologies which present papers delivered at international conferences on style. The first of these, published in 1960 by the MIT Press, is *Style in Language,* edited by Thomas A. Sebeok. Under eight distinct headings representing the three main viewpoints of linguistics, psychology, and literary criticism, this collection reprints twenty-six papers (six of them only in abstract) delivered at the 1958 conference on style held at Indiana University in Bloomington. Comments by the participants are reproduced at the end of each section, and an extensive bibliography is given on pp. 435–49. *Literary Style: A Symposium,* ed. Seymour Chatman (New York: Oxford University Press, 1971) reproduces the twenty-one papers delivered at a symposium on style that took place in Bellagio, Italy, in August of 1969. Some of the most distinguished stylisticians from America, England, and Continental Europe participated in this conference. Seymour Chatman presents his summary of the subsequent discussions of most of the papers immediately after the printed version of the paper. Of these two collections, I think teachers of composition would find more useful articles in the Chatman anthology.

In 1967, Houghton Mifflin published a distinguished collection of previously published articles on style, under the title *Essays on the Language of Literature,* ed. Seymour Chatman and Samuel R. Levin. The thirty-one essays in this collection are grouped under five headings: Sound Texture (four articles); Metrics (six articles); Grammar (six articles); Literary Form and Meaning (seven articles); Style and Stylistics (eight articles). Although most of the articles in this collection treat style as it applies to belletristic texts, teachers of composition will find at least ten of the articles useful for their purposes. This is the only anthology that reprints the two often-cited articles by Michael Riffaterre that will be discussed later on.

Glen A. Love and Michael Payne in their collection *Contemporary Essays on Style: Rhetoric, Linguistics, and Criticism* (Glenview, Ill.: Scott, Foresman, 1969) reprint twenty-five articles under the three headings indicated in the sub-title. If I were asked to recommend an anthology that would be most suitable for an introductory course on style on the undergraduate or graduate level, I would nominate the Love-Payne collection. It is the one that I first send my students to when they express an interest in the study of style.

Essays in Stylistic Analysis, ed. Howard S. Babb (New York: Harcourt Brace Jovanovich, 1972) reprints twenty-one essays, including some of the classic essays by Richard Ohmann, Morris Croll, and Josephine Miles. Professor Babb's wife has translated the three esssays that were written in German and has also translated the passages in French and Latin in the essays by Croll and Riffaterre.

Donald C. Freeman has reprinted twenty-three essays in his collection *Linguistics and Literary Style* (New York: Holt, Rinehart and Winston, 1970). The five essays appearing in the fourth section, Approaches to Prose Style, would be the ones most useful to the teacher of composition.

The anthologies in the next group have an historical bent. This orientation is reflected in the title of the collection that James R. Bennett, the editor of *Style,* put together in 1971—*Prose Style: A Historical Approach Through Studies* (San Francisco: Chandler, 1971). Starting out with three essays that deal with the Continuity of the Sentence and the Paragraph, Bennett arranges the remaining articles according to the period they deal with: II. The Old English and Middle English Periods; III. The Renaissance Period; IV. The Restoration and the Eighteenth Century; V. The Nineteenth and Twentieth Centuries. Each section carries Suggestions for Research, and sections III, IV, and V present Selections for Analysis. One of the most valuable features of this diachronic collection of essays is the Annotated Bibliography on pp. 253–80.

Louis T. Milic's *Stylists on Style: A Handbook with Selections for Analysis* (New York: Scribner's, 1969) also has an historical range, but the fifty-seven short selections in which various authors present their views on style are arranged in reverse chronological order, from Robert Graves in 1961 to Caxton in 1490. The second part of this collection presents forty-three selections for analysis from British and American authors. In the second edition of his *Modern Essays on Writing and Style* (New York: Holt, Rinehart and Winston, 1969), Paul C. Wermuth presents thirty essays on style and writing by contemporary authors, but the forty Sample Passages for Analysis and Discussion represent an historical range. In his *Style in English Prose* (New York: Macmillan, 1968), Carl H. Klaus traces the development of prose style in his introductory essay "Reflections on Prose Style" (pp. 1–14), but the rest of the collection merely reprints short selections for analysis. Perhaps the most inexpensive of the historically-oriented anthologies is the 288-page *The Problem of Style* (Greenwich, Connecticut: Fawcett Publications, 1966), which was compiled by J. V. Cunningham. This anthology carries thirty-five essays by such writers on style as Aristotle, Cicero, Longinus, Eric Auerbach, Morris Croll, René Wellek, Austin Warren, James Sledd, Frank Sullivan, and J. V. Cunningham himself.

The following anthologies have only a section of them devoted to style, but although they reprint considerably fewer essays on style than the anthologies devoted exclusively to style, the essays they do present are all pertinent to the composition classroom. In their *Teaching Freshman Composition* (New York: Oxford University Press, 1967), Gary Tate and Edward P. J. Corbett present five essays on style and two short bibliographies on style by James R. Bennett and Paul C. Doherty. In their later anthology, *Teaching High School Composition* (New York: Oxford University Press, 1970), they reproduce only three essays in the section on style, but they reprint Francis Christensen's "A Generative Rhetoric of the Sentence" and Bennett's annotated bibliography in two other sections of the book. In the section on style in his *New Rhetorics* (New York: Scribner's, 1967), Martin Steinmann, Jr. reproduces five of the oft-reprinted essays on style. In the most recent collection, *Contemporary Rhetoric: A Conceptual Background with Readings* (New York: Harcourt Brace Jovanovich, 1975), W. Ross Winterowd presents his own introductory essay on style (pp. 253–70) and seven previously published essays on style.

The value of collections like these is that they bring together a number of carefully selected pieces from widely scattered and sometimes inaccessible sources. Consequently, the teacher can add a number of these anthologies to his personal library and have available an ample body of material, in relatively inexpensive volumes, that he can prescribe as texts for a course he wants to teach. As recently as ten years ago, a teacher who wanted to teach a course in style would have had to send his students to bound periodicals in the library or to make xerox copies of the articles he wanted the students to read.

Bibliography

Not much needs to be said about the bibliographies of style. It will suffice to list them and say something about their scope, if their titles do not indicate their province. They fall into two general classes: selective listings published either as articles or as parts of books and book-length listings.

Four of the selective listings were mentioned in the previous section: (1) Thomas A. Sebeok's "Bibliography" in *Style in Language* (Cambridge, Mass.: MIT Press, 1960), pp. 435–49; (2) James R. Bennett's "Annotated Bibliography" in *Prose Style: A Historical Approach Through Studies* (San Francisco: Chandler, 1971), pp. 253–80; (3) James R. Bennett, "An Annotated Bibliography of Selected Writings on English Prose Style," *CCC,* 16 (December 1965), 248–55 [12, 13]; (4) Paul C. Doherty, "Stylistics—A Bibliographical Survey," *The CEA Critic,* 28 (May 1966), 1, 3–4, [4, 12]. Doherty prefaces his list of forty-four items with a brief essay in which he discusses the two main schools of stylistic studies—the "normative" and the "individual," to use his terms.

To these alphabetical listings of selected books and articles can be added Josephine Miles's extensive bibliography at the end of her book *Style and Proportion: The Language of Prose and Poetry* (Boston: Little, Brown, 1967), pp. 164–212; R. C. Alston's "Rhetoric and Style: A Bibliographical Guide," *Leeds Studies in English,* New Series, 1 (1967), 137–59; and James R. Bennett's

"Stylistic Domains: A Checklist," *Symposium in Rhetoric,* ed. J. Dean Bishop, Turner S. Kobler, and William E. Tanner (Denton, Texas: Texas Woman's University, 1975), pp. 18–24. The later the date of these selective bibliographies, the greater the chance that more recent stylistic studies are included in the listing.

Helmut Hatzfield's *A Critical Bibliography of the New Stylistics Applied to Romance Literatures, 1900–1952* (Chapel Hill: University of North Carolina Press, 1953) was the first of the book-length bibliographies of style. But although this compilation carries some 2000 items, most of the entries, as the title indicates, deal with literary texts written in the Romance languages. We now have two other book-length bibliographies. The first of these and the one that would probably be most useful to teachers of composition is *Style and Stylistics: An Analytical Bibliography* (New York: Free Press, 1967) compiled by Louis T. Milic. Milic lists the more than 800 items in his bibliography under five categories: I. Theoretical; II. Methodological; III. Applied (i.e., studies of particular authors, works, periods, etc.); IV. Bibliographies (separate bibliographies and bibliographies that are parts of other works); V. Omnibus (reference works and collections of essays on style). Three handy indexes aid the student of style in finding a particular item or a particular class of items: Authors as Contributors, Authors as Subjects, Subjects and Topics.

English Stylistics: A Bibliography, compiled by Richard W. Bailey and Sister Dolores M. Burton (Cambridge, Mass.: MIT Press, 1968), is comparable in its comprehensiveness to Hatzfield's bibliography of stylistic studies in the Romance languages. Its more than 2000 items are divided into three parts: I. A list of bibliographical sources (twenty-eight items); II. Language and Style Before 1900 (pp. 5–46); III. English Stylistics in the Twentieth Century (pp. 47–173). Sister Dolores, who compiled the bibliography in Part II, subdivided her area into five periods: Classical, Medieval, Renaissance, Neoclassic, and Nineteenth Century. In a prefatory section, Bailey provides a useful survey of modern stylistic activity and organizes his bibliography in Part III under topical headings.

For a year-by-year updating of these published bibliographies, Richard W. Bailey has been compiling the Annual Bibliography on Style that appears each year in the journal *Style,* which is published at the University of Arkansas and edited by James R. Bennett. The number of stylistic studies published in the last fifteen years is staggering.

History

As with most subjects, the study or the teaching of style can be enhanced by some acquaintance with the history of style. Most of the important studies of the history of style have appeared in books, but, as will be seen, treatments of a particular kind or period of prose style have also appeared in articles.

One of the earliest book-length treatments of English prose was George Philip Krapp's *The Rise of English Literary Prose* (New York: Oxford University Press, 1915), which traced the development of literary prose from Wyclif to Bacon. In *The Continuity of English Prose from Alfred to More and His School* (London: Oxford University Press, 1932), R. W. Chambers traced it back even further, to Alfred, and then forward through Aelfric to Thomas More. It is generally agreed, however, that the really pioneering studies of English prose style appeared in the series of essays that Morris W. Croll wrote in the 1920s to demonstrate his thesis that the development of "Attic Prose" and the Baroque Style in the seventeenth century represented a reaction to the development of "Ciceronian" prose style. Nine of Croll's essays, including "The Baroque Style in Prose," "'Attic Prose' in the Seventeenth Century," "Muret and the History of 'Attic Prose,'" and "Attic Prose: Lipsius, Montaigne, Bacon" have been conveniently gathered together in *Style, Rhetoric, and Rhythm: Essays by Morris W. Croll,* ed. J. Max Patrick and Robert O. Evans, with John M. Wallace and R. J. Schoeck (Princeton, N.J.: Princeton University Press,

1966). George Williamson, in his *The Senecan Amble: A Study in Prose Form from Bacon to Collier* (Chicago: University of Chicago Press, 1951), revealed himself to be a Crollian. The thesis that he argues in a book notable for its turgid prose style but sound scholarship is that the dominant prose style of the seventeenth century was modelled on the "Senecan Amble," a term that the Earl of Shaftesbury used to describe the kind of curt, easy, succinct prose style that developed as part of the anti-Ciceronian movement and that helped to establish many of the characteristics of modern prose style.

Croll's views are not as sacrosanct as they once were. They first were attacked by R. F. Jones, who in articles like "Science and English Prose Style in the Third Quarter of the Seventeenth Century," *PMLA*, 45 (1930), 977–1009, and "Science and Language in England of the Mid-Seventeenth Century," *JEGP*, 31 (1932), 315–31, argued that it was the new Baconian science that influenced the development of English prose style. Croll's thesis is further challenged in the latest book-length treatment of the evolution of prose style, Robert Adolph's *The Rise of Modern Prose Style* (Cambridge, Mass.: MIT Press, 1968). "Although my position," Adolph says, "is clearly closer to Jones than to Croll, the evidence suggests strongly that the ultimate influence on the new prose is neither 'science' nor 'Anti-Ciceronianism' but the new utilitarianism around which the values of the age are integrated."

Three of the more recent books on prose style are not so much historical treatments as they are analytical attempts to classify distinct types of prose style. In *Prose Styles: Five Primary Types* (Minneapolis: University of Minnesota Press, 1966), Huntington Brown distinguishes and exemplifies five types, which he labels the deliberative, the expository, the tumbling, the prophetic, and the indenture. In *Tough, Sweet, and Stuffy: An Essay on Modern American Style* (Bloomington: Indiana University Press, 1966)—a book that will be discussed below in another connection—Walker Gibson classifies three distinct styles which he regards as being reflections of the *ethos* of the writers. One of the best and most convincing book-length treatments of the development of a single kind of prose style is Richard Bridgman's *The Colloquial Style in America* (New York: Oxford University Press, 1966). Bridgman makes a good case for his thesis that Henry James, Mark Twain, Gertrude Stein, and Ernest Hemingway were the authors mainly responsible for the development of a truly colloquial prose style in America.

Theory

Although a number of promising methodologies have been developed, we still lack a fully developed, coherent theory of style. The closest we have come to a poetics of style is perhaps Longinus's *On the Sublime,* but the theory presented in that noted treatise deals with only one variety of style—the style that "transports" listeners or readers—and a great number of components of style are not dealt with at all. The kind of metatheory of style that I have in mind is exemplified in Louis Milic's article "Rhetorical Choice and Stylistic Options: The Conscious and Unconscious Poles" in *Literary Style: A Symposium,* ed. Seymour Chatman (New York: Oxford University Press, 1971), pp. 77–88. In that article, Milic makes a distinction between *stylistic options,* those choices we make unconsciously and habitually about lexicon and syntax while in the act of writing, and *rhetorical choices,* those decisions we make consciously and deliberately when we review and evaluate what we have generated. It is Milic's contention that "stylistic options taken together are the style of the writer and represent the primary field of inquiry for the analyst of style." "Where I differ from most investigators," he says, "is in the conviction that they have erroneously treated all decisions constituting style as conscious rhetorical choices, representing the realization of artistic intentions, or that they have mingled together habitual and artistic considerations." Accordingly, in his own book *A Quantitative Approach to the Style of Jonathan Swift* (The Hague: Mouton, 1967), Milic concentrates on the recurring stylistic features that he found in a large corpus of Swift's prose.

It is that kind of theory of style, with its implications for stylistic analysis, that has not been developed on a comprehensive scale. But I will review here some of the philosophical or linguistic orientations of stylisticians that might some day be incorporated into a comprehensive theory of style.

A number of Louis Milic's many articles on style have dealt with his objections to the usual bases for arriving at a typology of style, as in his "Against the Typology of Styles," in *Essays on the Language of Literature,* ed. Seymour Chatman and Samuel R. Levin (Boston: Houghton Mifflin, 1967), pp. 425–50 [3, 4], or with his attempts to classify the metaphysical underpinnings of the various schools of stylistic criticism, as in "The Problem of Style," a chapter in his *A Quantitative Approach to the Style of Jonathan Swift,* pp. 40–73 [15]. An article of the latter sort, which should be of special interest to the teacher of composition, is Milic's article "Theories of Style and Their Implications for the Teaching of Composition," *CCC,* 16 (May 1965), 66–69, 126 [4, 12]. In this article, he posits three basic theories of style:

(1) The theory of ornate form or rhetorical dualism (the theory that claims a separate existence for form and content—"ideas exist wordlessly and can be dressed in a variety of outfits").

(2) The individualist or psychological monism ("style is the man").

(3) The organic theory, the Crocean aesthetic monism, which denies the possibility of any separation of content and form.

Milic contends that acceptance of the second or third of these theories leaves little for the composition teacher to do. If "style is the man," all we can do is urge the student to express himself naturally and not tamper with his style at all; if form is inseparable from meaning, then we cannot encourage our students to consider alternative or synonymous ways of saying something, because a change in the form results inevitably in a change of meaning. Although the dualistic view has its shortcomings, especially in its potential implication that style is merely the dress of thought, it is, Milic contends, the only one among the three basic theories that justifies a teacher's efforts to help his students improve their style. "In the college composition course," Milic says, "which represents for most students their first formal training in rhetoric, an awareness must be instilled of the existence of alternatives, of different ways of saying the same thing, of the options that the language offers."

A good example of the organic or Crocean view of the inseparability of style and meaning is found in Monroe E. Beardsley's frequently reprinted "Style and Good Style," which first appeared in *Reflections on High School English: NDEA Institute Lectures 1965,* ed. Gary Tate (Tulsa, Oklahoma: University of Tulsa, 1966), pp. 91–105 [4, 13, 14]. Beardsley clearly lines up on the side of the organicist view of style: "My argument is that a difference of style is always a difference in meaning—though implicit—and an important and notable difference of style is always a sizable difference in meaning. . . . Style is nothing but meaning. . . . Good style is logical congruity of explicit and implicit meaning." One of the consequences of this view is that "if a teacher advises a change of words or of word order, he is recommending a different meaning. And if he says one stylistic feature is better than another, he is saying that it is better to mean one thing rather than another." From this philosophical standpoint, Beardsley takes issue with many of the stylistic pronouncements in William Strunk and E. B. White's widely used text *The Elements of Style* (New York: Macmillan, 1959).

In his earliest article on style, "Prolegomena to the Analysis of Prose Style," in *Style in Prose Fiction: English Institute Essays,* ed. Harold C. Martin (New York: Columbia University Press, 1959), pp. 1–24 [3, 4, 5], Richard Ohmann registered his dissatisfaction with this organicist view of style: "The [organicist] critic can talk about what the writer says, but talk about style he cannot, for his neat identity—one thought, one form—allows no margin for individual variation, which is what we ordinarily mean by style." Ohmann found that I. A. Richards's notion of "forms of thought" ["I see the tiger," "I kick the tiger"], as presented in *Interpretation in Teaching,* represented a happy compromise between dualism and monism, because it left form and content "neither quite joined nor totally separated." Ohmann adopted the view of style as *epistemic choice* ("a writer's method of dissecting the universe as expressed by the infinite number of choices he makes"), a view that resides somewhere in between the dualistic school and the style-is-the-man school. "If the critic," Ohmann says, "is able to isolate and examine the most primitive choices which lie behind a work of prose, they can reveal to him the very roots of a writer's epistemology." It was this theory of style as epistemic choice that informed Ohmann's study of George Bernard Shaw's style, *Shaw, the Style and the Man* (Middletown, Conn.: Wesleyan University Press, 1962).

Another influential early article by Ohmann was his "Generative Grammars and the Concept of Literary Style," *Word,* 20 (December 1964), 423–39 [4, 6, 12, 14]. At the beginning of this article, Ohmann outlined twelve different kinds of stylistic studies and claimed that none of them could yield "a full and convincing explication of the notion of style" because they lacked "an appropriate underlying linguistic and semantic theory." It was in this article that Ohmann espoused transformational grammar as the most promising linguistic theory for stylistic study, mainly because it gets at the "syntactic component" in style and at the "alternativeness" among constructions. His analyses in this article of short passages from Faulkner, Hemingway, James, and Lawrence presaged some of the stylistic analyses that will be reviewed in the next section of this essay.

Two important articles by Michael Riffaterre laid the theoretical groundwork for the development of a methodology of style analysis: "Criteria for Style Analysis," *Word,* 15 (1959), 154–74 [3] and "Stylistic Context," *Word,* 16 (1960), 207–18 [3]. Riffaterre's intention was to make stylistics as much of a science as possible by devising a heuristic that would permit objective determination of the linguistic facts of a text. Seeing style as a departure from a linguistic norm, he proposed to make use of an "average reader" as an informant to identify a convergence or cluster of "stylistic devices" (those unpredictable, contrasting linguistic elements in a text) and to replace the overall linguistic norm with "stylistic context" as a norm. The notion of "stylistic context" was the novel element in Riffaterre's theory. In the 1959 article, he defined the stylistic context as "a linguistic pattern suddenly broken by an element which was unpredictable"; "the contrast resulting from this interference," he went on to say, "is the stylistic stimulus." In the 1960 article, he refined his definition of context and differentiated between an interior context (the context that creates the opposition constituting the stylistic device) and an exterior or macrocontext (the context that modifies this opposition by reinforcing or weakening it).

In "On Defining Style," *Linguistics and Style,* ed. John Spencer (New York: Oxford University Press, 1964), pp. 3–56 [4, 9], Nils Erik Enkvist, a professor of English Language and Literature in Finland, picks up on this notion of context. "Style," he says, "is concerned with frequencies of linguistic items in a given context, and thus with contextual probabilities. To measure the style of a passage the frequencies of its linguistic items of different levels must be compared with the corresponding features in another text or corpus which is regarded as a norm and which has a definite contextual relationship with this passage." Enkvist too differentiates between two kinds of context: a textual context (phonetic, phonemic, morphemic, syntactic, lexical, and compositional elements) and an extra-textual context (period, type of speech, literary genre, speaker/writer, listener/reader, situation and environment, etc.). "The aim of stylistic analysis," he says, "is the inventory of style markers [those linguistic items that only appear in one group of contexts] and a statement of their contextual spread."

In his headnote to the section on style in *Contemporary Rheto-*

ric: A Conceptual Background with Readings (New York: Harcourt Brace Jovanovich, 1975), pp. 253–70 [15], W. Ross Winterowd divides his own discussion of style into two parts: *pedagogical stylistics* ("teaching students to develop style") and *theoretical stylistics* ("concerned with theory, definitions, place of style in literary studies"). In his discussion of the prevailing theories of style, Winterowd questions the concept of style as choice. He observes that transformationalists speak of "obligatory transformations" and "non-obligatory transformations" and concedes that we might call the latter "stylistic transformations." But a complication is introduced by Charles Fillmore's notions of case and modality (see Charles J. Fillmore, "The Case for Case," in *Universals in Linguistic Theory,* ed. Emmon Bach and Robert T. Harms [New York: Holt, Rinehart and Winston, 1968]). From the point of view of case grammar, *all* transformations are obligatory, and if so, the element of choice would be eliminated. Winterowd asks then, "What is it that we describe when we study style?" Like others, he sees transformational grammar as providing the best framework for the analysis of style, but in formulating his own schema of what we look at when we study style, he turns to speech–act theory as propounded by J. L. Austin in *How To Do Things with Words* (Cambridge, Mass.: Harvard University Press, 1962) and by John Searle in *Speech Acts* (Cambridge, England: Cambridge University Press, 1969). Searle divides Austin's *locutionary act* into two parts: the *utterance act* (the act of uttering strings of words) and the *propositional act* (consisting of referring [the subject] and predicating [the verb]). Positing that all aspects of the locutionary act can be subsumed under *transformations, lexicon,* and *figures of thought* (tropes such as metaphor, irony, and litotes rather than schemes like chiasmus, asyndeton, or alliteration, which would be studied under *transformations*), Winterowd proposes this schema of the proper objects of stylistic study:

Transformations

> Intersentence
>> Embedding
>> Subordinating
>> Conjunction
> Intrasentence

Lexicon

> Parts of speech
>> (content words, like nouns, verbs, etc.)
> Structure words
>> (conjunctions, prepositions)

Figures of Thought

> Those figures which involve a shift in normal meaning

It is significant that Richard Ohmann, who has written extensively on style as epistemic choice and on the usefulness of tranformational grammar for the analysis of style, has also in recent years been turning to speech-act theory for another basis of stylistic analysis. He has published at least three articles in which he points out the rhetorical and stylistic dimensions of speech-act theory: "Speech Acts and the Definition of Literature," *P and R,* 4 (Winter 1971), 1–19; "Instrumental Style: Notes on the Theory of Speech as Action," in *Current Trends in Stylistics,* ed. Braj B. Kachru and Herbert F. W. Stahlke (Champaign, Ill.: Linguistic Research, Inc., 1972), pp. 115–41; and "Speech, Action, and Style," in *Literary Style: A Symposium,* ed. Seymour Chatman (New York: Oxford University Press, 1971), 241–54 [2]. Basically, the speech-act theorists view an utterance not so much as *expressing* something as *doing* something, and they distinguish three major kinds of act that the speaker or writer performs: the *locutionary act*—the sounds or the graphic symbols that the speaker or writer produces; the *illocutionary act,* the act that the speaker or writer performs *in* saying something—e.g. stating, promising, endorsing, questioning, etc.; the *perlocutionary act,* the effect of the act of speaking or writing on the hearer or reader—e.g. informing, frightening, enraging, puzzling, etc. What is particularly fruitful about this method of analysis is not only that it allows the critic to range freely from word to sentence to larger units of discourse but that it allows him to unite the provinces of the linguist as he looks at the locutionary act, the semanticist as he looks at the illocutionary act, and the rhetorician as he looks at the perlocutionary act. It moves us from the rather atomistic study of isolated units of language to the larger social, political, aesthetic, and pragmatic contexts of the language.

Winston Weathers's "The Grammars of Style: New Options in Composition," which occupied the entire Winter 1976 issue of *Freshman English News,* is likely to increase our tolerance of a wider and more unorthodox range of styles than we recognized or permitted our students to cultivate in the past. Weathers's thesis is that many students write well when they find a "grammar of style" that works best for them, either because it fits their "chemistry" of composition or because it suits what they have to say. Today, we have prose styles that fall outside the established "grammars of style"—discontinuity replacing continuity, non sequiturs replacing transitions, synchronicity replacing diachronicity, etc. Until recently, we tended to apologize for the Gertrude Steins, the John Barths, the William Burroughses, the Donald Barthelmes— as though they fell outside our stylistic mainstream but got away with their strange styles because of some sort of dispensation given them by the culture. Weathers's point is that if we confront our students with these "unorthodox" styles and encourage them to cultivate such styles, they might prove themselves in ways previously denied them.

That is not quite the point, but it is akin to the point, that Martin Joos made in his *The Five Clocks* (New York: Harcourt, Brace and World, 1962), in which he claimed that all of us are in command of a variety of styles or registers—to use his terms, *frozen, formal, consultative, casual,* and *intimate*—and that we shift back and forth among these styles to suit the occasion and our audiences. Some of Joos's registers—especially the *casual* and the *intimate*—are so individualistic and unorthodox as to qualify as idiolects, and still they communicate perfectly well in certain settings and with certain audiences.

It is perhaps time that we move away from our exclusive interest in the style of those pieces of discourse that are enshrined in the literary pantheon. There is colorfulness and eloquence to be found in the speech of common folk too. The current interest in various dialects and registers of the language may promote the study of the stylistic features of *vox populi* and the study too of the style of spoken discourse.

Methodology and Application

Since behind every methodology there is an implicit or an explicit theory, many of the items reviewed in this section might just as well have been discussed in the previous section because the primary emphasis in them seems to be on methodology and/or application. Most of the items in this section propose a method of analyzing the style of a prose text that has already been composed, but in most cases, the method proposed can have at least an indirect effect on the synthetic process too—that is, in helping students generate stylistically improved sentences. However, a few of the items discussed here—like the items by Christensen, the items describing imitation exercises, and the items on sentence-combining exercises—deal primarily with methods for generating rather than analyzing sentences. In many of the items that outline a method of analyzing style, the author goes on to demonstrate the method by applying it to some piece of prose.

One of the questions many teachers ask is this one: "If I want

103

to engage my students in analyzing prose style, what do I have them look at?" That is an elementary question, and many of the items discussed here suggest very specific features that the student should observe, tabulate, and classify. I dare say that many teachers have overlooked the "readability formula" that Rudolf Flesch proposed in his bestselling *The Art of Readable Writing* (New York: Harper & Row, 1949, revised edition 1974). In the very first sentence of this book, Flesch says, "To come right out with it, this is a book on rhetoric." And indeed it is. The first eight chapters of the book deal with the larger aspects of composition—invention, arrangement, and audience. But he devotes thirteen chapters of the book to style. And it is in the chapters on style that he sets forth his formula for measuring the readability of prose. His readability formula consists of two components: a human-interest rating and a reading-ease rating. The human-interest rating measures the percentages of "personal words" (proper nouns, personal pronouns) and "personal sentences" (dialogue, questions, commands, requests, incomplete sentences) found in a piece of prose. The more "personal" words and sentences, the higher the human-interest rating. The reading-ease rating measures the length of words and sentences. According to Flesch, the longer the words and the sentences, the harder the prose is to read. One of the criticisms levelled against Flesch's system is that if applied strictly, these formulas would rate the kind of prose found in the Dick-and-Jane readers as being the "most interesting" and the "easiest to read." Whether that criticism is justified or not, one must concede that Flesch's formulas do give the student something definite and specific to observe and tabulate, and teachers might consider using them as an easy entree into stylistic study.

In *Tough, Sweet, and Stuffy: An Essay on Modern American Styles* (Bloomington: Indiana University Press, 1966), Walker Gibson proposes his Style Machine as a paradigm for the analysis and classification of prose style. His formula outlines sixteen grammatical-rhetorical qualities to look for in measuring the relative toughness, sweetness, or stuffiness of passages of prose. He looks at such features as the size of words (in syllables), the length of sentences (in number of words), the structure of sentences (grammatical types), the use of articles (definite and indefinite), the proportions of nouns, verbs, modifiers, and imagery. Throughout the book, Gibson demonstrates his method by looking at 200-word samples of contemporary American prose and arriving at some characterization of the personality of the writer behind the prose. Gibson's model suggests more features to look at than the Flesch formulas do.

As the title suggests, Edward P. J. Corbett's "A Method of Analyzing Prose Style with a Demonstration Analysis of Swift's *A Modest Proposal,*" in *Reflections on High School English: NDEA Institute Lectures 1965,* ed. Gary Tate (Tulsa, Oklahoma: University of Tulsa, 1966), pp. 106–24 [4, 12, 13] presents a method of analysis and then demonstrates the method by applying it in an analysis of a text familiar to most English teachers. Corbett suggests those features of diction (abstract/concrete, formal/informal, monosyllabic/polysyllabic, referential/emotive), of sentences (length and grammatical, rhetorical, and functional types), of paragraphs (length, methods of development, transitional devices) that an investigator can look at. Most of the analysis that follows the exposition of the method is given over to pointing out the rhetorical significance or effect of the raw data, most of which is given in statistical tables at the end of the essay. Corbett suggests that a great deal about the style of a prose piece can be learned simply by copying out a prose passage word for word, and he recommends that students be asked eventually to do an analysis of their own prose.

In "Teaching Prose Style Analysis: One Method," *Style,* 9 (Winter 1975), 92–102, John F. Fleischauer describes, along with a week-by-week syllabus, an undergraduate course in prose stylistics that he offered at two different universities. His assignments included short oral reports on the style of particular authors and on published criticism of those writers, and the reading of books and articles on general stylistic theory and of literary works themselves. The final paper in the course was a long one on the style of an author chosen by the student. He includes a bibliography of general works on style, of analyses of specific works or authors, and of the literary works studied in the course. Only one paragraph of the article tells us what kinds of things he had his students look at: "As for the technical matter of analysis, I asked the students to pick one paragraph which seemed to them to be typical (not outstanding) of the author after a thorough reading of the whole text. Then they identified the patterns in that passage, including sentence length and number, types of verbs and modifiers, conjunctions, clausal structures, images— whatever elements seemed both typical and significant based upon their reading of the whole work."

In a later article, "James Baldwin's Style: A Prospectus for the Classroom," *CCC*, 26 (May 1975), 141–48, Fleischauer gives us more specific information about what he has his students look at when they analyze prose passages: average length and variety of length of sentences and paragraphs; kinds of verbs used (active, passive, *to be*) and their proportions; diction; kinds and positions of subordination; repetition and parallelism; parenthetical structures; sentence–openers. In his analysis of James Baldwin's "Notes of a Native Son," he frequently compares the characteristics of Baldwin's prose with those of such other contemporary writers as Arthur Miller, Jack Kerouac, J. Edgar Hoover, Eldridge Cleaver, William Buckley, and some anonymous prose-writers in *Atlantic, Newsweek,* and *U.S. News.* Like the other authors reviewed above, Fleischauer uses the method of counting and classifying various linguistic features of the text, and like Louis Milic, he looks more for recurrent features than for rare and unusual ones.

As early as his article "Generative Grammars and the Concept of Literary Style" [4, 6, 12, 14] in the December 1964 issue of *Word,* Richard Ohmann was showing us how he made use of transformational grammar to analyze the style of prose texts. In that article, he looked at short passages from Faulkner, Hemingway,

James, and Lawrence and broke down the surface structures of their sentences into kernel sentences to show us the characteristic ways in which those authors constructed their sentences. Ohmann's article "Literature as Sentences," *CE,* 27 (January 1966), 261–67 [3, 4, 5, 15] is an extension of that earlier article in *Word.* In the latter article, he analyzes a sentence from Joyce's "Araby," a sentence from Conrad's "The Secret Sharer," and a sentence from Dylan Thomas's "A Winter's Tale," converting the surface structures into the separate kernel sentences that reflect the deep structures of the sentences. In the last paragraph of the article, Ohmann says, "But I hope that in loosely stringing together several hypotheses about the fundamental role of the sentence I have indicated some areas where a rich exchange between linguistics and critical theory might eventually take place. To wit, the elusive intuition we have of *form and content* may turn out to be anchored in a distinction between surface structures and the deep structures of sentences. If so, syntactic theory will also feed into a theory of style."

A surprising number of analyzers of style have resorted to the transformational model in their analysis of sentence structure and have thereby given us some sense of what makes an author's style distinctive. One of the best examples of this kind of analysis is found in Curtis W. Hayes's "A Study in Prose Styles: Edward Gibbon and Ernest Hemingway," *Texas Studies in Literature and Language,* 7 (1966), 371–86 [6]. Like Ohmann, he regards transformational grammar as one of the best systems for analyzing and differentiating styles, and like Milic, he holds that a style can best be defined by its characteristic, habitual, recurrent linguistic features. He applied the transformational model to a hundred randomly chosen sentences from Edward Gibbon and Ernest Hemingway, and as a result of his analysis, he confirmed his own "intuitions" that Gibbon's style is "grand," "majestic," and "complex" and that Hemingway's style is "simple." He discovered, for instance, that whereas Gibbon averaged 4.3 transformations per sentence, Hemingway averaged 1.3, and that whereas Gibbon's sentences frequently had transformational expansions and embedded structures, Hemingway's rarely did. The comparative statistical tables included in the article further point up the differences between the two styles. My own intuition has been that Hemingway's style is not as "simple" as many people suppose—and indeed it isn't—but what this study does confirm is that Hemingway's style is "simple" in comparison with Gibbon's.

Before going on to review some of the methods which are more generative than analytical, I would like to look at a few more systems of analyzing prose that has already been composed.

In her book *Style and Proportion: The Language of Prose and Poetry* (Boston: Little, Brown, 1967), Josephine Miles is more interested in observing and tabulating lexical proportions than in studying syntactical patterns of whole sentences. She defines her method in these words: "The chief specified pattern then is the proportion, in a sequential text of one thousand lines of poetry (six to eight thousand words) and eight thousand words of prose, of adjective to noun to verb, the referential pattern; and of these to connectives, the grammatical pattern. These proportions, simply established, allow us to see the overall structure of the text—its dominant subordination or its dominant qualification, for example—more easily than a closer structure-by-structure scrutiny could do." On pages 204–5 of her book, she records in a chart the changes in the proportion of adjectives, nouns, verbs, and connectives used by sixty poets and sixty prose writers in English in the past five centuries. "Our prose," she says, "has moved in good array from much clausal subordination to much phrasal subordination to much adjectival assumption, through three standard styles—plain, middle, and high." On the basis of the part-of-speech proportions, she distinguishes three predominant contemporary styles:

(1) *predicative* (heavy on verbs, a statement-making style that creates situations—e.g. D. H. Lawrence)
(2) *connective-subordinative* (heavy on connectives—e.g. Bertrand Russell)

(3) *adjectival* (heavy on adjectives, a style that *presents* rather than *states*—e.g. Huxley [Julian? Aldous?])

Miles's system of observing the proportions of lexical items could be a useful one for those teachers who want to look more at diction than at syntax in a text.

An extremely interesting and useful article, using traditional grammar as its orientation, is Richard W. Weaver's "Some Rhetorical Aspects of Grammatical Categories," in *The Ethics of Rhetoric* (Chicago: Henry Regnery, 1953), pp. 115–27 [13]. His thesis is that "a language has certain abilities or even inclinations which the wise user can draw into the service of his own rhetorical effort. . . . Language is not a purely passive instrument, but owing to this public acceptance, while you are doing something with it, it is doing something with you or with your intention." In the first half of the article, he takes the three basic grammatical types of sentence—simple, complex, and compound—and shows the rhetorical potentialities of each type. For instance: "Whereas the simple sentence exhibits the coexistence of discrete classes, the complex sentence reveals the hierarchy between things by the process of subordination. Subordination makes inevitable the emergence of a focus of interest." In the second half of the article, Weaver goes on to discuss the grammatical and rhetorical aspects of the parts of speech—noun, adjective, adverb, verb, conjunction, and preposition. I have never seen any other writer on style treat the rhetorical dimensions of the grammar of language in the way that Weaver does, and I highly recommend his article to teachers of writing.

Prompted by Weaver's article, Donald Davidson, in his "'Grammar and Rhetoric:' The Teacher's Problem," *QJS*, 39 (December 1953), 425–36 [12], takes single sentences, from writers like Agnes DeMille, Thomas Babington Macaulay, W. H. Hudson, Aldo Leopold, and analyzes not only the grammatical structures of the sentences but their rhetorical effects. One could not imagine that so many significant observations could be made about the stylistic flavor of a single sentence. I recommend this article to teachers of writing and also the analyses that Davidson does of a single sentence by James Joyce and one by William Faulkner at the end of his *Twenty Lessons in Reading and Writing Prose* (New York: Scribner's, 1953), one of the best little rhetoric texts ever published in this country.

An unusually brilliant example of the analysis of a single paragraph of prose is provided by Ian Watt's "The First Paragraph of *The Ambassadors:* An Explication," *Essays in Criticism,* 10 (July 1960), 250–74 [4, 5]. Starting out with the objectively observable idiosyncracies of Henry James's syntax and diction, Watt relates these features to their function in the paragraph, to their effects on the reader, to the character traits of Strether and the narrator, and ultimately to the cast of James's own mind. He attempts then to persuade us that the stylistic features of this one paragraph are not only characteristic of James's later prose but also indicative of James's complex vision of life and his conception of the novel as an art form.

Frank D'Angelo does a similar thoroughgoing analysis of five paragraphs, totalling ten sentences, from Thomas Wolfe's novel *You Can't Go Home Again* in his article "Style as Structure," *Style,* 8 (Spring 1974), 322–64. D'Angelo outlines for us what his examination of these paragraphs will include: (1) a brief discussion of the literary context of the passage; (2) a word-for-word tabulation of sentence length, paragraph length, and discourse length; (3) a sentence-by-sentence description of the potentially significant linguistic and rhetorical features within each sentence; (4) a description of the potentially significant features of relationships between each sentence and all the preceding sentences; (5) a description of the structural features of the whole passage; (6) an interpretation of the passage, including an explanation of the linguistic and rhetorical features and the rhetorical method in terms of the interpretation; (7) a summary of the generalizations implied about the conventions and devices of this kind of description. One disadvantage of this arrangement is that

D'Angelo has frequently to rehearse the same stylistic features as he moves from section to section. He says in the last paragraph of his article, "If the study of style is to advance beyond the identifying of easily classified features on the sentence level, much more attention will have to be devoted to holistic analyses of this sort."

Teachers who want to investigate figurative devices in prose may find the following three articles helpful: Laurence Perrine, "Four Forms of Metaphor," *CE*, 33 (November 1971), 125–38 [15]; Rosemarie Gläser, "The Application of Transformational Generative Grammar to the Analysis of Similes and Metaphors in Modern English," *Style*, 5 (Fall 1971), 265–83 [15]; Richard L. Graves, "A Primer for Teaching Style," *CCC*, 25 (May 1974), 186–90. Perrine points out that every metaphor has two components: a literal term (the thing actually being discussed) and the figurative term (the thing to which it is compared). Proposing that both the literal term and the figurative term of every metaphor or simile are ultimately reducible to substantives, Perrine arrives at his four-part classification on the basis of whether these terms are expressed or implied:

Form 1. When both the literal term and the figurative term are expressed. Takes the form of "A is B." ("All the world's a stage," *As You Like It*).

Form 2. The literal term occurs but the figurative term must be inferred. ("Sheathe thy impatience; throw cold water on thy choler," *Merry Wives of Windsor*).

Form 3. Only the figurative term is named; the literal term must be inferred. For this reason, Form 3 metaphors can easily be mistaken for literal statements. ("Night's candles are burnt out," *Romeo and Juliet*).

Form 4. Neither the literal nor the figurative term is named; both must be inferred. ("I like to see it lap the miles," Emily Dickinson—here the lit-

> eral term is represented by the pronoun *it,*
> whose antecedent is left unspecified).

In the latter part of his article, Perrine discusses the consequent problems students may experience in interpreting the metaphorical content of a passage.

Professor Gläser sets up a tree diagram of the semantic markers of the noun, and on the basis of this categorization of the semantic markers, she analyzes similes and metaphors as "violations" of the selectional rules for nouns. For instance, she considers these three sentences:

(1) John works as hard as a miner.
(2) John works like a horse.
(3) John works like a machine.

The first sentence compares John [+ human] with miner [+ human] and is therefore not a simile. The second sentence compares John [+ human] with a horse [+ animal] and is a simile because the comparison involves nouns of different semantic features. The third sentence presents an even stronger simile, because while the second sentence matches two [+ animate] nouns, the third matches John [+ human, + animate] with a machine [+ artifact, + inanimate]. She reminds us that not all deviations from selectional rules create metaphors or similes. "Random selections of lexical items," she says, "are not yet a metaphorical string. Apart from the semantic proximity or remoteness of the categorical semantic markers, there must be a minimum of semantic correspondence between the idiosyncratic semantic features of the lexical items compared."

Whereas the articles by Perrine and Gläser deal with the analysis of tropes (shifts in the meanings of words), Richard L. Graves's article shows how he teaches students to recognize and compose various schemes (patterns of words), like anaphora, epistrophe, isocolon, antithesis, chiasmus, polysyndeton. Using an overhead projector, he flashes on the screen the name of the figure, a one-sentence definition of the figure, a diagram of the figure (if it lends itself to graphic representation), and one or more examples of the figure. Then he asks the student to compose a similar scheme of his own. Apparently, the use of the visual aids helps the students to conceive of the pattern of the scheme.

The Graves article marks the transition to those methods that engage students in generating their own sentences instead of just analyzing the prose that others have written. The most widely known and maybe the most influential of these methods was first introduced by Francis Christensen in two articles: "A Generative Rhetoric of the Sentence," *CCC,* 14 (October 1963), 155–61 [4, 12, 13, 15]; "A Generative Rhetoric of the Paragraph," *CCC,* 16 (October 1965), 144–56 [4, 12, 14, 15]. Christensen later published these two articles, with some revisions, in a collection of six of his articles, *Notes Toward a New Rhetoric* (New York: Harper & Row, 1967), and they have often been reprinted in other collections. In the article on the sentence, Christensen says, "The typical sentence of modern English, the kind we can best spend our efforts trying to teach, is what we may call the *cumulative sentence.*" In defining a cumulative sentence then, he uses a cumulative sentence:

> The main clause, which may or may not have a sentence modifier before it, advances the discussion; but the additions move backward, as in this clause, to modify the statement of the main clause or more often to explicate or exemplify it, advancing to a new position and then pausing to consolidate it, leaping and lingering as the popular ballad does.

"The main clause [of the cumulative sentence]," Christensen goes on to say, "is likely to be stated in general or abstract or plural terms. With the main clause stated, the forward movement of the sentence stops, the writer shifts down to the lower level of generality or abstraction or to singular terms, and goes back over the same ground at this lower level. . . . Thus the mere form of the sentence generates ideas." In the latter part of this article, Christensen lays out a number of sentences, some of them written by professional writers, some of them written by students, in structured layers that show the direction of movement and the levels of generality in the sentences.

The thesis of Christensen's article on the paragraph is that the paragraph has a structure similar to that of the cumulative sentence: the topic sentence, and the other sentences are equivalent to the modifiers in the sentence. He defines the paragraph as a sequence of structurally related sentences. By a "sequence of structurally related sentences," he means a group of sentences related to one another by coordination or subordination. As in the article on the sentence, Christensen lays out several paragraphs in layered structures so that we can see how the various sentences of the paragraph are related either by coordination or by subordination. But in this article, he uses only paragraphs from expository writing, probably because of his sensitivity to the charge that in "A Generative Rhetoric of the Sentence" he had used sentences only from narrative and descriptive writing.

Judging from the testimony given by teachers in convention talks and in journal articles, the Christensen method really works. Christensen later expanded his system into a full-blown *Rhetoric Program,* complete with transparencies, that Harper & Row published in 1968. It might be fair to mention at this point Sabina Thorne Johnson's "Some Tentative Strictures on Generative Rhetoric," *CE,* 31 (November 1969), 155–65 [15]. The heart of Johnson's reservations about the Christensen method is that she cannot accept his claim that form can generate content, "especially if the content is of an analytical or critical nature." "The weaknesses I see in student writing," she says, "the paucity of thought, the monotony of style and structure, the superficiality of analysis and explanation, the insensitivity—all indicate to me that what students need first is training in how to attack a topic. . . . More experimentally, I would also like to see whether and to what degree his method of building sentences can be made to carry over from the narrative and descriptive to the expository essay." Readers should see the reply to Johnson's strictures that Christensen's widow, Bonniejean McGuire Christensen, published in the May 1970 issue of *College English* and also A. M. Tibbetts' response in the same issue.

Teachers interested in the generative potentialities of transformational grammar should consult John C. Mellon's report of his experiment with 250 seventh-graders in *Transformational Sentence-Combining* (Urbana, Ill.: NCTE, 1969) [15]. The hypothesis upon which this experiment was based was that "practice in transformational sentence-combining would enhance the normal growth of syntactic fluency." After students had had some instructions in basic transformational grammar, they were asked to transform a series of separate kernel sentences according to directions explicitly given to them, embedding these transforms as constituents in other sentences according to a simple formula that was used in all the exercises and finally writing out the results of all the transforms in a single fully-developed complex sentence. As a result of these exercises, these junior high school students did make significant advances in syntactic fluency. Teachers who may want to engage their students in this kind of sentence-combining practice can make use of the kernel-sentence groups that Mellon reproduces in the appendix of his book.

For an extension of Mellon's method, teachers can consult Frank O'Hare's *Sentence Combining: Improving Student Writing without Formal Grammar* (Urbana, Ill.: NCTE, 1973). O'Hare too conducted an experiment with sentence-combining practice as a way to improve student writing, but without giving students any formal instruction in grammar. He started out by exercising students in smaller sub-skills and then led them, through progressively more difficult steps, to a more mature style. In his book, he gives explanations of his sentence-combining methodology and reproduces sample lessons and several sentence-combining problems.

I will conclude this section with a glance at some items dealing with imitation as a way to improve students' prose style. Edward P. J. Corbett, in his article "The Theory and Practice of Imitation in Classical Rhetoric," *CCC,* 22 (October 1971), 243–50, gives a short summary of the history of imitative practices, and in his book *Classical Rhetoric for the Modern Student,* Second Edition (New York: Oxford University Press, 1971), pp. 510–38, he suggests three or four kinds of imitative exercises. In his article, "An Exercise in Prose Style," in *Rhetoric: Theories for Application,* ed. Robert M. Gorrell (Champaign, Ill.: NCTE, 1967), pp. 99–106 [13], Walker Gibson describes some imitative exercises that he has used with his students. On the first day of class, Gibson asks his students to write a few sentences describing the circumstances of their birth and early life. On the next day, he distributes dittoed samples of the students' prose and asks the class to define and classify the various voices heard in these excerpts. In the second step, Gibson distributes to the students, without revealing the authors' names, the first couple of paragraphs from autobiographical novels by Charles Dickens and Saul Bellow and asks the students to analyze the language of each selection to see how these different voices are created. In the third step, Gibson then asks his students to rewrite twice, according to specific instructions, the prose they wrote on the first day. On the first rewriting, for instance, they might be asked to turn half their verbs into the passive voice, half their sentences into subordinate clauses and to put half of these subordinate clauses before the subject of the main clause. "The point," Gibson says, "is to illustrate, even in this heavyhanded way, the fact of choice"—and also to illustrate how changes in diction and sentence structure effect changes in the voice of the writer.

In his article "Imitation and Style," *CCC,* 24 (October

116

1973), 283–90, Frank D'Angelo describes an approach he uses in helping students to improve their style:

> The approach consists basically in having the students follow a sequence of steps which may be described briefly as follows: a preliminary reading of the model in order to get an overview of the dominant impression; a careful analysis of the model, which should include quantitative descriptions and a sentence-by-sentence description of the potentially significant linguistic features within each sentence; an interpretation of the passage, including an explanation of the linguistic features and the rhetorical effects; and finally a close imitation of the model.

Readers will recognize this approach as essentially the one that D'Angelo demonstrated with his analysis of five paragraphs of Thomas Wolfe's prose in the article from *Style* discussed above.

Winston Weathers and Otis Winchester devote an entire book of 143 pages to this kind of imitative practice: *Copy and Compose: A Guide to Prose Style* (Englewood Cliffs, N.J.: Prentice-Hall, 1969). The authors display thirty-seven different kinds of sentences and twenty-eight different kinds of paragraphs. The pattern of their method is to reproduce a sentence—or a paragraph—written by a professional writer, to analyze the structure of the sentence and point out some distinctive stylistic features of it, and then to ask the students to write a sentence or a paragraph according to the model. Admittedly, this kind of imitative exercise is a form of finger-exercise, and it asks for the composition of sentences in isolation from a context of occasion, purpose, and audience, but like practice exercises in the acquisition of any skill, this kind of practice can pay off when a writer is called upon to engage in some real-life writing.

Even as I conclude this survey of style as it relates to the teaching of composition, I am apprehensive about having over-

117

looked some important books and articles. But I guess I will just have to be judged by what I remembered to include, not by what I neglected to mention. I derive some measure of assurance, how-ever, from the realization that many of the books and articles mentioned in this survey are those most often cited in studies on style and most often reprinted in anthologies of essays on style. It is comforting sometimes to ride the bandwagon.

1986

When I finished the original bibliography on style, I ac-knowledged my awareness that bibliographies soon date and my fear that I had overlooked a number of important studies of style as it related to composition. But that original bibliography proved to be not as ephemeral nor as deficient as I had antici-pated. In a talk entitled "Ventures in Style," which I delivered at an international conference on composition held at Carleton Uni-versity in Ontario, Canada, in May 1979 and which I later pub-lished in *Reinventing the Rhetorical Tradition,* ed. Aviva Freedman and Ian Pringle (Conway, Arkansas: Canadian Council of Teach-ers of English, 1980), I remarked that there was little evidence that the study or the teaching of style had caught on in the com-position classroom since the Tate bibliography had been pub-lished in 1976. Checking the twenty issues of *College Composition and Communication* published during the first five years of my edi-torship (1974–1978), I discovered that only about a dozen articles could be said to be dealing with style. Exercises in sentence-combining and in the Christensen-type of cumulative sentence seemed to be flourishing in the classroom, and psycholinguistics as it related to the reasons for the sentence errors that students made or to the readability of prose texts figured prominently in important new books like Mina Shaughnessy's *Errors and Expecta-tions: A Guide for the Teacher of Basic Writing* (New York: Oxford University Press, 1977) and E. D. Hirsch's *The Philosophy of Composition* (Chicago: University of Chicago Press, 1977). Except for those activities, however, there was little evidence that composition teachers were devoting much attention to style. And I had discovered only a few shameful omissions of important books and articles in my original bibliography.

But in the ten years since the publication of the Tate bibliography, there have been *some* developments in the teaching of style in relation to composition, and I will note some of the important developments in this 1986 update.

Collections

There have been only three new collections of articles on the teaching of style. Two of those, *The Writing Teacher's Sourcebook*, ed. Gary Tate and Edward P. J. Corbett (New York: Oxford University Press, 1981) and the second edition of *Rhetoric and Composition: A Sourcebook for Teachers and Writers*, ed. Richard L. Graves (Montclair, N.J.: Boynton/Cook, 1984), devote only one section to articles on style. The Tate and Corbett collection reprints five articles in its section on Style. Richard Graves reprints seven articles on style in his Part Three, The Sentence: A Reluctant Medium. Although neither anthology carries enough essays to support a quarter-long or semester-long course in style, the anthologies do serve to introduce students and prospective teachers to the study of style, and they conveniently gather together under two covers articles from a variety of sources.

The other new collection is a revised and expanded version of a collection of papers on style that was originally published by L & S Books of Akron, Ohio. *The Territory of Language: Linguistics, Stylistics, and the Teaching of Composition*, ed. Donald McQuade (Carbondale: Southern Illinois University Press, 1985) contains essays by a roster of thirty-one authors that reads like a Who's Who in Composition. A number of authors who were not represented in the original collection were invited to contribute to this new edition, and several of the original authors revised their essays. Now that the Love and Payne collection *Contemporary Essays on Style: Rhetoric, Linguistics, and Criticism* (1969) has gone out of print, the McQuade collection is likely to be the one most often used in undergraduate and graduate classes dealing with style.

Bibliography

As in the original bibliography, I will not have to elaborate very much on the items in this section because their titles sufficiently disclose the nature and scope of the coverage.

Research in Composition and Rhetoric: A Bibliographic Sourcebook, ed. Michael G. Moran and Ronald F. Lunsford (Westport, Conn.: Greenwood Press, 1984) is a new comprehensive bibliography containing discursive essays on various aspects of composition and rhetoric, followed by a Reference section that lists the items discussed in the essays. Only one essay here seems to be pertinent to style: Frank D'Angelo, "The Sentence," pp. 303–13 + References, pp. 313–17.

Max Morenberg and Andrew Kerek's "Bibliography on Sentence Combining: Theory and Teaching, 1964–1979," in *RSQ,* 9 (1979), 97–111, may be the most comprehensive bibliography on sentence-combining during its most flourishing period. James R. Bennett's "The Paragraph: An Annotated Bibliography," in *Style,* 11 (Spring 1972), 107–18, may prove to be the definitive bibliography for those stylisticians who include the paragraph in their studies. Eric D. Wallborn has compiled the definitive bibliography on stylistic imitation, ancient and modern, in his "Imitation: Its Theoretical and Practical Implications for Teaching Writing— A Twentieth Century Survey," unpublished M.A. thesis, Ohio State University, 1985. Those composition teachers who want to pursue the study of tropes will find God's plenty in Warren Shibles's *Metaphor: An Annotated Bibliography and History* (Whitewater, Wis.: The Language Press, 1971).

History

I want to call attention to only one item in this category. Although nineteenth-century England produced an uncommon number of distinguished prose stylists and although many modern literary critics or historians have noted or analyzed the prose styles of those writers, not many critics or historians have talked about the nineteenth-century writers who discussed the rhetoric of English prose style. Marie J. Secor has filled that gap with her article "The Legacy of Nineteenth-Century Style Theory," *RSQ,* 12 (Spring 1982), 76–94. By reviewing what Thomas DeQuincey, Herbert Spencer, George Henry Lewes, John Henry Newman, Robert Louis Stevenson, and Walter Pater had to say about style, she has put together a compendium of Victorian views on the rhetoric of style, views which have helped to shape contemporary attitudes toward style.

Those teachers who want to give their students an historical perspective on the development of English prose style would do well to add this item to their list of books and articles on the subject.

Theory

It has continued to be difficult for me to discern clearcut lines of demarcation between the category of Theory and the category in the next section, Methodology and Application. Somewhat arbitrarily I have put into the category of Theory those items that, in my view, lean more heavily toward theory than toward methodology.

In her article "Revitalizing Style: Toward a New Theory and Pedagogy," *FEN,* 14 (Spring 1985), 8–13, Elizabeth Rankin may have accounted for what I observed at the beginning of this update: there is very little evidence that the study of style has caught on in the composition classroom. She maintains that the "paradigm shift" that has been noted by such teachers as Richard Young, James Berlin and Robert Inkster, and Maxine Hairston has resulted in a decline in the teaching of style. "Style is out of style," she says.

So far, Rankin maintains, the New Rhetoric has not offered us "a sound, complete, and adequate theory of style." If we are to formulate a new theory that will restore the study of style to the classroom, it will have to meet the following criteria (p. 12): (1) A new theory of style would offer a broad yet workable definition of style; (2) A new theory of style would take into account the wide range of psychological operations that go into the making of stylistic decisions; (3) A new theory of style would be grounded in sound and consistent philosophical/epistemological assumptions about the nature of language. Most of the other items that I review in this section meet one or more of those three criteria.

In his long article "Prolegomenon to Pedagogical Stylistics," *CCC,* 34 (February 1983), 80–90, W. Ross Winterowd attempts to provide the underlying theory and the pedagogical rationale for sentence-combining and for the new technology of accessibility (*accessibility* being Winterowd's term for the relative ease with which a text can be read). According to Winterowd, the two areas of sentence-combining and accessibility constitute "the largest portion of a field that might justifiably be called 'pedagogical stylistics.'" By exploring the components of both sentence-combining and accessibility in modern linguistic theories, Winterowd shows how these two "technologies" can promote the acquisition of literacy in the realm of writing and the realm of reading. It may be significant that, as I observed in my "Ventures in Style" talk in Ottawa, the two areas of stylistic study which were getting some attention in the writing classroom were the practice of sentence-combining and the means of achieving relative readability.

In the May 1965 issue of the *CCC* journal, Louis T. Milic published his article "Theories of Style and Their Implications for the Teaching of Composition," which was often reprinted in subsequent years. Obviously echoing that title, John T. Gage, in his article "Philosophies of Style and Their Implications for Composition," *CE,* 41 (February 1980), 615–22, argues the thesis that our conception of style and the way in which we teach it depends fundamentally on whether "we consider language adequate or inadequate to the task of depicting reality." Gage traces the two prevailing views of the adequacy of language to represent reality back to two competing schools of Greek grammarians: the *analogists,* who believed that language was capable of directly and accurately manifesting an orderly reality; the *anomalists,* who believed that, at best, language could give us "a useful but imperfect (at any rate, indirect) manifestation of a reality maybe orderly, maybe not." Gage sees those differing views as being reflected in Milic's two categories of stylistic theory: the *dualistic* and the *monistic.* According to the dualistic theory, style is so intimately merged with content that any change in style results in a fundamental change in meaning.

The implications of these differing views of language for the teaching of composition are summarized in these two sentences from Gage's article (pp. 619–20):

> In the first place, by stressing revision, we are advocating a separation between the way a thing is said, in its unrevised form, and the ideas themselves, unclothed, that is, in words. In the second place, however, by stressing clarity and the "plain style"—the precise and the straightforward way of saying a thing—we seem to call upon precisely the opposite assumption, namely that there is an ideally suited linguistic formula for each idea.

In "Why Teach Style? A Review Essay," *CCC,* 34 (February 1983), 91–98, Ian Pringle questions whether we can teach style at all. The article starts out with a review of Joseph Williams's *Style: Ten Lessons in Clarity and Grace,* an important new textbook that I will talk about in the next section, but after praising Williams's treatment of style for its linguistic soundness, Pringle questions whether the pedagogy of even a sound text like Williams's can teach style. Pringle discusses the teachability of style in relation to the distinction that Stephen Krashen, a second-language specialist, makes between *acquiring* a language and *learning* a language. Pringle contends that "if students are to produce literate writing, they will do so primarily on the basis of what they have acquired, and what they acquire will come to them not through the explicit study of style (or for that matter, grammar), but from 'comprehensible input,' from reading good, relevant models, not because they are prescribed, but because they are interesting, intellectually engaging, exciting, new" (p. 94). Pringle further points out that students' writing abilities do not necessarily keep pace with their intellectual growth. "On the contrary," he says, "a frequent sign of a burst of intellectual growth is an apparent reversion to a lower level of writing ability" (p. 96). For that reason, books that engage students in a formal study of prose might do more good if they are put off until the end of, or even after, the undergraduate years.

Ian Pringle's contentions need to be seriously considered by all of us who engage students in the systematic study and exercise of style.

Methodology and Application

The most notable development in this area in the last ten years has been the publication of a number of textbooks designed to exercise students primarily in the stylistic aspects of the composing process. In fact, the publication of these textbooks is the first glimmer of evidence that the study of style may be gaining at least a toehold in the composition classroom. This section will be devoted principally to a review of those texts.

The first of those textbooks to be reviewed is the Joseph M. Williams book that Ian Pringle was discussing in the *CCC* article mentioned at the end of the previous section. Apparently, Williams's *Style: Ten Lessons in Clarity and Grace* (Glenview, Ill.: Scott, Foresman) was widely enough adopted in advanced-composition courses and in business and professional writing courses that the publishers were encouraged to bring out a second edition, in paperback, in 1985. The book gives students very practical advice about how to recognize flaccid, awkward, obscure prose in their own and others' writing and about how to write clear, graceful prose. Individual chapters deal with such lamentable stylistic infelicities as nominalizations, successions of prepositional phrases, heavy use of *be* verbs, sprawling sentences, strained coherence, and weak emphasis. The book makes all writers painfully aware of the bad habits they have acquired.

Richard A. Lanham has produced a number of books and articles on style in the last ten years. Two of the best of those publications are *Revising Prose* (New York: Scribner's, 1979) and *Analyzing Prose* (New York: Scribner's, 1983). The second of those texts might be more suitable for a graduate-level course, but if a teacher can devote a whole quarter or semester to the study of style, *Analyzing Prose* is the book to start with, because it shows students what to look for when they are analyzing style. Once students can recognize the felicities and blemishes of a prose style, they will be more disposed to cultivate the felicities and eliminate the blemishes in their own prose. At that stage, Lanham's *Revising Prose* can be helpful to students. The objective of that book is to get students to translate what Lanham calls "the Official Style" into the plain style. And he deals with much of the same kind of deadwood that Williams deals with in his book.

A wonderful little paperback book, which deserves to be better known, is Thomas Whissen's *A Way with Words: A Guide for Writers* (New York: Oxford University Press, 1982). The pedagogy of this text is solidly based on the imitative principle. Whissen introduces students to a wide variety of prose styles and with a series of ready-made exercises engages students in imitating those styles, even bad styles. What is especially delightful about this book is that it encourages students to play with language, and if you can get students in an academic setting to do what they naturally loved doing as children, they can learn a great deal about the characteristics of good and bad prose.

Frank D'Angelo, who has written a number of articles on style and deals with style in his own rhetoric text, has recently published an article describing the imitative activities that he engages his students in: "Imitation and the Teaching of Style," in *Fforum: Essays on Theory and Practice in the Teaching of Writing,* ed. Patricia L. Stock (Montclair, N.J.: Boynton/Cook, 1983), pp. 173–88. D'Angelo starts by getting his students to do a close reading of a piece of prose, then leads them to do an intensive study of the stylistic features of that text, and then engages them in two kinds of writing assignment: imitative exercises and stylistic analyses. He lays down eight guidelines for doing a stylistic analysis and displays a number of examples of imitations and analyses written by his students. D'Angelo claims that the imitation of models mediates between process and product, because it "mirrors the writer's cognitive processes, leading the student writer to a discovery of new effects" (p. 188).

Two notable developments that have taken place in relation to sentence-combining in the last ten years are that the practice of sentence-combining has moved up to the college level and that it has moved on to consider units larger than the sentence. The widely used sentence-combining texts by Frank O'Hare and William Strong—*Sentence Craft* and *Sentence Combining,* respectively—had their heaviest play originally in high-school classrooms. But those texts have moved up to college classrooms, and a number of new college-level rhetoric texts now have a section or a chapter devoted to sentence-combining. The text by Donald A. Daiker, Andrew Kerek, and Max Morenberg, *The Writer's Options: Combining to Composing,* 2nd ed. (New York: Harper & Row, 1982) was designed primarily for the college market, and, like the revised editions of the O'Hare and Strong texts, it moves on from the usual combining of short sentences to combining clusters of related sentences in the paragraph and the whole composition. Two results of this moving on to units larger than the sentence are that sentence-combining is now not just a finger-exercise with the minimal units of discourse but a technique that can be used by students to produce and revise sequences of related sentences in the larger units of the paragraph and the whole composition.

Another imitative exercise that is getting some play in college classrooms is "controlled composition," a technique appropriated from ESL. One of the successful texts of this kind is Helen Heightsman Gordon's *From Copying to Creating,* 2nd ed. (New York: Holt, Rinehart and Winston, 1985). This system gets students to copy a short passage of well-written prose and then asks them to rewrite the passage, changing some one feature of the text—such as changing all the past-tense verbs to present-tense verbs or changing all singular subjects to plural subjects or converting all adverb clauses to verbal phrases or all compound sentences to complex sentences. In making the prescribed changes, students of course have to make other changes in related parts of the sentence. For instance, if they are asked to change all singular masculine nouns in the passage to singular feminine nouns, all subsequent related pronouns have to be changed from masculine to feminine.

Winston Weathers has expanded the proposal he first made in his long article "The Grammars of Style: New Options in Composition" in the Winter 1976 issue of *Freshman English News* into a full-length book. His *Alternate Style: Options in Composition* (Montclair, N.J.: Boynton/Cook, 1980) encourages students to make appropriate and effective use of the kinds of stylistic features that English teachers commonly frown on: sentence fragments, labyrinthine sentences, verbal collages or montages, and "crots," those discrete units of prose somewhat comparable to stanzas in poetry. And incidentally, although Winston Weathers's book of more traditional imitative practice, *Copy and Compose: A Guide to Prose Style* (1969), has been allowed to go out of print, the essence of that book constitutes Chapter Twelve, "Sentence Models," of Winston Weathers and Otis Winchester's *The New Strategy of Style,* 2nd ed. (New York: McGraw-Hill, 1978).

Those teachers who make the recognition and the production of figures of speech a part of their regimen of stylistic exercise now have at least two handbooks available that identify, define, and illustrate the various schemes and tropes. The Language Press of Whitewater, Wisconsin, published in 1972 a paperback edition of Warren Taylor's 1937 doctoral dissertation at the University of Chicago under the title *Tudor Figures of Rhetoric*. The University of California Press in 1968 published Richard A. Lanham's *A Handlist of Rhetorical Terms: A Guide for Students of English Literature*. Both of these handbooks have an alphabetical list and a descriptive list. If you know the name of the figure, you can consult the alphabetical list; if you can recognize an unusual sentence pattern but don't know the name of the figure, you can consult the descriptive list and find the name of the figure that this pattern exemplifies. In the chapter on style in Edward P. J. Corbett's *Classical Rhetoric for the Modern Student,* 2nd ed. (New York: Oxford University Press, 1971), pp. 459–95, there is an abbreviated list of the schemes and tropes, with definitions and illustrative examples.

It is too early to say how much of a part the computer will play in the classroom study of style. But two recent articles in the collection *The Computer in Composition Instruction,* ed. William Wresch (Urbana, Ill.: NCTE, 1984) suggest the potential of the computer for the study of style: Michael E. Cohen and Richard A. Lanham, "HOMER: Teaching Style with a Microcomputer," pp. 83–90, and Kathleen Kiefer and Charles R. Smith, "Improving Students' Revising and Editing: The Writer's Workbench," pp. 65–82. The program HOMER automates the method that Lanham's book *Revising Prose* demonstrates. As the authors of the article say, "HOMER does the bean counting, leaving the student writer free for the big job" (p. 85). After the student types in a text, HOMER measures and displays such statistical data as the total number of words in the text, the number of sentences, the average number of words per sentence, and the number of prepositions, *to be* verbs, shun words, and woolly words. Kathleen Kiefer and Charles Smith discuss the use of Bell Laboratories' Writer's Workbench program in writing classes at Colorado State University in 1981 and 1982 to help students analyze their own writing style and to detect the errors in it. The Writer's Workbench analyzes and tabulates various features of style, such as the type and length of sentences, the kinds of sentence-openers, and the percentages of abstract words, nominalizations, passive verbs, and *to be* verbs. Both articles emphasize the point that although the computer programs spare the students the tedium of counting and tabulating raw data about their styles, the chief fruit comes from what the students do with their prose style in response to the stylistical analyses provided them.

A LIST OF THE COLLECTIONS MENTIONED
IN THE BIBLIOGRAPHICAL ESSAY

The collections are listed here in the order in which they are discussed in the essay. Numbers given within brackets after an item in the essay indicate that this item is reprinted in the collections bearing those numbers in this listing. For instance, the notation [1, 4, 6] after an item indicates that this item is reprinted in the Sebeok collection, the Love and Payne collection, and the Freeman collection.

(1) *Style in Language,* ed. Thomas A. Sebeok (Cambridge, Mass.: MIT Press, 1960).

(2) *Literary Style: A Symposium,* ed. Seymour Chatman (New York: Oxford University Press, 1971).

(3) *Essays on the Language of Literature,* ed. Seymour Chatman and Samuel R. Levin (Boston: Houghton Mifflin, 1967).

(4) *Contemporary Essays on Style: Rhetoric, Linguistics, and Criticism,* ed. Glen A. Love and Michael Payne (Glenview, Ill.: Scott, Foresman, 1969).

(5) *Essays in Stylistic Analysis,* ed. Howard S. Babb (New York: Harcourt Brace Jovanovich, 1972).

(6) *Linguistics and Literary Style,* ed. Donald C. Freeman (New York: Holt, Rinehart, and Winston, 1970).

(7) *Prose Style: A Historical Approach Through Studies,* ed. James R. Bennett (San Francisco: Chandler, 1971).

(8) *Stylists on Style: A Handbook with Selections for Analysis,* ed. Louis T. Milic (New York: Scribner's, 1969).

(9) *Modern Essays on Writing and Style,* ed. Paul C. Wermuth, Second Edition (New York: Holt, Rinehart, and Winston, 1969).

(10) *Style in English Prose,* ed. Carl H. Klaus (New York: Macmillan, 1968).

(11) *The Problem of Style,* ed. J. V. Cunningham (Greenwich, Conn.: Fawcett Publications, 1966).

(12) *Teaching Freshman Composition,* ed. Gary Tate and Edward P. J. Corbett (New York: Oxford University Press, 1967).

(13) *Teaching High School Compositon,* ed. Gary Tate and Edward P. J. Corbett (New York: Oxford University Press, 1970).

(14) *New Rhetorics,* ed. Martin Steinmann, Jr. (New York: Scribner's, 1967).

(15) *Contemporary Rhetoric: A Conceptual Background with Readings,* ed. W. Ross Winterowd (New York: Harcourt Brace Jovanovich, 1975).

(16) *The Writing Teacher's Sourcebook,* ed. Gary Tate and Edward P. J. Corbett (New York: Oxford University Press, 1981).

(17) *Rhetoric and Composition: A Sourcebook for Teachers and Writers,* ed. Richard L. Graves, 2nd ed. (Montclair, N.J.: Boynton/ Cook, 1984).

(18) *The Territory of Language: Linguistics, Stylistics, and the Teaching of Composition,* ed. Donald McQuade (Carbondale: Southern Illinois University Press, 1985).

Aims, Modes, and Forms of Discourse

FRANK J. D'ANGELO, Arizona State University

IN THIS ESSAY, I WILL BE PRIMARILY CONCERNED with surveying books and articles that deal with the classification of the aims, modes, and forms of discourse. Unfortunately, these terms have been subject to a bewildering variety of uses by teachers and scholars. For example, the term *aim* has been variously defined as "a plan that guides action," "ultimate purpose," and "the effect that the writer intends to achieve on his or her audience." The term *mode* has sometimes been referred to as "the way or manner in which something is done." At other times, it has been used as a synonym for *form, kind,* or *type*. According to the *Oxford English Dictionary,* a *form* is "the mode in which a thing exists, acts, or manifests itself" or "a kind, type, or variety of discourse." A *kind* is "a class or category of similar or related individuals," and a *type* is "a taxonomic designation, such as the name of a species or genus."

Because of this confusing overlapping of terms, unless the context or the source conveys a different meaning, I shall use the word *aim* to refer to "the *typical intention* of the writer" or to "*ultimate purpose*" and the word *purpose* to refer to "the *specific intention* of the writer in a particular rhetorical situation." By the term *form of discourse* I mean "a *generic kind*—a classification of discourse based on aims, audiences, subject matter, rhetorical situations, or formal characteristics of some kind," and by the phrase *mode of discourse* I mean "a *strategy of discourse*" or "a *manner or way* of developing ideas in a discourse."

Some teachers see little value in the classification of discourse types. To these teachers, each piece of writing is a unique creation. In this view, writers simply *express* themselves, and this expression constitutes the *form* of discourse. Therefore, there are as many *kinds* of discourse and aims as there are individual acts of writing. Yet it is clear that the forms of discourse have long been accepted as traditional ways of ordering experience. In addition, as historical phenomena, they can be understood and appreciated within the cultural context of which they are a part. At the very least, the types approach has arisen out of a need to organize textbooks and courses of study. To be ignorant of traditional approaches to the forms of discourse and of more recent developments in discourse theory and classification is to be a slave to someone else's textbook, course of study, or conceptual framework. What follows is a survey of these traditional approaches and of recent developments in the classification of discourse aims and types.

THE NINETEENTH-CENTURY FORMS OF DISCOURSE

The most important bibliographies that deal with the nineteenth-century forms of discourse are Albert R. Kitzhaber's "Rhetoric in American Colleges, 1850–1900" (dissertation, University of Washington, 1953) and James A. Berlin's "A Bibliography of Rhetoric in England and America in the Nineteenth Century: The Primary Sources," *RSQ*, 11 (Summer 1981), 193–203.

Some composition scholars trace the origin of the classification of forms of discourse to George Campbell's *The Philosophy of Rhetoric* (1776). In his discussion of the nature of eloquence, Campbell states that "all the ends of speaking are reducible to four; every speech being intended to enlighten the understanding, to please the imagination, to move the passions or to influence the will" (*The Rhetoric of Blair, Campbell, and Whately,* ed. James L. Golden and Edward P. J. Corbett [New York: Holt, Rinehart and Winston, 1968], p. 145). Like Campbell, John Witherspoon, a Scottish minister who came to America in 1768, did not actually classify *forms* of discourse. Instead, he classified *aims*. From Lecture XIII, cited in Virgil L. Baker's "Development of Forms of Discourse in American Rhetorical Theory," *Southern Speech Journal*, 18 (May 1953), comes this remark: "The ends a writer or speaker may be said to aim at are information, demonstration, persuasion, and entertainment" (p. 208).

In 1823, W. M. A. Russell published a text entitled *A Grammar of Composition* (New Haven: A. H. Maltby and Co.) which, as far as I can determine, was in fact the first composition textbook (Witherspoon's treatise was directed to both speakers and writers) to classify composition into basic *forms*. Russell divided all composition into three categories: *narrative, descriptive,* and *didactic* (p. 54). Russell's didactic category seems to include what later rhetoricians would label exposition and argumentation. Although Russell does not define his categories, the division of the didactic into exposition and argumentation can be inferred from the kinds of exercises he proposes in the section of his text dealing with "didactic pieces."

Samuel P. Newman was perhaps the first rhetorician to classify composition into the basic forms of discourse with which we are familiar today. In his book *A Practical System of Rhetoric* (New York: Mark H. Newman, 1827), Newman divides writing into five categories (*didactic, persuasive, argumentative, descriptive,* and *narrative*), each with a different aim: to convey instruction, to influence the will, to prove with reasons, to relate past occurrences, and to place objects and scenes before the mind (p. 27). Newman's "didactic" category corresponds roughly to the "expository" category in later composition texts. Richard Green Parker's *Aids to English Composition* divides composition into six categories: the *narrative, descriptive, didactic, persuasive, pathetic,* and *argumentative*. (The earliest edition I have seen was published by Harper & Brothers, 1854. Virgil Baker cites an earlier edition, published in Boston in 1844.)

In his text *Advanced Course of Composition and Rhetoric* (New York: D. Appleton and Co., 1855), George Payne Quackenbos lists five basic kinds of composition: *description, narration, argument, exposition,* and *speculation.* Of the five categories Quackenbos mentions, description, narration, exposition, and argumentation are the ones referred to today as the basic "forms of discourse."

Thus far, I have been primarily concerned with tracing the development of the traditional forms of discourse as we know them today. But the number and kinds of discourse types did not have the kind of uniform development that one might expect. More often than not, the categories of description, narration, exposition, and argumentation were embedded in broader classification systems. For example, James R. Boyd, in *Elements of English Composition* (New York and Chicago: A. S. Barnes & Co., 1860), classifies discourse into ten categories: *descriptive writing, narrative composition, biography, historical composition, letter writing, essays, dissertations,* the *oration, sermon writing,* and *poetry.* In his text *A Manual of the Art of Prose Composition* (Louisville: John P. Morton and Co., 1867), J. M. Bonnell lists *description, narration, letters, history, biography,* and *argumentation* as principal forms. A. D. Hepburn, in his *Manual of English Rhetoric* (New York: Van Antwerp, Bragg & Co., 1875), divides all composition into five principal classes: *dialogue, epistolary prose, didactic prose, historical prose,* and *oratorical prose.* He then subdivides each of these categories into numerous subcategories. The point is that the forms of discourse existed in embryonic form in the classification systems of a number of nineteenth-century rhetoricians or were embedded in larger classification systems. But it was Alexander Bain, the Scottish rhetorician and associationist psychologist, who seems to have gotten the credit for developing this conceptual system. (Bain includes *poetry* along with the four forms of discourse recognized today.)

In his book *English Composition and Rhetoric* (N.Y.: D. Appleton & Co., 1866), Bain based the classification of the forms of discourse on the faculties of the mind. According to Bain, the mind is divided into *three faculties:* the *understanding,* the *will,* and the *feelings*. The aims of discourse (to *inform*, to *persuade*, and to *please*) correspond to these three faculties. The forms of discourse are the kinds of composition that relate to the faculties of the mind, the aims of discourse, and the laws of thought. Thus, description, narration, and exposition relate to the faculty of understanding, persuasion relates to the will, and poetry to the feelings (p. 19).

William B. Cairns, in his text *The Forms of Discourse* (Boston: Ginn and Co., 1896), used the primary laws of association (*contiguity, continuity, likeness* and *contrast,* and *cause* and *effect*) as the basis of his classification of the forms of discourse. In Cairns's scheme, *description* is based on the law of contiguity, *narration* on the law of continuity, and *exposition* and *persuasion* on the laws of likeness and contrast and cause and effect (pp. 46–47).

Since Alexander Bain, many scholars and teachers have been interested in the forms of discourse approach to writing, but some have become dissatisfied with the traditional classification of these forms. For example, in 1914 Sterling Leonard, in his essay "As to the Forms of Discourse," which appeared in *EJ*, 3 (April 1914), 201–11, complained: "The difficulty I have most often met in attempting to organize . . . courses [based on the forms of discourse] has its roots in the present classification of the forms of discourse. For, useful as this doubtless is for sorting completed pieces of writing, it does not view the process of composition from the side of the thoughts or ideas the writer has to express, and particularly of his purpose in expressing these" (p. 202). For pedagogical purposes, Leonard assigned his students a sequence of forms, arranged in ascending order of difficulty and abstraction, beginning with themes based on sense impressions (using the forms of description and narration), moving through themes of simple explanation (exposition), and concluding with interpretative themes (using the forms of description, narration, interpretive exposition, and argument).

In my essay "Nineteenth-Century Forms/Modes of Discourse: A Critical Inquiry," *CCC,* 35 (February 1984), 31–42, I argue that the nineteenth-century forms of discourse should not be used as the basis of composition teaching "because they confuse forms of discourse [i.e. generic kinds] with modes of discourse [i.e. "strategies" of discourse], they present aims that are not equal in status, and they are based on an outworn faculty and associationist psychology" (p. 32). However, in her article "The Physics of Rhetoric," *CCC*, 25 (December 1974), 382–87, Therese B. Dykeman attempts to justify their use. She argues that four principles of physics—space, matter, time, and motion—can best explain the division of composition into the traditional forms of discourse. In her view, "space is concerned with the description of place; matter with the exposition of what is; time with sequence; and motion with change" (p. 382).

Like Sterling Leonard, Percival Chubb, in *The Teaching of English in the Elementary and Secondary School* (New York: Macmillan, 1903), would lead students "from the intuitive and unconscious practice of the simplest forms of discourse, to the conscious, ingenious mastery of the most elaborate and difficult forms" (p. 195). In practice, this means setting up a sequence of writing assignments that move from narration, to description, to exposition, culminating in argumentation and persuasion. William F. Irmscher sees a different use for the forms of discourse in the composition classroom. In his text *The Holt Guide to English,* 3rd ed. (New York: Holt, Rinehart and Winston, 1981), Irmscher presents the student with a sequence of questions, related to the forms of discourse, designed to encourage rhetorical invention (pp. 47–48). For example, under the category of narration, he includes questions such as "What happened?" "What is happening?" In my article "Advertising and the Modes of Discourse," *CCC*, 29 (December 1978), 356–61, I note that the kinds of writing described by copy writers for writing advertising copy between 1940 and 1950 are based on the four traditional forms of discourse. In that article, I give practical suggestions for using advertising and the forms of discourse in the classroom.

There have been several empirical studies that attempt to justify having students write in the traditional forms. For example, J. C. Seegars's essay "Forms of Discourse and Sentence Structure," *The Elementary English Review,* 10 (March 1933), 51–54, reports on a study conducted with elementary school children who were asked to write essays using the traditional forms of discourse. This study concluded that the form of discourse has a definite influence on clause structure. In their article "Thinking and Writing: Creativity in the Modes of Discourse," *Language Arts,* 54 (October 1977), 742–49, Ken Kantor and Jack Perron contend that "teachers who provide opportunities for children to explain situations and argue points of view—as well as tell stories and dramatize or depict scenes—will help them to expand linguistic and cognitive powers which are basic to their thinking and writing skills" (p. 748). Finally, the study conducted by Marion Crowhurst and Gene L. Piche on "Audience and Mode of Discourse: Effects on Syntactic Complexity in Writing at Two Grade Levels," *RTE,* 13 (May 1979), 101–9, provides evidence that "narration places fewest demands and argument greatest demands on writers to make use of their syntactic resources" (p. 107).

During the past few years, several important studies dealing with the intellectual history of the nineteenth-century forms of discourse have appeared. Among these are Robert J. Connors's "The Rise and Fall of the Modes of Discourse," *CCC,* 32 (December 1981), 444–55, which attempts "to explore the question of what makes a discourse classification useful or appealing to teachers" by examining "the rise, reign, and fall" of the forms of discourse (p. 444); my essay titled the "Nineteenth-Century Forms/Modes of Discourse: A Critical Inquiry" (previously cited), which looks at the psychological bases of the classification of discourse aims and forms; James A. Berlin's *Writing Instruction in Nineteenth-Century American Colleges* (Carbondale: Southern Illinois University Press, 1984), which analyzes "the epistemological assumptions underlying classical, psychological-epistemological, and romantic rhetoric" (p. ix); William F. Woods's "Nineteenth-Century Psychology and the Teaching of

Writing," *CCC,* 36 (February 1985), 20–41, which examines three psychologies implicit in early methods of teaching writing (Scottish common sense philosophy, Bain's associationist psychology, and William James's functionalist psychology); and Jon Harned's "The Intellectual Background of Alexander Bain's 'Modes of Discourse,'" *CCC,* 36 (February 1985), 42–50.

If the traditional forms of discourse do not work well for some teachers and scholars, others feel that some kind of classification of aims and forms can be useful as a way of guiding research and organizing textbooks and courses of study. One of the most influential of the more recent attempts to classify discourse aims and forms is James Kinneavy's *A Theory of Discourse* (Englewood Cliffs, N.J.: Prentice Hall, 1971; New York: W. W. Norton and Co., 1980).

JAMES L. KINNEAVY'S THEORY OF DISCOURSE

Kinneavy put forth his theoretical ideas in a series of publications which include "The Basic Aims of Discourse," *CCC,* 20 (December 1969), 297–304; "Theories of Composition and Actual Writing," *Kansas English,* 59 (December 1973), 3–17; *A Theory of Discourse* (previously cited); *Aims and Audiences in Writing* and *Writing—Basic Modes of Organization,* with John Q. Cope and J. W. Campbell (Dubuque: Kendall/Hunt Publishing Co., 1976); and a recent text, *Writing in the Liberal Arts Tradition* (New York: Harper & Row, 1985), with William J. McCleary and Neil Nakadate. Kinneavy's theory of discourse owes much of its theoretical justification to communications theory. In any act of communication, writes Kinneavy, four elements are involved: the *encoder* (the speaker or writer), the *decoder* (the audience or reader), the *reality* (the outer world) and the *message* (the text itself). Corresponding to each of the elements of the communication situation is an associated aim: *expressive, persuasive, referential,* and *literary.* These aims also translate into *kinds* of discourse, with referential discourse being subdivided into *exploratory, scientific,* and *informative.* In addition, Kinneavy includes a set of categories that he calls the *modes* of discourse: *description, narration, classification,* and *evaluation.* The modes of discourse are *strategies* that a speaker or writer uses to develop ideas for a particular aim in a particular kind of discourse. Kinneavy's scheme can be graphically depicted as follows:

Rhetorical Situation
  1. Speaker/writer
  2. Audience/reader
  3. Text
  4. Reality

Aims of Discourse
  1. Expressive
  2. Persuasive
  3. Referential
     a. Exploratory
     b. Scientific
     c. Informative
  4. Literary

Modes of Discourse
  1. Description
  2. Narration
  3. Classification
  4. Evaluation

Kinds of Discourse
  1. Expressive
     a. Of individual
     b. Of society
  2. Persuasive
  3. Referential
     a. Exploratory
     b. Scientific
     c. Informative
  4. Literary

Since the publication of Kinneavy's *A Theory of Discourse* in 1971, three textbooks based on his ideas have appeared: John J. Ruszkiewicz's *Well-Bound Words: A Rhetoric* (Glenview, Ill.: Scott, Foresman and Co., 1981); the second edition of *Four Worlds of Writing* (New York: Harper & Row, 1985), by Janice Lauer, Gene Montague, Andrea Lunsford, and Janet Emig; and Kinneavy's recent text, *Writing in the Liberal Arts Tradition* (New York: Harper & Row, 1985), coauthored by William J. McCleary and Neil Nakadate. Curiously, none of these texts deals with the literary aim. All three include sections dealing with expressive, persuasive, and referential aims. Since these texts will ostensibly be used in freshman composition classes, perhaps the authors feel that the literary aim might best be included in literature classes.

Of the scholarly articles dealing with Kinneavy's ideas, Tim Crusius's "A Brief Plea for a Paradigm and for Kinneavy as Paradigm," *FEN*, 12 (Winter 1984), 1–3, and "Thinking (and Rethinking) Kinneavy," *Rhetoric Review*, 3 (January 1985), 120–30, are the most enthusiastic. In "A Brief Plea," Crusius argues that "we should adopt Kinneavy's theory as the paradigm for our field, thinking with his concepts, developing his categories, extending his system in principled ways, until it either becomes adequate and complete or reveals innate shortcomings that call for a new . . . set of ideas" (p. 1). In "Thinking (and Rethinking) Kinneavy," Crusius contends that Kinneavy's theory can profit from internal development in two areas: the ends or aims of discourse and the relation of the modes to heuristic or topical systems. According to Crusius, we should discriminate, within the aims, more specific categories or sub-aims. Aims derive from the structure of discourse; purpose comes from the writer's experience, knowledge, interest, values, etc. The modes (description, narration, classification, and evaluation) can subsume and organize the topoi (e.g. partition, cause and effect, definition, etc.).

In addition to Crusius's articles, three articles that argue for the use of Kinneavy's ideas in the composition classroom are Elizabeth Harris's "Applications of Kinneavy's *Theory of Discourse* to Technical Writing," *CE*, 40 (February 1979), 625–32, and John Hagaman's "Using Discourse Analysis Scales to Encourage Thoughtful Revision in a Kinneavy-Framed Advanced Composition Course," *JAC*, 1 (Fall 1980), 79–85, and "A Comparative Analysis of Revisions Made by Advanced Composition Students in Expressive, Persuasive and Information Discourse," *JAC*, 3 (Spring and Fall 1982), 126–35.

Not all teachers and scholars, however, agree about the usefulness of Kinneavy's ideas for teaching writing or for guiding research. In an early review of *A Theory of Discourse* in the *Rhetoric Society Newsletter*, 3 (March 1973), 13–14, George Yoos posed these questions: "Why speak of a theory of discourse? What is Kinneavy doing in the name of theory when his theory seems no more than a classification based upon a definition of the nature of discourse?" (p. 14). More recently, John D. O'Banion, in his essay "A Theory of Discourse: A Retrospective," *CCC*, 33 (May 1982), 196–201, comments that Kinneavy's theory is unsatisfactory for those who teach composition "because he fails to account adequately for rhetorical choices and composing processes" (p. 196). And in his article "Kinneavy on Referential and Persuasive Discourse: A Critique," *CCC*, 35 (February 1984), 43–56, Richard P. Fulkerson complains that Kinneavy's "theoretical descriptions of the individual types are frequently unsatisfactory when compared to the reality of specific pieces of discourse" (p. 54).

In his essay "Teachers of Composition and Needed Research in Discourse Theory," *CCC*, 30 (February 1979), 39–45, Lee Odell criticizes Kinneavy for basing his assertions about "purpose" in discourse on the analysis of written products rather than on the choices writers actually make. Odell proposes a series of research questions designed "to examine and refine assumptions from current discourse theory" (p. 39). For example, "to what extent do students see composing as a process of making choices?" "Do students justify their choices by referring to their basic purpose in writing?" (pp. 40–41). C. H. Knoblauch's "Intentionality in the Writing Process: A Case Study," *CCC,* 31 (May 1980), 153–59, raises similar questions. Knoblauch takes Kinneavy to task for rejecting the notion of "operational purpose." To Knoblauch, "operational purposes are specific to real situations and often quite complex. Indeed, composing typically entails responding to multiple purposes, the interaction of which motivates and shapes performance" (p. 155).

JAMES BRITTON'S FUNCTION CATEGORIES

James Britton's discussion of the functions of discourse can be found in his article "What's the Use? A Schematic Account of Language Functions," *Educational Review,* 23 (1971), 205–17, in his book *The Development of Writing Abilities,* pp. 11–18, co-authored by Tony Burgess, Nancy Martin, Alex McLeod, and Harold Rosen, and in an article titled "The Composing Process and the Functions of Writing" which appeared in *Research on Composing,* edited by Charles R. Cooper and Lee Odell (Urbana, Ill.: NCTE, 1978), pp. 13–28. Unlike Kinneavy's theory of discourse which is self-consciously theoretical, Britton's classification scheme is an attempt to describe stages in the development of writing abilities of students from eleven to eighteen and to find a means of classifying discourse in relation to the writer's audience and the functions of discourse. Because he found the nineteenth-century aims and forms of discourse unsatisfactory as a conceptual framework to study the writing of these students, Britton (and his colleagues) settled on three main *function categories*—the *expressive,* the *transactional,* and the *poetic*—that are similar in some respects to Kinneavy's aims of discourse. Britton's expressive category matches that of Kinneavy. His transactional category, which is further subdivided into *informative* and *conative,* corresponds roughly to Kinneavy's referential and persuasive categories. And his poetic category closely matches Kinneavy's literary. Besides these categories, Britton has three main *audience categories:* the *self,* the *teacher,* and the *known wider audience,* and he sees the processes of language and audience awareness as moving through stages of increasing differentiation and abstraction.

Britton claims that there are two kinds of language roles: *participant* and *spectator*. As a participant, a writer uses language to interact with other people and to get things done. As a spectator, a writer uses a language to contemplate what has happened or what may happen to us and others. This distinction between spectator and participant roles underlies the functions of language (transactional, expressive, and poetic), which move on a continuum between the participant and spectator roles. The following scheme depicts these relationships.

Transactional	*Expressive*	*Poetic*
Participant role	. . . .	Spectator role

Although Britton's classification scheme was designed to study stages in the development of writing abilities of students from eleven to eighteen, his ideas have had some influence on the teaching of college composition. *Writing: Discovering Form and Meaning* (Belmont, Calif.: Wadsworth Publishing Co., 1984), by Charles W. Bridges and Ronald F. Lunsford, is a college text that moves from expressive to transactional writing, but like the texts previously mentioned based on Kinneavy's aims of discourse, this text does not deal with poetic discourse. Several articles follow Britton's lead in lamenting the lack of emphasis on expressive writing. In her article, "James Britton and the Pedagogy of Advanced Composition," *JAC*, 3 (Spring and Fall 1982), 1–9, Karen Pelz argues that since expressive writing is "the kind of writing best adapted to exploration and discovery" (p. 3), we ought to offer advanced writing courses in expressive writing. Toby E. Fulwiler in "Journal Writing Across the Curriculum," in *Classroom Practices in Teaching English, 1979–1980* (Urbana, Ill.: NCTE, 1979), pp. 15–22, and "Journals Across the Disciplines," *EJ*, 69 (December 1980), 14–19, contends that "expressive writing is a unique mode of learning" and advocates the use of journals across the curriculum. He and his former colleagues at Michigan Technological University make extensive use of Britton's ideas in their writing across the curriculum program. In a book edited by Fulwiler and Art Young, titled *Language Connections: Writing and Reading Across the Curriculum* (Urbana, Ill.: NCTE, 1982), Fulwiler, Young, and their colleagues present a sequence of articles that move from dicussions of the contribution that expressive writing can make to writing and learning, through transactional writing, to a discussion of the poetic function of language.

The most comprehensive criticism of the model of language learning proposed by Britton and his colleagues has been made by John Warnock in a review essay titled "Brittonism," which appeared in the *RSQ*, 9 (Winter 1979), 7–15. Warnock asserts that Britton and his associates make "the questionable assumption that there is such a thing as a taxonomy of discourse that is good for all occasions and purposes" (p. 8). He questions whether or not the British researchers have "proved" their hypothesis "that the development of writing abilities proceeds by the kind of progressive differentiation they embody in their taxonomy" (p. 12). In fact, Warnock contends that it is impossible for anyone to "prove" a taxonomy and that Britton's classificatory scheme is not a theory (i.e. an explanation), but a taxonomy (i.e. a description). C. H. Knoblauch, in his essay "Intentionality in the Writing Process: A Case Study" (previously cited), has the same reservations about Britton's scheme as he has about Kinneavy's. By reducing the notion of purpose to general types, he writes, both Britton and Kinneavy imply an ignorance of the complexity of *operational purposes*. Furthermore, "they encourage a static, monolithic view of such concepts as 'purpose' and 'reader,' oversimplifying them after the fact in a way that fails to preserve the vitality of their function in actual composing" (p. 154).

JAMES MOFFETT'S SPECTRUM OF DISCOURSE

Like Britton's classification scheme, Moffett's spectrum of discourse was intended for use in elementary and secondary school classrooms. But because his ideas relate to those of Kinneavy and Britton in interesting ways and because they are potentially useful in the college composition classroom, I am presenting them here. Moffett has articulated his ideas in a number of articles and books that include "I, You, and It," *CCC,* 16 (December 1965), 243–48; "A Structural Curriculum in English," *Harvard Educational Review,* 36 (Winter 1966), 17–28; *A Student-Centered Language Arts Curriculum, Grades K-13* (Boston: Houghton Mifflin Co., 1968; second edition, coauthored with Betty Jane Wagner in 1976); *Teaching the Universe of Discourse* (Boston: Houghton Mifflin Co., 1968); *Active Voice* (Montclair, N.J.: Boynton/Cook, 1981); and *Coming on Center* (Montclair, N.J.: Boynton/Cook, 1981).

Moffett proposes that the structure of discourse is a set of relations among a speaker ("I"), a listener ("You"), and a subject ("It"). There are accordingly four *kinds of discourse* based on the increasing distance in time and space between the speaker and his or her audience—*reflection, conversation, correspondence,* and *publication;* and four *modes of discourse* that emphasize the increasing distance in time and space between the speaker and his subject—*drama, narrative, exposition,* and *logical argument.* Moffett's modes correspond in part to the nineteenth-century forms of discourse and to Kinneavy's modes. Finally, Moffett puts all of his schemes together in a larger scheme that he calls the *spectrum of discourse:*

The Spectrum of Discourse

Interior Dialogue (egocentric speech)   P
Vocal Dialogue (socialized speech)
Recording, the drama of what is happening.
PLAYS   O

Correspondence
Personal Journal
Autobiography   E
Memoir
   Reporting, the narrative of what happened.
FICTION   T
Biography
Chronicle
History   R
   Generalizing, the exposition of what happens.
ESSAY   Y
Science
Metaphysics
   Theorizing, the argumentation of what will, may happen.

I was unable to find articles that apply Moffett's ideas to the college composition classroom, but Carol Kuykendall's "Sequence without Stricture," *EJ,* 61 (May 1972), 715–22 and Lou Willett Stanek's "Hesse and Moffett Team Teach the Theory of Discourse," *EJ,* 61 (October 1972), 985–93 discuss the relevance of Moffett's ideas for secondary school teachers.

ROMAN JAKOBSON'S ASPECTS AND FUNCTIONS OF DISCOURSE

Both Kinneavy's theory of discourse and Britton's functions of discourse seem to be indebted to Jakobson's aspects and functions of discourse. Jakobson was asked to make a few closing remarks at a conference on style at Indiana University in 1958. His comments were subsequently published as "Closing Statement: Linguistics and Poetics," in *Style in Language,* ed. Thomas A. Sebeok (Cambridge, Mass.: The MIT Press, 1960), pp. 350–77. Jakobson's task in his summary remarks was to comment on the relationship of poetics to linguistics. But in order to do this, he realized that he had to comment on language *in all of its functions,* not just the poetic function.

In every discourse act, asserts Jakobson, there is an *addresser,* an *addressee*, a *context*, a *message*, a *contact*, and a *code*. Each of these elements determines a function of language, so that corresponding to each aspect of discourse are associated functions: *emotive, conative, referential, poetic, phatic,* and *metalinguistic.* The verbal structure of a message "depends primarily on the predominant function." The six aspects of discourse, together with their associated functions, are listed below in a scheme that depicts their relationship:

Aspects of Discourse
    Addresser
    Addressee
    Context
    Message
    Contact
    Code

Functions of Discourse
    Emotive (or Expressive)
    Conative
    Referential
    Poetic
    Phatic
    Metalinguistic

The value of a functional model such as Jakobson's for the writer is that it demonstrates the processes through which rhetorical choices are made. Yet some critics contend that he uses too many categories and that there is a danger that someone else will come along and create new functions which could be multiplied endlessly.

WALTER BEALE'S PRAGMATIC THEORY OF DISCOURSE

One of the most ambitious attempts to classify discourse performances since Kinneavy's *A Theory of Discourse* (Beale would argue, however, that Kinneavy does not classify discourse "performances") is Walter Beale's pragmatic theory of discourse. Beale's ideas have not been widely promulgated because they appear in a single article, "On the Classification of Discourse Performances," *RSQ*, 7 (Spring 1977), 31–40, and an unpublished manuscript, *Rhetoric in Writing: A Pragmatic Theory*. Beale contends that any approach to discourse performances must use a *situational* approach. This involves constructing a *matrix of features* to identify kinds of discourse, so that any classification of aims, modes, forms, or genres must be based on normal *coalescences* of features, rather than on a single feature.

In contrast to the Kinneavian aims of expressive, persuasive, referential, and literary, Beale postulates four corresponding aims: *instrumental, poetic, scientific,* and *rhetorical*. But rather than base his classification on a single feature such as audience, Beale bases his on a combination of features including the purpose and functions of discourse performances, typical relationships of author and audience, the occasions of discourse, the norms of language, and so forth. According to Beale, the aims should be thought of as existing along the lines of a continuum, rather than as categories with distinct boundaries between them. There are four "kinds" or genuses of discourse: *deliberative, informative, performative* (or epideictic), and *reflective/exploratory*. These correspond respectively to rhetorical, scientific, instrumental, and poetic aims.

Whereas the aims have to do with the writer's purpose and the genuses with form or genre, the modes and strategies of discourse are "ways of conducting discourse" or "formal methods of proceeding coherently in written monologue." There are three *modes* of discourse (*discursive, narrative,* and *dramatic*) and six strategies of discourse (*generic, material, dialectical, dispositional, stylistic,* and *modal*). Actually, the strategies of discourse include the modes.

Needless to say, this kind of Aristotelian division, classification, and definition can be tiring, but Beale claims that his theory can account for the way certain categories conform or don't conform to the *actual products of discourse they are supposed to represent,* better, and in a less reductive way, than other theories. He calls his theory *pragmatic* because he is primarily concerned with "what human beings do with discourse." Not everyone will agree with Beale's classifications and definitions of the aims, modes, and forms of discourse. His ideas are often difficult and complex, and they do not always allow for easy summarization. Yet I believe that Beale's pragmatic theory, like Kinneavy's theory of discourse, will be provocative in the best sense of provoking discussion.

A MISCELLANY OF CLASSIFICATION SCHEMES

In addition to the approaches that I have discussed thus far, there are other approaches to discourse classification that are worthy of attention. The first comes out of speech communication, but has relevance for the composition classroom. In an article titled "Toward an Axiology of Rhetoric," *Q JS,* 48 (April 1962), 157–68, Ralph T. Eubanks and Virgil L. Baker argue that the teacher of public address must be a teacher of human values. In communication courses, therefore, values ought to be taught in conjunction with the aims of discourse. In their scheme, the values of well-being, affection, and rectitude are related to the aim *to inspire,* those of respect and power to the aim *to convince,* those of wealth and skill to the aim *to activate,* and the value of enlightenment to the aim *to inform* (p. 166).

An interesting attempt to combine literary modes with rhetorical modes has been made by Leo Rockas in *Modes of Rhetoric* (New York: St. Martin's Press, 1964):

Modes of Rhetoric

I.   The Static Modes
   A. Description
   B. Definition
II. The Temporal Modes
   A. Narration
   B. Process

III. The Mimetic Modes
    A. Drama
    B. Dialogue
IV. The Mental Modes
    A. Reverie
    B. Persuasion

In Rockas's classification scheme, the A categories make up the *concrete modes* (*description, narration, drama, reverie*), whereas the B categories constitute the *abstract modes* (*definition, process, dialogue,* and *persuasion*). There are four pairs of modes. Each pair contains a concrete mode and an abstract mode. The relationship between the modes is indicated by the superordinate categories: *static, temporal, mimetic,* and *mental.* The sequence of modes is from those abstracted from time and space to those embedded in past, present, and future actions (pp. ix, x).

George Bramer, in an article entitled "Like It Is: Discourse Analysis for a New Generation," *CCC,* 21 (December 1970), 347–55, maintains that although Rockas's system has attractive features, it "cannot promote discourse that tells it like it is" nearly as well as other systems. In its place, Bramer offers a system whose main features are schematically presented below:

Discourse

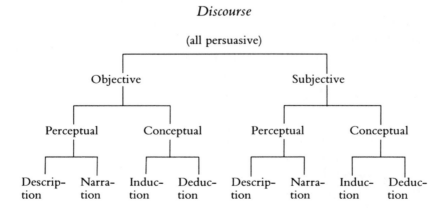

150

Bramer considers persuasion as fundamental. Therefore, all of the modes are subdivisions of persuasion. Each of the two main divisions, the *objective* and the *subjective,* is divided into the *perceptual* (or concrete) and the *conceptual* (or abstract). The subdivisions of these categories (*description, narration, induction,* and *deduction*) constitute the modes of discourse. The perceptual modes are description and narration. There are two kinds of description: *objective* (or technical) and *subjective* (or imaginative). There are also two kinds of narration: *objective* (expository) and *subjective* (imaginative). The abstract or conceptual modes are *induction* and *deduction.* Bramer does not subdivide these, but like Rockas, he sees these modes as operating in both imaginative and non-imaginative discourse.

Another interesting way of classifying discourse has been proposed by Winston Weathers and Otis Winchester in *The Attitudes of Rhetoric* (Englewood Cliffs, N.J.: Prentice-Hall, 1970). Weathers and Winchester argue that the writer's attitude toward his or her subject and audience constitutes an important part of the writer's message. They classify nine different kinds of discourse based on *attitude,* define each, and relate each attitude to style and tone. The *attitudes* of rhetoric are the *confident,* the *judicious,* the *quiet,* the *imperative,* the *impassioned,* the *compassionate,* the *critical,* the *angry,* and the *absurd.*

In his essay "Lloyd Bitzer's 'Rhetorical Situation' and the Classification of Discourse: Problems and Implications," *P and R,* 3 (Summer 1970), 165–68, Richard Larson comments that Lloyd Bitzer's concept of the rhetorical situation "calls attention to what seemingly unrelated instances of discourse have in common, and helps differentiate rhetorical from nonrhetorical discourse" (p. 168). Larson believes that Bitzer's ideas can provide the basis for classifying and evaluating the success of particular instances of discourse.

In "The Spectrum of Rhetoric," *CCC,* 25 (May 1974), 181–85, Daniel Marder suggests that "we can view all rhetoric as

151

a spectrum of persuasiveness," with "simple descriptions of objects or reports of observations at one end and the most esoteric poetry at the other" (p. 184). Marder believes that all discourse seeks agreement between the writer and his or her audience, and he maintains that discourse can be classified according to the means used to achieve agreement.

In his discussion of "Primary Trait Scoring" in *Evaluating Writing*, ed. Charles R. Cooper and Lee Odell (Urbana, Ill.: NCTE, 1977), pp. 33–66, Richard Lloyd-Jones contends that "in order to report precisely how people manage different types of discourse, one must have a model of discourse which permits the identification of limited types of discourse and the creation of exercises which stimulate writing in the appropriate range" (p. 37). Lloyd-Jones favors a three-part model that focuses on the writer, the audience, and the subject, in relation to the purpose of the discourse. The following is a graphic depiction of this three-part model:

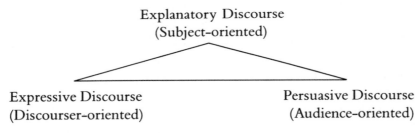

Explanatory Discourse
(Subject-oriented)

Expressive Discourse   Persuasive Discourse
(Discourser-oriented)   (Audience-oriented)

Lee Odell, Charles R. Cooper, and Cynthia Courts are interested in the implications of discourse theory for research in composing. In their essay "Discourse Theory: Implications for Research in Composing," in *Research on Composing*, ed. Charles R. Cooper and Lee Odell (Urbana, Ill.: NCTE, 1978), pp. 1–12, Odell, Cooper, and Courts suggest *four kinds of questions* that can help researchers test assumptions about purpose, writer, subject, and audience—questions about the *process of composing*, about *published writing*, about *writing done at different age levels*, and about *eliciting* and *assessing writing performance*. For example, is the claim that a primary purpose guides a writer's choice of form and content "borne out by the actual practice of writers" (p. 6)?

Caroline Eckhardt and David Stewart believe that their taxonomy of composition has a greater resemblance to "real writing" outside the classroom than do other taxonomies. In an essay entitled "Towards a Functional Taxonomy of Composition," *CCC*, 30 (December 1979), 338–42, they identify four basic *purposes* for writing: to *clarify* what the subject is, to *substantiate* a thesis, to *evaluate* the subject, and to *recommend* that something be done about it. They maintain that these purposes are incremental. Each builds on the preceding one.

Richard Fulkerson, in "Four Philosophies of Composition," *CCC*, 30 (December 1979), 343–48, advances the idea that the four theories of literature proposed by M. H. Abrams in *The Mirror and the Lamp* might be relevant to composition. Abrams's four categories are the *pragmatic,* the *mimetic,* the *expressive,* and the *objective.* With a slight change of wording, Fulkerson comes up with these categories, suggestive of Kinneavy's aims of discourse: *expressive, rhetorical* (i.e. persuasive), *mimetic* (i.e. referential), and *formalist* (i.e. literary).

In his article "Tactics of Discourse: A Classification for Student Writers," *CE*, 43 (February 1981), 168–78, Richard H. Haswell indicates that he is looking for a classification system that will help beginning writers "produce" writing. He believes that current systems are too abstract and too difficult for the student writer and that, more importantly, they describe formal properties instead of strategies. He defines a *tactic* as "any conscious decision of the writer to add to, subtract from, or alter in any way what he or she is writing" (p. 170). Haswell classifies tactics into *tactics of understanding, tactics of knowing, tactics of language-sense,* and *tactics of audience-sense.* Each of these categories is further subdivided and explained in this article.

Finally, in her article, "Genre as Social Action," *QJS,* 70 (May 1984), 151–67, Carolyn Miller complains that "rhetorical criticism has not provided firm guidance on what constitutes a genre" (p. 151). Yet she believes that classification is necessary to language and learning. Her thesis is that "a rhetorically sound definition of genre must be centered not on the substance or the form of discourse, but on the action it is used to accomplish" (p. 151). She proposes to base a classification of discourse "upon recurrent situation or, more specifically, upon exigence understood as social motive" (p. 158). She would have teachers study the "typical" uses of rhetoric and the "forms" it takes in those uses (p. 158).

As might appear evident in this survey of approaches to the aims, modes, and forms of discourse, teachers and scholars disagree about the value of particular approaches to discourse classification. Although at times the various ways of classifying kinds of writing seem simply the result of a need or an impulse to get experience in order, at other times such classifications seem to represent linguistic, psychological, and cultural processes at work on the writer's attitudes and intentions. Whether discourse types are taken as genres, modes, aims, attitudes, or conventions of a particular kind, they must not be thought of as unchangeable and immutable archetypes. They are rather a cluster of changing conventions classified for specific purposes. At its best, the forms of discourse approach to writing forces us to attend more closely to differences in rhetorical purpose, attitudes, values, and audience. At its weakest, it may develop into a mere formalism, with undue emphasis on static conventions, rather than with a more proper emphasis on the processes of discourse.

Tests of Writing Ability

RICHARD LLOYD-JONES, University of Iowa

THE ASSESSMENT OF WRITING ABILITIES IS ES-sentially a managerial task. It represents an effort to record quantitatively the quality of the writing or writing skills of a group of people so that administrators can make policies about educational programs. Tests are given and scores are assigned to individual performances of people as parts of large groups. As a rule the scores then are used in aggregate.

Grading is basically the same activity, but the term suggests a classroom limit. Grades are the record of a teacher's evaluation of work by each pupil. Sometimes they are confused with or even substituted for the teacher's response to student writing. Both are evaluations, but responses are primarily directed to the improvement of the writing and the general skill of the writer, while grading exists primarily to provide records within a mass school system. As a rule grades are reported to the pupil on an individual basis.

A teacher may respond to writing as does a common reader by showing concern for what the writer actually says. Since most writers seek to be understood, being taken seriously is a powerful incentive for improvement. Each misunderstanding by the reader is an invitation to the student for revision, so long as the misreading is not perceived as a form of heckling. Similarly, teachers may respond as editors, or may use a class group as a board of editors. Talk about the writing as writing suggests the importance of the text as an expression. Serious discussion of the reason for alternatives in writing is flattering to the writer, for it implies that the text and its message are worth being concerned about, although some editors manage to suggest that mere conformity is the goal. "Correctness" is important when it can be related to the reaction of an audience the writer really wants to impress.

Response is a teaching activity, a human engagement rather than a bureaucratic rite even though class overloads tempt some teachers to use managerial shortcuts. Given the nature of a school system one must always be ready to defend judgments of a paper. Still, one's principal concern should be helping the student acquire skill and knowledge. The best descriptions of how to make responses are those which describe ordinary decent human relationships. Pedagogical tact takes into account the personal investment of the writer in the text, and ordinary skill in discourse requires a teacher to adjust explanations for the student's lack of vocabulary, other experience, and objectivity about the situation which called for the writing in the first place.

Not a lot has been written systematically on how teachers should respond to writing, despite its centrality to teaching, probably because response is merely a special form of the general teaching relationship. Brooke K. Horvath summarized the best available material in "The Components of Written Response: A Practical Synthesis of Current Reviews" in the *Rhetoric Review* of January 1984. His bibliography lists 81 items, but his nine pages of commentary raise the central issues and offer a suitable taxonomy of kinds of response.

In a sense the material can be epitomized as advice on how to keep the writer eager to try again in a never-ending process. Provide information, but don't fuss about error. Be ready with questions and suggestions so that the writer's motor doesn't stall out. On the whole comparative studies of different specific ways of responding are unsatisfactory because in order to narrow advice sufficiently to frame useful rules, the studies isolate acts which are meaningless without reference to the whole context of student-teacher relationships. The taxonomy at least provides a teacher with a useful framework for self-examination, and the best essays are those which deal with response in ethical terms.

The need to respond to the actual writing of an intelligent human being is crucial to teaching, but it should not make one forget that managing a classroom or a writing program is also a serious part of education. Fair and perceptive management of programs is basic to a mass educational system. Responding to student writing and managing a system for teaching writing both require complex acts of evaluation. In simple terms, reading and responding require judgments of quality if a teacher is to encourage a writer to continue on a sound path or to undertake a different one, but the response is ordinarily in the same language as the text. Grading or assessing by tests is obviously evaluative, and the verdicts are ordinarily recorded in numbers. A judgment reported in English can readily be questioned in English; a judgment recorded in numbers is highly abstract and usually very hard to challenge. The abstractness is what makes it a useful managerial tool, for abstractions can be manipulated efficiently, but that also is what makes it dangerous, for one easily acquires excessive confidence in the scores or is tempted to read results far beyond what is implied by the test itself.

Because managerial or political convenience strongly tempts people to over-read scores, one should always take into account the situation in which the testing of writing abilities is to take place, so as to forestall misinterpretation. Scores are used to justify programs or change appropriations, and scores may be used to penalize or reward students, so they have important public effects. They are easily used out of context, so in frustration the victims cry out against all testing.

Before deploring all uses of testing, two particular conditions should be noted: the word "test" is valued highly in our society, and the social goal of universal education has made the numbers of students so large that management requires proof of

157

accomplishment. These conditions make calls even for restraint seem to some people to be obstructionist. Consider societal preconceptions about testing.

The positive value assigned to the word "test" is apparent in popular usage and in broad acceptance of tests in general discussions of education. One learns to "test the water," either with a toe or an elbow, to check the temperature. Practically the test may be bad. The water may be layered, so a test at the top will mislead one about the temperature below the surface. Or one may have a numb toe, a bad measuring instrument. But still the notion of a trial is built into the adage, and we often do use the tests carefully if we are to bathe a child or swim in an unknown pond.

The value attached to the word is seen even more aptly in the idea of "testing oneself" in strenuous or dangerous activity. Athletics may serve for exercise, but much of the motive surely is to win, to prove one's competence, one's ability to endure pain and hardship. Campers go out in sub-zero weather when staying in the heated house would be safer and more pleasant, just to test themselves. Presumably the test leads to confidence, for we need to prove to ourselves that we really are the people we brag about. One of the main reasons for a classroom test is to prove to pupils that they have learned, that they are ready to move on to new ideas. The teacher may want the same information for managerial reasons, but the justification of the test in real educational terms is self-definition.

To some extent any test requires risk and is threatening. The risk in a test of the water or a plank across a ditch seems mild, for the consequence of failure in the test is slight compared with the consequences of a boiling bath or a fall. The test is so clearly related to our good and the failure to make a test is so clearly related to pain that we affirm the value of testing. As we move to more abstract tests imposed by others we are less sure of their goodness, but even if we complain we pay attention. We sometimes believe the test when our fuller experience suggests a different evaluation, and we don't seriously begin major activities without making tests.

Marketing, for example, requires testing customer interest. A good marketing director is very careful to observe the limits of the test, but it would be foolish to invest large amounts without some preliminary discovery. So also almost any modest political campaign nowadays depends heavily on polling as a means of directing the campaign strategy. The polls in the newspaper are but the tip of the iceberg, and although editorialists may thunder about the accuracy or the effect, the test is essential if the campaign is to be managed well. In this sense, mass testing in the schools is just another polling technique, sometimes sampling the work of one person in order to make a judgment about her or his total work, sometimes sampling the work of individuals in order to make a judgment about the group.

However we make the comparison, we must note that society takes testing in most of its varieties as given. In fact, we have such a large educational establishment that some sort of testing is probably essential as a means of cost control. The traditional classroom test is so much a part of teaching technique that few teachers or administrators are ready to challenge the idea of testing even though they may be persuaded that a particular kind of test is inadequate for its stated purpose. Our population shifts, so we need to be able to place students in new environments, we need to transfer credit. Those who put up the money but who have almost no direct contact with students want to be assured that the money is well spent or that pupils are not being cheated. With large numbers of pupils and huge bodies of knowledge, some kind of sampling is probably necessary. When an individual teacher has more than a hundred pupils a day probably the test score or grade is a necessary substitute for actual personal knowledge. The question is not whether to test but what kind to use. How much error of measurement can be tolerated and how can the damage of mismeasurement be contained?

For a writing teacher the issue is unusually difficult. Everyone writes, or so it seems, and yet the craft is extremely complicated. One learns it lifelong, mostly out-of-school, in widely various ways. Few are expert as writers in the same way, and yet many may be expert at writing some things. As in many complex activities, the whole is greater than the sum of the parts, so merely testing separate writing skills ordinarily is misleading. To understand writing itself is difficult, and many simply take it for granted because what so many people do seems to be ordinary. Still more difficult is understanding what one does to teach the craft, even though many seem to teach it, because a large part of the learning takes place in ordinary human transactions not labeled as educational. We learn much in the market place. Then to require that one learn the arts of testing, another complicated craft, is enough to make most administrators and many researchers despair.

The best advice I can give to any writing teacher or administrator is to take a psychometrist into partnership. Learn enough about the arts of testing yourself to give good instructions to test makers and to challenge their recommendations, but have the help of a specialist at hand. Be sure that the psychometrist is ready to give you similar respect—to allow you to talk about the nature of writing and to insist on appropriate limits. Testmakers like to limit the focus of what is being tested so as to increase their control, but the nature of writing requires a broad look. Tension between a psychometrist and rhetorician will be inevitable, so the partnership must be carefully established.

The best place to begin to acquire a working knowledge of how to examine writing performances is with Edward M. White's *Teaching and Assessing Writing* (San Francisco: Jossey-Bass, 1985). For most readers his book makes earlier works unnecessary except for historical reasons, although he identifies and discusses most relevant works previous to his own, thus allowing me more space for discussing some of the broad issues relating to testing. White's list of references is a sufficient guide for those who want to go farther. For those who want to go just a bit beyond White's compendium, Paul B. Diederich's *Measuring Growth in English* (Urbana, Ill.: NCTE, 1974) and *Evaluating Writing: Describing, Measuring, Judging* (NCTE, 1977), edited by Charles Cooper and Lee Odell, still offer useful amplifications. White takes a comprehensive view of the general character of indirect and relatively direct forms of testing. Then he concentrates on the more direct forms, which use writing samples and the analytic and holistic methods for judging them. He properly concentrates on what is required in using holistic scoring.

In a sense, all testing of writing is indirect because even a test essay is always a limited sample taken under abnormal conditions, but there is still a useful contrast to be made between tests which are based on a sample of writing and tests which focus on a single element of language examined by means of some "objective" testing format. A direct test ordinarily does not require sampling. If one assigns a ten-word spelling list and then requires the student to reproduce all ten words, the test is direct. If one has a one-hundred-word list and tests only ten words, the sampling implies a degree of indirectness. Which ten words are chosen? the hard ones? every tenth word in alphabetical order? the most frequently used ten? The decision will markedly affect the result and thus affect what can be said about the mastery of the spelling of the whole list. The mastery has been tested inferentially.

A test of swimming skills which requires one to swim lengths of a pool is indirect as a measure of the ability to swim in the ocean, although perhaps not seriously so, but is direct as a measure of the ability to swim laps. The direct test is really something of a tryout, and if subsequent situations are quite like the sample, the test is quite direct. If one has no pool and therefore gives a paper and pencil test of a swimmer's knowledge of the psychology and physics of swimming, then one has an indirect test. Implicitly the test maker assumes that a knowledge of theory and practice are closely related. An employer of technical writers might have a prospective employee write a set of technical direc-

161

tions as a relatively direct test of the ability to produce additional instruction manuals, and the same test might serve indirectly as an indication of whether the person could write technical proposals. Still, the writing situations are different—that is, they are not exactly parallel—so errors will creep in. A test over knowledge of rules from a writer's handbook is even less helpful. Writing like swimming depends on more than theoretical knowledge.

The most common indirect tests of writing skills are those which focus on some limited subset of writing skills—most often vocabulary or usage. These really are measures of the correlation between two variables (say, vocabulary and writing ability) even though the particular item (size of vocabulary) seems plausibly a writing skill.

We often confuse correlations with demonstrated connections. Most of us believe that smoking is a cause of cancer even though so far we can't exactly explain why. We know that people who smoke get cancer more often than those who don't, but some smokers do not get cancer, and some non-smokers do. The correlation is not by any means perfect. We speak knowingly of SAT and ACT scores as though they reported something certain about the educational level of young people going to college. All the test makers claim is that the scores correlate with grades earned in the first year of college, but with a rather large margin of error. In both examples the correlations are good enough to be useful, but the errors are great enough to force us to be restrained in interpreting any particular case. When we say that the correlation is believeable at a rate of 0.4, as we do say with the admissions tests, we imply that we must leave a lot of room for adjustments in individual cases. (A correlation of 1.0 or -1.0 is perfect, 0.0 is random. In the physical sciences 0.9 would seem shaky.)

On the face of it, a large vocabulary would seem to indicate writing abilities. Vocabulary tests are very helpful in predicting most academic performances, and since words are so clearly basic to writing, we might expect a vocabulary test to tell a lot about writing skills. Still, we know of people with large vocabularies

162

who write very badly—read almost any academic journal. Government regulations are sometimes similarly unreadable. Some kinds of unintelligible prose almost require large vocabularies. Yet, people with limited vocabularies and very clear purposes can sometimes write powerful and useful prose. Although doubtless there is a positive correlation between vocabulary and good writing, it is not perfect.

Much the same can be said of usage tests. A nation brought up on the notion of correctness values standard usage highly in the abstract even though considerable variation is allowed in practice. Probably usage tests measure social identification, social class, in a society that doesn't like to talk about classes. Correct usage requires the language forms comfortably used most of the time by most of the people who exercise power in a given society. The standard of correctness changes according to time and place and social dominance, for the language is an invention of the society which uses it. Since the people who have power determine the norm, those who aspire to power and who want to identify with the values of the dominant group must acquire control of standard usage. A test of such mastery will ordinarily identify who has paid the dues and therefore will be ready to produce according to the values represented by educational institutions and acceptable to the people who teach in them. Such students will write with manners that are socially pleasing regardless of whether the intellectual content of the writing is remarkable. The usage test will probably correlate quite well with what is understood as writing skill even though it is measuring something else.

For me none of the indirect tests is really a measure of writing ability although several may be adequate for placement in a college writing course, especially if there are provisions for appeal from unsatisfactory decisions. The tests are relatively cheap and can be administered in relatively adverse conditions, such as those common during the first few days at college or during the summer pre-registration visit. They provide another kind of information which can be added to records of courses and grades as well as general experience out of school to help a student decide about her or his own competence. But in the end if such tests are to be described as tests of writing ability they should be correlated to actual samples of writing. Then we have entered the difficulties of mass scoring, for in order to make a correlation with actual writing, we must first score some writing.

Mass scoring of writing samples requires that one get the samples and then devise a system of scoring. It is easier to think of the problem backwards. Examining systems of scoring will partly reveal why it is difficult to get good samples that are also comparable. When one gets suitable samples, essentially one may decide that the quality of a piece of writing can be reported as the sum of its parts. Then one creates a guide describing the parts, the features to be observed, and asks readers to score each part separately. The separate scores added together indicate the quality of the whole sample. Or one may decide that the quality of a piece of writing is dependent upon the complex interaction of the parts within the situation which evokes it. The score must represent what a sophisticated reader interprets as a total effect. This is much more than a "general impression," for it implies a complex interpretive act. The first assumption about what makes good writing leads to "analytic scoring" and the second leads to "holistic scoring."

Analytic scoring in a systematic way may be traced to E. F. Lindquist's doctoral work after World War I, although it has classroom parallels of longer standing. For example, the impulse to give separate grades for content and mechanics is related to it. Textbooks have used rating guides tied to the chapters of advice in the books. Some of the usual categories are focus, organization, evidence, diction, point of view, sentence variety, and mechanics. Paul B. Diederich (with John French and Sydell Carlton) in 1961 identified for ETS five factors which influenced the ratings of judges. These (ideas, organization, wording, flavor, mechanics) became the basis for some analytic scales. In fact almost any system used to describe style can be modified to create an analytic scale. With the help of the computer memory some extremely complex scales can be created, like the one with dozens of categories designed by Rosemary Hake with the assistance of Joseph Williams at the University of Chicago. All that is required is that each sub-category of description be defined precisely and assigned a range of possible scores.

This cursory list suggests the chief problem with analytic scales. Getting agreement on the suitability of any scale and on the points assigned to the categories is difficult. For example, some people don't want any points given for mechanics and others consider mechanics "basic." Those who claim that each writing situation is unique and requires its own mixture of skills and strategies refuse to accept any scale (or at least any allocation of points among categories) as applying to more than one exercise. Still, the scales are explicit. Outsiders can see what is being judged, although in truth most test scores seem to be accepted at face value by general public readers. Teachers can show students why they are being judged as they are. Analytic scales surrender subtlety in order to gain explicitness, but perhaps most of the time subtlety is wasted anyway.

Holistic scoring, probably now the system most used for mass testing, is divided into two types according to restrictions placed on development of exercises and scoring guides, although the types actually blend and perhaps should be identified as extremes on a scale. The original system developed by Diederich and others for ETS emphasized tasks which stimulated writers to present their best efforts. The scoring made use of the full experience of skilled readers to adapt their judgments to signals about intentions and strategies embedded in the sample of writing thus produced. This is a useful approach for handling large numbers when the principal desire is to rank the papers in relatively large categories of quality. It is a variant of "grading on the curve" or "norm scoring."

A second holistic system was developed for the National Assessment of Educational Progress (NAEP). Fewer papers had to

165

be read, and the need was primarily to provide research information about groups of writers. Ranking was less important than detailed descriptions. Exercises to generate writing were designed to show what writers would do in precisely limited situations, and the scoring guides were extremely elaborate so as to approximate the explicitness of analytic scoring or of "criterion referenced scoring," a system requiring standards based on predetermined needs of the situation. Because the purpose implied in the task was crucial in evoking the writer's strategy of response, the scoring guide was framed to indicate success in accomplishing that specified purpose. The score could be described as indicating a specified level of achievement in using writing purposefully. In theory, at least, all of the papers in a set might be judged successful. They could satisfy the criteria established in accord with the demands of the situation.

This system was called "Primary Trait Scoring" (PTS) in order to suggest that the scoring scale was designed to fit the dominant purpose implied in the writing. If the exercise was supposed to explain a problem, then the scoring reported how that dominant goal was achieved, although of course most writing exhibits concern with a large number of secondary goals, often specific to separate paragraphs or even sentences or words. The word "primary" should alert one to the existence of secondary purposes.

In both holistic systems the quality of the paper is identified as a function of the interactions of the parts. The popular designation, "general impression" scoring, misleads in suggesting quick off-handedness. To be sure, papers are ordinarily read quickly so that scorers avoid becoming excessively self-conscious. If the readers are properly experienced and trained, their knowledge should become tacit, below the surface, like the knowledge one exhibits in riding a bicycle. Thinking about how to steer often causes one to fall off. So too, thinking about how to balance two examples against one metaphor will throw off a scorer, yet examples and metaphors in relation to structure, and the personality of the author, and the point to be made, and more specific qualities fused together make up the basis of judgment. The experienced reader automatically balances the separate elements into a single judgment of a text. The process is not in question; the problem is how to make the reporting of the process consistent among several readers—or even for one reader over a period of time and fatigue—and informative.

If one imagines a reader to be just another meter—like a thermometer or a water meter—it is evident that one must calibrate the reader/meters to a universal scale, which in turn must be devised. One begins with a range of numbers, although letters and pluses-and-minuses could be substituted. Numbers permit arithmetic manipulation more conveniently. A four-point scale is common, for it reflects the grossness of human judgments of writing. Even numbers force readers away from a large class of middle-quality papers—the ordinary "C." The four point scale permits an initial separation into better and worse and then a secondary decision about each of the resultant groups into better and worse piles. In short, it permits a rough ranking of the papers by quality even though there may be differences about the border between two classes. The greater the number of score points in the scale, the greater the problem of agreement. Teachers used to grading "A" to "F" with pluses and minuses find such limited scales deny them distinctions they are fond of, but probably they over-rate their ability to make fine and consistent divisions. Since usually two readers examine each sample, scores are sometimes added to make one report and suggest a larger range of rating.

PTS designers occasionally use slightly larger ranges, partly to make clear that they are not simply ranking the papers. They may have "1" represent unsuccessful papers, "2" marginal papers, and "3" through "6" different degrees of success—or different kinds of success. Both systems may have additional code numbers to represent unreadable papers or papers showing no intention to engage the exercise. PTS also encourages secondary readings to report on how writers handled particular strategies such as point of view or evidence or mechanics or syntax or metaphor while actually creating text as opposed to responding within the frameworks of an objective test. Error rates on mechanics, for example, are much different when writers can choose syntactic patterns which are familiar to them. The actual scales, then, are established for PTS to fit the immediate need of the testing situation. A given set of papers may have several scores.

Establishing the border between scores is the difficult task. Administrators of the test pick papers representative of each score point and suggestive of problems to be faced in the reading. In the original ETS system, that was enough, for then the readers were gathered together and led through group readings until all—or most—generated the same scores assigned by the test administrators. Since the actual decisions were necessarily tacit, the only issue was to make sure that readers drew divisions at the same point defined by essays selected for the practice readings. Their reasons might have been different.

PTS administrators have a more elaborate task. Since each task is designed to reveal how a writer handles a particular mixture of purposes, the scoring guide requires more explanations even though in the end the readers are supposed to internalize what they learn. The designers are obliged to offer a rationale for the exercise, showing how each phase of the test assignment is supposed to evoke a particular response in the writer and why that special response is useful to know.

Then each score point requires a detailed description so that readers can know what kind of success is indicated. These descriptions usually include hypotheses about specific strategies or devices the writers will use, not to suggest formal requirements for an answer but to make concrete any general description of what the score point means. Readers are supposed to have not only similar scores, but similar reasons. Some literalists among the scorers will be tempted to think that the illustrative forms are intended as the standard itself, so it is important to have a number of sample papers discussed in detail. Some should exhibit useful solutions to the problem different from the illustrations tied to the score points. Finally there must be sample papers with scoring and discussion kept separate from the samples so that the papers can be presented to readers untouched while the administrators have systematic advice for the sessions to calibrate the readers. The resulting guide may be twenty to thirty pages long, and that implies that much extensive training of readers is important for PTS scoring.

As White observes, the two systems have drifted toward each other. PTS is more elaborate than most administrators can afford to deal with, and the ETS system has accepted some of its general constraints in order to make more informative statements about what has been measured, but still the differences are worth observing as indications of what can be done in different testing situations. One of the best discussions of the usefulness of various systems is that by Lee Odell and Charles Cooper in "Procedures for Evaluating Writing: Assumptions and Needed Research," *CE,* 42 (Sept. 1980), 35–43.

Both systems depend upon getting good samples of writing. All of us are better writers on certain topics under certain circumstances. Some of us write good poems and bad memos. More of us write pleasant personal letters and fuzzy philosophical speculations. Some of us write well in the morning, others at night. Some need silence, some distractive music, some a typewriter, some green ink, and so on. We all develop special needs and aids to composition to fit our personalities and habits and pattern of life. Writing, more than most skills, is tied to our lifelong development of social and intellectual practices so it is difficult to observe in a "standard" way as required for test comparability. By the nature of our individual approaches to our common language we will favor some writers over others in a test, but we try to be institutionally fair as part of the compromises of management. The fairness of an institution is to some extent being unfair to all but attempting to balance out the unfairness; we remind ourselves to allow for errors in interpreting what we discover.

If we simply asked writers to offer us samples of their best work, as we might if we were hiring a writer or running a contest, we would acquire documents we couldn't really compare in a large way. An employer is usually looking for one person to fit a particular slot and can therefore afford to eliminate all sorts of competent people. A contest is to some extent a lottery among those who are quite good. Even selecting material for publication in a magazine combines specificity of need and chance in selection. But test makers are not allowed such laxity. They must have samples as much alike as possible so as to permit generalizations leading to policy or fair rewards to individuals in a large group. They must find topics about which the writers can be expected to have knowledge and opinions, but which do not favor any one segment of the group. Could city children write about detasseling? Could groups of girls write about big time football? For that matter would girls be handicapped if they were asked to write a letter to be signed by a person named "William"?

The nature of the task is specially important for PTS designers because the implied purpose becomes the basis for determining success. Some literary critics may claim that we can not discover the intention of a writer from looking at the text, but most transactions in writing are insistently purposeful. Our purposes may be to relieve our feelings or play games with language for the fun of it as well as to sell or explain ideas, but we expect our labor to be rewarded some way, and the point of PTS scoring is to judge the appropriateness of the response in accomplishing a stated purpose. That is likely, also, to be the purpose of a classroom teacher in designing tasks, to encourage the students to experiment with language in satisfying different needs. The experiments enlarge their range of skills so that they can imagine more writing situations and adapt to them.

One relationship between purpose and writing has been amply explored by Carl H. Klaus and a battalion of associates working for CEMREL, a regional education laboratory in St. Louis. Two of Klaus's books, *Composing Childhood Experience*

and *Composing Adolescent Experience,* were designed to show
teachers how to use the strategies of PTS exercise design in the
classroom, but in the demonstration reveal much about PTS
scoring and philosophy. The books were elaborately field-tested
in various short courses, and, as federally financed works, are in
the public domain, but they are hard to find because CEMREL
ceased effective functioning before the books were finally dis-
tributed. One hopes that they will be reissued, but in the meantime business in relation to them is being handled by the Mid-
Continent Regional Educational Laboratory (McREL) at 470 N.
Kirkwood Rd., Second Floor South, St. Louis, Missouri, 63122
(telephone 314-821-1700). They deal primarily with the expressive functions of writing, often neglected in secondary schools,
and imply the importance of associating the goals of teaching and
testing. They suggest how test exercises are created.

The issue of sampling goes beyond the choice of subject. To
ensure comparability we ask that all write at one time in similar rooms with similar light and ventilation. We limit the time
allowed. Even putting aside the problems of people who develop
particular quirks about where, when, and with what instrument
they write, we still have to deal with people who compose
quickly and neatly and those who labor over each phrase, those
who muddle their way into a draft and depend on second and
third thoughts for finished prose and those who have a formula
for everything. Any test sample favors those who extemporize
well, but we may want to know who polishes well. Furthermore,
on a given day and hour a good writer may be blank. Bad days
hamper people who take objective tests, too, but sheer chance
may reduce the problem of hitting the right answer. Writers, almost by definition, always perform at less than their level of competence, so the reported scores will penalize them; their off days
may be extremely bad and a particular performance may seem to
be extremely bad as a result of a relatively minor choice of details.

One of the most frustrating decisions is how much advice to
offer as part of the task. Letting the writer have a wide choice is

171

often no help at all, for it increases the time spent on deciding what to do. Some test makers offer a first sentence as a way of setting a direction to the writing. At best the prescribed sentence reduces initial fussing by reducing choices, for each element of a text establishes patterns which reduce the options at all subsequent points. By offering something specific to start with, it may reduce writing block. At worst, if the suggested opening strikes the writer as wrong, then the whole effort is lost. The writer wallows in misdirection. In general most teacherly advice, which might be standard on an assignment of homework, simply distracts in a test situation.

Two rules are crucial in thinking about scores derived from a sample of writing. First, the sample must be understood as having limited application, showing at least how well a writer can perform. Other situations might produce quite different results, so interpreters must be careful about over-generalization from a single sample. Second, even the most clever designers of tasks make mistakes. Every task should be field-tested and retested after each revision. In fact, each scoring guide should probably be tried out on sample readers before the actual scoring begins. Guides composed by the most astute editors are sometimes misleading and always omit some sensible solutions to the problems posed, so readers should be encouraged to view unusual responses with open minds.

All of the preparation comes to naught if the readers are not well cared for. The guides and training sessions are crucial, but these scorers are human and must be treated with consideration. They tire, they get hungry, they feel abused. Most of all, they have individual quirks or loss of attention. Test administrators create a pleasant social situation with breaks, food, and signs of appreciation. If the readings last for several days, it is important to see that evenings are pleasant (and not excessively alcoholic) so that mornings are fresh.

But even so papers are routinely examined by two readers, the second reader not seeing the score of the first. When the scores are the same, no problem exists. When the scores differ by one place, usually no problem is perceived even though in fact major differences may exist. When the two scores disagree by two, a referee must settle the difference either by negotiation or by a third reading. The score then is that of the two readers most in agreement. This process provides statistics showing a high level of agreement among readers, a necessary condition if such scoring is to be believed. In fact, on most papers most of the time conversation will show that the readers do agree, or do quickly when conversation restores a flagging attention level. Still, a four-point scale is crude; a low 2 and a high 3 are almost half the scale apart. The scores can agree even when major differences exist about the quality of the writing.

Each kind of testing can provide useful information, but no kind is sufficient as a measure of writing ability. For most purposes combinations of test scores and other information should be used as a basis for practical decisions. Most objective tests are marketed with detailed descriptions of what is being tested in relation to whom, although one should be wary of decisions about how particular questions are designed to represent bodies of information being tested. So too one should be careful of how correlations are checked. Still, within the stated limits the tests can provide one kind of information about writers subject to specified kinds of error. Setting those scores with scores obtained by a different method, and then putting both with information about school records, one can begin to make sound judgments. Given enough different kinds and sources of information we can discover the moot cases for closer personal examination. The point is not to depend on single measures.

Current work on testing is often presented orally at conferences and thus is hard to find. The Educational Testing Service of Princeton and the American College Testing Program of Iowa City conduct continuous research and offer relevant studies of their own work. The National Assessment of Educational Progress has produced a series of reports dealing with their findings on the testing of reading and writing since the late sixties. Earlier NAEP reports can be purchased from the Education Commission of the States, 1600 Lincoln Street, Denver, Colorado 80298. New reports published since the contract for administering NAEP was assigned to ETS can be obtained from NAEP, CN 6710, Princeton, New Jersey 08541 (telephone 800-223-0267). "Writing Trends Across the Decade, 1974–1984" appeared in midsummer of 1986. Additional analyses of the 1984 results will be presented later. One should always be cautious about depending upon newspaper accounts of the reports because problems of condensation from data to reports, from reports to news releases, from releases to actual stories cause the elimination of crucial qualifications of general remarks.

The Instructional Resource Center, Office of Academic Affairs, The City University of New York, publishes a series of research monographs primarily on the experiences of their own extensive program of testing. Marie Jean Lederman, Susan Remmer Ryzewic, Michael Ribaudo, Karen L. Greenberg, and Lynn Quitman Troyka are among the principal researchers. Greenberg, Harvey S. Wiener and Virginia Slaughter have organized a National Network on Testing as a way of keeping current on relevant issues.

Edward White and Linda Polin, under an NIE grant administered through the California State University system, have reported extensively on testing of writing as part of the evaluation of writing programs. The findings are generally explained in a series of essays appearing in 1984 and later in the *Bulletin of the Writing Program Administrators* (WPA). The Education Commission of the States monitors most work in the mass testing of writing, primarily under the direction of Rexford Brown, who also chairs a standing committee on testing for the National Council of Teachers of English. Individual states with statewide assessments also make reports of results of their testing, although rarely do they have much to say about the general practices.

Since mass testing is a managerial tool, it is also a public relations concern. It invites simplified comments on results—usually viewing them with alarm—or accusations of conspiracy and abuse. Even news releases by departments of the agencies doing research work in testing are suspect. In condensing the results of work done by their own people, they often omit significant qualifications in the results or interpretations. Simplifications turn up in headlines. Yet it is the public alarm aroused by the sensational findings that justifies additional funding of basic work. Furthermore, the original justification of funds for the study probably called for information to support present practices or to argue for change. The data are evidence in a debate, and that leads to extreme statements.

Scores are also important for individuals as evidence of achievement, allowing for placement or credit. Ordinarily that means some score is established as a cut-off point even though all scores are approximate. Administrators find their lives quieter if they act as though scores were precise, but they should in the long run always doubt and check so as to prevent a major dislocation caused by overconfidence. Those who take the tests are in no position to challenge in the short term, for almost everyone will assume that any complaint is just sour grapes. The test takers may very well accept the scores as a final statement, and become victims of a self-fulfilling prophecy by thinking of themselves as incompetent, so it is important that they understand its limitations. Or they may with others discover that they have been victims of ill-based judgments and become angry and alienated.

At the level of individual actions and public policy the fear of political consequences distorts our understanding of the information produced by tests. That statement is not a condemnation of tests, but rather an exhortation to resist pressure. In particular it is an exhortation to resist pressures to choose simple measures and treat them as final as well as to avoid making tests an end in themselves.

In a proper educational world tests are devised to check whether or not students have achieved desired goals. The goals should come first. But testing programs sometimes develop their own momentum. The test becomes its own excuse, and educational programs are adapted to fit the test. Such adjustments are always questionable, but for writing the danger is exceptionally serious because writing itself is so complicated. The tests are at best approximate measures, simplifications which can redefine the program of teaching into something trivial. Even if we say that we know there is more to writing than spelling, if we give only spelling tests, then the system will devote an inordinate amount of time to teaching spelling. For all practical purposes, then, writing becomes spelling.

In the end, tests should be part of a larger program of evaluation. The best judgments are those made over a long period of time—a semester, a year, several years—and based on many efforts at writing for many purposes. Ideally several experienced readers or editors will be involved. If that sounds like how a professional writer expects to be judged, it is no coincidence, for it is probably the most accurate way to do the testing. We want to approach it as closely as we can.

Basic Writing

MINA P. SHAUGHNESSY, The City University of
New York

1976

I

THE TEACHING OF WRITING TO SEVERELY UN-
prepared freshmen is as yet but the frontier of a profession, lack-
ing even an agreed upon name. "Remedial" writing is out of favor
for good reasons: it seems inaccurate to speak of beginners,
whether on the tennis court or in a writing class, as remedial, and
the students we are concerned with have generally had but token
instruction in writing; the medical metaphor suggests a disease,
and indeed students assigned to "remedial" classes do get sent to
writing "labs" or "clinics" where their problems are "diag-
nosed"; but worse, it is a soiled word with unhappy associations
that go back to grade school, where many college remedial students began the losing game of "catching up."

Still, the word persists. "English for the disadvantaged"
and "handicapped" English are worse; "compensatory" is only
slightly more neutral; and "developmental" or "basic" writing
tends to get translated into "remedial" when the chips are down. I
will use "basic writing" in this essay, but "remedial" will slip
in often.

There is another problem with identifying the subject; even
where programs and teachers use the word "remedial," we cannot be at all certain that they mean the same thing by it. One

school's remedial student may be another's regular or even advanced freshman. The English A that Sabina Thorne Johnson describes so impressively in her article about remedial English at Berkeley, "Remedial English: The Anglocentric Albatross?" *CE,* 33 (March 1972), 670–85, or the persona paraphrasing recommended by Phyllis Brooks for the same students in "Mimesis: Grammar and the Echoing Voice," *CE,* 35 (Nov. 1973), 161–68, would doubtless strike many teachers from inner-city colleges as unrealistic for their "remedial" classes. Nor can we assume that courses called "freshman composition" are *not* remedial, for many schools, particularly several two-year colleges, have eradicated all labels that carry the old connotations even though their students have the old problems. We cannot be guided by the type of institution either. Some two-year colleges accept no remedial students and some four-year colleges with open admissions policies now have over fifty per cent of their freshmen in remedial classes. Finally, there are distinctions to be made across time. Most colleges have always had some freshmen who couldn't write as well as their peers and often such students ended up in classes that were called remedial, or more crassly, "bonehead" English. L. W. Michaelson's "'Bonehead' Grammar," *Education,* 80 (Jan. 1960), 283–85, catches something of the quality of the course and of the attitudes that shaped it. But this type of course was waning, along with Freshman English, when the new remedial population began to appear in the sixties. In 1964, the first year of the War on Poverty, the headings "cultural deprivation" and "cultural differences" appeared for the first time in *Education Index.* By the next year, they were among the most heavily itemed headings in the *Index.* We can date the "new" remedial English from then.

Given the confusion of terms, therefore, I must try to define the population of writers I have in mind when I refer to basic writing students. K. Patricia Cross in *Beyond the Open Door: New Students to Higher Education* (San Francisco: Jossey-Bass, 1971) has provided the fullest portrait of the "new" students who entered colleges under the open admissions revolution of the sixties.

178

Among the students she describes are many, however, whose skills are beyond the level I would call basic. Nonetheless many of the traits she mentions are familiar—non-academic interests, pragmatic educational goals (credentials and vocational preparation), and fear of failure (although I would prefer to say the expectation of failure in academic situations without necessarily implying a lack of confidence and sense of self in other settings). I would add to this list certain features that define their writing. First, they tend to produce, whether in impromptu or home assignments, small numbers of words with large numbers of errors (roughly from 15 to 35 errors per 300 words) that puzzle and alarm college teachers when they see them for the first time, errors with the so-called regular features of standard English (the past tense of regular verbs, for example, or the plural inflections of nouns), misspellings that appear highly idiosyncratic, syntactic snarls that often seem to defy analysis, and punctuation errors that reflect an unstable understanding of the conventions for marking off the boundaries of sentences and little or no acquaintance with the uses of colons, semi-colons, parentheses, or quotation marks. Second, they seem to be restricted as writers, but not necessarily as speakers, to a very narrow range of syntactic, semantic, and rhetorical options, which forces them into either a rudimentary style of discourse that belies their real maturity or a dense and tangled prose with which neither they nor their readers can cope.

From these features alone we can infer much about their backgrounds. We can infer that they have never written much, in school or out, that they have come from families and neighborhoods where people speak other languages or variant, non-prestigious forms of English and that, while they have doubtless been sensitive to the differences between their ways of speaking and their teachers', they have never been able to sort out or develop attitudes toward the differences that did not put them in conflict, one way or another, with the key academic tasks of learning to read and write and talk in standard English. This situation in turn generated such a maze of misunderstandings of every kind throughout their school years that the one attitude a teacher has come to expect when he steps into his basic writing class is an attitude of mistrust. It is a mistrust only peripherally related to the ideological mistrust of the "establishment" that was cultivated in the sixties. It is rather a less deliberate but more deeply conditioned pessimism about the possibility of ever learning anything or ever being understood in school. It comes from experience, the experience of not having been noticed or respected or heard in too many classrooms, the experience of becoming used to not understanding what books and teachers are saying, of being passed on but never encouraged, of feeling dumb and bored in school. The typical silence of those first days of class is the silence of seasoned watchers of teachers who are trying to determine whether the class is going to be different from all the others and, if not, what strategy will best insure survival.

To recount the conditions that led to the entry during the sixties of large numbers of these students into college classrooms is not within the scope of this essay, but it is important to note that there were urgent conditions, both political and economic, that led administrators to create, often without much forethought or grace, entire remedial wings to their departments or even separate departments that were charged with the task of bringing these deeply unprepared men and women (usually with only a semester or two of low-intensity teaching) to a level of competence that placed them at no great academic disadvantage in regular college classes.

The teachers of these special courses, who were drawn usually from the untenured, junior ranks of English departments, set out to accomplish this task without knowing much about their students or the skills that were to be acquired so swiftly. Having little sense at that point of the ways in which the imperatives of the academy might collide with the social imperatives of the sixties, they simply started trying to teach their students to write. Usually they did first what *their* English teachers had done—or what they wished they had done—and then, as the classroom delivered its data, began to move outward, trying what seemed to be working for others, modifying, inventing, elaborating, but rarely stopping (or having the time to stop) to formulate theories or carry on systematic research.

It was a situation in which teaching clearly *had* to make a difference. So long as one's students could write the kind of prose that gets people through high school there was no pressing need for them to improve. Their writing would not be an embarrassment in academia—merely more of the depersonalized, institutional prose everyone was used to. A sobering analysis of the origins of this prose can be found in Carl Nordstrom, Edward Friedenberg, and Hilary A. Gold's *Society's Children: A Study of Ressentiment in the Secondary School* (New York: Random House, 1967). But here were young adult students, many of them with an experience of the world outside academia and with hard responsibilities in that world which their teachers had not encountered and probably never would. They could write neither in their own voices nor in what Friedenberg has called the "pasteurized prose" of high schools. Nor was it clear to teachers just why their errors and reluctancies did not give way easily under instruction.

Doubtless the richest materials from this period of groping and discovery are unpublished and unpublishable—teachers' journals, class materials (some of which is working its way into textbooks now), departmental memos on pedagogical issues, in-house evaluations, and the records of conference sessions with students. But in English there is no tradition of observation and cumulative publication, as there is in the sciences. Teachers and administrators of writing programs seldom keep systematic files of student writing or of conferences. They keep grade books and return the data to their students. Team research is rare. There are few case studies of student writers (none, to my knowledge, of basic writers), no longitudinal descriptions of writing progress that would enable us to credit successive approximations of good writing or determine sequences of instruction that might help avoid what I. A. Richards once called English teachers' "hugger-mugger, promiscuous leave-it-to-nature style in which the seeds of all things are being strewn over the would-be student's mind" (*Speculative Instruments* [New York: Harcourt, 1955], p. 106).

Without an accumulation of published information across a range of experiences with the new students, we are left with a highly circumscribed literature, essentially the bits and pieces of information that make their way back from a frontier, tempting us to premature judgments about the students and how or what they are learning. The literature consists largely of articles and dissertations which concentrate on two subjects: the students, how they write and what they appear to need; and programs and methods, what they are or how well they are working. I will describe each of these categories briefly, suggesting articles or studies that a basic writing teacher might find useful.

So far, we know the new students mainly through statistical reports on attrition rates, grade-point averages, performance on nationally normed tests, and responses to questionnaires. One wishes for more studies of the sort Rex M. Newton has undertaken in "An Exploratory Study of a Small Group of Disadvantaged Students' First Year on a College Campus" (dissertation, Univ. of Oregon, 1971), in which he recorded and interpreted the behavior of a small group of students for a year. His findings remind us that far more central than statistics on attrition to an understanding of the students is the fact of their being in a new environment which appears to them unrelated to anything in their own backgrounds.

Statistics tell us little directly about the students as writers or even as learners. Surprisingly little effort has been made to analyze the content of their essays, perhaps out of concern for their privacy. Yet Marie Jean Lederman's memorable piece on the self-images of remedial and composition students who were asked on a placement test, "What would you like to come back as if you were re-born tomorrow?" has a resonance few tests could yield.

("A Comparison of Student Projections: Magic and the Teaching of Writing," CE, 34 [Feb. 1973], 674–89). Adrienne Rich, in an essay describing her experiences as a SEEK and open admissions teacher, "Teaching Language in Open Admissions: A Look at the Context," *Harvard English Studies,* 4 (1971), 257–73, has written with exceptional insight of her students' backgrounds and responses to literature. Robert Cumming, in the same issue (pp. 245–55), has given a sensitive account of the literature that "worked" in his classes. The students have written of themselves, often in powerful, generous ways in the transient anthologies that writing classes generate. I recommend the *Basic Writing Anthology* (New York: English Department of City College of N.Y., 1972) because it is the one I know and have used in classes. But beyond this there is little direct description of the students. One seeks a portrait with the depth and complexity of Richard Hoggart's *The Uses of Literacy* (New York: Oxford, 1970), a description of working class culture in England, or a volume such as the Schoolboys of Barbiana wrote in their *Letter to a Teacher* (New York: Random House, 1971), a classic expression of the disadvantaged student's mistrust of the educator and his respect for an education.

Few attempts have been made to describe the writing of the new students. John A. Higgens, in "Remedial Students' Needs Versus Emphasis in Text-workbooks," *CCC,* 24 (May 1973), 188–92, has surveyed writing errors among remedial students at York College and reports that spelling, diction, and sentence logic pose greater problems for the students than grammaticality. He then goes on to demonstrate that current text-workbooks do not address the students' needs. We also have little information about the high school preparation of the students, but it seems safe to assume that their instruction has been not only inadequate but often alienating. A 1963 study of University of Nevada students, Robert McQueen, A. Keith Murray, and Fredericka Evans's "Relationships Between Writing Required in High School and English Proficiency in College," *Journal of Experimental Education,* 31 (Summer 1963), 419–23, shows a clear correlation between the amount of writing done in high school and performance in Freshman Composition. Little has been done to gather from the students themselves their recollections of learning to write in school, but Bonnie Rubenstein's "Say Something in English," *Junior College Journal*, 38 (Oct. 1967), 7–12, with its record of student responses to the word "English," suggests that we might learn much simply by asking students to describe how they learned to write.

While it is clear from direct experience if not from surveys that remedial-level students are reluctant writers, it does not follow that they are not motivated to learn to write. Many of them see the usefulness of this skill not only for college work but in the careers they hope to follow. They may, however, be skeptical about the possibility of acquiring the skill in an English class. (A good case might be made for a very different argument: namely, that teachers are not highly motivated to require writing of students in non-English courses, and that many English teachers still view an assignment to basic writing as a punishment.) Gerald A. Silver, in his study "A Comparative Investigation of Motivation in the Achievement of Remedial and Non-Remedial Students at Los Angeles City College" (dissertation, Univ. of California, 1961), found among 608 remedial and non-remedial students few motivational differences between the two groups but did find that faculty members had a tendency to consider students with high verbal and quantitative skills as highly motivated. Geraldine McMurray Bartee, in another study of student perceptions, "The Perceptual Characteristics of Disadvantaged Negro and Caucasian College Students" (dissertation, East Texas State Univ., 1967), found no support for the assumption that disadvantaged freshmen have lower self-concepts than other students. In fact, in her research a control group of "advantaged" students showed the lowest self-concept of all the groups, and two of the Negro groups of disadvantaged freshmen showed the highest self-concept scores. Such findings point to the need for a better understanding of the ways in which both students and teachers perceive the task of learning to write and how these perceptions serve to supply or cut off the energies needed to do their work.

It has been difficult so far to discover what makes a difference in basic writing teaching. The four-year colleges have produced practically nothing in the way of program evaluations, although many colleges have described their programs as successful. Among the two-year colleges, LeRoy Joseph Dare reports in his "A Study of Remedial Programs in Public Two-year Colleges" (dissertation, Univ. of North Carolina, 1970) that the few colleges that have made studies of their programs are often unwilling or unable to produce statistical data. Meanwhile individual reports on programs are seldom decisive. Thomas J. Farrell has ably reviewed the literature of evaluation in his own study of the general program at Forest Park Community College, "Opening the Door: An Analysis of Some Effects of Different Approaches to Educating Academically High-Risk Students at Forest Park Community College, 1971–1972," (dissertation, St. Louis Univ., 1973). John E. Roueche and R. Wade Kirk have written about junior college programs that have made a difference in *Catching Up: Remedial Education* (San Francisco: Jossey-Bass, 1974). But such studies are evaluations of the over-all remedial efforts of colleges and tell us little about how or how well the students in these programs learn to write.

Where teachers have attempted to evaluate specific methods of writing instruction, the results have generally shown no significant difference among approaches. Allan Lee Slay's "A Comparison of the Effectiveness of Programmed, Handbook, and Non-Formalized Grammar Instruction in Remedial College Freshman English Composition" (dissertation, St. Louis Univ., 1968) found some progress among all groups but no statistically significant differences in writing skills among them. Richard M. Bossone and Max Weiner, in "Three Modes of Teaching Remedial English: A Comparative Analysis" (New York: City University of New York, 1973), found little improvement under any method. Doris G. Sutton and Daniel S. Arnold, comparing the grade-point averages and attrition rates of students in conventional and individualized (writing lab) remedial courses, reported in "The Effects of Two Methods of Compensatory Freshman English," *RTE*, 8 (Feb. 1974), 241–49, that over a two-year period the writing lab students did somewhat better than the conventionally trained students, but the differences, while statistically significant, were not impressive.

Where teachers have reported positive results with specific techniques or course designs (as they have for a range of strategies including card playing, pattern practice, simulation gaming, etc.), their experiments have rarely been replicated. One suspects they are rarely noted. Lucille G. Shandloff's study of the relation between teacher practice and research in written composition suggests little connection between the two ("The Relationship of Freshman Composition Curriculum Practices in Florida Public Community Junior Colleges to Research in the Teaching of Written Composition" [dissertation, Florida State Univ., 1973]).

Despite some excellent individual studies of programs or methods, one is left after reviewing the literature with the sense that there is something premature, repetitive, and unavoidably reductive about our attempts so far to evaluate instruction in writing. Few teachers have been trained for this kind of research. Few schools or programs are organized to generate or process information about their effectiveness, with the result that the individual researcher is overburdened by clerical and administrative duties that quickly discourage experimentation. Furthermore, writing is a slow-developing skill that should be measured over longer periods than a semester, but no system for collecting longitudinal data on writing performance exists to my knowledge in any program. We lack information and the habit of getting information about individual students that would enable us to isolate outside influences such as previous training or career commitments from methods of instruction. We lack adequate (i.e., precise and economical) instruments for measuring writing and then for controlling the unruly variables that swarm about the classroom situation. In the jargon of the systems analysts, we have difficulty measuring output (writing) and even greater difficulty relating output to input (teaching). Finally, we lack a tradition of collaborative research, within colleges as well as among them, that would enable us to combine resources and conduct more systematic experiments. Nowhere in the profession of teaching writing is the frontier more wide open.

Teachers must nonetheless keep pursuing their hunches and describing what "works," even though they lack the means to prove it. And this is largely what the literature in basic writing is—a miscellany of articles on what has been working, or appears to the teacher to have been working, in a variety of places with a variety of teachers and pedagogies. We find among the articles much that has been going on in Freshman English for years. The magic adjective "innovative" should be withheld until one has reviewed Gary Tate and Edward P. J. Corbett's *Teaching Freshman Composition* (New York: Oxford Univ. Press, 1967) and Michael F. Shugrue's summary of curricular programs that were developing in the early sixties under the support of the Office of Education, "New Materials for the Teaching of English: The English Program of the USOE," *PMLA*, 81 (Sept. 1966), 3–38.

Three concentrations among the articles on basic writing seem important to note: an emphasis upon creating what is often called a "humanistic" environment in the classroom; an interest in working out detailed sequences of instruction accompanied by unit tests; a concern with the pre-writing or beginning stages of the composing process. I will suggest readings in each of these areas.

Because he knows little about his students—what they can be expected to find difficult, what their individual silences or reluctancies may mean—the basic writing teacher needs a classroom that encourages open response. Yet, given the amount of work the student must do in order to reach even minimal proficiency within the timetable of the college, the teacher cannot afford to risk the waywardness and easy solipsism that often follow the collapse of the teacher-centered class. Jerome Bruner, in an essay with the misleading title "The Uses of Immaturity," *Intellectual Digest,* Feb. 1973), stresses the importance of employing the socially mature elements in student character for better learning. He recommends collaborative approaches to learning, especially among open admissions students. Basic writing teachers, if one is to judge by the attention they give in their articles to classroom organization, would agree that the teacher-centered model which most of their students associate with school is ineffective. It triggers stereotyped responses that impede learning and is especially unsuited for the highly social activity of writing.

Despite these inadequacies, the traditional classroom, as well as the relationships it fosters, is difficult to replace. Kenneth A. Bruffee has alerted us in "The Way Out: A Critical Survey of Innovations in College Teaching," *CE,* 31 (Jan. 1970), 457–70, to the ways in which the old authoritarianism reappears in the garb of the "decentralized" class, demonstrating that the real barriers to innovation lie within students and teachers and can be removed only by a deeper understanding of the learning process itself and by skill in organizing people to work collaboratively at learning. In "Collaborative Learning: Some Practical Models," *CE,* 34 (Feb. 1973), 634–43, Bruffee offers four models for teaching literature and composition. M. L. J. Abercrombie, reporting in *Anatomy of Judgement* (New York: Basic Books, 1960) on a course she developed to improve the diagnostic judgment of medical students, reviews the fundamental research on the use of group learning in teaching judgment, much of which has obvious relevance to teaching writing. She has also provided a useful short survey of practical methods of group teaching in university education, *Aims and Techniques of Group Teaching,* 3rd ed. (London: Society for Research into Higher Education, 1974, available through Pendragon House, Palo Alto, California).

Implicit in the move to open colleges to students who are not prepared for college work is the assumption that it is both practicable and possible to prepare them once they arrive at college.

Support for this assumption can be found in the writings of several learning theorists, most particularly in John Carroll's "A Model of School Learning," *Teachers College Record,* 64 (May 1963), 723–33, and Jerome Bruner's *Toward a Theory of Instruction* (Cambridge, Mass.: Harvard Univ. Press, 1966). Both writers hold that, given sufficient time and adequate instruction, most people (they would except those with severe learning disabilities and agree that the pace is reduced as learners get older) can learn any subject or master any task whatever its complexity. They may differ greatly, however, in the ways they learn and in the rate at which they learn. Aptitude, Carroll would say, is simply the *amount of time* required by the learner to attain mastery of a learning task, not a limit on the types of tasks a person can successfully undertake. Such a view shifts radically the way a teacher might view achievement, heightening his awareness of the content of instruction and of the importance of individual styles and rates of learning.

Even when teachers are unaware of the theories underlying so-called "mastery" learning, their approaches to teaching basic writing often parallel the approaches recommended by mastery theorists such as Benjamin S. Bloom in "Learning for Mastery," *Evaluation Comment,* 1 (May 1968), published by the Center for the Study of Evaluation of Instructional Programs, Los Angeles. The approach involves breaking the course or subject into smaller units of instruction, each of which is then analyzed into a number of elements and arranged hierarchically for learning. There is frequent testing after each unit (called formative testing) to determine mastery or, where mastery is not achieved, to select a different approach to the lesson.

The analytic approach is not new. Good teachers always decide carefully "what comes after what" and tailor their methods of instruction to their individual students. Still, the mastery system is a more rigorous, conscious attempt at systematized instruction which encourages a scrutiny of the learning-teaching process much needed in basic writing, where many of the tasks yield to sharp definition and measurement. The approach can of course lead to gross simplifications of complex and little-understood skills, but wherever highly definable conventions and patterns are to be acquired (as they are in basic writing, where the conventions of both standard and academic written English usually make up a major part of the content), the principles of mastery learning appear applicable.

They underlie the approaches of many teachers, even those who are not acquainted with the term "mastery teaching." Gilbert Schechtman and William McGannon, in papers delivered at the March 1975 CCCC Conference in St. Louis, described the mastery program in composition that has been developed at Olive-Harvey College, Chicago. Their report, "Mastery Learning," March 14, 1975, includes a sketch of a typical work week in a mastery writing course. The ambitious computer-assisted learning system now under development at Brigham Young University, described in a progress report by Victor C. Bunderson entitled "Team Production of Learner-Controlled Courseware" (Provo, Utah: Brigham Young Univ., May 1973), will incorporate the main features recommended by Bloom for mastery teaching. Helen Mills, in "Individualized Instruction: A Shift in Perspective," an address delivered at the Workshop on Teaching Composition, Appalachia State University, May 10, 1974 (available in ERIC Reports), has described the evolution of her method of teaching the sentence and the paragraph through a sequence of individualized lessons.

Given the reluctance of many basic writing students to risk themselves on the written page and their ignorance of the ways of writers, it is not surprising that basic writing teachers have concentrated on understanding and teaching the art of getting started. Ken Macrorie's description of pre-writing in *Uptaught* (Rochelle Pk., New Jersey: Hayden, 1970) and Peter Elbow's model of the writing process as he develops it in *Writing Without Teachers* (New York: Oxford Univ. Press, 1973) have by now had their effect upon basic writing teaching. In addition, basic writing teachers themselves have proposed imaginative ways of helping students gain access to themselves through written words. Many of their articles support some form of narrative or autobiographical writing as the most "natural" place for the inexperienced writer to begin. Don M. Wolfe, in "A Realistic Writing Program for Culturally Diverse Youth," in *Education of the Disadvantaged,* ed. A. Harry Passow (New York: Holt, 1967), 415–23, has made a strong argument for autobiographical writing. Harvey Wiener, in "Media Compositions: Prelude to Writing," *CE,* 35 (Feb. 1974), 566–74, has proposed media exercises that stimulate students to express their responses as a prelude to writing them down. Again in "The Single Narrative Paragraph and College Remediation," *CE,* 33 (March 1972), 660–69, Wiener stresses the importance of beginning work on the essay with the form that allows for the greatest use of concrete detail from the writer's own experience. Michael Paull also locates "beginning" at the moment of perception and provides in "Invention: Understanding the Relationship between Sensation, Perception, and Concept Formation," *CCC,* 25 (May 1974), 205–09, a sequence of steps for moving from that point into conceptualization.

It would be difficult to argue against the accumulation of experience in basic writing that suggests autobiographical content, expressive forms, and write-think or feel-think models of composing as most effective for beginning writers, even where the intent is to end up with formal academic writing. Certainly experience with children supports a method that encourages the development of both a personal and formal style of writing, with the personal coming first in the sequence of instruction. A pedagogy supporting this idea has been developed at the Institute of Education, University of London, in a project entitled "Writing Across the Curriculum," which has by now generated curricular materials as well as several important books, the latest of which is *Understanding Children Writing,* Tony Burgess, ed. (Middlesex, England: Penguin, 1972), an analysis of students of various ages writing both expressive and formal papers on a range of subjects.

Still, the special conditions of the remedial situation, that is, the need to develop within a short time a style of writing and thinking and a background of cultural information that prepare the student to cope with academic work, create a distinctive tension that almost defines the profession—a constant, uneasy hovering between the imperatives of format and freedom, convention and individuality, the practical and the ideal. Just where the boundaries between these claims are to be drawn in basic writing is by no means clear. Some would argue for a gradual exposure of academic subjects and skills through the extension of the remedial concern (but not the remedial structures and styles) into other courses, as in block programming and interdisciplinary curriculums, or into the entire college experience; others would press for a concentrated, direct approach to the distinctive tasks of academia, arguing that for students to lay claim to their critical and analytical powers and to cultivate the formal discursive style associated with academic work is no less "creative" or "personal" than the activities (poetry, stories, etc.) usually associated with those words.

The debate has not yet surfaced among basic writing teachers in formal or scholarly ways. It is more an undercurrent that unsettles staff meetings and most probably confuses students who must often move between semesters from one pedagogy to another. As I will suggest later, a better understanding of the nature of academic writing may help teachers move more effectively and imaginatively into the thick of the task their students face in learning to write for diverse audiences.

II

Experience with the new students so far suggests that at least some of the premises that governed the teaching of writing in the past, premises that most English teachers inherited from their own training, are problematic in the basic writing class. I have mentioned the problem, for example, of mistrust which results when students define their situations in the classroom very differently from the way teachers define them. Whether a teacher uses games or computers or a grammar book to teach standard inflections, whether the need for evidence in academic discourse is illustrated by slides or dialogues or rules, the student who experiences the grammars and logics of academia as competitive with those he has acquired on his own is certain to have difficulty mastering his lessons unless his teacher is prepared to mediate between the two worlds.

This is a problem college teachers rarely thought about in the past. Criticized individually, perhaps, for being tough or easy or boring or unapproachable, they rarely felt called upon to justify their subject matter as well. They taught "the King's English," not a standard dialect, the universals of sound reasoning, not "linear causality." They assumed a cultural trust, a vast body of unspoken but shared routines and information, which freed them from the need to explain what they were up to.

But once having discovered that he and his students do not share a universe of discourse but must discover one another's, the teacher begins to look with different eyes at his subject matter, much as a traveler begins to discover the assumptions and features of his *own* culture by observing someone else's. This transforms his task, which is no longer simply to make the old lessons clearer and simpler nor yet to abandon the goal of teaching students the national language and its uses but to try to understand why the conventions and routines that seem so simple to him are not simple to his students. Thus he does not so much simplify as go deeper into his subject. It is no longer enough, for example, to ask, "How do I teach students to write correctly?" He must first ask, "What is correctness?" Not "How do I get students to be logical?" but "What is the context within which the logic and modes of academic discourse have developed?" Not "How do I get more adverbs or embedded clauses or free modifiers?" but "What are the conditions that give rise to greater sentence complexity?"

Such questions lead the teacher far beyond the immediate problem he is attempting to solve, even beyond the territory of his expertise. Thus the "simple" *s* inflection upon which so many hours are spent in remediation may involve the teacher in larger considerations than he might expect if he views himself as only a sentence mechanic. The teacher must know more about language and learning than English teachers have had to know in the past— more about how people acquire languages, how language functions in different social settings, what writing is as a product and a process, and what theories of learning might inform his pedagogy. The teacher faces, in short, the formidable task of extrapolating from a number of complex, even turbulent, fields whatever insights and information will serve him in his work with his students.

In what remains of this essay, I will suggest readings I would expect to be helpful to teachers as they attempt to close the gap between Monday morning and the large themes of inquiry that now dominate the study of langauge.

Classic Studies of Language

While the documents of science are always superseded, the outstanding documents continue to be worth reading. Not only does much of what the scientist said continue to be valid, but the way he observed and thought is communicated in his work, and the reader is thus apprenticed to him through what he wrote. Among the outstanding documents in the study of language are four which seem of special value to the writing teacher. Leonard Bloomfield's *Language* (New York: Holt, 1933) was the handbook for American linguists for at least twenty years. Historically it is the link between the "old" and the "new" grammars, but beyond that, an example of a brilliant linguistic intelligence at work. Edward Sapir's *Language* (New York: Harcourt, 1921) is a philosophical effort to get at the nature of language by describing its variability, its elements and processes, and its relation to thought and culture. With its combination of grammatical and cultural insights and its non-technical discussion of the relation of sound to the development of language it is still perhaps the most stimu-

194

lating and re-orienting book a writing teacher can find. Benjamin Lee Whorf's reflections on the influence of native languages upon thought in *Language, Thought and Reality*, ed. John B. Carroll (New York: Wiley, 1956) have been argued over for years, but his sensitivity to the ways in which particular languages order and shape our perceptions along culturally important lines is of importance to a basic writing teacher. Finally, Otto Jespersen's attempt in *The Philosophy of Grammar* (New York: Norton, 1965) to explore the ideas underlying grammatical concepts such as tense or number and, beyond that, to suggest the outlines of a universal grammar, remains a tremendously invigorating work for the English teacher.

Readings in Grammar

The objectives of linguists and teachers are of course quite different. The linguist, seeking to describe the neutral possibilities in language, develops an ideal model of the language that serves as his instrument of analysis; the teacher, seeking to control certain features of a student's language in the interest of clarity, style, and correctness, develops an ad hoc grammar that draws from whatever grammatical models serve him in particular situations. Thus the linguist is committed to *a* system and the teacher to whatever works, which at one point may be traditional grammar or just plain drill and at another some aspect of transformational or structural grammar.

With the stormy allegiances that have developed among linguists, however, and the great complexity of their theories, teachers have tended either to become discipled to one grammatical system, whatever its inefficiencies in certain areas, or to piece together their classroom grammars on the sly, somewhat embarrassed about their eclecticism, even when it appears to be working. The wisest and clearest statement on the uses of grammatical theories in the English class is James Deese's "The Psychology of Learning and the Study of English," in *The Learning of Language,* ed. Carroll E. Reed (New York: Appleton-Century-

Crofts, 1971), pp. 157–85. This should be read before a teacher ventures into current linguistic theory. Following Deese's essay, I recommend a general guide to theoretical linguistics such as John Lyons's *Introduction to Theoretical Linguistics* (Cambridge: Cambridge Univ. Press, 1969), which is comprehensive and assumes no previous knowledge of the field. Then the teacher might turn to two individual works that have been of value to basic writing teachers. Charles Fries' *The Structure of English* (New York: Harcourt, 1952) demonstrates the difference between a normative and a descriptive approach to language, specifically to the sentence, and proposes a break-up of old grammatical categories, thereby refreshing one's response to the sentence even where it does not produce a conversion to Fries' terminology. Noam Chomsky's *Syntactic Structures* (The Hague: Mouton, 1957) is the key to understanding all subsequent interpretations and applications of his grammatical theories. Because of the conceptual density of this work, the reader may also want to consult John Lyons's explication of Chomsky's theories in *Noam Chomsky* (New York: Viking, 1971). I would add two works on semantics: Stephen Ullman's *Semantics: An Introduction to the Science of Meaning* (Oxford: Basil Blackwell, 1970), particularly chapter 4 on transparent and opaque words, which illuminates many of the vocabulary difficulties that arise in basic writing; and Geoffrey Leech's *Semantics* (Middlesex, England: Pelican, 1974), which is also an introduction to the science but one that devotes more time to theoretical semantics.

Attempts to study the relationship of traditional grammar study to writing go back at least to 1906 and suggest with unusual consistency that traditional grammar has not made a difference. J. Stephen Sherman has summarized this long history of research in *Four Problems in Teaching English: A Critique of Research* (Scranton, Penn.: International Textbook, 1969), pp. 116–35. Studies of the effect of the study of more recent grammars, namely structural and transformational grammars, upon writing are somewhat more encouraging. Jean McColley reports some positive results for structural grammar in "Effects of a Method of Teaching Sentence Structure upon Sentence Structure Used in Writing," in *RTE*, 8 (Spring 1967), 95–97, as does Eva Klauser in her comparison of structural and traditional methods in "A Comparison of a Structural Approach and a Traditional Approach to the Teaching of Grammar in an Illinois Junior High School" (dissertation, Univ. of Colorado, 1964). The history of experiments in sentence-combining has been well summarized by Sandra L. Stotsky in "Sentence-Combining as a Curricular Activity: Its Effect on Written Language Development and Reading Comprehension," *RTE*, 9 (Spring 1975), 30–71. Among the works she mentions, John C. Mellon's *Tranformational Sentence Combining*, Research Report No. 6 (Champaign, Ill.: NCTE, 1966), and Frank O'Hare's *Sentence Combining*, Research Report No. 15 (Champaign, Ill.: NCTE, 1971) are the most useful sources of information on sentence-combining as a method of instruction. James Wesley Howell has studied transformational approaches among remedial writers and reports positively on the results in "A Comparison of Achievement of Students in Remedial English Using a Linguistic and a Traditional Approach" (dissertation, New York Univ., 1973).

Many teachers claim impressive results among remedial students from grammar study of all kinds. Unfortunately their claims are seldom supported by reliable research descriptions, but the special constraints within which they teach and the special uses to which they would put grammar suggest that yet another study of the relation between grammar study and writing may be in order. At this point, one can simply report a remarkable kind of eclecticism among basic writing teachers. Some hold to the effectiveness of traditional grammar drill; others subscribe to the total course designs developed by linguists such as Paul Roberts and Robert L. Allen; still others report various applications and adaptations of more recent grammars to remedial-level instruction. Elaine Chaika's description of how she leads her students to a discovery of sentences, reported in "Who Can Be Taught?" *CE*,

35 (Feb. 1974), 575–83, is sensitive and linguistically enlight-ened. Jacqueline Griffin's description of her eclectic grammar, combining insights from Robert Allen's sector analysis, Chom-sky's transformations, and Francis Christensen's multi-level sen-tences, demonstrates well how the ways of teachers must depart from the ways of linguists ("Remedial Composition at an Open Door College," *CCC,* 20 [Dec. 1967], 360–63).

Both structural and transformational grammars have offered teachers more open, more potentially productive ways of view-ing student sentences. They have affirmed, as prescriptive gram-mar did not, the resourcefulness of speakers, whose intuitions about their native languages provide the linguistic data from which grammatical rules are derived. "A speaker of language," writes Wayne O'Neill in his foreword to N. R. Cattell's excellent introduction to present-day grammar, *The New English Grammar* (Cambridge, Mass.: MIT Press, 1969), p. xiv, "has a knowledge of it in a way that he has knowledge of few other things. The knowledge . . . can be tapped in ways that his knowledge of American history, say, cannot be until he is filled full of the facts of American history. Moreover, in grammar there are no un-challenged or unchallengeable explanations; the teacher does not and cannot hold the secret in his back pocket."

Readings on Language in Various Social Settings

Many recent events have turned our attention to the fact of diversity in language and to the controversies that arise when the social and political hierarchies that have held languages and dia-lects in their "places" begin to give way. The basic writing class-room is simply one of the places where the fact of diversity has become not merely an "academic" topic but a complex and trou-bling issue affecting what English teachers teach and how they teach it. The literature on diversity can be divided into works that attempt to analyze the problems that arise out of diversity and works that describe the languages that are the sources of this di-versity, but the borderlines tend at times to be obscure.

Among the first group are three collections of essays on aspects of diversity I would recommend for basic writing teachers. *Language and Poverty,* ed. Frederick Williams, Institute for Research on Poverty Monograph Series (Chicago: Markham Pub. Co., 1970) is valuable for the variety of views and issues it explores through the papers of linguists, sociolinguists, and educators who disagree among themselves about the ways in which poverty affects language. Three essays in particular serve to articulate basic differences: William Labov's much anthologized essay "The Logic of Nonstandard English" (Chapter 9); Siegfried Engelmann's behavioristic proposal for teaching standard English, "How to Construct Effective Language Programs for the Poverty Child" (Chapter 6); and Basil Bernstein's attempt to define the differences in language styles according to class styles of socialization, in "A Sociolinguistic Approach to Socialization: With Some Reference to Educability" (Chapter 3).

The Summer 1973 issue of *Daedalus,* entitled *Language as a Human Problem,* gathers the views of leading anthropologists, educators, and linguists on the phenomenon of linguistic diversity. It is a much broader treatment of language than the *Language and Poverty* collection, with several essays on language variations in other countries. The collection includes Dell Hymes's powerful essay "On the Origins and Foundations of Inequality Among Speakers" (pp. 59–86), with its appeal for a shift from the study of languages in the interest of cultural hegemony to the study of languages in contexts of inequality for the purpose of transforming these inequities "through knowledge of the ways in which language is actually organized as a human problem and resource."

A third collection, *Functions of Language in the Classroom,* ed. Courtney B. Cazden, Vera P. John, and Dell Hymes (New York: Teachers College Press, 1972), attempts to promote an anthropological perspective on the language problems that arise in the classroom. Directed largely toward elementary-school situations, the essays nonetheless pierce many of the myths that follow students to college.

The literature on social dialects has not concerned itself directly with the college-enrolled adult so much as with children or with youths who for social reasons have resisted the assimilation of standard forms of English. What research we have on second-language and dialect interference suggests that college-level remedial students, whatever their native dialects or languages, end up with a common stock of difficulties with standard English. Marilyn S. Sternglass reported in "Similarities and Differences in Nonstandard Syntactic Features in the Compositions of Black and White College Students in Freshman Remedial Writing Classes" (dissertation, Univ. of Pittsburgh, 1973) that the differences in frequency of nonstandard linguistic patterns between the two groups of freshmen were not significant enough to require separate language materials for each group. Samuel A. Kirschner and Howard G. Poteet's study, "Non-Standard English Usage in the Writing of Black, White, and Hispanic Remedial English Students in an Urban Community College," RTE, 7 (Winter 1973), 351–55, also found similar types of non-standard English usages, generally with the same frequency.

To what extent more subtle problems in syntax, vocabulary, and organization are related to dialect at this level we do not know and probably will not until teachers become their own ethnographers. The most useful model for this kind of study remains William Labov's Language in the Inner City (Philadelphia: Univ. of Pennsylvania Press, 1972), particularly the final chapter of that study where Labov examines across a range of ages the devices in the vernacular for indicating the main point in a narrative. Through such insights it should be possible to help students see analogies between what they know and do and what academic tasks demand.

Valuable facts about specific dialects can be found in the collection Culture, Class, and Language Variety (Urbana, Ill.: NCTE, 1972), particularly William Card and Virginia McDavid's listing of the main problem areas in grammar (Chapter 6) and Al Davis's "English Problems of Spanish Speakers" (Chapter 9). The Spring

1975 issue of the *Basic Writing Journal* contains three useful articles on dialect interference in the writing of remedial-level students of college age: Barbara Quint Gray's "Dialect Interference in Writing: A Tripartite Analysis," pp. 14–22, which proposes three categories of interference that call for different types of instruction; Betty Rizzo and Santiago Villafane's "Spanish Influence on Written English," pp. 62–71; and Nancy Lay's "Chinese Language Interference in Written English," pp. 50–61. John Joseph Collins has measured deviations from standard written English among sixty-six disadvantaged college freshmen, ninety percent black, and presents a useful list of the most frequent deviations in "Deviations from Standard English in Written Compositions of Disadvantaged College Freshmen and Regular Admissions Students at Glassboro State College" (dissertation, Temple Univ., 1971). A convenient list of Black English features appears in Ralph W. Fasold and Walter A. Wolfram's "Some Linguistic Features of Negro Dialect," in *Contemporary English,* ed. David Shores (Philadelphia: Lippincott, 1972), pp. 53–85. Mary Jane Cook and Amy Sharp have described specific interference problems among Navajo students in "Problems of Navajo Speakers in Learning English," *LL,* 16, nos. 1 and 2 (1966), 21–29.

Because of the quasi-foreign nature of the difficulties basic writing students have with formal English, many of the techniques developed in foreign-language teaching seem to be applicable to basic writing. Among these techniques, contrastive analysis, a method that uses a common analytic frame to describe the mother tongue and the target language at those points where differences between the languages produce errors, has been much discussed but not well researched. A full curriculum using contrastive materials has been under development for several years at Brooklyn College, New York, under the direction of Carroll E. Reed and Milton Baxter. In a project conducted at Clafin College in the early sixties the techniques of oral-aural pattern practice proved effective in teaching standard forms to speakers of Black dialect. San-Su C. Lin has reported on the project in "An Experiment in Changing Dialect Patterns," *CE,* 24 (May 1963), 644–47. For a wider perspective on the possibilities and problems with ESL approaches in the teaching of English to natives, I recommend two essays: Peter Strevens's "Second Language Learning," *Daedalus* (Summer 1973), 149–60, and J. C. Catford's "The Teaching of English as a Foreign Language," in *The Teaching of English,* ed. Randolph Quirk and A. H. Smith (London: Oxford Univ. Press, 1964), pp. 137–59.

Readings on Writing

In his excellent table of specifications for writing in "Evaluation of Learning in Writing," in *Handbook on Formative and Summative Evaluations of Student Learning,* ed. Benjamin S. Bloom, J. Thomas Hastings, and George F. Madaus (New York: McGraw-Hill, 1971), p. 770, Joseph J. Foley lists eighteen items under "content" and eighteen under "behavior." Each item could in turn be elaborately subdivided. But even with such refinements, the complexity of the writing act would barely be suggested. Somehow people of ordinary abilities nonetheless learn to write. Most of them acquire the skill over such a long period and in such a variety of contexts that we can't claim to know how they learned. But the question of training becomes crucial when we face the basic writing student, who must acquire through explicit instruction what others absorbed unconsciously over many years. One seeks therefore to know more precisely how writing differs from the other language skills the student has already acquired as a speaker and reader and how the skills he has support or interfere with his attempts to write.

Some stress the continuity between speaking and writing and encourage easy transitions between the two forms of language. John Hawkes's Voice Project, described in "An Experiment in Teaching Writing to College Freshmen" (Stanford University, California, 1967), was one of the early efforts to develop writing skills among unprepared students through a talk–write method. Where orality and literacy are perceived as vastly different forms of expression that have in the past given rise to different cultures, there is a more deliberate attempt to build careful transitions between talk and formal writing. Thomas J. Farrell, pursuing the distinctions that Walter J. Ong has developed in his broad cultural histories, has proposed a curriculum that uses such techniques as glossing and oral reading to prepare students to comprehend and produce academic literature in "Open Admissions, Orality, and Literacy," *Journal of Youth and Adolescence,* 3 (1974), 247–60.

There is a sense in which writing is itself a special dialect, with not only its own syntax and vocabulary but even its own cognitive style, as Lev Vygotsky suggests in *Thought and Language* (Cambridge, Mass.: MIT Press, 1962), pp. 98–101. This means that while the student's competence as a speaker serves as a bridge to writing, his real models for written language are probably absorbed through reading. Thus reading is inextricably linked to writing, much as the talk of adults is linked to the infant's acquisition of speech. The influence is doubtless subtle and pervasive. John M. Broderick's analysis of formal and informal texts by proficient and non-proficient writers, reported in "Usage Varieties and Writing Competencies" (dissertation, Georgetown Univ., 1972), not only finds that the vocabularies of proficient writers are larger and include verbs that increase the syntactical options of the writers but also suggests that the sense of how to use these words is acquired through careful readings of formal texts. I. A. Richards has written both practically and philosophically on the interrelatedness of reading and writing and on writing as a distinctive instrument with which the learner "can examine at another tempo and in another form and for the first time the miracles he has been accomplishing fleetingly in speech" ("Instructional Engineering," in *The Written Word* by Sheridan Baker, Jacques Barzun, and I. A. Richards [Rowley, Mass.: Newbury House, 1971], p. 67).

The writer is also engaged as a peculiar sort of reader in relation to his own text, shifting from the persona of the writer to that of the reader as he writes and then becoming his own copy editor after he has finished composing. Many of the students' writing problems are reading problems: inflectional and mechanical errors, syntactical snarls, and many misspellings. We need to know more about the perceptions and coordinations involved in such reading. Kenneth Goodman's *Miscue Analysis* (Urbana, Ill.: NCTE, 1973) suggests techniques of diagnosis that might be applied to the good proofreader as well as the good reader. Frank Smith's *Understanding Reading* (New York: Holt, 1971) analyzes the reading process in the light of recent research in such areas as cognition, perception, and linguistics. There exists as yet no analysis of the spelling problems of basic writers and therefore no adequate way of tending to a difficulty that seriously handicaps students both as readers and writers.

Little attention has yet been given also to the kind of writing students are expected to produce and read while they are in college and afterwards in most professions. Yet only by understanding the situation of the writer in an academic community can the student grasp the purpose behind those features of academic writing that give him difficulty. The attention to examples and evidence, the well-marked routes of reasoning, the tone of "fairness," the predictable formats of essays and research papers—all arise from the nature of the task: namely, to present to an anonymous, critical audience ideas that are both new and possibly unsound. (Again, unless the student has played the role of critical reader, the conventions of academic writing can but appear arbitrary.) As I have mentioned, teachers disagree about which sequence of lessons leads most efficiently to the mastery of academic writing. Some would even abandon the goal. It is an old argument, but the issues that underlie it might be clarified by a closer look at the literature on discourse analysis and the writing process.

James L. Kinneavy's *A Theory of Discourse* (Englewood Cliffs, New Jersey: Prentice-Hall, 1971) helps sort out the differences between the aims and modes of discourse, the first referring to what he calls referential, literary, persuasive, and expressive forms of discourse and the second to ways of thinking about reality (narrating, describing, classifying, etc.) that are used in all types of discourse. This useful distinction suggests a sequence in which each mode might be taught across a range of discourse, from expressive to referential so that the student is repeatedly exposed to the critical stance and analytical methods of academic writing and yet not cut off from the resources he brings to the classroom, the experience of having classified, compared, and described features of the world he has lived in for eighteen or more years.

A better understanding of the writing process might similarly save us from false dichotomies between content and correctness or creativity and convention, for what little we understand about the process suggests that writing includes both generative and administrative actions, the proliferation of subordinate levels of generality and the control of these powers in the interest of making a point. Janet Emig's pioneering study *The Composing Processes of Twelfth Graders,* Research Report 13 (Urbana, Ill.: NCTE, 1971) reveals that students do not compose the way they or their teachers think they do, that in fact schools have failed to create the conditions that encourage both the impulse and ability to write. If the composing processes of competent writers are little known, we can be certain that even less is known about the ways incompetent writers set about writing their papers. We can observe that the characteristic behaviors of good writers which Charles K. Stollard lists in his study "An Analysis of the Writing Behavior of Good Student Writers," *RTE*, 8 (Summer 1974), 206–18, are foreign to basic writers and often to the circumstances in which they must write—spending time contemplating the assignment, extensive revising, contemplating the work at intervals, and having a clear purpose for writing.

We know little about how student writers typically behave or how they ought to behave, however. Among the works on language learning, three should be mentioned, and with these I will conclude my recommendations. Jean Piaget's *The Language and Thought of the Child* (New York: World, 1955) has already influenced many writing teachers but no effort has as yet been made to determine how accurately the developmental model Piaget describes for children fits the experience of the young adult learning to write for college. Robert Selman has pointed up the difficulties that arise when Piaget's theory is applied to education in his review of Hans Furth and Harry Wach's *Thinking Goes to School* in the *Harvard Educational Review*, 45 (Feb. 1975), 127–34. Robert Zoellner's monograph, "A Behavioral Pedagogy for Composition," *CE,* 30 (Jan. 1969), 267–320, is a model of the kind of rigorous and informed thinking that must take place before there is any substantial yield for writing from current learning theory. The pedagogy he proposes is in many ways supported by the experience in basic writing classrooms. Finally, James Britton's *Language and Learning* (Middlesex, England: Penguin, 1970) is a sensitive attempt to trace the development of language in the child and to distinguish the different functions of language that develop as the child matures. Many of the strands of research we have touched upon here are brought together in Britton's work in a way that makes them seem close to the concerns of the teacher.

I began by saying that the teaching of writing to unprepared college-age students is but the frontier of a profession. The readings I have cited in this essay must suggest that this is so. For basic writing teachers, the world is indeed all before them. The skill they have contracted to teach is itself among the most complex of human activities and the students who sit in their classrooms, young, intelligent, and miseducated men and women, depend as students have never depended before upon having good teachers. The "remediation" of their teachers may, in fact, be the most important education going on today.

An Update of the Bibliography on Basic Writing

ANDREA LUNSFORD, Ohio State University

1986

MINA SHAUGHNESSY CLOSES THE PRECEDING essay by reiterating her belief that "the teaching of writing to unprepared college-age students is but the frontier of a profession." Insofar as we have been able to explore and expand the boundaries of this frontier in the last ten years, we have done so largely on the basis of the chartings and directions pointed to in Shaughnessy's own writing. Any review of basic writing in the last decade, therefore, must begin with her *Errors and Expectations* (Oxford University Press, 1977). This classic text has been widely praised for its method, its meticulous attention to student writing, its search for order and pattern amid seeming chaos. But many commentators have also noted what seems finally its most important contribution: its attitude toward students, teachers, and research. This attitude is a revolutionary one, respectful of the intelligent but unprepared students, infinitely patient with teachers who are bewildered by this startling new frontier, and ultimately demanding that basic writing research be rigorous, sound, academically respectable.

Shaughnessy's attitude toward the welter of incomprehensible errors confronting her is a case in point, and she made that attitude the cornerstone of her book. Convinced that basic writers are not "handicapped" or "ineducable," she began a systematic search for the logic of the errors, for the reasons informing them. In her insistence that "Basic writing students write the way they do not because they are slow or non-verbal, indifferent to or incapable of academic excellence, but because they are beginners and must, like all beginners, learn by making mistakes" (p. 5), she applied the insight of philosophers such as Michael Polanyi and Gilbert Ryle that error is a way of learning, and hence she caught our attention and our interest. Errors were, in this view, not mistakes to be rubbed out or deplored but exercises in competence. This is a profound and, for many writing teachers, a radical view of error, and it has not only challenged basic writing teachers to "transcend their deficiencies" (p. 294) and to chart new territory; it has challenged our traditional view of accessibility to college and our assumptions about literacy as well.

The association of intelligence (and indeed of moral value as well) with literacy has strong historical precedent in the United States. In "Literacy and the Direct Assessment of Writing: A Diachronic Perspective," in *Current Issues in the Assessment of Writing,* ed. R. Donovan, K. Greenberg, and B. Schier-Peleg (Longman, 1986), Stephen P. Witte and his co-authors trace this association, noting in particular M. B. Hillegas's 1912 "Scale for the Measurement of Quality in English Composition by Young People." Hillegas's scale and the conclusions he draws on the basis of it assign high value to "literary writing" about works in the accepted literary canon and relegate writing about everyday life in "ordinary" language to the low end of the scale. In this way, the scale implicitly equates literacy with intelligence and literariness, and illiteracy with "low" topics and low intelligence.

This equation has been vigorously attacked in the last twenty years by those who have sought to describe non-traditional students and point out the inadequacies of educational institutions that exclude them from higher education. As Robert Lyon has pointed out, when Shaughnessy wrote, "It was clear from several essays on Open Admissions and from several letters to the *Times* that examples of unskilled writing by nontraditional students were considered a powerful weapon by those opposed to the broadening of higher education" ("Mina Shaughnessy and the Teaching of Writing," *JBW*, 3 [Fall/Winter 1980], 5). In such an atmosphere, Mina Shaughnessy's courage in publicly attending to such infelicitous writing is important, and her interest in and commitment to an expanded understanding of literacy lead us to consider a number of important works on that subject.

In "The Language of Exclusion: Writing Instruction at the University," Mike Rose addresses the question of accessibility to higher education as he attempts to loosen some of the linguistic binds that surround remediation in general and basic writing in particular (*CE*, 47 [April 1985], 341–59). "Remediation" and "illiteracy" are two of the terms he tries to release from reductive definitions and the negative semantic freight they traditionally carry: "If we fully appreciate [Shaughnessy's] message, we see how inadequate and limiting the remedial model is. Instead, we need to define our work as transitional or as initiatory, orienting, or socializing to what David Bartholomae and Patricia Bizzell call the academic discourse community. This redefinition is not just a semantic sleight-of-hand. If truly adopted, it would require us to reject a medical-deficit model of language, to acknowledge the rightful place of all freshmen in the academy, and once and for all to replace loose talk about illiteracy with more precise and pedagogically fruitful analysis" (p. 358). (See Bartholomae's "Inventing the University," in *When a Writer Can't Write: Studies in Writer's Block and Other Composing Process Problems*, ed. Mike Rose [New York: Guilford Press, 1985]; and Bizzell, "College Composition: Initiation into the Academic Discourse Community," *Curriculum Inquiry*, 12 [1982], 191–207.)

Rose's work points up concerns over definitions and pseudo-definitions of literacy, and clearly the term is very much in flux. Harvey Graff, for instance, argues that we are today in the midst of a "literacy myth. We do not know precisely what we mean by literacy or what we expect individuals to achieve from their instruction in and possession of literacy. . . . We continue to apply standards of literacy that—owing to our uncertainties—are inappropriate and contradictory. . . ." (*The Literacy Myth* [New York: Academic Press, 1979], p. 323; for more historical discussion of literacy, see Graff's *Literacy and Social Developments in the West: A Reader* [Cambridge: Cambridge University Press, 1981]). The debate over definition is carried forward in a number of volumes published recently. John Oxenham's *Literacy*, for example, suggests that the study of literacy is a young branch of investigation searching for form and goes on to question whether current notions of literacy will not simply become irrelevant "to large areas of everyday communication, commerce, politics, administration, domestic life, and leisure. . ." (London: Routledge and Kegan Paul, 1980, p. 133). Other definitions and arguments are offered in *Perspectives on Literacy*, ed. Richard Beach and P. David Pearson (College of Education, University of Minnesota, 1978; see especially John R. Bormuth's "Literacy Policy and Reading and Writing Instruction," pp. 13–41), and in Robert Pattison's *On Literacy* (New York: Oxford University Press, 1982), in which he identifies a "new literacy": its "commitment is to the immediacy of the Word, its art form is lyric poetry, its spirit is set against the formal impositions of the old literacy" (p. 122). Other writers concentrate on relating the traditional concept of literacy to biliteracy (A. L. Becker, "Literacy and Cultural Change: Some Experiences," in *Literacy for Life: The Demand for Reading and Writing*, ed. Richard W. Bailey and Robin Melanie Fosheim [New York: MLA, 1983], pp. 45–51) or to the mass media (Donald Lazere, "Literacy and the Mass Media: The Political Implications," forthcoming in *New Literary History*) or to new computer technologies (Paul A. Strassmann, "Information Systems and Literacy," in *Literacy for Life*, pp. 115–21). Still others debate whether (and how) print literacy is related to the way students think and write (Thomas J. Farrell, "Developing Literacy: Walter J. Ong and Basic Writing," *JBW*, 2 [Fall/Winter 1978], 30–51; Frank J. D'Angelo, "Literacy and Cognition: A Developmental Perspective," in *Literacy for Life,* pp. 97–114; and D'Angelo, "Luria on Literacy: The Cognitive Consequences of Reading and Writing," in *Literacy as a Human Problem,* ed. James C. Raymond [University: University of Alabama Press, 1982], pp. 154–69).

If we can find no current consensus on definitions of literacy, there does seem to be general agreement that, as James Raymond points out in the introduction to *Literacy as a Human Problem,* "we must be more cautious and less doctrinaire in our deliberations about literacy and its human consequences" (p. x). In addition, most writers in this new field of literacy studies agree that questions of literacy can never be separated from questions of economic, social and political power. Thus teachers of basic writing need to be aware of the debate over definitions of literacy and, more importantly, need to examine their own definitions, the ones they use to inform their classes, and the ones their colleges and universities use to provide, or to limit, enrollment and hence access to higher education.

Defining the population of student writers we refer to as "basic" also presents difficult problems, which were first clearly elucidated in Shaughnessy's work and in the sources she cites in the preceding essay in this book. During the last few years, Lynn Troyka has done much to elaborate on this work. In "Perspectives on Legacies and Literacy in the 1980's," *CCC,* 33 (Oct. 1982), 252–62, Troyka tells us that our decade's non-traditional students are older, that "they usually represent the first generation in their families to go to college," that they are often parents and often women, that they have jobs, that many barely finished high school, and that "not a few are foreign born" (p. 253). (Troyka reports that "currently 300,000 foreign students attend America's colleges and universities; by the early 1990's at least 1,000,000 such students are expected." The growing foreign student population and the even faster growing number of students whose native language is not English greatly complicate definitions both of basic writing and of literacy. As Richard Lanham of UCLA notes, this shift in population will surely present one of the greatest challenges our discipline has had to face.) The legacies Troyka identifies are also helpful in describing basic writers: they are "highly gregarious and social" (p. 256); they are "more comfortable in an oral rather than a written mode"; they "are holistic thinkers," (p. 258); and they are "ambivalent about learning" (p. 260). Explaining and exemplifying each of these legacies in turn, Troyka provides a balanced and helpful view of these students, their strengths as well as their weaknesses. As Troyka recognizes, however, descriptions of basic writing populations shift from college to college, setting to setting, and we need to know much more about what constitutes basic writing in particular settings. Toward that end, Troyka has gathered a national sample of the prose of basic writers from two- and four-year institutions in order to draw an inductive definition of "basic writing" based on analysis of their texts (see Lynn Q. Troyka, "Context for Basic Writing," in *A Sourcebook for Basic Writing Teachers,* ed. Theresa Enos [New York: Random House, 1986]; for further descriptions—and challenges to descriptions—of basic writers, see Andrea Lunsford, "What We Know—and Don't Know—About Remedial Writing," *CCC,* 29 [1978], 47–52; and George H. Jensen, "The Reification of the Basic Writer," *JBW,* 5 [Spring 1986], 52–64).

Error, Dialect, Grammar

Shaughnessy's breakthrough in studying the products and particularly the errors of basic writers has paid off in a number of studies which have helped us understand these error patterns better. Among those following Shaughnessy's lead in viewing error as an active part of learning are Barry Kroll and John Schafer, whose "Error Analysis and the Teaching of Composition," *CCC,* 29 (Dec. 1978), 242–48, provides practical advice on how to shift our own attitudes to error and thus help our students identify sources of mistakes. Others provide help in understanding the kinds of errors often found in basic writing (David Carkeet, "Understanding Syntactic Errors in Remedial

Writing," *CE*, 38 [1976–77], 682–95; Lunsford, "An Historical, Descriptive, and Evaluative Study of Remedial English in American Colleges and Universities" [dissertation, Ohio State University, 1977]). The study of error, so important to Shaughnessy's work and to basic writing in general, became the subject for the inaugural issue of the *Journal of Basic Writing*. In the introduction to this first issue, Shaughnessy says that while "Error may seem to be an old place to begin a new discussion about teaching writing, . . . few [English teachers] have been in the habit of observing them fruitfully, with the intent of . . . understanding why intelligent young adults who want to be right seem to go on, persistently and even predictably, being wrong" (Spring 1975, pp. 4–5). This first issue of what has become the most important journal in the field of basic writing attempts to "get in the habit" of careful observation. While the entire issue is important, of special interest for their insights on error are Patricia Laurence's "Error's Endless Train: Why Students Don't Perceive Errors" (23–42); Valerie Krishna's "The Syntax of Error" (43–49); and Isabella Halsted's "Putting Error in its Place" (72–86).

One of the most thoughtful and provocative observers of basic writers has been David Bartholomae, whose work attempts to map more precisely the territory Shaughnessy explored. In "The Study of Error," *CCC*, 31 (Oct. 1980), 253–69, Bartholomae borrows from research on error analysis, and particularly miscue analysis (see Kenneth Goodman, ed., *Miscue Analysis: Applications to Reading Instruction* [Urbana, Ill.: ERIC, 1977]) to compare student errors in writing with those that occur while reading aloud. Starting with the theory that "allows us to see errors as evidence of choice or strategy among a range of possible choices or strategies" (p. 257) and a definition of error analysis as "the double perspective of text and reconstructed text [which] seeks to explain the difference between the two on the basis of whatever can be inferred about the meaning of the text and the process of creating it," Bartholomae argues that studying students' oral reconstructions of their own texts will provide "a diagnostic tool, . . . a means of instruction, . . . [and a way to] chart stages of growth in basic writers" (p. 267).

In spite of the amount of research on error during the last decade, we are still far from understanding its sources. No current subject, in fact, is fraught with more contention than that of the relationship between dialect interference and error in student writing. Most research on dialect interference, of course, has been conducted with speakers of second languages. (See Nancy Lay, "Chinese Language Interference in Written English," *JBW*, 1 [Spring 1975], 50–61, and Betty Rizzo and Santiago Villafane, "Spanish Influence on Written English," pp. 62–71 in the same issue, for discussion of second language interference in the context of a basic writing class. And for two opposing views on whether non-native and native student speakers should be mixed in basic writing classes, see Alice M. Roy, "Alliance for Literacy: Teaching Non-Native Speakers and Speakers of Nonstandard Dialect Together," *CCC*, 35 [Dec. 1984], 439–48; and James R. Nattinger, "Second Dialect and Second Language in the Composition Class," *TESOL Quarterly*, 12 [March 1978], 77–84.)

In a comprehensive overview of the debate over grammar and instruction in writing ("Grammar, Grammars, and the Teaching of Grammar," *CE*, 47 [Feb. 1985], 105–27), Patrick Hartwell concludes that his analysis "makes the question of socially non-standard dialects, always implicit in discussions of teaching formal grammar, into a non-issue. Native speakers of English, regardless of dialect, show tacit mastery of the conventions of Standard English, and that mastery seems to transfer into abstract orthographic knowledge through interaction with print. Developing writers show the same patterning of errors, regardless of dialect. Studies of reading and of writing suggest that surface features of spoken dialect are simply irrelevant to mastering print literacy" (p. 123). Hartwell concludes that teaching formal grammar is ineffective in the classroom. (For another discussion of this issue, including a lengthy set of grammar exercises, see Sarah D'Eloia, "The Uses—and Limits—of Grammar," *JBW*,

1 [Spring/Summer 1977], 1–38.) An opposing view is taken by Mary Epes in "Tracing Errors to their Sources: A Study of the Encoding Processes of Adult Basic Writers," *JBW,* 4 (Spring 1985), 4–33, in which she presents extensive evidence for the argument that "the influence of nonstandard dialect on writing is . . . even greater than has been assumed, [and thus] direct instruction in the grammar of standard written English is essential for nonstandard dialect speakers" (p. 31). These two essentially opposing articles simply point up for us an area of great uncertainty and confusion in the teaching of basic writing.

In "IQ and Standard English," *CCC,* 34 (December 1983), 470–84, Thomas Farrell takes the extreme view that "abstract thinking depends on learning (1) the full standard deployment of the verb 'to be' and (2) embedded modification and (3) subordination," that "IQ test scores reveal that black ghetto children have not developed the power of abstract thinking, and they do not speak standard English." Farrell's hypothesis, and his solution to the problem, is that we should teach formal grammar because "the mean IQ scores of black ghetto students will go up when they learn to speak and write Standard English" (p. 481). To say that Farrell's argument is controversial is a vast understatement (see, e.g., the responses by Karen Greenberg, Patrick Hartwell, Margaret Himley, and R. E. Stratton in the December 1984 issue of *CCC*). But the central issue—whether and how to include formal grammar instruction in basic writing classes—is one that is still being hotly debated in theory. In practice, meanwhile, my sense is that many, many basic writing classes depend primarily on grammar workbooks for their class structure and "lessons."

The Process of Composing

Following again on leads from Shaughnessy, researchers in the last decade have concentrated on the writing processes of basic writers, with very informative results. Studies of student attitudes and their relation to writing appear in Lunsford's dissertation (previously cited); in Muriel Harris's "Individual Diag-

noses: Searching for Causes, Not Symptoms of Writing Deficiencies," *CE,* 40 (Nov. 1978), 318–23; and especially in the
work of Mike Rose. In "Rigid Rules, Inflexible Plans, and the
Stifling of Language: A Cognitivist Analysis of Writer's Block,"
CCC, 31 (December 1980), 389–99, Rose categorizes types of
writing blocks as they relate to student attitudes and offers elo-
quent student testimony to their importance. In *When Writers
Can't Write* (New York: Guilford Press, 1985), Rose further explores this issue and its relation to performance in basic writing
classes. In addition, a recent dissertation by Pamela Gay ("Sources
of Negative Attitudes Toward Writing: Case Histories of Five Unskilled College Freshman Writers," New York Univ., 1983), examines how attitudes are formed and demonstrates the powerful
role such attitudes play in writing performance.

When Shaughnessy wrote, we had no significant case studies
of basic writers, no studies of their composing processes. Sondra
Perl's dissertation ("Five Writers Writing: Case Studies of the
Composing Processes of Unskilled College Writers," New York
Univ., 1978) provides just the sort of study Shaughnessy called
for. In this dissertation and in subsequent essays ("The Composing Processes of Unskilled College Writers," *RTE,* 13 [December
1979], 317–36; "Understanding Composing," *CCC,* 31 [De-
cember 1980], 363–69; and "A Look at Basic Writers in the Process of Composing," in *Basic Writing: Essays for Teachers, Researchers, Administrators,* ed. Laurence W. Kasden and Daniel R.
Hoeber [Urbana, Ill.: NCTE, 1980]), Perl reports that, contrary
to traditional assumptions, the basic writers she observed "had
stable composing processes which they used whenever they were
presented with a writing task. While this consistency argues
against seeing these students as beginning writers, it does not
necessarily imply that they are proficient writers. Indeed their
lack of proficiency may be attributable to the way in which premature and rigid attempts to correct and edit their work truncate
the flow of composing without substantially improving the form
of what they have written" ("The Composing Processes," p. 328).

Nancy Sommers reports somewhat similar findings in "Revision Strategies of Student Writers and Experienced Adult Writers," *CCC*, 31 (December 1980), 378–88. Her study revealed that basic writers generally regard revision as rewording, that they have been "taught to [revise] in a consistently narrow and predictable way," that they have strategies for handling words and phrases . . . [but] lack strategies for handling the whole essay, . . . heuristics to help them render lines of reasoning or ask questions about their purposes and readers" (p. 383). Sommers's findings are corroborated and elaborated on in Sandra Schor's "Revising: The Writer's Need to Invent and Express Relationships" (in *The Writer's Mind: Writing as a Mode of Thinking,* ed. Janice Hays, Phyllis Roth, Jon Ramsey, and Robert Foulke [Urbana: NCTE, 1983], pp. 113–25), and the concept of revision is further explored in a full issue of the *Journal of Basic Writing* (Fall/Winter 1981). A number of the essays in this issue link revision with questions of audience and hence with traditional concerns of invention and planning (see Sommers's "Intentions and Revisions," pp. 41–49; Thomas Newkirk's "Barriers to Revision," pp. 50–61; Linda Flower's "Revising Writer-Based Prose," pp. 62–74; and David Rankin's "Audience and the Composing Process," pp. 75–80), thus emphasizing the fact that composing is a recursive, nonlinear activity and that the "stages" of this process are frequently recapitulated, shifted, repeated, as a piece of writing develops.

Linda Flower's research has been most instrumental in helping us to view the writing process as fluid, and problems of revision as being directly related to problems of audience and planning. In "Writer-Based Prose: A Cognitive Basis for Problems in Writing," *CE,* 41 (September 1979), 19–37, reprinted in *The Writing Teacher's Sourcebook,* ed. Gary Tate and Edward P. J. Corbett (New York: Oxford Univ. Press, 1981), she identifies the characteristics of writer-based prose ("written by a writer to himself and for himself"); assesses its uses as well as its problems; and provides ways to help student writers transform writer-based to reader-based prose. This attention to audience and planning and the way such concepts will later aid editing and revising allows us to see our basic writers as competent at one form of self-expression while they are moving to another. Other important articles include four by Flower and John R. Hayes: "The Dynamics of Composing: Making Plans and Juggling Constraints," in *Cognitive Processes in Writing,* ed. Lee Gregg and Erwin Steinberg (Hillsdale, N.J.: Lawrence Erlbaum, 1979); "Problem Solving Strategies and the Writing Process," *CE,* 39 (1977), 449–61; "Problem Solving and the Cognitive Processes of Writing," in *Writing: The Nature, Development, and Teaching of Written Communication,* ed. C. H. Frederiksen, M. F. Whiteman, and J. F. Dominic (Hillsdale, N.J.: Lawrence Erlbaum, 1981); and "The Cognition of Discovery: Defining a Rhetorical Problem," *CCC,* 31 (1980), 21–32.

The technique developed by Flower and Hayes for their research, protocol analysis (see "Uncovering Cognitive Processes in Writing: An Introduction to Protocol Analysis," in *Research on Writing,* ed. P. Mosenthal, S. Walmsley, and L. Tamor [London: Longmans, 1982], 207–20), has not been used extensively with basic writers. One recent dissertation, however, makes use of the technique to compare basic writers' performances in differing contexts and to study the way the students represent the contexts to themselves both during writing and, later, in a text (see Deborah Louise Brandt, "Writer, Context, and Text," Indiana Univ., 1983).

Content

Shaughnessy reported in 1976 that "surprisingly little effort has been made to analyze the content of [basic writers'] essays" (above, p. 182), and to a large extent this is still true. Both David Bartholomae's and Mike Rose's work present a number of excerpts of such writing, accompanied often by insightful discussion of content, but their primary focus is on process rather than written product. In "The Basic Reading and Writing Phenomenon: Writing as Evidence of Thinking," *The Writer's Mind*, pp. 103–12, Karen Hjelmervik and Susan Merriman offer examples of such writing, but concentrate primarily on error and its effect on the composing process. Lunsford's "The Content of Basic Writers' Essays," *CCC*, 31 (October 1980), 278–90, provides a preliminary analysis of content and its relation to evaluation, but little has been done to follow up on this tentative research.

The issue of content, of course, is related not only to student texts but to what texts they should read, to what they should know. Over this issue there is currently great debate. Robert Pattison (*On Literacy*, p. 210) summarizes the essence of the debate, albeit in an extremely biased fashion:

> This [current] curriculum tends to be "humanistic." It encourages discussion of moral values found in various short stories, essays, and poems while it teaches the basics of grammar and spelling. In fact, this training makes students minimally functional in the mechanics of literacy while it deprives them of the essential language discipline they need in order to make the mechanics of literacy effective. After their exposure to a succession of tawdry literature anthologies from grade school through college, students may be full of beautiful values and charming ideas, but they lack the ability to manipulate these ideas in language, and values or ideas without a means of realization are useless.

The issue put so baldly here is between "content" in the sense of students' passive consumption of the texts of the literary canon, and "content" in the sense of active participation in creating a "content" of their own. On one side of this debate stands E. D. Hirsch ("Culture and Literacy," *JBW*, 3 [Fall/Winter 1980], 27–47), who argues for the necessity of teaching the canon by calling for "back to content, shared knowledge, cultural literacy. Cultural literacy involves, does it not, teaching shared knowledge about ourselves, our history and our world, our laws, our political, economic, and social arrangements, our classical texts. . . ." (p. 45). For Hirsch, whose arguments are impassioned and sincere, knowledge and literacy are commodities to be taught. Many teachers hold this same view. Robert Scholes, however, presents an opposing viewpoint, one eloquently argued in *Textual Power: Literary Theory and the Teaching of English* (New Haven: Yale Univ. Press, 1985):

> What students need from us—and this is true of students in our great universities, our small colleges, and our urban and community colleges—what they need from us now is the kind of knowledge and skill that will enable them to make sense of their worlds, to determine their own interests . . . to see through the manipulations of all sorts of texts in all sorts of media, and to express their own views in some appropriate manner. That they need both knowledge and skill is perhaps a matter worth pausing to consider. (pp. 15–16)

For Scholes, the texts students read are not commodities. Instead, they are always and foremost "occasions for other textuality" (p. 6). In other words, they are the means whereby students come to critical insights of their own, the means by which they create a world of textual meaning and significance for themselves.

These questions of content, of what is to be taught and how, are crucial ones for our entire profession, and they have myriad layers and powerful spokesmen all around. They are questions to which basic writing teachers especially must attend in order to enter the debate.

Classroom Practices

In the last two chapters of *Errors and Expectations,* Shaughnessy provided a brief sketch of how a basic writing class might be organized. Since then, a number of writers have addressed the question of what the focus of such classes should be.

In "Remedial Writing Courses: A Critique and a Proposal," *CE*, 45 (Feb. 1983), 109–28, Mike Rose argues that "a remedial writing curriculum must fit into the intellectual context of a University. Topics should have academic substance and, when possible, should require the student to work from text" (p. 128). He demonstrates an alliance between "reflexive" and "expository" discourse, and criticizes the "flat" remedial courses that stress skills and workbook exercises over meaning and whole discourse. (For another discussion of similar issues, see Jerrold Nudelman and Alvin H. Schlosser, "Experiential vs. Expository: Is Peaceful Co-existence Really Possible?" *Teaching English in the Two-Year College*, 8 [Fall 1982], 17–23.) Rose's work grows out of his experience in directing the Freshman Writing program at UCLA. Further east on the basic writing map, David Bartholomae's work at the University of Pittsburgh provides another model of how to organize basic writing classes. In "Teaching Basic Writing: An Alternative to Basic Skills," *JBW*, 2 (Summer 1979), 85–109, and especially in "Facts, Artifacts, and Counterfacts: A Basic Reading and Writing Course for the College Curriculum" in *A Sourcebook for Basic Writing Teachers*, ed. Theresa Enos (New York: Random House, 1986), Bartholomae describes the sequence of courses he and his colleagues have developed, courses which are designed "to enable students to locate ways of perceiving and describing themselves as writers" ("Teaching Basic Writing," pp. 89–90).

A variety of basic writing programs and their organizational bases appear in the Spring/Summer 1979 issue of the *Journal of Basic Writing* (in addition to Bartholomae's Pittsburgh courses, descriptions are included of programs at York College, CUNY, Illinois Central College, and Ohio State University); in *Basic Writing: Essays for Teachers, Researchers, Administrators* (programs at J. Sargeant Reynolds Community College, Boston University's College of Basic Studies, the Western North Carolina Consortium, and the University of Michigan–Flint); and in Alice Trillin's *Teaching Basic Skills in College: A Guide to Objectives, Skills, Assessment, Course Content, Teaching Methods, Support Ser-*

vices, and Administration (San Francisco: Jossey-Bass, 1980). In addition, Marie Ponsot and Rosemary Deen provide both a well-reasoned and a practically articulated framework for a basic writing course in their *Beat Not the Poor Desk: What to Teach, How to Teach It, and Why* (Montclair, N.J.: Boynton/Cook, 1982).

While most basic writing theorists are agreed that basic writers should engage challenging texts and produce whole discourses, such theory does not always inform practice, and many basic writing classes continue to rely on drills of "sub-skills" and workbook exercises. This is one of the basic dichotomies examined in Lunsford's "Assignments for Basic Writers: Unresolved Issues and Needed Research," *JBW*, 5 (Spring 1986), 87–99. Other areas of classroom controversy are not hard to find. How useful, for example, are traditional conferences with basic writers? (For differing views, see Harvey Wiener, *The Writing Room* [New York: Oxford Univ. Press, 1981], pp. 204–6; and Mary P. Hiatt, "Students at Bay: The Myth of the Conference," *CCC*, 26 [1975], 38–41.) Or what kind of response is most helpful and effective with basic writers? (For an alternative to the mark-every-error school, see John Butler's "Remedial Writers: The Teacher's Job as Corrector of Papers," *CCC*, 31 [October 1980], 270–77; or Mary Beaven's "Individualized Goal-Setting, Self-Evaluation, and Peer Evaluation," in *Evaluating Writing*, ed. Charles Cooper and Lee Odell [Urbana: NCTE, 1978], 135–56.)

The entire issue of assessment, of course, is particularly problematic for basic writers, who must often master a series of competency exams. Here again, agreement is hard to find. Marie Jean Lederman and her CUNY colleagues, who have surely mounted one of the most effective mass essay testing programs in the history of our discipline, argue fervently for the need to base placement and exit decisions on actual student writing (see Lynn Q. Troyka, "The Phenomenon of Impact: The CUNY Writing Assessment Test," *Writing Program Administration*, 8 [Fall/Winter 1984], 27–36). But many others disagree, arguing instead that standardized tests are perfectly adequate for such tasks (see

Hunter M. Breland, "Multiple-Choice Test Assesses Writing Ability," *Findings* [ETS], 5 [1977], 1–4). These questions and others are explored in a number of resources on evaluation. The Spring/Summer 1985 issue of the *Journal of Basic Writing* includes articles on evaluation by Rexford Brown, Joseph Williams, Edward White, Rosemary Hake, Roberta Matthews, Elizabeth Metzger, and Muriel Harris, as well as a selected annotated bibliography by Richard Larson. Cooper and Odell's *Evaluating Writing* presents descriptions and discussions of various methods of scoring essays as well as an insightful article by Lee Odell ("Measuring Changes in Intellectual Processes as One Dimension of Growth in Writing," pp. 107–32) which demonstrates how student writing can be analyzed to reveal various processes that will aid teachers in understanding and responding to student texts. Finally, Edward M. White's recently published *Assessment in Writing* (San Francisco: Jossey-Bass, 1985) presents an overview of the testing issue and some practical advice about how to ensure that our tests do what we want them to do.

Other resources specifically designed for the basic writing teacher include, in addition to Ponsot and Deen's *Beat Not the Poor Desk,* Harvey Wiener's *The Writing Room* (Oxford Univ. Press, 1981), and the largely unsatisfactory collection *Basic Writing* (NCTE, 1980). *A Sourcebook for Basic Writing Teachers,* ed. Theresa Enos (New York: Random House, 1986), containing essays by Troyka, Bartholomae, and Lunsford, promises to be more helpful. Additional resources, while still not plentiful, are far more accessible than they were ten years ago. Most importantly, the *Journal of Basic Writing* provides numerous examples of fine classroom practice (see especially the issue on Vocabulary [Fall/Winter 1979] and on Applications: Theory into Practice [Fall/Winter 1978]). *Teaching English in the Two-Year College* provides another important resource for basic writing teachers; the May 1985 issue, for instance, includes a special section on Basic Writing Resources edited by Sarah D'Eloia Fortune. Perhaps less well known but extremely helpful are the issues of *Resource,* a publication of the Instructional Resource Center, Office of Academic Affairs, CUNY. And of course the ERIC system continues to provide valuable unpublished materials having to do with basic writing classroom practices.

This review of work in basic writing has necessarily touched on many points of controversy and disagreement, as is predictable in a young, poorly-charted discipline whose place names were hardly even known ten years ago. I believe, however, that two noticeable and important trends have emerged during the last few years, and that they characterize the best potential for our discipline. The first, exemplified in the course proposals of both Bartholomae and Rose, is a new emphasis on reuniting the arts of speaking, writing, reading, and thinking. This trend is evident in a number of works relating thinking to the writing classroom: Kroll and Schafer, previously cited; Elaine Lees, "Building Thought on Paper with Adult Basic Writers," *The Writer's Mind*, pp. 145–52; Janice Hays, "The Development of Discursive Maturity in College Writers," *The Writer's Mind*, pp. 127–44; William Costanzo, "Writing and Thinking in a Postliterate Society," *The Writer's Mind*, pp. 181–90; A. Lunsford, "Cognitive Development and the Basic Writer," *CE*, 41 (1979), 38–47; Paul Ranieri, "A Descriptive Study of the Correlation Between Freshman English Students' Cognitive Development and Selected Measures of Their Writing Ability," (dissertation, University of Texas, 1983); Mary Quinn, "Critical Thinking and Writing: An Approach to the Teaching of Composition," (dissertation, University of Michigan, 1983); and the work of Flower and Hayes already cited. In addition, a growing number of works explore the many interconnections between reading, speaking, and writing. Marilyn Sternglass has particularly pursued these connections, most notably in "Assessing Reading, Writing, and Reasoning," *CE*, 43 (1981), 269–75, but this emphasis also characterizes work by Lynn Q. Troyka ("The Writer as Conscious Reader," in *A Sourcebook for Basic Writing Teachers;* "Classical Rhetoric and the Basic

Writer," in *Essays on Classical Rhetoric and Modern Discourse,* ed. Robert Connors, Lisa Ede, and Andrea Lunsford [Carbondale: Southern Illinois University Press, 1984], pp. 193–202); Lisa S. Ede ("New Perspectives on the Speaking-Writing Relationship: Implications for Teachers of Basic Writing," in *A Sourcebook for Basic Writing Teachers*); Charles Bazerman ("A Relation Between Reading and Writing: The Conversational Model," *CE,* 41 [1980], 656–61); A. Lunsford, ("Assignments for Basic Writers," *JBW* [Spring 1986], 87–99); and in *Exploring Speaking-Writing Relationships,* ed. Barry Kroll and Roberta Vann (Urbana: NCTE, 1981).

The second closely related trend emphasizes the role that collaboration and a sense of community play in all learning. One of the best–established principles of learning theory is that learning most often occurs as part of an interaction, either between the learner and the environment or, more frequently, between the learner and peers. The tendency to emphasize drills and workbooks, which has worked against a collaborative classroom community and against bringing reading, writing, speaking, and thinking together, may finally give way to these trends. If so, we will have a number of teacher/scholars to thank. Among those arguing that basic writers need primarily to be introduced to and made familiar with the academic discourse community, Patricia Bizzell's work has been particularly helpful ("Cognition, Convention, and Certainty: What We Need to Know About Writing," *Pre/Text,* 3 [Fall 1982], 213–44); additional work on discourse conventions appears in Bazerman's "What Written Knowledge Does: Three Examples of Academic Discourse," *Philosophy of the Social Sciences,* 11 (September 1981), 361–87.

Ken Bruffee has been instrumental in helping teachers understand why collaboration can and should work in the writing class and in providing models for teachers to try in their own classes ("The Brooklyn Plan: Attaining Intellectual Growth Through Peer-Group Tutoring," *Liberal Education,* 64 [December 1978], 447–68; "Writing and Reading as Collaborative or Social Acts," *The Writer's Mind,* pp. 159–71). An interesting study which supports Bruffee's concept of peer groups is Miriam Hoffman's "A Writer's Identity: An Effect of the Small Peer Writing Group," (dissertation, Rutgers Univ., 1983). Work in progress by Anne Gere promises to answer many questions about the history of writing groups in America and to draw implications from her research for current pedagogy. In addition, Andrea Lunsford and Lisa Ede argue, on the basis of a two-year study of collaborative writing in seven major professions, that students should be given more opportunity to write collaboratively in their classes (see "Let Them Write—Together," *English Quarterly*, 18 [Winter 1985], 119–28; and "Why Write Together: A Research Update," forthcoming in *Rhetoric Review*).

Such hopeful trends would help to re-focus the teaching of basic writing in the way most theorists recommend: eschewing the pejorative medical metaphor so long attached to basic writing and moving it from the fringes of concern into the full academic community where it becomes not what Mina Shaughnessy referred to as a "band-aid station" but an opener of long-closed doors to academic discourse, to intellectual rigor, to the way writing helps create ourselves and our worlds. While such a re-focusing seems to be taking place in a number of two-year and in some four-year colleges, the entire structure and hierarchy of our major universities militates against such a change because it demands a full reexamination of those structures and, in the bargain, new definitions not only of literacy but of our responsibility to and for literacy. At this time, I cannot be overly sanguine about the university's capacity for self-criticism and change. But clearly basic writing, with its urgent political issues of accessibility to higher education and of what constitutes literacy in the late twentieth century, presents the most powerful challenge and perhaps agent for such change. That is why the next ten years of research and pedagogical practice in basic writing may be more crucially important than those of the last decade.

Language Varieties and Composition

JENEFER M. GIANNASI, Northern Illinois University

COMPOSITION RESULTS FROM WRITERS' DETER-
mined uses of the oral and written language varieties at their
command. Effective composition results from writers' determina-
tions of effective rhetorical choices and effective sociolinguistic
options. Whether the intention is to produce a facsimile of oral
discourse or written discourse itself, sociolinguistic competence
is the issue and rhetorical competence is the goal. To achieve such
competence, however, is an uneasy task. The subject of language
varieties cannot be separated from the political, economic, and
social issues that breed our concern for it. Thus, it remains vola-
tile, emotion–inducing, and stressful. Language varieties reflect
our world–national–regional–local conceptions of status, our
valuations of spoken versus written discourse, our beliefs about
propriety, error, and class, and our understandings about what
language performance demonstrates about intentionality.

LANGUAGE VARIETIES AND LITERACY

The number of scholars attempting to explain the volatility
of our social and rhetorical responses to language varieties and
the ramifications of such responses has grown in the last several
years. Their efforts have contributed to an expanding literature of
literacy within which to focus still other scholarly attempts to
explain the actual workings of language varieties and the implica-

tions of recent findings for the teaching of composition. In *Literacy as a Human Problem,* edited by James C. Raymond (University, Ala.: University of Alabama Press, 1982), the issues of language use (Middleton, Davis, Simon, McPherson), writing competence (Newkirk, Lloyd-Jones), and literate culture (Corbett, D'Angelo, Ong) are explored and rationales examined. *English in the Eighties,* edited by Robert D. Eagleson (Adelaide, Australia: Australian Association for the Teaching of English, 1982), focuses attention on multicultural environments, curricula for negotiation skills, patterns of and constraints on writing, and assessment of writing. Statements by Britton, Rosen, Mawasha, Diamond, Watts, Wagner, Dixon and Stratton, Hay, Johnston, Moffett, Graves, Spencer, O'Donnell, Boomer are featured. Underlying each thesis is concern for the rhetorical and sociolinguistic competencies that result from understanding language varieties.

Literacy for Life, edited by Richard W. Bailey and Robin Melanie Fosheim (New York: Modern Language Association, 1983), provides a forum for the discussion of literacy—in politics and policy (Robinson, Power, Bailey, Becker, Delattre), in its forms (Fleming, Salomon, Tannen, D'Angelo, Strassmann), in the marketplace (Weisz, White, Redish, Odell, Goswami, Quick), and in education (Tyler, Cohen and Brawer, Carsetti, Fader, Coles, Morris). Harvey A. Daniel's *Famous Last Words* (Carbondale: Southern Illinois University Press, 1983) approaches the issues of literacy and language variety through an attack on the "language crisis" argument, seeking to put that argument to rest by appealing to available knowledge of language theory, practice, and attitudes. And Dennis E. Baron's *Grammar and Good Taste* (New Haven: Yale University Press, 1982) focuses on our attempts at American language reform, its history, our correctness doctrine, and our suspicion of regulating procedures and agencies. Spelling, vocabulary, grammar, and usage options and constraints are dealt with historically.

Yet, even while these attempts to define and argue literacy issues have been developing, all interested parties—teachers, students, writers, and readers—have had to continue searching in often unlikely places for the language information that would lead toward competence. Language varieties, as they must be dealt with by the student and the teacher of composition, pose problems of definition, of what constitutes data, and of field of concern. Is a variety oral or written, dialectal or diatypic? Are the descriptions of speaker-hearer attitudes, the analysis of linguistic components, or observations of socio-cultural interactions all to be considered useful, legitimate data? Should the study of varieties be accomplished by linguists, rhetoricians, socio-linguists, anthropologists, or psychologists (to name only a few specialist areas)? And should the resulting statements be prepared for classroom teachers, students, theorists, researchers, or the general public?

The study of language varieties, of their users and uses, and of their importance in written composition is being considered at the present time from a mixed yet strongly sociolinguistic perspective. Such study attempts to focus attention on language as a part of culture and society. It embraces contributions from linguistics, dialectology, ethnography, sociology, psychology, anthropology, communications theory, componential analysis, ethnoscience, ethnomethodology, paralinguistics, kinesics, folklore, pragmatics, and stylistics. As the body of literature has grown within the past three decades, it has taken the study of language varieties beyond the development and publication of linguistic atlases, has expanded the study of usage beyond the listing of rules and etiquette options, has focused attention on proficiency and competence, has begun explaining the differences and similarities between spoken and written language, has placed our conceptions within an international setting, and has made us internationally aware of speaker-audience negotiation.

The speaker of broadcast English utters a language code accepted for general, public reportage and consultation. The writer of technical English composes in a language code used to convey the data of a referent-oriented world. The speaker of Black En-

229

glish Vernacular renders a language code which reflects a distinct cultural orientation to time, space, and people involved in social contact. The writer of Edited American English records through a language code which seeks to render for general use the thoughts of people involved in the conduct of behavior in the public world. Each is concerned about using a variety (or varietal mix) of language that will most accurately reflect speaker intention, respond to audience expectation, and reinforce social and cultural attitudes. Each is concerned about appropriate and effective choice of the usage options available within the habit patterns allowed for each code. Each is involved in exhibiting communicative competence—performance in a situation that exhibits practical control of the grammar of a variety. And each strives for rhetorical competence.

No less involved in this process is the teacher of written composition. For example, the teacher who commits a group of students to the writing of a business letter is involving both student and teacher in a complex set of sociocultural and linguistic concerns. The student must take into account the audience's attitudes and expectations. The teacher and the student must answer many questions before each letter is ready for "publication."

Which language variety usually informs such writing?

What are the written conventions of that language variety?

Which language variety mix would the audience consider acceptable?

Which usage options of the speaker's language variety and the audience's language variety can be drawn into the more neutral, required written pattern?

What social distance should be maintained through the choice of appropriate code markers?

Suppose that a student, using text materials, class directives, and past experience, begins the orientation paragraph with this sentence:

In answer to your request for names of witnesses to the accident, didn't nobody see it.

As a statement that conveys mutually intelligible information, it succeeds. But as a statement that exhibits competence in showing speaker intention and in answering to expected behavior patterns and social sensibilities, it works against itself. The pre-comma prepositional phrases increase the formality of this written style of Edited American English while the post-comma statement suggests the informal oral style of Black English Vernacular. This particular mix of oral and written code markers and varietal habit patterns would interfere in the consultation process. The audience would react to the mix of patterns rather than receive the message. Effective consultation and negotiation depends on a careful balance of linguistic and extra-linguistic components, all of which must be considered by the teacher and student who seek rhetorical competence and by speaker and audience who expect rhetorical competence. Thus, all are involved in a process which encourages them to accept or seek multi-varietal proficiency. As listeners and speakers or as readers and writers, they are faced with the need to understand inter-varietal (that is, standard versus nonstandard; middle class versus lower class; Middle Atlantic versus Appalachian) and intra-varietal (that is, spoken versus written; formal versus informal; consultative style versus intimate style) differences and similarities.

For these reasons, the researcher, teacher, and composer of written composition must be aware of the scope, influence, and uses of the many varieties of the language. Questions about variety status, code switching, mutual intelligibility, and social attitudes may be answered only if the researcher, teacher, and composer differentiate varieties and institute adequate controls to avoid cross-cultural interference. Projections about changing social and linguistic conventions and constraints can be provided only if the history and values of the users and uses of the many varieties are understood. Thomas Kochman's "Cross-cultural Communication: Contrasting Perspectives, Conflicting Sensibilities," *Florida FL Reporter*, 9 (Fall/Spring 1971), 3–16, 53–54, explained this growing understanding of the early 1970s: "Cross-cultural interference occurs when communicants who operate from different codes interpret the same behavior according to respectively different, and often conflicting, code perspectives." As he discusses some types of interference and communication failure which result from black and white Americans' cultural differences, Kochman shows that these problems result from lack of understanding of the ramifications of dialect as a manifestation of both linguistic and social habits and expectations. Cultural codes determine the value to be given to linguistic habit patterns in situational context. Also, working from the cross-cultural perspective of English as a Second Language instruction (an important dimension of the varieties/composition issue), Christina Bratt Paulston's "Linguistic and Communicative Competence," *TESOL Quarterly*, 8 (December 1974), 347–62, focuses attention on the "international" problems of teaching the social rules of communicative competence within dual language and language varieties situations.

SOCIOLINGUISTIC ORIENTATIONS

Publications of the early 1970s dealing with language varieties reflected the growth of our need to address the linguistic, cultural, and rhetorical negotiation necessary to communication. The scope and influence of sociolinguistic studies were summarized by Pride and Labov. J. B. Pride's "Sociolinguistics," in *New Horizons in Linguistics,* edited by John Lyons (Baltimore: Penguin Books, 1970), surveys the field through a review of some of the major contributors and their contributions. Pride concludes that sociolinguistics (a) encourages "reciprocal validation" through interdisciplinary work; (b) recognizes the "interpenetration of language . . . with almost all walks of life and varieties of experience"; (c) seeks "criteria for the demarcation of boundaries (or recognition of irrelevance of boundaries) among languages, dialects, and styles"; (d) produces studies of code-switching between languages and between dialects; (e) establishes methodologies for observation of private and public verbal behavior; and (f) characterizes cultural values which determine verbal transactions. William Labov's "The Place of Linguistic Research in American Society," in *Linguistics in the 1970's* (Washington, D.C.: Center for Applied Linguistics, 1970), outlines the major results and new theoretical questions that sociolinguistic study was then encouraging. He explains that "within the past fifteen years, there has been a noticeable movement away from the extreme asocial position in theoretical work towards a view of linguistic structure and evolution which includes the evidence of every-day speech outside of the university community." He sees five major research areas which warrant development: (a) field studies of linguistic diversity in urban communities, (b) investigations of the social implications of dialectology, (c) identification of coexistent systems and bilingualism, (d) attitudinal studies of the social evaluation of language, and (e) reconsideration of the relation of language and thought.

The need to understand and respond to the influence of language varieties in written composition was pointed out also in the 1970s by those involved in the teaching of composition. Walt Wolfram and Marcia Whiteman, in "The Role of Dialect Interference in Composition," *Florida FL Reporter,* 9 (Spring/Fall 1971), 34–38, 59, discuss interference problems which arise in written composition because of dialectal differences in grammatical and pronunciation features. The features are inventoried, and manifestations of hypercorrection are illustrated through Black English writing samples. The authors stress that writing Standard English is a productive skill which must be taught as a separate communicative skill and that the deliberate style of writing is quite different from spoken style.

R. W. Bailey's "Write Off versus Write On: Dialects and the Teaching of Composition," in *Varieties of Present-Day English,* edited by Richard W. Bailey and Jay L. Robinson (New York: Macmillan, 1973), suggests how the teacher of composition can establish a set of priorities which will build toward concentration on writing. The teacher must help the student draw distinctions between written and spoken varieties of language, extend his linguistic resources, and recognize that he is involved in translation from speech act conventions to writing act conventions. "The primary task that the composition teacher should set for himself is the development of skills in controlling the large patterns that unify discourses. Such study must acknowledge the important differences between the organization appropriate to a piece of writing and that natural in speech, and it must come to terms with the role of the teacher as both participant and spectator."

Mary Newton Bruder and Luddy Hayden, in "Teaching Composition: A Report on a Bidialectal Approach," *LL,* 23 (June 1973), 1–15, describe a bidialectal approach designed to teach formal composition style to students whose repertoires lack a formal standard speaking style. The objectives of the approach are to teach how black dialect and Standard English differ, how to recognize situational appropriateness, how to distinguish register features (especially the formal written register), how to recognize the functional interrelationship between registers and dialects and the speech community, how to write compositions in the standard dialect using standard rhetorical techniques, and how to carry out research in acceptable academic form.

Carroll E. Reed's "Adapting TESL Approaches to the Teaching of Written Standard English as a Second Dialect to Speakers of American Black English Vernacular," *TESOL Quarterly,* 7 (September 1973), 289–307, describes a bidialectal teaching program intended to develop functional, productive competence in Standard English. Through extensive contrastive analysis (adapted from second-language teaching procedures) and dialogue exercises, speakers of Black English Vernacular are encouraged to identify vernacular features and cross-dialectal interferences in their writing. Directions for the teaching of such a curriculum unit are provided. The intention is to verify understanding of the second dialect through appeals to the students' own cultural tradition and acknowledgment of the legitimacy of the BEV system.

Samuel A. Kirschner and G. Howard Poteet, in "Non-Standard English Usage in the Writing of Black, White, and Hispanic Remedial English Students in an Urban Community College," *RTE,* 7 (Winter 1973), 351–55, report the results of a study of the writing of students in remedial classes. The authors analyzed papers for the presence of thirteen nonstandard grammatical and mechanical features. Their conclusion is that "up to now, instructors of remedial English composition have believed that there were significant differences between the writing of blacks, Hispanics, and whites, even though their socio-economic backgrounds were similar. This study suggests that in the main there are no significant differences in the type and frequencies of non-standard English usage between black, white, and Hispanic students."

Marilyn S. Sternglass, in "Close Similarities in Dialect Features of Black and White College Students in Remedial Composition Classes," *TESOL Quarterly,* 8 (September 1974), 271–83, and in "Dialect Features in the Compositions of Black and White College Students: The Same or Different?" *CCC,* 25 (October 1974), 259–63, reports the results of a study of the writing of students in remedial classes. She analyzed papers for the presence of seventeen nonstandard grammatical features. All but one of the nonstandard features appeared in the papers of both black and white students, though she found that black students employed all the nonstandard features more often. This study indicates that separate language materials are not needed for white and black students in college level remedial writing classes.

235

Wallace Douglas's "On the Crisis in Composition," *ADE Bulletin,* 40 (March 1974), 3–11, surveys attitudes and approaches to teaching composition up to 1974. He points out that the then-present school composition rationale encouraged teaching techniques and textbooks which assume that students' speech is similar to, or the result of familiarity with, written texts. He advocates a move toward the use of contrastive analysis and the development of the ability to see a dialect system or dialect interference at work. Turning to the needs of minority students, he states that "our first task is to teach ourselves the need and possibility of learning how to read the writing codes developed by minority students."

Dennis E. Baron's "Non-Standard English, Composition, and the Academic Establishment," *CE,* 37 (October 1975), 176–83, first concentrates on reviewing major distinctions between spoken and written language and the constraints that are basic to each. Baron then considers the problems of translating a nonstandard spoken dialect into writing. Finally, he argues that "the function of the composition teacher, then, should be to focus the student's attention on the intelligibility requirements of the written code, rather than to attack the student's use of language. The arbitrary standards of correctness must be ignored, the relative means of effectiveness must be stressed, the student must develop a self-confident attitude toward his language." Language etiquette is not the teaching goal.

Michael D. Linn, in "Black Rhetorical Patterns and the Teaching of Composition," *CCC,* 26 (May 1975), 149–53, focuses on the ways Black English Vernacular and the oral culture in which it is used interact to create and reflect verbal contests (such as *shucking, rapping,* and *stylin' out*) which are constrained by their respective rhetorical devices. He suggests that an understanding of idiom and oral situational formats will enable the composition teacher to develop a program of "high context" and "low context" writing situations. In such a setting, the student can learn to translate the "styles" (see Joos) appropriate to various oral contexts into those appropriate to written situational formats.

Reflecting the rhetorical orientation of Linn, Marshá Taylor and Andrew Ortony's "Rhetorical Devices in Black English: Some Psycholinguistic and Educational Observations," *LCHC*, 2 (April 1980), 21–26, approach translation activities from another perspective. The work of Kochman, Mitchell-Kernan, and Labov on signifying, marking, and sounding serves as the basis for discussion of nonliteral language and metaphor and the possibilities of focusing on metaphor as a means of improving school performance.

The views, positions, and research results presented in the 1970s articles are representative of the major concerns that continue to be expressed by teachers of composition. All demonstrate that greater understanding of varieties differentiation is crucial to the teacher of composition in a pluralistic society. But they also focus attention on the need to carefully define written versus spoken language, analyze discourse, distinguish code-switching versus linguistic etiquette, identify situational formats, employ contrastive analysis, recognize the pervasiveness of nonstandard features, understand variety differentiation, and seek rhetorical competence. In this way, they set the shifting dialectal-diatypic perspective of the 1980s statements (see Taylor and Ortony) in motion and build toward the intention to develop rhetorical competence.

LANGUAGE VARIETIES DIFFERENTIATION

The teacher and researcher seeking an outline of the interconnections between language varieties and composition can find a focus for study in Michael Gregory's "Aspects of Varieties Differentiation," *JL*, 3 (October 1967), 177–98. This article summarizes the research which led to our understanding of varieties differentiation at that point in time. Gregory carefully delineates situational and contextual categories for *dialectal varieties*, which are "the linguistic reflection of reasonably permanent characteristics of the USER in language situations" and for *diatypic varieties,* which are "the linguistic reflection of recurrent characteristics of user's USE of language in situations." He demonstrates, for example, that *users* are characteristically governed by temporal, geographic, and social provenance and dialects while *use* is characteristically governed by role, relationship, and discourse requirements. He encourages more careful distinctions between spoken and written MODES. As he develops his argument, he clarifies some of the "current terminological confusion in this area of study." This early attempt at clarification was later expanded and explained in Michael Gregory and Susanne Carroll's *Language and Situation* (London: Routledge & Kegan Paul, 1978). The authors discuss dialect, fields (purpose)–mode (medium)–tenors (formality range) of discourse, register, and code in order to define textual varieties, meaning, and social context. These works signaled a division and classification procedure that has influenced subsequent approaches to language varieties and their differentiation.

Such categorization procedures obviously help the teacher of composition to approach language varieties in a more reasoned way—conscious of overlap of concerns yet able to focus on dialectal versus diatypic varieties and varieties versus usage problems. And they also show that, as the study of dialectal varieties tends to focus on community and *lect* (dialect), so diatypic varieties study tends to focus on the individual and *lect* (idiolect). G. W. Turner, in *Stylistics* (Middlesex, England: Penguin, 1975), explains the shift in focus that diatypic studies encourage regarding sound, syntax, context, register, functions, and the uses of stylistics.

Dialectal varieties

The study of dialects focuses attention on the social, geographical, and temporal conventions and constraints of language varieties as the members of their respective sociolinguistic communities render them. Such study (a) distinguishes pronunciations, vocabularies, and syntax available to various habit pattern sets (dialects), (b) emphasizes the primacy of speech, and (c) draws attention to the differences between spoken and written language varieties. As a result, dialect study is intimately involved with the rhetorical problems of speaker-audience contact *in situation*—a problem of first importance to the teacher and researcher of composition.

Dialect definition, identification, and differentiation fit into a larger pattern of varieties differentiation. But, as the work of the 1950s, 1960s, and early 1970s shows, the number of definitions places the term *dialect* within a series of shifting perspectives. From one perspective, it is treated as a nonjudgmental linguist's term. Raven I. McDavid, Jr.'s "The Dialects of American English," in W. Nelson Francis's *The Structure of American English* (New York: Ronald Press, 1958), surveys the specific nature of American English dialects. He discusses dialect differences and causes, dialect geography, linguistic atlases, forces underlying dialect distribution, principal dialect areas (sample maps are provided), foreign language influences, class dialects, and literary dialect. Roger Shuy's *Discovering American Dialects* (Champaign, Ill.: NCTE, 1967) presents a simplified introduction to dialects as regional, social, and literary varieties. He considers how and why they differ and introduces the problem of foreign language influence.

Considering the term from the perspective of its misuse, Raven I. McDavid, Jr., in "A Theory of Dialect," *Linguistics and the Teaching of Standard English to Speakers of Other Languages or Dialects,* edited by James E. Alatis (Monograph Series on Languages and Linguistics, No. 22; Washington, D.C.: Georgetown University Press, 1969), reviews the uses of the term "dialect" while pointing to misuses of the designation, redefining the functions and limitations of the dimensions of language varieties, and considering various standards. Attempting to clarify the definition, Jean Malmstrom's "Dialects—Updated," *Florida FL Re-*

porter, 7 (Spring/Summer 1969), 47–49, 168, considers the general nature of dialect, outlining and discussing its components and variables and its socioeconomic and geographic determinants. Joshua A. Fishman, in *Sociolinguistics* (Rowley, Mass.: Newbury House, 1970), suggests that the term "variety," a nonjudgmental designation, allows more objective consideration of dialect function. He distinguishes among dialect, variety, and language and considers all three within a sociolinguistic definition which considers attitude and behavior toward linguistic change, constraints, and repertoire range. Carroll E. Reed, in *Dialects of American English,* rev. ed. (Amherst: University of Massachusetts Press, 1977), provides an introduction to dialect study which concentrates on the geographical movements of American English across the country and points to the future of American dialect studies.

Still others point out the difficulties of understanding and using the term when the definers attempt to distinguish standard and nonstandard dialects. In "Variations in Standard American English," *EE,* 45 (May 1968), 561–64, 608, Raven I. McDavid, Jr., narrows his discussion to our "standard" variety, considering those historical and current variations in phonology, vocabulary, and syntax which reflect regional differences yet represent Standard American English. Randolph Quirk, in *The Use of English* (New York: St. Martin's Press, 1968), points out that a standard variety may be viewed as "basically an ideal, a mode of expression that we seek when we wish to communicate beyond our immediate community with members of the wider community of the nation as a whole, or with members of the still wider community, English-speakers as a whole." But he cautions that members of different speech communities may produce different realizations. Albert H. Marckwardt's "The Concept of Standard English," in *The Discovery of English* (Urbana, Ill.: NCTE, 1971), considers the historical basis for the development of a standard dialect and the reasons for determining and defining one. From an alternative perspective, William Labov, in "The Logic of Nonstandard English," *Linguistics and the Teaching of Standard English to Speakers of Other Languages or Dialects,* edited by James E. Alatis (Monograph Series on Languages and Linguistics, No. 22; Washington, D.C.: Georgetown University Press, 1969), carefully illustrates the habit-pattern organization of nonstandard English and argues that nonstandard English is neither an illogical variety of speech nor a manifestation of verbal deprivation.

The difficulties of defining from the perspective of standard versus nonstandard are the central concern of *Contemporary English,* edited by David L. Shores (Philadelphia: Lippincott, 1972). In this reader, aimed at prospective and in-service teachers, the problems of establishing "accurate concepts and realistic attitudes toward standard and nonstandard varieties of English" are considered through the statements of twenty-one contributors. Temporal, regional, and social variations in standard and non-standard English (Shuy, Bloomfield, Malmstrom, McDavid, Fasold and Wolfram, Stewart, Davis), partial definitions of Standard English (Gove, Pyles, Kenyon, Kilburn, Joos, DeCamp), and problems of learning and teaching standard and nonstandard English (Feigenbaum, Bloomfield, Hill, Allen, Shuy, Dillard, Goodman, Troike, Sledd) are the major concerns of the collection.

Two early introductory readers serve to establish the definitional perspective of the dialectologists in the 1970s. *Readings in American Dialectology,* edited by Harold B. Allen and Gary N. Underwood (New York: Appleton-Century-Crofts, 1971) presents forty-one articles about regional and social dialects. Regional dialects are defined through methodology and attitudinal overview (Atwood, McDavid), area studies (Thomas, Duckert, Marckwardt, Allen, Reed, Wood, Norman), single feature studies (Hempl, Atwood, Ives, McDavid, Avis, Bloch, Pace), comparative approaches (Orton, Francis, Kurath, Reed), and dialect theory (Bottiglioni, Weinreich, Stockwell, Troike, Hill). Social dialects are defined in articles on interrelationships, structural differences, sociolinguistic factors, and social features (McDavid, Kurath, Sawyer, Pederson, Bailey, Loflin, Stewart, Labov, Maurer and Vogel). Subsequent editions of this reader are of special value as they demonstrate the gradual shift in orientation into greater sociolinguistic concerns. *A Various Language,* edited by Juanita V. Williamson and Virginia M. Burke (New York: Holt, Rinehart and Winston, 1971), surveys the history and scope of dialect studies. Fifty contributors discuss origins and varieties (Scott, Kurath, Krapp, Kenyon, Currie, McDavid), inherited features (Pyles, Hill, Kurath, Francis, Turner, Brooks), literary representations (Ives, Bowdrie, Harrison, Stockton, Rulon, Blackburn), regional and social aspects (Kurath, Atwood, Morgan, Howren, Thomas, La-Ban, Norman, Klipple, Davis, McDavid and McDavid, Allen, Reed), sound and forms (Avis, Wetmore, Kurath, Atwood, Williamson, Levine and Crockett, Sledd, McMillan); and urban dialect studies (McDavid, Pederson, DeCamp, Sawyer, Williamson, Parslow, Bronstein, Labov).

The now-classic, early 1970s work of William Labov places *dialect* within a clearly sociolinguistic perspective which reflects consistent treatment of the socio-economic and linguistic variables that affect social interaction. Intent on the development of methodology, field study, and accurate reportage, Labov focused primarily on social dialects in the New York City area. *The Social Stratification of English in New York City* (Washington, D.C.: Center for Applied Linguistics, 1966) is an in-depth analysis of one multi-level speech community. Social context, social stratification, and contextual styles were surveyed through interviews; class and linguistic variables were differentiated; personal and public attitudes toward New York City speech were evaluated. The New York City vowel system was identified. Labov outlines the continuous social and stylistic variation of language influenced by socio-economic stratification and the transmission of prestige patterns. He considers the nature of social control of language variety and shows identification of linguistically discrete social dialect boundaries in New York City to be impossible because of the influence of social variables.

For teachers, Labov developed two major statements. He treats dialects as conceptual systems in *The Study of Nonstandard*

English (Champaign, Ill.: NCTE, 1970). He surveys the theoretical and educational issues surrounding the controversy about nonstandard English. Nonstandard English is considered within the context of the nature of language, sociolinguistic principles, educational implications, and needed in-school research. Reasons are given for studying nonstandard language; nonstandard dialects are viewed as self-contained systems; the relationship between standard and nonstandard English is described. Social stratification, linguistic rules and norms, sex differences, and acquisition stages are reviewed. The importance of sociolinguistic research to reading, speech, and vocabulary instruction and to classroom speech events is described. Labov then considers informal and formal approaches to testing for presence of varieties of language in order to determine types of dialect differences, and to testing students' perceptual competence, grammatical competence, and speech competence. "Variation in Language," in *The Learning of Language,* edited by Carroll E. Reed (New York: Appleton-Century-Crofts, 1971), pp. 187–221, presents Labov's organizational perspective through consideration of regional differences in language, urban language differences, language differences in age levels, learning of language differences, and the structure of linguistic variation. He discusses those language features which reflect the parameters of social mobility, demonstrate social stratification as it functions, and evidence those sub-cultural determinants which affect change in linguistic habit patterns.

Sociolinguistic Patterns (Conduct and Communication, No. 4; Philadelphia: University of Pennsylvania Press, 1972) presents a nine-essay collection of Labov's research into social change and motivation in language and discusses contextual style and the subjective dimensions of change. His thesis is that "the basis of intersubjective knowledge in linguistics must be found in speech—language as it is used in everyday life by members of the social order." His chapter sequencing of now-classic articles reveals his key terms and demonstrates his concern for movement from particularity to synthesis: "The Social Motivation of a

Sound Change," "The Social Stratification of (r) in New York City Department Stores," "The Isolation of Contextual Styles," "The Reflection of Social Processes in Linguistic Structures," "Hypercorrection by the Lower Middle Class as a Factor in Linguistic Change," "Subjective Dimensions of a Linguistic Change," "The Study of Language in Its Social Context," and "The Social Setting of Linguistic Change."

Language in the Inner City: Studies in the Black English Vernacular (Conduct and Communication, No. 3; Philadelphia: University of Pennsylvania Press, 1972) is a collection of nine essays in which Labov presents a reorganization and rewriting of several earlier statements into a sequenced study of the *structure* ("Some Sources of Reading Problems for Speakers of the Black English Vernacular," "Is the Black English Vernacular a Separate System?" "Contraction, Deletion, and Inherent Variability of the English Copula," and "Negative Attraction and Negative Concord"), *social setting* ("The Logic of Nonstandard English," "The Relation of Reading Failure to Peer-Group Status," "The Linguistic Consequences of Being a Lame"), and *uses of the Black English Vernacular* ("Rules for Ritual Insults" and "The Transformation of Experience in Narrative Syntax").

The organized, integrated work of Labov raised the problem of identifying social codes, a concern already taken up by Basil Bernstein. His largely theoretical studies served to broaden the implications of Labov's field studies. *Class, Codes and Control, Volume 1: Theoretical Studies Towards a Sociology of Language* (London: Routledge & Kegan Paul, 1971) is a collection of the British social psychologist's articles on the interaction of social class and language behavior. Spanning thirteen years of conceptualizing, these chronologically arranged statements demonstrate the development of Bernstein's theories and empirical studies. It is Bernstein's contention that "elaborated" and "restricted" language codes (that is, those principles which regulate the selection and organization of speech events) are learned by the members of the middle and lower classes respectively, that each of these codes determines the linguistic and social competence of their speakers, and that speakers of restricted codes are confined to "public" language while speakers of elaborated codes have access to both "public" and "formal" language. The behavioral characteristics which result manifest themselves in the speaker's cognitive processes and responses to social and natural events and reflect the speaker's concept of reality. The linguistic and social characteristics of the codes are investigated throughout.

In a companion volume, *Class, Codes and Control*, Volume 2: *Applied Studies Towards a Sociology of Language* (London: Routledge & Kegan Paul, 1973), Bernstein and others, working within the framework of his theories, investigate aspects of maternal orientations to communication and the speech of five-year-old children and seven-year-old children for contextual specificity, discretion, and cognitive socialization, for perceptual and verbal discriminations of code users, and for the influence of sex, social class, and pause-location in hesitation phenomena. Of special interest in this volume is R. Hasan's "Code, Register and Social Dialect" in which she investigates the three terms in an attempt to further define their meanings, interrelationships, and the correlation of the latter terms with Bernstein's category of *code*.

The defining of dialect from the perspective of Black English studies has required still another approach. The study of Black English dialects has been quite extensively developed in response to the needs of black students in public school classrooms and in an effort to define total sociolinguistic contexts. There is first the issue of uniqueness and competence. Thomas Kochman, in "Culture and Communication: Implications for Black English in the Classroom," *Florida FL Reporter*, 7 (Spring/Summer 1969), 89–92, 172–74, makes cross-cultural comparisons between black culture and white middle-class culture. In the process, he considers communication channels, prestige forms, mechanisms and networks, audience dynamics, speech styles, and the goals and assumptions for language programs. He states that increasing language skill in black children is not dependent on teaching them the ability to perform in standard dialect. Joan C. Baratz, in "Should Black Children Learn White Dialect?" *ASHA,* 12 (September 1970), 415–17, argues that "standard English" is not "white dialect" but the lingua franca of the "American mainstream" culture to which the black student has a right. Standard English is defined as "that dialect which uses a set of grammatical patterns in oral production that are similar to those used in the written form of the language." She acknowledges the "mutual intelligibility" argument used to oppose teaching Standard English, defends the bidialectal teaching approach, and explains the interference problems which arise from imperfect understanding of the oral and written systems. Geneva Smitherman's "God Don't Never Change: Black English from a Black Perspective," *CE,* 34 (March 1973), 828–34, argues for the uniqueness of black expression as it lies in the situational context from which the style of the Black Idiom develops. The argument is placed in historical context.

The issue of uniqueness, setting, and history is also considered. In *A Sociolinguistic Description of Detroit Negro Speech* (Washington, D.C.: Center for Applied Linguistics, 1969), Walter A. Wolfram reports the results of an urban language field study, showing the interaction of social setting and linguistic (phonological and grammatical) variables which produce "nonstandard Negro English" specific to Detroit. *Black-White Speech Relationships,* edited by Walt Wolfram and Nona H. Clarke (Washington, D.C.: Center for Applied Linguistics, 1971), presents eight viewpoints on the possible social and historical influences in the development of black-white varieties of English. Considered are Gullah (Turner), black-white speech relationships (McDavid and McDavid), Negro English dialectology (Bailey), historical continuity-change factors (Stewart), dialect research (Davis), Afro-American communication (Dalby), and black-white speech differences (Wolfram). J. L. Dillard's *Black English: Its History and Usage in the United States* (New York: Random House, 1972) considers the ramifications of Black English, its historical development, and its cultural validity. He discusses the implications of such information for teacher training and classroom practices. Chapter VII stresses the harm done black students by failing them on the basis of dialect. *Language, Communication, and Rhetoric in Black America,* edited by Arthur L. Smith (New York: Harper & Row, 1972) is a collection of twenty-nine essays by communication specialists and educators who discuss the communication process in its totality, that is, dialect, styles, tone, situational context, and rhetorical intention. Consideration is given to black language (Baratz, Green, Erickson, Wolfram), ethnicity (Holt, Davis, Kochman, Mitchell), rhetorical case studies (Smith, Dick, Harris and Kennicott, Campbell, Illo, Brockreide and Scott, Bosmajian), criticism and social change (Smith, Epps and Gregg, McCormack and Pedersen), and social-historical dimensions (Smith, Hannerz, Jones, Larson, Brooks, Richardson, Garret). F. Erickson's comparison of white and black college students in rap sessions is especially valuable.

The issue of uniqueness of grammar, especially of verb tense and aspect, is an ongoing concern. Representative approaches include Joan G. Fickett's *Aspects of Morphemics, Syntax and Semology of an Inner-City Dialect* (West Rush, N.Y.: Meadowood Publications, 1970) which is devoted to fully documenting the cultural validity of Black English. Her more accessible "Tense and Aspect in Black English," *JEL,* 6 (March 1972), 17–20, extends the concern for cultural validity into the identification of tense and aspect of the Black English verb system, showing how tense and aspect reflect cultural attitudes and values. Through representative illustrations, she demonstrates that "Black English has five aspects, four relative past tenses, two relative future tenses and a true present tense. It has combinations of tense and aspect, but only one tense may appear in a predicator. As many as three aspects are possible in the same phrase. It is clear that the system is present oriented." Attempts to identify and explain continue into the present in such focused analyses as John Baugh's "*Steady:* Progressive Aspect in Vernacular Black English," *American Speech,*

59 (Spring 1984), 3–12, which attempts to explain special aspectual uses and to provide adequate data for making pronouncements about what the user of BEV *steady* intends.

As can be seen, all attempts to define dialect for practical purposes have been clouded by attitudes toward the nature of dialects, the users and uses of dialects, and the standard versus nonstandard argument. Concern for this led early to attitude studies that concentrate specifically on types of subjective reactions to language. Charles Billiard, Arnold Lazarus, and Raven I. McDavid, Jr., in *Identification of Dialect Features Which Affect Both Social and Economic Opportunity Among the Urban Disadvantaged, Final Report* (Washington, D.C.: Office of Education, 1969), report the results of a study undertaken to determine (a) dialect features associated with three ethnic groups (Anglo, Black, Latin American) and four social classes which were unacceptable to a dominant, urban culture (Fort Wayne, Indiana), (b) social markers which might handicap such speakers socio-economically and culturally, and (c) the implications of this for teacher preparation and classroom teaching. The results offer specific illustrations of code markers which may affect socio-economic mobility. The authors suggest that "greater emphasis should be given to [the] nature of usage and study of social dialects, problems of motivating students to learn a second dialect, and the techniques of developing two dialectal skills." Walt Wolfram's "Sociolinguistic Premises and the Nature of Nonstandard Dialects," *ST*, 19 (September 1970), 177–84, presents sociolinguistic considerations which affect teacher evaluation of speech behavior and teacher attitudes toward nonstandard speech behavior. Verbal options as arbitrary and/or established by custom, adequacy of a dialect as a communicative system, and language as learned in a community context are discussed. Raven I. McDavid, Jr.'s "Dialect Differences and Social Differences in an Urban Society," in *Sociolinguistics,* edited by William Bright (The Hague: Mouton, 1971), discusses the class markers by which speakers are tagged by their listeners and the resulting prestige or lack of it which is attributed to the speakers and their linguistic utterances. Nancy Hewett's "Reactions of Prospective English Teachers Toward Speakers of a Non-Standard Dialect," *LL,* 21 (December 1971), 205–12, tests "the hypothesis that prospective English teachers have unfavorable stereotypes of speakers of non-standard dialects." Standard and nonstandard pronunciation styles (taped) of black and white speakers were judged for personality characteristics, race, and probable occupation of the speakers. Prospective teachers participating in this matched-guise experiment exhibited common, culturally determined responses which produced the expected stereotyping.

A collection which serves the double purpose of (a) identifying the major directions taken in attitude research and (b) displaying methodologies developed and employed is *Language Attitudes: Current Trends and Prospects,* edited by Roger W. Shuy and Ralph W. Fasold (Washington, D.C.: Georgetown University Press, 1973). Twelve research statements consider subjective reactions to language. Attitudes, beliefs, and values held toward language varieties are investigated in studies dealing with such problems as dialect attitudes and stereotypes, teacher attitudes toward dialects, linguistic correlates of speech style, subjective reactions toward accented speech, anatomical and cultural determinants of male and female speech, stereotyped attitudes and dialect communities, reactions to various American-English dialects, objective and subjective parameters of language assimilation, bilingual attitudes and learning, and a conceptual framework for dealing with language, speech, and ideology.

Studies such as the above-listed encouraged the publication of "Students' Right To Their Own Language," *CCC,* 25 (Fall 1974), an explanation of the CCC's original resolution. This statement attempts to help teachers of composition and communication review then-current attitudinal problems and linguistic knowledge so that they may more effectively respond to the variety of dialects they face in the English classroom. The focus of the text and the extended bibliography is on the development of rational teaching positions based on then–present knowledge of language and its cultural effects.

Diatypic varieties

The study of diatypic varieties focuses attention on the intentionality of the speaker and the ways in which a speaker-writer adjusts discourse to create proximity with an audience in a given context. Written language varieties are emphasized. As a result, diatypic varieties study is intimately involved with speech events, cohesive procedures, stylistic variations, and stylistic considerations of written rhetorical competence—issues of first concern to the teacher of composition.

In varieties differentiation, studies of "levels," "styles," "keys," and "register" are viewed as intra-dialectal and are of special importance to the teacher of composition who must teach how variations and options within a dialect are used to create social distance or proximity. John Kenyon's "Cultural Levels and Functional Varieties of English," *CE,* 10 (October 1948), 31–36, was an early and incomplete attempt to draw a distinction between *cultural levels* and *functional varieties*—to establish the independence of style and class stratification of language. Unfortunately, the article does not recognize that the same linguistic variables may mark social distance and stylistic functions. The statement serves, however, to demonstrate the problems involved in delineating dialectal and diatypic varieties. In his now-classic *The Five Clocks* (New York: Harcourt, Brace & World, 1961, 1967), Martin Joos defines levels of functional style which he labels *frozen, formal, consultative, casual,* and *intimate.* He is careful to point out that in the case of the last four styles he is dealing with transcripts of speech. Through this set of five usage scales, which Joos matches against age, breadth, and responsibility scales, he attempts to direct concern toward the sets of linguistic features and constraints by which speakers establish degrees of intimacy in varieties of dyadic relationships. He also encourages a tolerant view of varying linguistic patterns by illustrating the complexities of usage.

H. A. Gleason, Jr., adapts Joos's functional styles identification in his chapter on "Language Variation," in *Linguistics and English Grammar* (New York: Holt, Rinehart and Winston, 1965). He identifies speech "keys" (*consultative, casual, deliberative, oratorical,* and *intimate*) to which the speaker appeals for signals by which to control the amount and length of required interaction and the structure of utterances. He also presents hearer adjustment features (status, assumed knowledge, polish of language, socially approved grammatical norms) that affect the keys. He distinguishes dialects as systems of keys. He also identifies written keys which he labels "literary": *formal,* corresponding to deliberative; *semiformal,* corresponding to consultative; *informal,* corresponding to casual. He then considers how they approximate equivalent speech keys. Albert H. Marckwardt's chapter on "Usage: Varieties, Levels, and Styles," in *Linguistics and the Teaching of English* (Bloomington: Indiana University Press, 1966), summarizes historically the many attempts to define and label hierarchies of usage, the confusion of terms that has resulted, and the shift in focus that each definer has encouraged. His summary, which ends with considerations of Kenyon, Joos, and *Webster's Third,* attempts to demonstrate the pedagogical problems that face the teacher who must deal with dialect variations and options.

Even cautionary studies reflect the importance of diatypic theory and research. Robbins Burling's "Standard Colloquial and Standard Written English: Some Implications for Teaching Literacy to Nonstandard Speakers," *Florida FL Reporter,* 8 (Spring/Fall 1970), 9–15, 47, investigates differences between written and spoken varieties of English and considers some of the ways in which they interact. He balances this information against the cautionary advice that teacher attitudes toward, and knowledge of, nonstandard habit patterns are the important factors in teaching literacy. Problems in teaching language usage are clarified. Burling points

out lexical, phonological, and grammatical variables (both constraints and options), considers what happens when standard,
nonstandard, and literary styles are mixed, and advocates teaching
for understanding of lexical variability, contraction and deletion,
homonymity, the colloquial passive, and shifting negation. The
teacher must know other dialects, but teaching Standard English
as a second dialect will only exacerbate the problem. His is a plea
for teaching varieties differentiation dialectally and diatypically.

M. A. K. Halliday, Angus McIntosh, and Peter Strevens's *The
Linguistic Sciences and Language Teaching* (Bloomington: Indiana
University Press, 1964) approaches the problem of social distance
and use through the term *register*. In the chapter "The Users and
Uses of Language," *register* is defined as a category "needed when
we want to account for what people do with their language. When
we observe language activity in the various contexts in which it
takes place, we find differences in the type of language selected as
appropriate to different types of situation." Out of this concern for
register have come style studies such as David Crystal and Derek
Davy's *Investigating English Style* (Bloomington: Indiana University Press, 1969). This text, geared to the university student, identifies features of language that characterize several major spoken
and written varieties of the present–day English of everyday life.
The authors' stylistic analyses isolate linguistic features of one
variety from another. The concern is to identify linguistic features
restricted to specific social contexts. To help the reader of this text
identify spoken and written varieties by functional orientation,
the authors encourage comparative linguistic analysis of language
samples (that is, of conversation, unscripted commentary, religious statements, newspaper reporting, legal documents) within
the dimensions of situational context.

The implications of *register* studies for multi–lingual composition classrooms quickly became apparent in the TESL field.
Appealing to the work of Gregory, Halliday, and Crystal, Ronald
V. White's "The Concept of Register and TESL," *TESOL Quarterly,* 8 (December 1974), 401–16, shows how the insights available

from this work can be used by the ESL teacher-as-researcher to identify items by frequency and range of occurrence in order to encourage diatypic varieties development in the ESL writer.

In addition to such attempts to analyze discourse diatypically, a body of literature on text coherence has been developing for text construction. M. A. K. Halliday and Raqaiya Hasan's *Cohesion in English* (London: Longman, 1976), provides a basic—though sophisticated and often difficult—introduction into the elements of substitution, ellipsis, conjunction, and lexical relations that constitute cohesion. This work alone has encouraged research studies aimed at verifying the usefulness of the system for analysis and production of composition. Patricia A. Carrell's "Cohesion Is Not Coherence," *TESOL Quarterly*, 16 (December 1982), 479–87, criticizes "the concept of cohesion as a measure of the coherence of a text." She argues against accepting cohesion studies as a panacea for ESL composition problems, explaining that broader theories taking the reader into account and denying the belief that coherence resides in the text must be considered. Robert J. Tierney and James H. Mosenthal's "Cohesion and Textual Coherence," *RTE*, 17 (October 1983), 215–29, presents the results of cohesive analyses of twelfth graders' essays, states that "a cohesion index is causally unrelated to a text's coherence," and explains how to base and present statements about the function of cohesive elements in coherent texts." Using Halliday and Hasan's (and others') theory to describe semantic relations between clauses, Jeanne Fahnestock's "Semantic and Lexical Coherence," *CCC*, 34 (December 1983), 400–16, offers yet another taxonomy for explaining semantic relations as they are developed in the grapholect which uses Standard English. Also working with Halliday and Hasan's theory, Robin Bell Markels offers and discusses four possible cohesion paradigms for expository paragraphs in "Cohesion Paradigms in Paragraphs," *CCC*, 45 (September 1983), 450–64. And in *A New Perspective on Cohesion in Expository Paragraphs* (Carbondale: Southern Illinois University Press, 1984), she pursues her considerations of cohesion, the relationship of the reader and cohesion, and single-term and multiple chain paragraphs.

USAGE AND ACCEPTABILITY

Attempts to identify social distance "levels," "styles," "keys," and "registers" have refocused attitudes toward usage theories and studies and have encouraged new definitions of usage. Also, controversy about standard and nonstandard varieties has encouraged new approaches to the gathering of usage data. An important usage article which directed attention quite early to doctrinal shifts in attitudes toward English usage is Charles V. Hartung's "Doctrines of English Usage," *EJ*, 45 (December 1956), 517–25. Hartung defines the four "propriety of language usage" doctrines (rules, general usage, appropriateness, and linguistic norm) that have informed statements on English usage. According to Hartung, the "rules" doctrine depends on an "assumed correspondence of the rules of grammar with basic principles of reason" and the "supposed correspondence of the rules with the usage of the best writers." The "general usage" doctrine takes its authority from those "language habits which have attained the most social acceptability." The "appropriateness" doctrine depends on "the satisfactory communication of thought and feeling" in social situations. It assumes knowledge of the community's language habits. The "linguistic norm" doctrine takes its authority from the need to "hold in balance the intention of the speaker, the nature of the language itself, the probable effect on the audience." He concludes that the linguistic norm doctrine with its concern for "maximum expression" would seem suitable for the classroom. Hartung's 1956 statement established a perspective for viewing subsequent statements about usage.

Standard sources of propriety–oriented, traditional usage information have been handbooks. *Current American Usage,* edited by Margaret M. Bryant (New York: Funk & Wagnalls, 1962) is most representative and offers a carefully researched, alphabetical usage handbook which bases decisions about acceptability on data collected from such varied sources as linguistic atlases, specialist journals, newspapers, popular magazines, radio broadcasts, formal grammars, and dictionaries. The aim is always to distinguish what has been identified with "Standard English" and what deviates from it. Distinctions are often rendered with "variety" labels of *informal, colloquial,* or *formal.* Items which represent divided usage are marked. Another type of handbook, designed to inform teachers about acceptability rules, is Robert C. Pooley's *The Teaching of English Usage,* second ed. (Urbana, Ill.: NCTE, 1974). This directive statement discusses English usage through consideration of the "problem of correctness," historical backgrounds, standard and nonstandard varieties of English usage, and "the nature of communication." Sources of specific information about usage and problems related to inflections and word order and to propriety are considered. The teaching of standard usage at the elementary, junior/middle, and high school levels is considered and suggestions for types of items to be used at each level are given. Procedures for evaluating what has been taught are offered.

The definition and study of usage as propriety is explained in much detail in Marvin K. L. Ching's recent, fine bibliographical essay, "Usage," in *Research in Composition and Rhetoric,* edited by Michael G. Moran and Ronald F. Lunsford (Westport, Conn.: Greenwood Press, 1984). Linguistic atlases, dictionaries, language history, and sex differences in communication are among the topics covered from the purview of usage, propriety, and judgmental procedures.

The need to deal with usage *in situation,* as it displays rhetorical intention, however, has become crucial as varieties differentiation has expanded. Reflecting concerns of the 1970s, James L. Funkhouser's "A Various Standard," *CE,* 34 (March 1973), 806–27, presents a discussion of how nonsituational handbook rules were superseded in the actual classroom by the writing of situational rules for effective communication of the ideas being developed by the students involved. Rule consistency is illustrated through Black English writing samples. Mary Vaiana Taylor's "The Folklore of Usage," *CE,* 35 (April 1974), 756–68, describes an attempt to make teacher-training students "conscious of the multiplicity of factors involved in judgments about usage." Students conducted a "field" study using a usage survey questionnaire in an effort to determine usage acceptability and the ways in which informants determined ultimate sources of authority. An awareness of the sociolinguistic forces that affect usage variations and options resulted.

Such willingness to test and question paved the way for Robert Gorrell's "Usage as Rhetoric," *CCC,* 28 (February 1977), 20–25. He states that (a) the mistake we make is in our basic attitude toward usage, (b) we misinterpret information and descriptions as precepts, (c) the linguistic information is only preliminary to the rhetorical decision, (d) *usage is a matter of rhetoric*—the art of making choices among available alternatives—and we must know the linguistic data bases from which to draw those choices. The importance of Gorrell's article is reflected in Jane R. Walpole's "Style as Option," *CCC,* 31 (May 1980), 205–12, which investigates the rhetoric-usage-grammar-style link in her discussion of how to improve student writing. Adding to the broadened definition of usage (as rhetoric) presented by Gorrell, Randolph Quirk's *Style and Communication in the English Language* (London: Edward Arnold, 1982) considers the interactions of usage and attitude with such concerns as broadcasting, nationhood, sexual permissiveness, and racial susceptibilities when people attempt to communicate. The rhetorical role of usage and its effect on rhetorical competence is a most serious issue here.

Another development of our changing approaches toward usage is the growing redefinition of error. Usage statements that question our definition of error and take into account the rhetorical and stylistic issues of discourse and rules of error analysis are proliferating. Mina Shaughnessy's *Errors and Expectations: A Guide for the Teacher of Basic Writing* (New York: Oxford University Press, 1977) sets one pattern for investigation into the nature of error and for redefinition of what constitutes usage error. Joseph M. Williams's "The Phenomenology of Error," *CCC*, 32 (May 1981), 152–68, deals with problems of usage, grammar, social error, and the perceptions of error in writing. He calls for greater care in rule making and acceptance. Williams's chapter, "Style and Usage," in *Style: Ten Lessons in Clarity & Grace*, second edition (Glenview: Scott, Foresman, 1985), provides a simple yet sophisticated discussion of rules (violations of Standard English) and nonrules (proscriptive folklore). Sidney Greenbaum and John Taylor's "The Recognition of Usage Errors by Instructors of Freshman Composition," *CCC*, 32 (May 1981), 169–74, discusses teachers' inabilities to identify and correct errors in a controlled experiment. They call for more work in this area.

The importance and accurate use of data-gathering methodologies is focused in Sidney Greenbaum's "Language Variation and Acceptability," *TESOL Quarterly*, 9 (June 1975), 165–72, in which he points out that attitudes toward and use of language do not always coincide. He provides reasons for unacceptability in both language variation and stylistic variation. The problem of surveying attitude and acceptability is displayed in Maxine Hairston's "Not All Errors Are Created Equal: Nonacademic Readers in the Professions Respond to Lapses in Usage," *CCC*, 43 (December 1981), 794–806. She describes non-teachers' responses to an informal questionnaire. Responses demonstrated that perceptions of the professionals surveyed were skewed to the conservative end of the spectrum. Why choices were made was sometimes a mystery.

As a result of changing attitudes toward authority and acceptability, knowledge of data-gathering methodologies is needed. Existing methodological texts include Randolph Quirk and Jan Svartvik's *Investigating Linguistic Acceptability* (The Hague: Mouton, 1966), which investigates "acceptability" and "grammaticality" and concentrates on "establishing degrees and kinds of acceptability in English sentences. Reasons are given for using "operation" and "selection" tests with informants. Problems of lexical and grammatical deviance and divided usage are discussed, and conclusions are presented. Sidney Greenbaum and Randolph Quirk, in *Elicitation Experiment in English* (Coral Gables, Fla.: University of Miami Press, 1970), explore the methodological problems involved in designing adequate elicitation procedures for determining use (performance) and attitude (judgment) responses to types of sentence tasks. "Acceptability" of utterance with regard to the grammatical and semantic constraints an informant feels bound to is investigated. Kinds of tests are described. The implications of this work for the gathering of usage data and facts are great. Rodney D. Huddleston's *The Sentence in Written English* (Cambridge: Cambridge University Press, 1971) is "a syntactic study based on an analysis of scientific texts." He does not attempt comparison study with other written varieties. Instead, he provides an intra-variety study which uses data samples from specialist journals, undergraduate textbooks, and popular works in the sciences. His intention is to investigate areas of the grammar of "common-core" English through his samples and to present a description of his findings, thereby producing a grammar on which to base further study.

COMMUNICATIVE COMPETENCE

The focusing on language varieties as a matter of literacy, of dialectal and diatypic differentiation, and of usage and acceptability requires the composition teacher to understand the nature and demands of communicative competence and the ethnography of communication. Communicative competence is a concept arising from ethnographic studies which seek to determine the social significance of competence *and* performance in speech and writing events. Dell Hymes in the Preface to *Directions in Sociolinguistics* (see later discussion) defined communicative competence as:

> what a speaker needs to know to communicate effectively in culturally significant settings. Like Chomsky's

term on which it is patterned, communicative competence refers to the ability to perform. An attempt is made to distinguish between what the speaker knows—what his inherent capacities are—and how he behaves in particular instances. However, whereas students of linguistic competence seek to explain those aspects of grammar believed to be common to all humans independent of social determinants, students of communicative competence deal with speakers as members of communities, as incumbents of social roles, and seek to explain their use of language to achieve self-identification and to conduct their activities. While for linguistic theory in the former sense the ability to formalize sentences as grammatically acceptable is the central notion, for sociolinguistics as represented in the book, the central notion is the appropriateness of verbal messages in context of their acceptability in the broader sense.

Several master collections of theoretical and research articles are available to acquaint the teacher of composition with this view of users and uses and to provide immediate access to the breadth and depth of sociolinguistic concerns. *Language in Culture and Society,* edited by Dell Hymes (New York: Harper & Row, 1964), arranges the now-classic statements of sixty-nine contributors into a ten-division discussion of (a) the scope of linguistic anthropology; (b) equality, diversity, relativity; (c) world view in grammatical categories; (d) cultural focus and semantic field; (e) role, socialization, and expressive speech; (f) speech play and verbal art; (g) social structure and speech community; (h) processes and problems of change; (i) relationships in time and space; and (j) historical perspectives. Definitions of the fields of study, comments on methodologies, language and dialect studies, mode-of-address studies, levels of usage studies, and standard language and vernacular language studies are presented and illustrated through a variety of languages and dialects.

259

Explorations in Sociolinguistics, edited by Stanley Lieberson (The Hague: Mouton, 1967), is a collection of thirteen articles which represent various views of the purposes of language and dialect. Through, among others, discussions of the effects of social mobility (Labov), elaborated and restricted codes (Bernstein), social stratification and cognitive orientation (Bright), social status and attitude (Heise), and social uniformation (Hertzler), the collection describes those components which contribute to prestige or nonprestige forms.

Readings in the Sociology of Language, edited by Joshua A. Fishman (The Hague: Mouton, 1968) provides an introduction to the general categories through the collected articles of forty-five contributors who present perspectives on the sociology of language (Sebeok, Lounsbury, Ervin and Miller, Hymes, Halliday), on language in small-group interaction (Lennard and Bernstein, Marshall, Joos, Ervin-Tripp, Bock), on language in social strata and sectors (Bernstein, Labov, Brown and Gilman, Nader, Geertz, Zengel, Weinreich), on language through sociocultural organization (Epstein, Leopold, Garvin and Mathiot, Ferguson, Weinreich, Conklin, Frake, Basilius, and Gumperz), on language within the scope of multi-lingualism (Lambert, Gardner, Olton and Tunstall, Herman, Rubin, Stewart, Lieberson, Mackey), on language maintenance and shift (Jakobson, Deutsch, Taylor, Hofman, Kloss, Samarin), and on language planning (Haugen, Goodman, Berry, Ray, Guxman). This introductory reader serves to orient the reader to the milieu within which varieties of language may be considered. The following articles are of special value: Dell H. Hymes's "The Ethnography of Speaking" defines speech in cognitive and expressive behavior, seeks a descriptive analysis of speaking, explains "speech event" as composed of seven factors (that is, sender, receiver, message form, channel, code, topic, and setting), and considers the function of speech events. Susan M. Ervin-Tripp's "An Analysis of the Interaction of Language, Topic, and Listener" defines setting, participant, and topic and explains their functions in dyadic interactions. Changes of form (formal features) which occur when one or another of these factors dominates are considered. Joshua A. Fishman's "The Sociology of Language" defines the combined field of linguistics and sociology as inquiry into "the co-variation of diversity and of pattern in these two fields." Language is explained as consisting of codes, regional varieties, social class varieties, and stylistic varieties.

Sociolinguistics, edited by William Bright (The Hague: Mouton, 1971) introduces the papers of thirteen participants in the 1964 UCLA Sociolinguistics Conference. The purpose of the collection is to present perspectives on the dimensions of sociolinguistics. Included are statements on folk-linguistics (Hoenigswald), the ethnology of linguistic change (Gumperz), linguistics and language planning (Haugen), urban dialect and social differences (McDavid), the effect of lower middle class hypercorrection on linguistic change (Labov), types of linguistic relativity (Hymes), syntax and social structure (Fischer), self-annulling prestige factors (Samarin), structural implications of pronominal usage (Friedrich), writing systems development for preliterate peoples (Sjoberg), language status (Rona, Kelly), and national sociolinguistic profile formulas (Ferguson).

In *Directions in Sociolinguistics,* edited by John J. Gumperz and Dell Hymes (New York: Holt, Rinehart and Winston, 1972), an ethnography of communication is developed through nineteen articles which explain (a) the socio-cultural shaping of ways of speaking, (b) procedures for discovering and stating rules of conversation and address, and (c) the origin, persistence, and change of varieties of language. The aim is "to present evidence documenting the existence of a level of rule-governed verbal behavior which goes beyond the linguists' grammar to relate social and linguistic constraints on speech, to illustrate the type of data that must be collected for its analysis and the elicitation methods by which it can be gathered." As in so many of these collections, the contributions reflect work done in many different languages and dialects. Thus, the chapter on ethnographic description and explanation contains a study of the Yakan concept of litigation and a study of Afro-American signifying and marking procedures. The chapter on discovering structure in speech contains a study of sequencing in conversational openings and a study of the social context and semantic features which are illustrated through Russian pronominal usage. The chapter on genesis, maintenance, and change of linguistic codes contains a study of code switching in Norway which demonstrates social meaning in linguistic structures and a description of the mechanisms of linguistic change in the Martha's Vineyard and New York City areas.

More recently, Charles A. Ferguson and Shirley Brice Heath's *Language in the USA* (Cambridge: Cambridge University Press, 1981) focuses on the need to expand ethnographic data to verify the numbers and importance of speakers and varieties involved in American English (Heath, Kachru, Wolfram, Nichols, Whatley), languages before English (Leap, Walker, Taylor, Craddock), languages after English (Zentella, Correa-Zoli, Gilbert, Gold, Henzl, Beebe and Beebe, Beltramo), and language in use (O'Barr, Cicourel, Gumperz and Gumperz, Cazden and Dickinson, Paulston, Waggoner, Fishman). The key issues here are ethnicity, language differences, and language maintenance.

Language and Social Identity, edited by John J. Gumperz (Cambridge: Cambridge University Press, 1982), provides insights into "communication processes that underlie categorization, intergroup stereotyping, evaluation of verbal performance and access into public resources in modern societies." Discourse structure and strategies—from courtroom testimony to male-female communication—are discussed by Gumperz, Cook-Gumperz, Aulakh, Kaltman, Mishra, Young, Hensell, Ajerotutu, Bennett, Heller, Akinnaso, Maltz, Borker, Tannen, Jupp, Roberts.

The above-listed collections introduce the reader to broad aspects of communicative competence and at the same time demonstrate cross-cultural investigative procedures. Two important works which narrow their procedures and illustrations to present intra-cultural approaches show the development of a new direction. *Rappin' and Stylin' Out: Communication in Urban Black America*, edited by Thomas Kochman (Urbana: University of Illinois Press, 1972), presents a study of communication in the urban black situation through the views of twenty-seven contributors. The spectrum of black communication from non-verbal and verbal expression to vocabulary and culture and from expressive uses of languages to expressive role behavior is reviewed. Visual and verbal illustrations are abundant. Through his collection, Kochman attempts "to identify some of the communicative and behavioral norms of urban black Americans and (wherever possible) their source." He has "deliberately and consistently chosen to examine those contexts where the vernacular culture has been most pervasive and articulated and where mainstream cultural norms are likely to have penetrated *least*." This ethnic portrait presents descriptions of street, church, clubhouse, shoeshine stand, park, pool hall, and cafe behavior. Its contributors employ a variety of methodologies to consider nonverbal communication, vocabulary and culture, expressive language, and expressive roles. A more recent ethnographic study which expands the intra-cultural approach is Shirley Brice Heath's *Ways with Words* (Cambridge: Cambridge University Press, 1983). This single-author ethnographic study attempts to provide a complete methodology for studying whole communities, singly and by comparison. Orality versus literacy and the ways children learn to talk in Trackton (black working-class community) and Roadville (white working-class community) in the Piedmont Carolinas are studied. Brice gives special attention to types of uses of reading and writing.

A review of the divisions of this essay verifies that in 1985, after several decades of the gathering of forces, language varieties and composition are indeed fields of study with a history, with sets of concerns that require divisions and classifications, and with a various subject matter. Many gaps still exist in data, practices, and theories. Some of this appears to be the result of scholarly and political shifts in interests and concerns which preclude adequate updating. There remain terminological confusions—some due to idiosyncratic needs to refine distinctions; some due to absorption from other fields and use without adequate concern for the "freight" the terms bring with them. There are conflicts in positions—some tied to firmly held beliefs; others resulting from the tentativeness of research results. However, the importance of this study to the development of rhetorical competence is firmly established and its value to us is clear.

Literacy, Linguistics, and Rhetoric

W. ROSS WINTEROWD, University of Southern California

THE NATURE OF A FIELD GIVEN TO THE STUDY of language (i.e., linguistics) will depend on the definition of language accepted by practitioners in the discipline. If "language is in the main muscular movement, either voluntary or involuntary, determined by changes in the nervous system of the communicator" (Walter B. Pillsbury and Clarence L. Meader, *The Psychology of Language* [New York: D. Appleton and Company, 1928], pp. 4–5), then linguistics will ultimately be a branch of physiology. However, if you define language as symbolic action (Kenneth Burke, *Language as Symbolic Action* [Berkeley and Los Angeles: University of California, 1966]), then linguistics will be a branch of rhetoric. And the latter is, as a matter of fact, the definition that I stipulate in this essay.

The essay that follows, then, is a rhetorician's survey of linguistics. I have not dealt with, for instance, syntax or phonology because I feel that those subjects relate more tangentially—or hardly at all—to the concerns of rhetoricians.

As I was preparing to write this essay, three colleagues at the University of Southern California availed me of their wisdom, knowledge, and good fellowship: Professors Elinor Ochs, Stephen Krashen, and Edward Finegan, all members of the Linguistics Department. I thank them for their invaluable help. John and Tilly Warnock of the University of Wyoming read a draft of the essay and made valuable suggestions. As usual, my colleague Louise Wetherbee Phelps helped me in various ways with her perceptive advice.

Some will argue, no doubt, that I have cast too wide a net, bringing in not only literacy in general, but reading theory and other matters not usually conceived as belonging directly to linguistics. However, in a volume such as the present one there must be a place where composition theory is located in literacy theory, of which the former is a part. Compositionists must also take account of reading theory, particularly now with the movement beyond the current-traditional "process" model toward what might be called a "transactional" model of composition. In 1975, I said,

> Any view of the composing process that limits itself just to the discourser . . . is likely to be warped, for the discourse itself is shaped not only by the discourser's mental and kinetic abilities but also by other factors in the discourse complex. Aside from an addressee (or addressees) to be adjusted to, there are also the context of composing . . . the sort of contact that is established, and the limits and possibilities of the code to be taken into account. . . . There can be no "Skinner box" studies of the composing process, for isolating the composer and limiting his or her activity to one segment of the whole process simply falsifies what actually goes on (*Contemporary Rhetoric: A Conceptual Background with Readings* [New York: Harcourt Brace Jovanovich]. See also Louise Wetherbee Phelps, "Dialectics of Coherence: Toward an Integrative Theory," discussed below in "Form.")

LITERACY

In regard to the rhetoric of written composition, linguistics is meaningless outside the context of literacy, a term which in this discussion includes any act of reading or writing, from the most basic to the most sophisticated. For this reason, the essay begins with "literacy" and works toward increasingly more specific areas of concern.

In *Literacy: Writing, Reading and Social Organisation* (London: Routledge & Kegan Paul, 1980), John Oxenham presents a brief (135-page), readable, and perceptive introduction to the field, including a history of writing systems. This work is particularly valuable because of its focus on the social needs for and consequences of literacy.

Studies and theories of literacy tend to fall into one of two areas: the effects of literacy on cognition and the social ramifications of reading and writing. A now-classic work that deals with literacy and cognition is Eric A. Havelock's *Preface to Plato* (Oxford: Basil Blackwell, 1963), a book that raises many of the key issues.

Havelock begins by asking why Plato banished poetry from the Republic and postulates that the Greeks had a completely different view of poetry from ours.

In fact, argues Havelock, Plato is at the transition between a pre-literate and a literate society. For him, poetry represented an educational method and body of lore, not a form of higher pleasure, let alone higher truth. To preserve the cultural tradition, poets composed metrical narratives—metrical so that they would be easier to memorize and narrative because that was a way both of knowing and of telling. These poems—the "Homeric" epics, for example—were "encyclopedias" of history, public policy, community values, and so on.

Committing this traditional lore—in the form of poems— to memory demanded intense involvement; the learner was not separated from the learning, but participated in it, much as an actor assumes roles in dramas, a sort of *mimesis*.

In order for the concept of individuality to emerge, argues Havelock, it was necessary for the Greek mind to make itself independent of poetic knowledge—to "stop identifying itself successively with a whole series of polymorphic vivid narrative situations" (p. 200)—and thus gain the freedom to say "I am I," not an agglomeration of the characters in the poetry that has made up my total heritage.

Concomitant with the separation of the knower from the known comes the recognition that the known is an object. In the poetic "encyclopedia," knowledge was a series of events, but now with literacy it is possible to know the law, and the individual acts and events become irrelevant. "They should be discarded; they are the accidents and incidentals of place, time, and circumstance. What we require to think about and to know is 'the law itself'" (p. 217). For Plato's philosophy and mindset to develop, it was clearly essential that poetry in the "classical" sense be banned from the Republic.

The concept of self and the inevitable alienation from community, the separation of the knower from the known, the birth of abstract knowledge—these are perhaps the principal motifs that run through works on literacy and mind. (As a prime example, see Walter J. Ong, S. J., *Interfaces of the Word* [Ithaca: Cornell University Press, 1977]. The boldest claims regarding the effects of literacy are those of Marshall McLuhan in *The Gutenberg Galaxy* [Toronto: University of Toronto Press, 1962].)

The social-scientific study of literacy and cognition begins with Lev S. Vygotsky (*Thought and Language* [Cambridge, Mass.: MIT Press, 1962]; *Mind in Society: The Development of Higher Psychological Processes,* ed. M. Cole, V. John-Steiner, S. Scribner, and E. Souberman [Cambridge, Mass.: Harvard University Press, 1978]), who, in the 1920s and 1930s, proposed universal psychological processes (generalization, abstraction, inference) that vary according to the symbol systems used and the societies in which they are used. Following Vygotsky in the 1930s, A. R. Luria (*Higher Cortical Functions in Man* [New York: Basic Books, 1966]; *Cognitive Development: Its Cultural and Social Foundations* [Cambridge, Mass.: Harvard University Press, 1976]; *Making of Mind* [Cambridge, Mass.: Harvard University Press, 1979]) tested literates and non-literates in a rapidly developing region of central Asia. He found that the non-literate, unschooled population responded to his tasks in context-bound, concrete ways. The most highly schooled group, on the other hand, dealt in abstractions and discovered logical relationships among items. In short, Luria's results would lead us to believe that literacy fosters the ability to carry out abstract, logical thinking.

However, two works serve as cautions against sweeping conclusions regarding the effects of literacy on cognition: Jack Goody, *The Domestication of the Savage Mind* (Cambridge, Eng.: Cambridge University Press, 1977) and Sylvia Scribner and Michael Cole, *The Psychology of Literacy* (Cambridge, Mass.: Harvard University Press, 1981)—both of which argue against the "great divide theory" that literacy radically changes the structure of human cognition, domesticating the "savage" mind.

Goody begins with a critique of Lévi-Strauss, who develops the great divide theory in *The Savage Mind* (Chicago: University of Chicago Press, 1966). According to Goody's argument, Lévi-Strauss commits the typically structuralist fallacy of dichotomizing, viewing the world from a binarist standpoint: modern–neolithic, science of the abstract–science of the concrete, scientific thought–mythical thought, engineering–bricolage, history–myths. Yes, literacy does change the nature of human cognition, Goody argues, but not as drastically as the "great divide" theory would hold. "The boy brought up as a bricoleur becomes an engineer. He has his difficulties, but they do not lie at the level of an overall opposition between wild and domesticated minds, thoughts or approaches, but on a much more particularistic level" (pp. 8–9).

Scribner and Cole studied the Vai, a group of people living on the border of Liberia and Sierra Leone. The Vais have three literacies: the native (with a unique syllabic script), learned through traditional socialization; English, learned in school; and Arabic, learned through memorizing the Qur'an and perhaps subsequently in school. Some members of the group have all three literacies; some have none; and the level of skills varies, from the most "basic" to the relatively sophisticated. Here was an opportunity to study literacy precisely at the "great divide" between savage and civilized. The results of the study suggest that schooling, not literacy *per se,* brings about the most dramatic cognitive changes. In a chart adapted from Scribner and Cole (p. 253), Figure 1 presents a summary of results.

Additionally, urbanization, not literacy, seems to facilitate the ability to sort and classify.

A collection that addresses the dichotomy of literacy is *Spoken and Written Language: Exploring Orality and Literacy,* ed.

Figure 1

BROAD CATEGORY OF EFFECT	Type of Literacy			
	English/ school	Vai Script	Qur'anic	Arabic language
Categorizing (form/number sort)	xxxxx	xxxxx		xxxxx
Memory — Incremental recall			xxxxx	xxxxx
Memory — Free recall	xxxxx			
Logical reasoning (syllogisms)	xxxxx			
Encoding and decoding rebuses — Reading	xxxxx	xxxxx		
Encoding and decoding rebuses — Writing	xxxxx	xxxxx		xxxxx
Semantic integration — Words	xxxxx	xxxxx	xxxxx	xxxxx
Semantic integration — Syllables		xxxxx*		
Verbal explanation — Communication game	xxxxx	xxxxx		
Verbal explanation — Grammatical rules	xxxxx	xxxxx		
Verbal explanation — Sorting geometric figures	xxxxx			
Verbal explanation — Logical syllogisms	xxxxx			

*It should be remembered that Vai script is a syllabary.

Deborah Tannen (Advances in Discourse Processes, No. IX; Norwood, N.J.: Ablex, 1982).

For both the teacher and the theoretician, the work of Paulo Freire is massively important. *Education for Critical Consciousness* (New York: Continuum, 1981) first appeared in 1969 in Rio de Janeiro; *Pedagogy of the Oppressed* (trans. Myra Bergman Ramos; New York: Continuum, 1982) was first published in 1968, again in Rio de Janeiro.

Freire developed a pedagogical method which Winterowd ("Black Holes, Indeterminacy, and Paulo Freire," *RR*, 2, No. 1 [Sept. 1983], 28–36) explains as follows:

> The literacy teacher begins with a *generative word*, such as *favela* (slum) and breaks it down into syllables: *fa-ve-la*. These syllables in turn generate phonemic groups: *fa-fe-fi-fo-fu, va-ve-vi-vo-vu, la-le-li-lo-lu*. However, the word *favela* is not presented visually until the group "discusses the problems of housing, food, clothing, health, and education in a slum and . . . further perceives the slum as a problem situation. . . ." Other generative words are presented, and ultimately the group is using its newly acquired knowledge of phonemic combinations to read and then write other words. [See Freire, *Education for Critical Consciousness*, p. 82.]

The method involves what might be called *technic*: the phonics learning, for example. Far more important, however, is rhetoric: placing the technic squarely in the area of human concerns, making literacy valid and vital.

Freire goes beyond literacy as such to a whole theory of education, in which teacher and students learn together, cooperatively. The teacher does not "deposit" knowledge with the students, but works with them to develop it.

Literacy and Revolution, edited by Robert Mackie (New York: Continuum, 1981), is a useful collection of essays on Freire and his work.

Literacy for Life: The Demand for Reading and Writing (New York: MLA, 1983), edited by Richard W. Bailey and Robin Melanie Fosheim, is a particularly interesting collection, containing essays by, among others, A. L. Becker, Gavriel Salomon, Deborah Tannen, Frank D'Angelo, and James Boyd White. This book has great political significance, marking the entry of the MLA into mainline studies of literacy. (For discussions of the professional politics of literacy, see W. Ross Winterowd, "The Politics of Meaning: Scientism, Literarism, and the New Humanism," *Written Communication*, 2 [July 1985], 269–92; "The Paradox of the Humanities," *ADE Bulletin*, 64 [May 1980], 2–4.)

PSYCHOLINGUISTICS

In *Psychology and Language: An Introduction to Psycholinguistics* (New York: Harcourt Brace Jovanovich, 1977), Herbert H. Clark and Eve V. Clark have synthesized the field; their book is accessible to the layperson, adequately comprehensive for the purposes of non-specialists, and lucidly written.

What are the boundaries of psycholinguistics? The field starts with such minutiae as the identification of isolated speech sounds (pp. 191–210) and extends through meaning and thought (pp. 407–558). Along the way, one finds that ordinary language philosophy (Austin, Searle, and Grice, discussed in the "Pragmatics" section of this essay), transformational generative grammar, schema theory, learning theory, and a host of other areas make up the territory of psycholinguistics. It is a comment on the discipline, not a criticism of Clark and Clark, to mention that the book is totally devoid of rhetorical theory, either classical or modern. Among the unmentioned: Aristotle, Cicero, Quintilian, Blair, Campbell, Kenneth Burke, Chaim Perelman, Wayne Booth, Roland Barthes, Jacques Derrida. . . . Rhetoric is beginning to make use of psycholinguistics, but psycholinguistics has not yet discovered rhetoric.

READING

To get under way, we must establish two points. In the first place, reading theory has developed through two separate traditions, the *social-scientific* and the *humanistic*. Second, even though reading and writing are not mirror images of one another, it is inconceivable that one should study composition/rhetoric without taking account of reading, a point that is, in effect, our *Leitmotif* and that Stephen L. Kucer develops in "The Making of Meaning: Reading and Writing as Parallel Processes," *Written Communication*, 2 (July 1985), 317–36: "Drawing from a common pool of cognitive and linguistic operations" (p. 319), both activities produce what Kucer calls text worlds, make meaning. The literacy model in which the writer actively creates meaning and the reader passively absorbs it obscures the roles of both parties in the transaction.

We could begin our story with Edmund Burke Huey, who in 1908 published *The Psychology and Pedagogy of Reading,* reissued in 1968 by MIT Press, with an introduction by George Miller, who says that, by and large, Huey's amazing work still serves as a good introduction to the problems of reading. In fact, after a long period during which reading theory was predominantly behavioristic, Huey's "cognitivist" view has reemerged.

Undoubtedly the best introduction to current work is Frank Smith's *Understanding Reading* (Third edition; New York: Holt, Rinehart and Winston, 1982). In a couple of hundred pages, this well-written book takes one through the essential topics in its field, from a brief general introduction to language and linguistics through cognitive processes such as memory to letter and word identification and on finally to teaching. Because it is thorough (though not detailed), reliable, and "basic," this book is excellent for either beginners or laypersons.

Encyclopedic, and representative of what might be called the "current-traditional" model of reading, is Eleanor J. Gibson and Harry Levin's *The Psychology of Reading* (Cambridge, Mass.: MIT

Press, 1975). The three sections of the book deal with "Concepts Underlying the Study of Reading" (such as cognitive strategies and language development), "The Study of Reading" (e.g., the development of prereading skills, beginning to read, learning from reading), and "Questions People Ask About Reading."

In the "current-traditional" model that *The Psychology of Reading* represents, reading is the extraction of information from text in order to reduce uncertainty, with the focus squarely on the informational and "utilitarian," to the exclusion of what Louise Rosenblatt calls "afferent" reading (*Literature as Exploration* [Third edition, New York: Noble and Noble, 1976]) or "aesthetic" reading (*The Reader, the Text, the Poem: The Transactional Theory of the Literary Work* [Carbondale: Southern Illinois University Press, 1978]).

In a book also called *The Psychology of Reading* (New York: Academic Press, 1983), Insup Taylor and M. Martin Taylor cover all the territory staked out by Gibson and Levin, and then go well beyond those boundaries.

Taylor and Taylor are, of course, more up to date than Gibson and Levin, taking account, for instance, of work by Walter Kintsch and Teun A. van Dijk ("Toward a Model of Discourse Comprehension and Production," *Psychological Review* 85 [1978], 363–94) and D. E. Rumelhart ("Understanding and Summarizing Brief Stories," in D. LaBerge and J. Samuels, eds., *Basic Processes in Reading and Comprehension* [Hillsdale, N.J.: Lawrence Erlbaum Associates, 1977]). But this 1983 book has other strengths.

In the first place, Taylor and Taylor's discussion of writing systems is superb, including analyses of Oriental systems as well as Western. (From Gibson and Levin, one gathers the impression that literacy is strictly an Occidental phenomenon.)

Yet more significant is "the bilateral cooperative model of reading" that the authors develop. According to this model,

> The *LEFT track* deals with functional relationships, sequentially ordered material, phonetic coding, syntax,

and most functions we commonly think of as "linguistic." It is the analytic and logical track. The *RIGHT track* performs pattern matching functions, seeks out similarities between the input patterns and previously seen patterns, evokes associations, and relates the meanings of words and phrases with real-world conditions. Its functions tend to be global, parallel, and passive. (p. 233)

But, Taylor and Taylor admonish us, left and right track are not to be confused with left and right hemispheres of the brain. The left-right split is a way of schematizing, a mnemonic device. Yet the categories of functions do square with current notions about hemispheric specialization. (See W. Ross Winterowd, "Brain, Rhetoric, and Style," in *The Territory of Language,* ed. Donald McQuade [Carbondale: Southern Illinois University Press, 1986].)

Smith, Gibson and Levin, and Taylor and Taylor, then, represent the social-scientific bands in the spectrum of reading theory and research. The humanist side can be termed "post-structuralist," a general category that splits (not very neatly) into "reader-response" and "deconstructionist."

Two collections present the range of reader-response theory: *Reader-Response Criticism: From Formalism to Post-Structuralism* (Baltimore: Johns Hopkins University Press, 1980), edited by Jane P. Tompkins, and *The Reader in the Text: Essays on Audience and Interpretation* (Princeton: Princeton University Press, 1980), edited by Susan R. Suleiman and Inge Crosman.

The reader-response movement (if such it can be called) is appositely summed up by Stanley Fish (*Is There a Text in This Class? The Authority of Interpretive Communities* [Cambridge, Mass.: Harvard University Press, 1980]):

Whereas I had once agreed with my predecessors on the need to control interpretation lest it overwhelm and obscure texts, facts, authors, and intentions, I now believe that interpretation is the source of texts, facts, authors, and intentions. Or to put it another way, the entities that were once seen as competing for the right to constrain interpretation (text, reader, author) are now all seen to be the *products* of interpretation. (pp. 16–17)

In other words, reader-response theory is, in a sense, at the opposite pole from the older objective (i.e., "New") criticism. One can see that in their view of meaning and its sources, literary and psychological theories (such as those outlined by Kucer above) arrive at virtually the same point: the reader makes the meaning, and the text exists only in the mind of the reader.

It is possible to claim that reader-response criticism began in 1938 when Louise Rosenblatt published *Literature as Exploration* (cited above), an excellent book that seems to have had no influence on the mainline literary theorists working today.

In *Is There a Text in This Class?* (cited above), Stanley Fish argues the case for reader-centered criticism. Interpretation can be nothing other than subjective in one sense, for meaning is clearly not "in" the text. However, the reader is a member of an interpretive community, necessarily or else interpretation would be impossible; it is community that makes possible the development and sharing of meaning. By invoking the idea of interpretive community, Fish avoids the pitfall of pure subjectivity, the ultimate solipsism.

In *The Act of Reading: A Theory of Aesthetic Response* (Baltimore: Johns Hopkins University Press, 1978), Wolfgang Iser focuses on the interaction between text and reader, text being in effect a set of instructions for the derivation of a meaning, which is the meeting place of four perspectives: "those of the narrator, the characters, the plot, and the fictitious reader [i.e., the persona that the real reader assumes]" (p. 34).

David Bleich's *Subjective Criticism* (Baltimore: Johns Hopkins University Press, 1978) is a systematic and thoroughgoing argument regarding the epistemology of reader-response theory.

Bleich and Fish both hold that the reader creates the meaning and the purposes of literature, but that those judgments are validated by a community. Hence, the interpretive community is the ultimate source of meanings. (See also by Bleich, *Readings and Feelings: An Introduction to Subjective Criticism* [Urbana: NCTE, 1975] and "The Subjective Character of Critical Interpretation," *CE*, 36 [March 1975], 739–55.)

The preeminent name in deconstructionist criticism is, of course, Jacques Derrida, whose work is largely a reaction against the doctrine of presence and structuralism. In "Post-Structuralism and Composition," *Pre/Text*, 4, no. 1 (Spring 1983), 79–92, I sum up this way:

> In the Western tradition—from Plato to Walter Ong—writing has been considered the signifier (secondary) of the signifier (primary), which is speech. But Derrida argues that there is no *logos* behind the words. And suppose there were. How could you get at it except through language? So the problem is that meaning is built of *traces,* and traces are nothing but structures of differences and hence are not "something" (p. 82).

As Derrida himself puts it,

> It is because writing is *inaugural,* in the fresh sense of the word, that it is dangerous and anguishing. It does not know where it is going, no knowledge can keep it from the essential precipitation toward the meaning that it constitutes and that is, primarily, its future. . . . Meaning is neither before nor after the act. ("Force and Signification," in *Writing and Difference,* trans. Alan Bass [Chicago: University of Chicago Press, 1978], p. 11.)

Derrida's central work is *Of Grammatology* (trans. Gayatri Chakravorty Spivak [Baltimore: Johns Hopkins University Press, 1974]). A collection that gives a fair sampling of post-structuralist thinking is Josué V. Harari, ed., *Textual Strategies: Perspectives in*

Post-Structuralist Criticism (Ithaca: Cornell University Press, 1979).

The whole of post-structuralism raises the question of meaning's indeterminacy. If meanings are in readers, not in texts, can we talk about authorial intention and the "real" meaning to be found in the writer's ostensible inscription of that intention? The main proponent of the principle of determinacy is E. D. Hirsch, Jr., (*Validity in Interpretation* [New Haven: Yale University Press, 1973]; *The Aims of Interpretation* [Chicago: University of Chicago Press, 1976]), whose argument, in barest outline, runs like this: since language is a human action, it must have a purpose or *semantic intention;* it is the obligation of the reader to attempt to find that intention, in other words, to capture the author's meaning, which is expressed in or through the text.

Finally, two books that set forth the background needed to make sense of post-structuralism: Jonathan Culler's *Structuralist Poetics* (Ithaca: Cornell University Press, 1975) and Frank Lentricchia's *After the New Criticism* (Chicago: University of Chicago Press, 1980).

ENGLISH AS A SECOND LANGUAGE

In a widely reprinted and highly influential essay, "Cultural Thought Patterns in Inter-Cultural Education," Robert B. Kaplan has argued that thought patterns differ among cultures and that this difference manifests itself in written discourse, in coherence, especially at the paragraph level. This work appears in *Composing in a Second Language* (Sandra McKay, ed. [Rowley, Mass.: Newbury House, 1984]), along with other standard and important pieces, each followed by discussions and applications: Linda Flower, "Writer-Based Prose: A Cognitive Basis for Problems in Writing"; Bonnie J. F. Meyer, "Reading Research and the Composition Teacher: The Importance of Plans"; Nancy Sommers, "Responding to Student Writing," among others. According to my colleague Stephen Krashen, this 169-page collection pretty much covers literature relevant to composition in ESL.

Krashen's own book, *Second Language Acquisition and Second*

Language Learning (Oxford, Eng.: Pergamon Press, 1981), is an important statement concerning not only second-language learning, but also, by easy and inevitable extension, learning how to write. In fact, for discussions of just such an extension, see W. Ross Winterowd, "Developing a Composition Program" (in A. Freedman and I. Pringle, eds., *Reinventing the Rhetorical Tradition* [Conway, Ark.: L&S Books, 1980]) and "From Classroom Practice into Psycholinguistic Theory" (in A. Freedman and I. Pringle, *Learning to Write: First Language/Second Language* [London and New York: Longman, 1983]).

Krashen's point is that two processes are involved in language learning: conscious learning and unconscious acquisition. Of the two, acquisition is by far the more powerful; hence, teachers should provide environments, use methods, and choose materials that foster acquisition.

PRAGMATICS

In 1938, C. W. Morris divided the kingdom of semiotics into three provinces: syntactics, the study of "the formal relations of signs to one another"; semantics, the study of "the relations of signs to the objects to which the signs are applicable"; and pragmatics, the study of "the relation of signs to interpreters" (*Foundations of the Theory of Signs,* in O. Neurath, R. Carnap, and C. Morris, eds., *International Encyclopedia of Unified Science* [Chicago: University of Chicago Press], p. 6). Since Morris advanced his definition, the term *pragmatics* has undergone remodeling and overhauling by philosophers and linguists, but for our purposes "the study of the relation of signs to interpreters" is perfectly adequate.

From the point of view of linguistics, what areas of inquiry constitute pragmatics? In an excellent introduction to the field, Stephen C. Levinson (*Pragmatics* [Cambridge, Eng.: Cambridge University Press, 1983]) charts five: deixis (reference), conversational implicature, presupposition, speech acts, and conversational structure.

Of primary interest to rhetoricians are implicature, speech acts, and conversational structure.

In a series of lectures at Harvard in 1967, H. P. Grice had outlined the main ideas of implicature ("Logic and Conversation," in P. Cole and J. L. Morgan, eds., *Syntax and Semantics 3: Speech Acts* [New York: Academic Press, 1975], pp. 41–58; P. Cole, ed., "Further Notes on Logic and Conversation," in *Syntax and Semantics 9: Pragmatics* [New York: Academic Press, 1978], pp. 113–28). The "cooperative principle" that he worked out consists of four maxims:

> *The maxim of Quality*
> try to make your contribution one that is true, specif-
> ically:
> (i) do not say what you believe to be false
> (ii) do not say that for which you lack adequate evidence
> *The maxim of Quantity*
> (i) make your contribution as informative as is required
> for the current purpose of the exchange
> (ii) do not make your contribution more informative
> than is required
> *The maxim of Relevance*
> make your contribution relevant
> *The maxim of Manner*
> be perspicuous, and specifically:
> (i) avoid obscurity
> (ii) avoid ambiguity
> (iii) be brief
> (iv) be orderly (Levinson, *Pragmatics,* pp. 101–02)

These maxims set forth what John Searle (*Speech Acts* [Cambridge, Eng.: Cambridge University Press, 1969]) would call the "constitutive rules" of the conversational game. Though phrased as imperative sentences, the maxims are descriptive of language norms, the violation of which creates figures of speech such as irony or, on the other hand, mere confusion. For example, the following sentence violates the maxim of manner:

Miss Singer produced a series of sounds corresponding closely to the score of an aria from *Rigoletto*.

The violation was either intentional or unintentional. If the addressee takes the violation to be intentional, he or she interprets the sentence as irony: if the violation is taken to be unintentional, the sentence is judged inept.

Grice's work, then, enables us to account, at least in part, not only for figurative language, but also for cohesion and coherence. Employed instructionally, the maxims enable teachers to explain economically and powerfully many of the weaknesses in student texts (or, for that matter, in any texts). One can point out to students that when they write, as when they talk, they are entering into a Gricean "contract" with the reader; unintentional violations of that contract are extremely dangerous, but intentional violations are the very moves that allow one to use language figuratively.

Speech act theory begins as a recognizable entity with J. L. Austin (*How to Do Things with Words* [Oxford: Clarendon Press, 1962]), whose work, in a sense, was formalized by John Searle (*Speech Acts* [Cambridge, Eng.: Cambridge University Press, 1969]). A host of other linguists have entered the lists, which are growing exponentially. Levinson says, "Of all the issues in the general theory of language usage, *speech act theory* has probably aroused the widest interest" (p. 226)—not only among linguists, but among psychologists (e.g., Jerome Bruner, "The Ontogenesis of Speech Acts," *Journal of Child Language,* 2 [1975], 1–20), anthropologists, literary theorists (e.g., Stanley Fish, "Speech-Act Theory, Literary Criticism, and *Coriolanus,*" *Centrum,* 3, no. 2 [Fall 1975], 107–11; Richard Ohmann, "Speech Acts and the Definition of Literature," *P and R,* 4 [1971], 1–19; Mary Louise Pratt, *Toward a Speech Act Theory of Literary Discourse* [Bloomington: Indiana University Press, 1971]), and rhetoricians: e.g.,

Dorothy Augustine and W. Ross Winterowd, "Intention and Response: Speech Acts and the Sources of Composition," in *Convergences: Transactions in Reading and Writing,* ed. Bruce Peterson (Urbana: NCTE, 1986); Walter H. Beale, "Rhetorical Performative Discourse: A New Theory of Epideictic," *P and R,* 11 (Fall 1978), 221–46; Robert E. Sanders, "Utterances, Actions, and Rhetorical Inquiry," *P and R,* 11 (Spring 1978), 114–33; W. Ross Winterowd, "The Rhetoric of Beneficence, Authority, Ethical Commitment, and the Negative," *P and R,* 9 (Spring 1976), 65–83.

The mere term "speech acts" is revolutionary, implying as it does that speaking is acting, a way of doing (which, of course, Kenneth Burke has maintained for most of his long career). The kinds of actions that speakers (and writers) perform are, to use the jargon, utterance (the mere physical act of saying or writing), propositional (predicating and referring), and illocutionary (projecting an intention); the response by the hearer or reader is perlocution.

In this essay there is no space for a detailing of the premises of speech act theory and the controversies surrounding it, but one point is necessary: classical concepts of rhetoric square nicely with speech act theory, making them mutually illuminating. We can fairly equate *ethos*-illocution, *pathos*-perlocution, and *logos*-proposition, which, in fact, is one of the premises in the article by Augustine and Winterowd cited above.

Speech act theory comes from the philosophical tradition and is largely rationalistic and deductive. Conversational analysis, on the other hand, is empirical. In Levinson's view (*Pragmatics,* p. 285), the future of pragmatics lies in the direction of empirical, inductive work.

Conversational analysis involves such apparently straightforward matters as turn-taking, adjacency pairs (e.g., question-answer, greeting-greeting), and overall organization (Levinson, pp. 296–318), concerns that take one, via the methods of rigorous empirical observation, toward the philosophical questions about *ethos* and *pathos* that are central to the rhetorical tradition.

In *Forms of Talk* (Philadelphia: University of Pennsylvania Press, 1981), Erving Goffman, who, according to his own account, works in "the naturalistic study of human foregatherings and comminglings, that is, the forms and occasions of face-to-face interaction" (p. 162), performs "frame analysis" on replies and responses, response cries, footing (which roughly translates as "rhetorical stance"), the lecture, and radio talk. By and large, the book details the features of speech events, that is, does pragmatic analysis of how language works. Goffman recognizes that some aspects of these events can be formalized, but that a great many—for example, "back channel" communication, such as audience facial reaction—cannot be formally accounted for.

Goffman's work is valuable heuristically, suggesting directions for the pragmatic analysis of written discourse—for instance, as ritual, as self-talk, as a series of "moves," and so forth.

No work more clearly illustrates the blurred categories of our field than Thomas Kochman's *Black and White Styles in Conflict* (Chicago: University of Chicago Press, 1981). Depending on your point of view, its subject is rhetoric, anthropology, or linguistics: the communicative strategies of the black community in conflict with those of the whites. This richly textured book details the misunderstandings created when one cultural rhetoric confronts another. For example:

> Present-day whites relate to their material as spokesmen, not advocates. This is because they believe that the truth or other merits of an idea are intrinsic to the idea itself. How deeply a person cares about or believes in the idea is considered irrelevant to its fundamental value. . . . Because blacks admit that they deal from a point of view, they are disinclined to believe whites who claim not to have a point of view, or who present their views in a manner that suggests that they do not themselves believe what they are saying. That is why they often accuse whites of being insincere. (pp. 23–22)

In fact, blacks find "truth" through dialectic and the consensus achieved thereby; in contrast, whites appear to take "truth" as a given and thus argue in its behalf. Though Kochman does not take up this point, one can say that the Western metaphysic of presence is not part of black rhetoric, which, in just this sense, is "deconstructionist." (See, for example, Jacques Derrida, *Of Grammatology,* trans. Gayatri Chakravorty Spivak [Baltimore: Johns Hopkins University Press, 1976].)

Another interface is the blurred area between developmental studies and pragmatics, occupied by such scholars as Elinor Ochs and Bambi B. Schieffelin (eds., *Developmental Pragmatics* [New York: Academic Press, 1979] and *Acquiring Conversational Competence* [London: Routledge & Kegan Paul, 1983]).

Finally, a volume that does not strictly fall into the pragmatics category is worth mentioning. *Observing the Language Learner,* ed. Angela Jaggar and M. Trika Smith-Burke (Newark, Del.: International Reading Association; Urbana: NCTE, 1985) is a good, largely non-technical overview of developmental studies.

The moves in pragmatics have taken us at least to the fringes of anthropology, developmental psychology, and ordinary language philosophy—into a disciplinary Tower of Babel that seems to be the permanent home of the rhetorician, a locus not too different, after all, from the *agora,* where symbolically and historically rhetoric has been located.

FORM

Form—or, as the Latin rhetoricians would have said, *dispositio*—is one of the five traditional departments of rhetoric, the two subdivisions of which might now be termed "coherence" and "cohesion."

In the realm of coherence, Teun A. van Dijk's *Macrostructures: An Interdisciplinary Study of Global Structures in Discourse, Interaction, and Cognition* (Hillsdale, N.J.: Lawrence Erlbaum Associates, 1980) pursues the distinction between *local* and *global* structures, the local being, for example, the syntax of a sentence or the sorts of cohesion relationships dealt with by Halliday and Hasan (discussed below), in contrast with such global structures as gist, thesis, theme. Clearly a *text*, "the abstract underlying structure of a discourse" (p. 29), has properties that local analysis cannot account for—primarily a macrostructure or, in fact, a hierarchical series of macrostructures, depending on one's point of view.

Van Dijk distinguishes between the *semantic* macrostructure and the *formal* superstructure, which can be represented by an outline, for example.

The following passage is not coherent and thus, in fact, does not have a perceptible macrostructure, for in this sense macrostructure and coherence are virtually synonymous:

> (1) John was ill, so he called the doctor. But the doctor could not come, because his wife wanted to go to the theater with him. They were playing Othello, which she thought they could not miss because Shakespeare is one of the few dramatical authors who. . . .

In one sense, the passage does "hang together": the FACT-sequence is clear; the individual clauses are not *non sequitur*. ("A fact is an event, action, state, or process in some possible world," p. 32.) On the other hand, the passage has no topic, no center of gravity. Is it about John, the doctor, Othello, Shakespeare?

The problem with (1) is that it has no controlling *macroproposition*, "a propositional *common denominator* that describes a situation or course of events *as a whole*, such that the constituent sentences denote *normal component actions* of this overall episode" (p. 42). One sort of macrostructure, then, is the macroproposition (which may or may not appear in the passage but which must be, in any case, derivable therefrom).

As we should expect, there are also *macrospeech acts*, or, to use van Dijk's own terminology, "local" and "global" speech acts. The example that van Dijk gives (pp. 187–89) is too long for quotation here, but it is easy enough to cook up a brief illustration:

> (2) A husband at a cocktail party is in conversation with two friends. His wife joins the group and begins to speak.
> Wife: "I apologize for butting in this way." (expressive)
> Husband: "We were talking about tomorrow's football game." (representative)
> Wife: "Don't miss that game under any circumstances." (directive)
> Husband: "I certainly won't!" (commissive)
> Wife: "It is now half past twelve." (representative)
> Husband: "I hereby pronounce you my timekeeper." (declaration)
> Wife: "I repeat: it is now half past twelve." (representative)

Though the series of individual speech acts—expressive, representative, directive, commissive, representative, declaration, representative—do not, by some equation, add up to a clearcut macrospeech act, we can assume that the overall intent of the exchange adds up to a directive: "Go home."

As there are macrostructures, there are, of course, macrorules, namely *construction, deletion, evaluation, generalization, interpretation, selection,* and the *zero*-rule.

Macrostructures is an interesting and useful book, particularly if one overlooks the unfortunately few attempts to do formal analysis of passages. In the first place, van Dijk systematizes and gives vocabulary for our intuitions regarding form; in the second place, he raises central issues about *dispositio* that are traditionally the concern of rhetoricians.

In *Cohesion in English* (London: Longman, 1976), M. A. K. Halliday and Ruqaiya Hasan tell us that

286

Cohesion occurs where the *interpretation* of some element in the discourse is dependent on that of another. The one *presupposes* the other, in the sense that it cannot be effectively decoded except by recourse to it. When this happens, a relation of cohesion is set up, and the two elements, the presupposing and the presupposed, are thereby at least potentially integrated into a text. (p. 4)

Cohesion in English is a definitive "grammar" of its subject, the features of which can be simply exemplified:

reference
Three blind mice. See how THEY run.
substitution
THE LITTLE DEVILS ran after the farmer's wife.
ellipsis
She cut off the tails of all three [MICE] . . .
conjunction
. . . AND used a carving knife to do it.
lexical cohesion
From this tale, we learn that VERMIN should not fool around with RURAL WOMEN (vermin relating semantically to "mice," and "rural women" to "farmer's wife").

For teachers of composition, *Cohesion in English* is a useful book in that it enables one to specify exactly where and how the links are missing in incohesive student texts.

In "The Grammar of Coherence," *CE,* 31 (May 1970), 828–35, I proposed that *coherence* results from the workings of six relationships among T-units ("terminable units," or, roughly, clauses), failing to distinguish between cohesion and coherence. As a grammar of *cohesion,* the argument stands up pretty well, though it has been roundly attacked by Gary Sloan in "Transitions: Relationships Among T-Units," *CCC,* 34 (Dec. 1983), 447–53.

In "Dialectics of Coherence: Toward an Integrative Theory," *CE,* 47 (Jan. 1985), 12–29, Louise Wetherbee Phelps builds toward a *transactional* theory of composition, beyond the current-traditional process model, which "has no principled way to account for the role of texts in discourse events because it was constituted initially by a contrastive opposition between composing (dynamic process) and texts (inert product)" (p. 12). This model—which, as Phelps indicates, has momentous consequences—results from the simple gambit of viewing the text as a source of "cues" whereby the reader can build a satisfactory macrostructure, one that he or she feels squares with the intentions of the writer.

USAGE

We are not so much concerned with standard guides to usage (e.g., Margaret M. Bryant, ed., *Current American Usage* [New York: Funk & Wagnall's, 1962]; Henry W. Fowler, *A Dictionary of Modern English Usage,* 2nd ed. rev. by Sir Ernest Gowers [Oxford: Oxford University Press, 1965]) as with what Edward Finegan titles *Attitudes Toward English Usage: The History of a War of Words* (New York: Teachers College Press, Columbia University, 1980), that is, the politics and rhetoric of usage. In his exceptional book, Finegan recounts the history of the "war of words," starting with Jonathan Swift and Samuel Johnson in the eighteenth century and ending with the transformational-generative linguists.

Of the many battles in the long war, two are most instructive. The first might be called the "correctness versus appropriateness" campaign.

Between 1875 and 1952, scholars began to "face the facts," that is, to survey actual usage, an activity that crescendoed with the development of structural linguistics and the establishment of linguistics as a discipline. Sterling Leonard's *Current English Usage,* NCTE English Monograph No. 1 (Chicago: Inland, 1932) was based on a ballot of 102 items judged by seven "juries," including linguistic experts, businessmen, authors, editors, MLA members, NCTE members, and speech teachers. In *Facts About Current English Usage,* NCTE English Monograph No. 7 (New York: Appleton-Century-Crofts, 1938), Albert H. Marckwardt and Fred G. Walcott classified Leonard's items according to level of usage: literary, American literary, colloquial, American colloquial, dialect, and archaic. The most revolutionary of the studies based on usage surveys was Charles C. Fries's *American English Grammar: The Grammatical Structure of Present-Day English with Especial Reference to Social Difference or Class Dialects,* NCTE English Monograph No. 10 (New York: Appleton-Century-Crofts, 1940). Fries argued that usage cannot be judged out of context, cannot be valued on an absolute basis: appropriateness—to situation and audience—rather than mere "correctness" is the criterion. Furthermore, students should be exposed to the usage of educated persons, but should not be drilled in the abstract rules of grammar.

These and other pioneers entered a debate that is ongoing, the opposing sides represented most vividly by John Simon (*Paradigms Lost: Reflections on Literacy and Its Decline* [New York: Clarkson N. Potter, 1980]) and James Sledd (for example, "In Defense of *The Students' Right*," *CE,* 45 [Nov. 1983], 667–75). In a typical passage, Simon tells us that David B. Guralnik, editor-in-chief of *Webster's New World Dictionary,* concludes that

"The language in any period accurately reflects the culture in which it is used. Let's not try to treat a fever by tampering with the thermometer." If Guralnik's analogy means anything, it is that our culture is a sickness (fever), and that we must not take it out on language (thermometer) if we don't like what it registers. But suppose that the thermometer has become infected by mouths diseased with ignorance; should we stick it into every other mouth as well, including our own, and so have all of us sicken?

The test case for the logomachy is *Students' Right to Their Own Language,* published as a special issue of *CCC,* 25 (Fall

289

1974), which, in a sense, reaffirmed Fries's earlier position that appropriateness, not "correctness," is the valid standard for judging language use; students should not be penalized—indeed, excoriated and ghettoized—because of their language, and all students should have the opportunity to develop versatility in language use and dialect.

The second great battle in our century came with the publication of *Webster's Third New International Dictionary,* which, as Finegan puts it, "provoked a surly storm" (p. 116). Many critics, such as Mario Pei, thought that the dictionary was the product of modern linguistics, the "scientific," objective study of language, which according to Professor A. M. Tibbetts, "subtly corrupts a man. He becomes less a moralist . . . and more a pedant . . playing with tape recorders and other gimcrackery" ("The Real Issues in the Great Language Controversy," *EJ,* 55 [1966], 28–38, quoted in Finegan, p. 123). In the view of its critics, *Webster's Third* would corrupt not only language, but all of society. Unsurprisingly, James Sledd was also part of this battle ("The Lexicographer's Uneasy Chair," *CE,* 23 [1962], 682–87; Sledd and Wilma R. Ebbitt, eds., *Dictionaries and THAT Dictionary* [Chicago: Scott, Foresman, 1962]).

The two parameters of language variation are, on the one hand, user (according to region, social class, and so on) and, on the other, use (according to situation). In effect, *Language in the USA,* edited by Charles A. Ferguson and Shirley Brice Heath (Cambridge, Eng.: Cambridge University Press, 1981)—a densely printed 592-page book—in its four sections contains discussions of both parameters: "American English," "Languages before English" (e.g., "American Indian Languages," by William L. Leap), "Languages after English" (e.g., "The Speech and Writing of Jews," by David L. Gold), and "Language in Use" (e.g., "Ethnic Differences in Communicative Style," by John J. Gumperz and Jenny Cook-Gumperz).

Language in the USA is an excellent collection of primary sources for the rhetorician.

Literary Theory and Composition

JOSEPH J. COMPRONE, The University of Louisville

I. CRITICAL AND PROFESSIONAL BACKGROUND

For years teachers of English have divided themselves into composition-language and literature-criticism categories. My job in this essay does not include a specific account of the origins of this split, which recent research into the history of modern rhetoric suggests had its origins in post-romantic divisions between the scholarly-critical classical tradition, centered on rhetoric, and a more literary-organic criticism, centered on twentieth-century perspectivism and focus on process. But my job *will* include an account of recent theoretical overlap between the areas of composition and literary theory, an overlap which has the potential of synthesizing these up-to-now divergent categories of modern English studies. Composition teachers have come in the mid- and later twentieth century to carry the burden of service, literature teachers the banners of interpretation and criticism. While writing and reading teachers taught skills, the literature teacher "taught" sensibility and taste, what the seventeenth- and eighteenth-century philosopher might have termed judgment and wit. This dichotomy centered itself in the mechanistic context or Newtonian world, in which form and content could be divided, and in which learning *how* and learning *what* were different acts of body and mind. This split, often politically motivated but philosophically rooted, encouraged a parallel split in the academy between those who served and those who enriched.

In America, we might use Susan Sontag's *Against Interpretation* (New York: Farrar, Straus & Giroux, 1966) as an arbitrary dividing line. Naomi Schor in "Fiction as Interpretation: Interpretation as Fiction," in *The Reader in the Text,* ed. Susan Suleiman and Inge Crosman (Princeton, N.J.: Princeton University Press, 1980, pp. 165–82), uses Sontag's book to mark a shift from modern, New Critical, text-bound interpretation to the more open, pluralistic forms of interpretation found in the work of Roland Barthes and Jean Ricardou. Sontag, Schor argues, attacked traditional interpretation: the kind that "translated" a text as if it were an arbitrary assemblage of symbols rather than a construction of both the writer's and reader's minds (p. 165). Such interpretation, she argued, reduced reading to after-the-fact meanings. What was needed then, and what since has been developed in French criticism, is what Sontag called for in 1964: a "poetics of the novel" (Schor, p. 166), a criticism focused on questions of *how* we write and read rather than on *what* that writing and reading produced in terms of meaning or objective knowledge.

As criticism itself came to be seen in more functional terms, as all acts of interpretation came to be rooted in the hermeneutic circle, the acts of writing and reading began to be perceived as interdependent with acts of mind, and with criticism, evaluation, analysis, and the construction of knowledge in general. American literary criticism of the late 1960s, 1970s, and early '80s has often come to use the classroom, the basic processes of reading and writing, as illustrative ground for construction of these new theoretical models. These models explain generic processes, not individual acts of criticism. At the same time, composition research and theory has begun to venture beyond the traditional classroom and its error lists, mechanical exercises, and empirical studies of experimental, control, and placebo groupings of students. Composition has come to synthesize the study of student texts with the study of composing processes, just as literary theory influenced by the French, during this period, has subsumed text, writer, reader, and critic—in one, overall interpretive process. These shifting emphases have created confusion and some paranoia, but they have also created the potential for a new rapprochement between the formerly divided camps of literature and composition. Doing and thinking have become part of one interdependent process; literary theory comes to require the illustrative power of the classroom; the classroom comes to rely on the intellectual flexibility provided by theory.

Revisions in theory that emphasize the interdependency of function and meaning have coincided in recent years with changes in the English profession's sense of itself. Composition, long the service-oriented stepchild of English departments, has begun to develop its own specialists, some of whom read the same theoretical books as their literary theory colleagues. These shifts in English department perspectives is succinctly summmarized in two recent publications: Winifred Bryan Horner's collection of essays entitled *Composition and Literature: Bridging the Gap* (Chicago: University of Chicago Press, 1983) and a special *Profession 84* issue of the *ADE Bulletin* (Modern Language Association, 1984). A brief review of several essays in these sources will provide the kind of professional context that my review of literary theory and composition studies will require for full understanding.

Richard Lanham places this need for synthesis of theory and practice in the larger context of cultural literacy and the changing nature of English studies in American colleges and universities ("One, Two, Three," in *Composition and Literature*, pp. 14–19). Lanham answers three central questions for English teachers in the late twentieth century—What is the relationship between teaching literature and teaching composition? Should English departments take an interest in teaching composition? How does question one relate to question two?—by arguing for an integrated English curriculum in which composition and literature teachers use each other's research and theory to solve the problems created by a new pluralism of language and culture in American society. The implications in Lanham's article go beyond simple mutual appropriation of research and theory, however, in that the English teacher who wishes to be able to face the challenges of students with diverse linguistic and cultural backgrounds must in the future be able to understand the relationships between general discourse and particular utterance and between the general functions of literacy and the operation of those functions in particular situations. Composition teachers, Lanham suggests, have too often been their own worst enemies because they have restricted the acts of reading and writing to narrow and artificial contexts such as the five-hundred-word theme or the academic paragraph. Literature teachers have, in contrast, too often refused to examine or teach actual rhetorical situations: the audiences and purposes of the literature they limited themselves to teaching existed only on the highest and most abstract of cultural planes.

Essays by Walter Ong, Winifred Horner, E. D. Hirsch, Jr., and David Kaufer and Richard Young combine with Lanham's in this collection (*Composition and Literature*) to provide a composite of the historical context within which college English teachers must decide their professional futures. Ong, in "Literacy and Orality in Our Times" (*Composition and Literature,* pp. 126–40) reviews his long-standing research into the relationships among primary oral, secondary oral, and literary cultures. He argues that writing teachers must take their recently developed understanding of writing and reading as composing processes and contrast them to the cognitive habits and styles of people in primary and secondary oral cultures. The result, Ong suggests, would be a new insight, among writing teachers, into the "completely and irremediably artificial" (p. 129) set of skills and mind-sets within which writers operate. Untouched by immediate audience response, forced to create and work with a fictional audience as he or she writes, usually isolated from human activity, and cut off from the proverbial lore that supported the oral composer or conversationalist, the serious writer is culturally schizophrenic, making public utterances out of a fictionalized and private sense of community. Ong closes his essay by encouraging writing teachers to mix media, to contrast oral, written, and visual forms of expression. Ong faces the new academic pluralism that Lanham describes with a media-sensitive curriculum in which writers learn by reading, and by contrasting their responses to visual and verbal media.

Professor Horner, in her introduction to *Composition and Literature* (pp. 1–13), outlines the historical reasons behind the division between literature and composition. Her review makes it clear that the teaching of writing, reading, and literature has always been reflective of cultural attitudes and patterns. Classical and traditional rhetoric, by the sixteenth century, had allowed itself to be reduced to mechanistic stylistics, to long lists of figures and tropes that were not used in "ordinary" conversation but were added to everyday language to create more refined forms of language. This reductive emphasis on rhetoric as style combined later in the eighteenth century with the elocutionary movement, which reduced oral rhetoric to a dramatized form of public performance, and with the emphasis in the same century on the separate study of English literature, in place of classical literatures, to produce an overall context in which the way was prepared for the modern shift from what Horner calls "the creative act to the interpretive act" (p. 3). This developing split resulted in a separation of the teaching of reading from that of writing that has only recently begun to be addressed in literary theory and composition research.

E. D. Hirsch, Jr. has written two recent articles that supplement Lanham, Horner, and Ong's perspectives on the relationship between literacy and the teaching of literature and composition. Hirsch, earlier a literary theorist most known for his work on hermeneutics,[1] later published *The Philosophy of Composition* (Chicago: University of Chicago Press, 1977), in which he argued that composition was a formalistic discipline, a set of skills to be learned. The purpose of *The Philosophy of Composition* was to narrow the skills of writing down to a small number of principles and maxims that were based upon empirical, psycholinguistic research. Then, Hirsch hypothesized, teachers could learn how to base their pedagogies on this restricted set of principles and maxims and the literacy crisis would be a crisis no more.

Hirsch has radically revised this position in his two later essays. In "Reading, Writing, and Cultural Literacy" (in *Composition and Literature,* pp. 141–47), Hirsch explains that his extended research into the reading and writing abilities of secondary students had pointed out to him the inadequacy of formalistic approaches to teaching reading and writing. The reason behind this inadequacy was that students who read at the same general level did not respond in similar ways to different texts at the same level of reading difficulty. Hirsch explained this, to him, surprising finding by pointing to differences in "cultural literacy"—to, in other words, the different kinds and amount of background knowledge and experience student readers possessed on the topics about which they were reading. This recognition, in turn, led Hirsch to argue that the modern literacy crisis had begun to establish itself when, shortly after the turn of the last century, the American school curriculum began to move away from a common textual canon.

Hirsch carried this argument a step further as he proposed a solution to current literacy problems in a recent *American Scholar* essay ("Cultural Literacy," 52 [Spring 1983], 159–69). Here Hirsch proposes a national board that might recommend a canon of books from which a school might choose in filling out the specific contents of its curriculum. This kind of move toward uniformity of content would not, Hirsch makes clear, be necessitated by the need to hold certain texts or literatures above others as paradigms of excellence, but by a need for a commonality of background in the teaching of reading and writing. Without this common background, Hirsch contends, students are unfairly disadvantaged by topical constraints in the writing assignments to which they are asked to respond. Composition teachers, Hirsch argues, must replace formalism and its separation of style from content with a methodology that emphasizes the interaction of form and content, of competence in culture and competence in language. This argument parallels recent emphasis in literary theory, by Stanley Fish and others, on the interpretive strategies of literary communities (*Is There a Text in this Class?* [Baltimore: Johns Hopkins University Press, 1982]).

Hirsch's methodical discovery of a truism articulated much earlier by Susan Sontag represents once again the convergence of perspectives in current literary and composition theory. Literacy, whether approached by a classically trained pluralist such as Lanham, a Catholic-educated philosopher of language and culture such as Ong, or a conservative hermeneuticist such as Hirsch seems to produce a similar drive toward rapprochement. The focus of this rapprochement is most often a strident refusal to give any one of the three major components of the reading-writing transaction—text, writer, or reader—the upper hand in the composing process. Readers write texts by supplying the background experience which fills in the gaps the text itself contains, Hirsch's recent emphasis on "cultural literacy" seems to imply. In one way or another, a complete understanding of the acts of reading and writing must include strategies for connecting the reader's mind, the texts's signs and symbols, and the writer's cultural and linguistic competence.

David Kaufer and Richard Young summarize the pedagogical implications of this rapprochement of literature and writing teachers by reviewing the nineteenth- and twentieth-century history of English department assumptions toward writing. The first two assumptions dominated the teaching of composition from the early nineteenth century in American higher education. The first assumption separated "writing from thinking," treating writing as a relatively trivial craft concerned largely with the conventions and mechanics of good prose ("Literacy, Art, and Politics in Departments of English," in *Composition and Literature,* p. 150). The second assumption, existing alongside the first, supported a belief that writing could be learned but not taught, that "writing and thinking are inseparable" (p. 151).

The first assumption led to what Kaufer and Young call the

297

"craft" approach to teaching writing, the second to what these authors call the "art" approach to writing. Both assumptions together controlled the beliefs and methods of most composition teachers through the early nineteenth and twentieth centuries, with students often moving from one type of teacher to another in haphazard fashion. In the past twenty years, however, Kaufer and Young argue that a new paradigm for the teaching of writing has gradually begun to contest the control of the art/craft dualism over the teaching of writing. This new paradigm Kaufer and Young define by the term "competence" (p. 153). A competence paradigm is based on the assumption that writing is both art and craft, that "a continuum of activities that includes not only those associated with the conventional notion of craft but those we would characterize as creative as well" provides a more useful model of composing (p. 152). Kaufer and Young then explain how this paradigm might produce writing classrooms based on the use of both art- and craft-oriented heuristics, rather than on either the rule-governed strategies of the pure-craft or the mysterious impulses of the pure-art paradigms.

This emphasis on a competence paradigm brings us back to the literature and composition relationships. Recent literary theory, with its drive toward process and away from product, with its emphases on describing and creating explanatory models of the act of reading, has also begun to emphasize competence rather than particular performances. Key questions in current literary theory are ones of competence: What kinds of knowledge do readers share? How does this knowledge constrain the act of reading? How does this knowledge lead to a shared, community sense of the act of interpretation? How does this shared competence control the acts of composing texts? To return to Susan Sontag's call for greater emphasis on "how" rather than "what" questions, currently literary and composition theories are coming together around research and theory into the processes of reading and writing, rather than around the results of those processes. The work of Jonathan Culler, Wolfgang Iser, and Roland

Barthes serves as cornerstones in this edifice of explanatory rather than traditional, interpretive criticism, just as Donald Murray, Peter Elbow, Linda Flower, and Janet Emig have become recognized markers in composition's recent excursions into the processes of producing texts. This research and theory has yet, however, to influence the majority of English teachers, who often demonstrate superficial comprehension of the deeper relationships among literary, academic, and professional discourses.

There are, however, signs of a new insight into these relationships. An excellent, recent example is contained in the *Profession 84* issue of the *Association of Departments of English (ADE) Bulletin* (1984), published by the Modern Language Association. All of the essays (by Richard Lanham, Thomas R. Whitaker, Sandra M. Gilbert, Herbert Lindenberger, Art Young, Dorothy James, Gerald Prince, Murray Sachs) in this issue address the evolving, functional emphasis on the interactions of writing, reading, and criticism in departments of English and foreign languages. Four of the essays in this issue are especially significant to English studies because they carry the discussion of relationships between literature and composition a step farther than the items previously discussed. These articles offer two unifying concepts around which the various converging strains of literary and composition theory can function. The first concept involves a redefinition of and reemphasis on the process of interpretation; the second focuses on the concept of community as it affects the act of interpretation in its many forms.

It is this reconception of interpretation that can provide an organizing frame for an integrated literature and composition curriculum. Previously, theorists and critics considered interpretation an act that followed upon reading comprehension and thinking and writing. Now, however, we have the theory and research to support a much broader and more interdependent yet equally systematic definition of interpretation. Thomas Whitaker, in the previously mentioned issue of the *ADE Bulletin,* describes interpretation, in its broadest terms, as "conversation by design"

(p. 1). This conversation includes all forms of discourse, and it relies on our competences as members of different discourse communities, and on the general competence de Saussure ascribed to all users of a particular language (*Course in General Linguistics,* ed. C. Bally and A. Seehehaye, trans. Wade Baskin [New York: Philosophical Library, 1959]). Whitaker, Chair of the English Department at Yale, joins with Herbert Lindenberger ("Toward a New History in Literary Study," *Profession 84,* pp. 16–23) and Gerald Prince ("Literary Theory and the Undergraduate Curriculum," *Profession 84,* pp. 37–40) in asking that English teachers come to know "what it should mean . . . to be teachers of interpretation" (p. 1). Lindenberger explicitly relates this search for a broader, working theory of interpretation to the sense of academic community that lies behind and controls interpretation as it is carried out in different fields, and with different canons of texts:

> In view of the upheavals to which canons have been subjected in recent years, custodianship of a fixed canon would seem at best a tribal occupation . . . these very upheavals have suggested a project for the new historians . . . tracing the changes in canons at various moments in the past, seeking out the motivations behind these changes, studying the ideological and institutional framework that creates a particular canon at a particular time. (pp. 16–17)

Lindenberger posits a perspective in which the histories of critical reception and textual variance are used to explain the theoretical perspectives that underlie the interpretations shared by different communities. Art Young ("Rebuilding Community in the English Department," *Profession 84,* pp. 24–32) carries Lindenberger's perspective on the relationships between acts of interpretation and the critical communities that support them into the context of writing across the curriculum, where the general need to comprehend interpretive strategies as writers move from one academic discipline to another links up with the rhetorician's concern with shifting audiences. Writing workshops in which faculty share and discuss different disciplines' approaches to writing become Young's means of reeducating faculty for the job of teaching writing across the curriculum.

This introduction serves to contextualize my general discussion of literary theory and composition in the rest of this essay. This context must include both professional and theoretical concerns, for both literary theory and composition, if they are to be integrated, must find a way to eliminate the gap between what writing and literature teachers do as they teach and what they think when they develop theory and research.

Section II of this essay will build upon the professional context described in this section by categorizing current literary theory into three general perspectives, all of which will be organized under a model of the interpretive process. Elements within this model of interpretation will then be connected with significant perspectives in recent composition research. Section II, then, should provide both literature and composition teachers with a somewhat oversimplified but useful understanding of current literary theory and its implications.

Section III will describe the curricular implications of an interpretation-based perspective on reading and writing, particularly as this theoretical perspective might influence writing across the curriculum programs. This section will begin with a review of literary theorists who organize recent explanations and descriptions of reading and writing processes into a theory of interpretation, and it will conclude with references to several articles in which composition specialists consider the pedagogical implications of this revised hermeneutic model of the composing process.

II. PERSPECTIVES ON CURRENT LITERARY THEORY

American literary theory of the past decade can be loosely fitted into three categorical perspectives—the *subjective,* the *transactional,* and the *objective.* For the purposes of this essay, these perspectives are useful because they provide writing teachers with elements of theory that they can plug into their developing models of the writing and reading processes. We can create a context for descriptions of these perspectives by first explaining how they might be used by teachers of literature and composition to assure that students learn to read and write by actually engaging in the processes of composing, rather than simply analyzing the products of others' composing processes.

Picking up on the cue provided by my earlier reference to Susan Sontag's focus on "how" rather than "what" questions in *Against Interpretation,* I shall at this point relate Sontag's emphasis on the functional to those recent literary theorists who have taken a phenomenological approach to describing the acts of reading and writing. Wolfgang Iser, a German critic whose work evolves from that of Roman Ingarten in aesthetics and Edmund Husserl in earlier phenomenology, has centered current theory squarely on readers as they interact with texts.[2] Two of Iser's essays, both of which appear as chapters in his two most prominent books, do a good, basic job of outlining his model of the act of reading. In "The Reading Process: A Phenomenological Approach," *The Implied Reader* (Baltimore: Johns Hopkins University Press, 1974), pp. 274–94, Iser describes the playing off, within the temporal act of reading, of a *horizon* of meaning that readers hold in the back of their minds as they read, and a *theme,* which readers construct from their immediate response to the particular parts of a text. Interactions and frictions between horizon—what Frank Smith in *Understanding Reading* (2nd ed., New York: Holt, 1978) might call "non-visual" information that readers bring to a text as they read—and theme cause readers, Iser says, to perceive "gaps" and "negations" in their processing of a text. At the point of perceiving these gaps, readers are driven to examine text more specifically, and to scrutinize their constructed horizons in order to fill gaps and counteract negations.

Iser, then, posits a reader who constructs meaning out of a constant tension, during reading, between points of textual disappointment and counterpointing moments of insight in which social and cultural information is brought in to fill the holes in a text. Iser's ideal reader is above all active, always relating cultural frames of reference to holes or gaps in a text, seeking a balance between subjective and objective perspectives.

Iser carries this descriptive model of the ideal reader a step further in *The Act of Reading* (Baltimore: Johns Hopkins University Press, 1978), chapters 7–8, pp. 163–231, when he contrasts the "good continuation" of expository reading with the friction, the "dash of images," of literary reading. In most expository texts, Iser suggests, writers use a textbound type of cohesion in which readers follow an outline that imposes an artificial and abstract order on mental events and subjects. Flow or "good continuation" occurs when such expository texts result in readings in which there is little dissonance or friction in the reader's mind. But in literary reading substantive narrative, lyrical, or dramatic images clash with one another, causing readers, Iser says, to juxtapose immediate imagery and shifting frames of reference ("wandering viewpoints") in ways that disjoint and fracture this "good continuation." An ideal reader of literature, then, learns to question, to expect friction, even contradiction, to feel uneasy with the ideas and experiences of others as they are written.

I shall carry this discussion of Iser's transactional perspective on the act of reading further in the next section of this essay. At this point, we need emphasize only the fact that Iser's concept of textual gaps that are filled by non-visual or extra-textual information brings us once again to a focus on what readers do as they read rather than on what their reading means. Stanley Fish, particularly in his earlier *Self-Consuming Artifacts* (Berkeley: University of Calif. Press, 1972), supplements Iser's focus on the question of how readers read. Fish's approach is specifically illustrated in the Appendix ("Literature in the Reader: Affective Stylistics," pp. 383–428) to *Self-Consuming Artifacts*. Readers of literature, Fish argues, expect to be consumed by a text; they learn to accept the cognitive dissonance that derives from the reversals, contradictions, clashes of images, and shifts in viewpoint that they experience in their involvement with the syntactical and rhetorical forms of a text.

> It is characteristic of . . . [self-consuming artifacts] first to involve the reader in discursive activities—evaluating, deducing, interpreting—and then to declare invalid or premature the conclusions these activities yield. The result is a disturbing and unsettling experience in the course of which a reader is continually revising his understanding until . . . the very possibility of understanding is itself called into question. (*Self-Consuming Artifacts,* p. vii)

In this Appendix, Fish goes on to assert that quantitative stylistics is not useful in describing literary reading because context, what Iser would call "horizon," plays such a large part in the reader's perception of any given linguistic structure (what Iser would call "theme"): The process of reading is rooted in the mind of the reader, which—when it is functioning aesthetically—gives ordinary language extraordinary meaning.

What is important here is not the details of Fish's approach, which I shall deal with later, but the essential purpose behind Fish's reader-oriented stylistics. Fish, like Iser, tries to describe the mental processes of readers *as* they read, just as current composition theorists wish to develop descriptive models of what writers do *as* they write. Before, however, we conclude this essay with references to several professional articles that illustrate how these two functional perspectives on reading and writing might come together in the classroom, we should take a quick look at the general implications for the integration of composition and literary theory in the work of Roland Barthes.

Barthes's later post-structural work, particularly *S/Z* (transl. by Richard Miller, New York: Hill and Wang, 1974) and *The Pleasure of the Text* (transl. by Richard Miller, New York: Hill and Wang, 1975) speaks explicitly against "the pitiless divorce which the literary institution maintains between the producer of the text and its user, between its owner and its customer, between its author and its reader" (*S/Z*, p. 4). Barthes's *tour de force* in *S/Z* is one of combined scientific precision and ludic impulse. His adumbration of five reading codes—the hermeneutic, semantic, proairetic, cultural, and symbolic—which Barthes then applies to each of the 561 "lexias," or perceptual units of reading in Balzac's *Sarrasine,* enables him to provide readers with a system that explains how reading is socially and culturally controlled and simultaneously capable of producing playful, synthetic responses. Readers must play the game of reading within the cultural and linguistic roles that are defined by the literary institution while they maintain their self-conscious control over these subjective and objective perspectives. The play among these perspectives provides the individual with full expression through the pleasure of the text, which because it *is* controlled by each of the five basic codes, is always fully human in its manipulation of these cultural/social codes.

Barthes's perspective provides the composition teacher with a means of seeing part and whole in constant balance. Anyone who has written knows the alarming sense one has, when looking too closely at a sentence or clause in the act of composing, of having lost one's general sense of direction. Barthesian analysis opposes this fragmentation of our sensibilities during the act of composing—in *both* the acts of reading and writing—by refusing to isolate our senses of sentences from our sense of their place within the whole fabric of discourse. How does the reader see syntax?—as lexias in the process of perceiving meaning, not as separate entities in a left-right linguistic scansion. The codes of knowing that we inherit from social, cultural, and linguistic contexts combine to help us "see" chunks of meaning as we read. Here, again, we find evidence in literary theory of the interdependency of subject and object, of the acts of doing and knowing, and of the relation between the how and the what in all our interactions with written texts.

I have attempted to make this connection between Barthes's

emphasis on coded play in reading and current composition research in an article ("Syntactic Play and Composing Theory") that appears in Daiker, Kerek, and Morenberg's *Sentence-Combining: A Rhetorical Perspective* (Carbondale: Southern Illinois University Press, 1985) pp. 219–31. Sentence-combining research, focused as it has been on syntactical units at the expense of whole discourse, has suffered from the problems that occur when language is studied and used in decontextualized forms. Students learn to do linguistic tricks, to make longer and more embedded but not necessarily better sentences, because "better" is always judged by readers *in context*. Recently, in several innovative texts,[3] composition researchers specializing in sentence-combining have begun to encourage rhetorical choice in the context of whole-discourse composing. My essay uses Barthes's sense of a playful use of codes to bring this rhetorical choicemaking a step further: "The real trick, the essential trick, is to know these codes so well that we can, as readers [of our own texts], allow each line we read to call forth a playful, subconscious response to all the codes" (pp. 230–31).

Other essays have done a more specific job of combining recent composition and literary theory in ways that emphasize the processes of reading and writing. Louis Ceci, "The Case for Syntactic Imagery," *CE,* 45 (1983), 431–39, uses the frame of phenomenological thought to describe the phases a writer goes through in using his or her cultural and linguistic competence to transform a personal experience into a public utterance. Ceci, following thinkers such as Barthes, suggests how linguistic and cultural competence subconsciously controls even the early reflections and plans of a writer. James Hoetker, in a *College English* article ("A Theory of Talking About Theories of Reading," 44 [1982], 175–81), characterizes the contribution of reader-oriented theory by pointing out that it contrasts with the approaches of education-school and psychological-readability studies of reading. Rather than striving to economize, as the educationists and psychologists often claim, the mature reader "makes the *maximum* use of even the smallest details . . . in the various cue systems, and . . . generates and elaborates information, rather than continually reducing it" (p. 180). The mature reader, like Barthes's literary reader, writes a good deal of every text that he reads.

Several recent journal articles carry the idea of intertextual play by readers who rewrite the texts they read into the composition classroom. Anthony Petrosky, in "From Story to Essay: Reading and Writing," *CCC,* 33 (February 1982), 19–36, argues that ". . . writing about reading is one of the best ways to get students to unravel their transactions [with texts] so that we can see how they understand and . . . help them learn to elaborate, clarify, and illustrate their responses by reference to the associations and prior knowledge that inform them" (p. 24). For Petrosky, writing interacts with the actual process of reading, helping students connect personal response with public knowledge. Students, according to Petrosky, learn to analyze critically by writing as they read. But Petrosky, relying primarily on David Bleich's subjective theory, gives little attention to Barthes's concept of play among the public codes readers brings to texts. For Petrosky, the writing is useful as a way of filling out critical responses, but it is not a means of creative expression.

An article of my own ("Literature and the Writing Process: A Pedagogical Reading of William Faulkner's 'Barn Burning,'" *College Literature,* 9 [1982], 2–21) provides a more complete account of how writing might be used to facilitate a reader's movement through the major stages of the reading process. This article posits a *progressive* stage, where readers create perceptual patterns by responding in personal and public ways to textual cues, a *transitional* stage, where readers draw these cues and their related associations together into blueprints to direct the construction of meaning, and a *symbolic* stage, where readers make statements of significance out of textual cues and reader responses by connecting them with more abstract social and cultural experience. In this essay, I explain how expressive discourse can combine with transactional as readers move through these states of response to construct meaning from a reading experience.[4]

Norman N. Holland and Murray Schwartz ("The Delphi Seminar," *CE,* 36 [March 1975], 789–800) add a perspective on revision and drafting to my own and Petrosky's discussion of writing about and during reading. Holland and Schwartz describe a course in which students wrote brief responses to readings during an initial five-week period and, subsequently, wrote more complete responses that were based on these initial responses during a followup five-week period. Students, Holland and Schwartz found, defined their own identity themes in reaction to literary texts during the first period, while they filled the space between subjective and objective responses by negotiating with peers and writing fuller interpretations during the second period. Of most significance for writing teachers is Holland and Schwartz's implied strategy of teaching students to revise their more expressive response drafts into more transactional pieces of criticism.

In a very recent essay ("Carlos Reads a Poem," *CE,* 46 [September 1984] 478–92), Holland joins with Eugene R. Kintgen to construct a method of analyzing the reading protocols of a mature reader. Their aim is to identify "the separate cognitive processes involved in the act of reading" (p. 478). Their method involves using an I-Test to enable the researcher to define the dominant personality traits of the reader-subject, and it involves the analyses of a student subject's reading protocols in the light of these dominant traits. The result of the analysis that is described in this article is a realization that ". . . the human activity called literary interpretation consists of a personal selection [depending on dominant personality traits as they are defined by identity theme] and use of communal tools [derived from the reader's background as a member of a particular interpretive community]" (p. 491).

At this point we can return to the subjective, transactional, and objective categories of current literary theory and their relevance to the teaching of writing. Each of these categories represents a perspective on the acts of reading and writing that must be considered in the context of the process orientation I have described in the last few pages. What we come to know from theory and research about the cognitive acts of reading and writing must be sorted into a set of perspectives that teachers can use to organize their interventions into the reading-writing processes of their students.

Norman Holland in *The Dynamics of Literary Response* (New York: Oxford University Press, 1968, now available in a Norton paperback ed., 1975), *5 Readers Reading* (New Haven: Yale University Press, 1975), and *Poems in Persons* (New York: Norton, 1973) develops a perspective and method focused on the relationship between a reader's "identity theme" and the fantasy world existing in a literary work. Each reader brings his or her identity theme, which is itself constantly changing, into a dynamic relationship with the fantasy structure of a literary work. In the resulting transaction, both the reader's identity and the work are transformed into new and mutually significant forms. Authors work from their personalities and backgrounds, using learned literary forms to construct public utterances out of personal fantasies. Readers use the forms they share with others in a literary community as defenses against the projected fantasies of authors, while critics serve as referees in this defensive and offensive struggle between fantasies. Critics, to Holland, do not read texts, they "read" readers as they operate on texts. Holland supposes a world of shared literary convention and knowledge, but he consistently frames those conventions in a picture whose essential organizing strategies are subjective and psychologistic. Holland believes that critics and teachers can and should interpret readers' personalities and literary texts together as phenomena that help us construct, but do not themselves constitute, a literary text. Writers, readers, and critics, for Holland, are engaged in the public construction of subjectively generated meanings.

Readers who wish to examine Holland's specific applications

of psychoanalytic personality theory and literary dynamics to the classroom should consult two of Holland's articles: "Transactive Teaching: Cordelia's Death," *CE,* 38 (1977), 276–85, and Norman Holland and Murray M. Schwartz, "The Delphi Seminar," *CE,* 36 (1975), 789–800. In these articles, Holland and his co-author explain in detail how identity themes can be established through interpretations of draft responses and protocols of student-readers. (This process of interpretation is described in greater detail in *5 Readers Reading,* where the protocols of five student readers are, first, analyzed in order to define the students' identity themes and are, second, applied to a literary text— Faulkner's "A Rose for Emily"—in order to explain each student's interpretation of the text.)

Holland's subjectivism seems most questionable in its sometimes impressionistic and unsystematic way of encouraging teachers and critics to perform psychoanalysis of student readers. Although Holland's books on literary response are grounded in the theories of respected, recent psychological figures such as Erik Erikson and Otto Fenichel, Holland often plays fast and loose with those theories as he transforms them into critical and pedagogical methodology.[5] Eugene Kintgen, both in his own work and his collaborations with Holland, attempts to provide a more precise and systematic method behind the teacher-critic's interpretation of student-reader's protocols and responses. In an article that I described in the previous section ("Carlos Reads a Poem") Kintgen and Holland use a flexible personality test (the "I-test" developed by Holland) and their own interpretive abilities to define Carlos's dominant personality traits. These traits are then used to interpret Carlos's responses to William Gibson's poem "Winter Piece." Although the test has not yet been subjected to a great deal of reliability and validity testing, it would seem to begin the process of refining instruments that teachers and critics can use to read readers as well as texts. In "Perceiving Poetic Syntax," *CE,* 40 (1978), 17–27, Kintgen combines recent work in psycholinguistics and reading with Holland's more psychoanalytical perspective to explain how students come to "chunk" poetic structures according to a combination of cognitive and affective strategies, and to suggest ways in which these same student respondents use interpretive sets to control and organize their reading of a poem. Kintgen summarizes the results of the studies that produced both these articles in *The Perception of Poetry* (Bloomington: Indiana University Press, 1983). He also integrated into one theory the reading of both syntactical chunks and whole texts in this book.

David Bleich, however, provides what is probably the most coherent general account of both the epistemological implications and the pedagogical practices of the subjective perspective. In *Subjective Criticism* Bleich argues the essential subjectivity of all critical activity, indeed of all knowledge.[6] We cannot, as readers or knowers, ignore the fact that our subjective selves—personalities and linguistic-cultural competences combined—instigate and control acts of reading and interpretation. Bleich describes the institution of language study and literature as one in which individual knowers involve themselves in a process of symbolizing and re-symbolizing their personal experience. This experience becomes knowledge when these individual processes of re-symbolization have been negotiated with the reader's community. Objective knowledge is possible only when this negotiation of reader responses gains the authoritative backing of the community. All ways of knowing—reading, writing, criticism, and interpretation—are, to Bleich, interrelated; they cannot be separated from one another in the process of constructing knowledge. All are also subjective in origin.

Bleich describes the pedagogy that he believes is implied by this subjective epistemology in *Readings and Feelings* (Urbana, Ill.: NCTE, 1975). In this book, Bleich proposes a series of reading-writing assignments that include what he calls "affective and associative" verbal responses and sets of negotiated written meaning and interpretation statements. Each verbal and written sequence in this series overlaps with the others as a reader reads, responds to, and interprets a text. Always the individual response is both respected for its essential subjectivity and confronted by the responses of others in a classroom community. In this process the class molds itself into a community that is capable of giving authority to individual readings of a text by regulating the interaction of responses that it has negotiated.

Bleich, then, provides a simple but potentially useful frame for writing teachers as they attempt to incorporate literary theory and recent composition research in the classroom. Composition's recent emphasis on theories of audience (Bleich's negotiating community), on revision (Bleich's response process as it is influenced by a negotiating community), and on the uses of expressive and transactional discourse (Bleich's series of expressive then transactional response statements) all have their counterparts in the subjective perspectives of Holland, Kintgen, and Bleich. Also, as we view current literary theory from the vantage point of composition research, we come to see the degree to which differences among literary theorists are more those of perspective than substance. Subjective theory works from the perspective of reader–critic and writer back to text, community, and systems of knowledge, rather than from text back to author's intentions or social context.

Transactional theorists, in contrast, place their emphases squarely between readers and their texts. Louise Rosenblatt in *The Reader, the Text, the Poem* (Carbondale: Southern Illinois University Press, 1978) posits a reader who transforms literary texts into "events."[7] Literary readers recognize a piece of literature as literary and proceed to shift their stance on the text from the more ordinary "efferent" (reading for information) one to the extraordinary, or special, "aesthetic" stance. This new stance, Rosenblatt says, causes the reader to emphasize the experience before the meaning or significance of a literary work, which, in turn, enables an evocation of a reading event rather than the simple transference of new information. Readers must "live through" (p. 132) the transaction with the text.

Rosenblatt's approach provides numerous theoretical possibilities for the placing of composing exercises within rather than after the reading experience. Readers, according to Rosenblatt, must spend more time on developing, or *evoking,* the event or experience of reading, and they must be encouraged to understand the experience of reading as a process that comes before and creates the foundation upon which later critical interpretation of meaning and significance rests.

Stanley Fish's work also fits into the transactional perspective. In his earlier work, discussed earlier in this essay, Fish focuses our attention on the reader's line-by-line experience of literary texts, which he suggests is different from ordinary reading in that readers reading literature are more prepared to revise than when they are reading non-literary texts. Whereas Rosenblatt emphasizes the literary event as holistically experienced, Fish emphasizes the reader's immediate perceptual processing of literary syntax. Both critics, however, define the reader's role as a re-creative one rather than as one of finder and definer of meaning and significance. Both suggest that criticism must help readers experience a text before they interpret it.

In his later work, Fish becomes much more involved in questions of interpretive authority. His earlier work (*Self-Consuming Artifacts*) had posited an "informed" reader who shared the linguistic and literary competences of the author, who knew, as he or she wrote, how the game of reading literature was played. But in his latest book, *Is There a Text in This Class?* (Baltimore: Johns Hopkins University Press, 1980), Fish collects a series of essays in which the use of interpretive strategies as they are defined by interpretive communities becomes his primary concern. The book begins by reemphasizing Fish's earlier arguments against objective stylistics and for an "affective," or subjective stylistics. Syntactic structures as they appear in texts do not exist during the actual act of reading; only the reader's perception of frames or units of meaning controls the construction of interpretations.

In the middle part of this book, Fish assembles several essays on reading Milton in which he demonstrates how the reading of particular lines is conditioned by the interpretive strategies that are shared by the critics doing the reading. Fish locates the reasons behind this transactional perspective in the speech-act theories of John R. Searle and J. L. Austin.[8] He agrees with Searle and Austin that interpretive frames stand behind our interpretations of all verbal utterances, but he does not agree with those literary critics who apply Austin and Searle's distinction between illocutionary and perlocutionary forces to literary discourse. Illocutionary speech acts are performative and require contexts to communicate meaning; the perlocutionary effects of speech acts result from the force of illocutionary acts as they are recognized by hearers or readers. Illocutionary acts are governed by linguistic conventions; they are, to Fish, stable. But they are not always in some kind of defined or stable relationship with their perlocutionary effects. These effects, Fish suggests, are defined by the interpretive community to which the reader of a text belongs.

This community of readers and writers controls the reader's perspective on the text and provides particular strategies for solving textual problems. Different reading contexts produce different applications of these strategies, with the interpretive community to which a reader belongs providing the authority behind various readings. If a reader has appropriately used writing, reading, and interpretive strategies that are approved by an established interpretive community, his or her interpretation will be given authority in that community. This separation of communication act from effects in the processing of discourse is important to Fish because it explains why distinctions between literary and ordinary discourse are false, and it buttresses his argument that interpretive communities, not the linguistic or literary conventions in texts, control the acts of reading and interpretation (see "How to Do Things with Austin and Searle: Speech-Act Theory and Literary Criticism," *Is There a Text in This Class?*, pp. 197–245). Fish seems to ignore the influence of literary competence and the interpretive community on writers, who, in his model, are unaware of or lack control over the reader's response. Despite this slighting of the writer, however, Fish provides those in composition with a rationale for writing about literature that moves away from the sense of interpretive authority held by those New Critics who assume that a special kind of interpretive process must be part of our responses to literary discourse. All language, Fish suggests, can be subjected to the special kind of attention we, as members of a literary community, give to literature, and it is that special kind of attention that we impart when we teach reading and writing as interpretation. It is not a different kind of language that teachers of writing through literature teach.

Wolfgang Iser, whose work has been introduced earlier in this essay, rounds out our category of transactional theorists. Iser, much like Rosenblatt, is primarily interested in the process through which a literary experience is "realized." Drawing on earlier work by Roman Ingarten and Edmund Husserl in aesthetic phenomenology, Iser explains the interaction of text and reader as a process of "virtuality." The meaning of a literary work evolves from the reader's responses to "blanks" and "negations" in the text. Readers are driven by their competence as experienced readers to use the schemas embodied in the text and their own experience to fill these blanks and eliminate these negations: "They [blanks and negations] make it possible for the fundamental asymmetry between text and reader to be balanced out, for they initiate an interaction whereby the hollow form of the text is filled by the mental images of the writer" (*The Act of Reading,* p. 225).

Both transactionalists and subjectivists reject the objectivist position that determinate meanings are contained *in* texts. They, in contrast to objectivists, focus their attention on readers and the process of reading; their ideas contribute directly to the writing teacher's understanding of how readers and transactive processes become part of an overall interpretation, and how that process of interpretation can be enriched and made more coherent when different kinds of writing exercises are interspersed in the reading process.

Objective theorists, in contrast, share a focus on text as the container of meaning within the act of interpretation. Different objective critics have different reasons for their objectivity. E. D. Hirsch, Jr. (*Validity in Interpretation* [New Haven: Yale University Press, 1968]; *The Aims of Interpretation* [Chicago: University of Chicago Press, 1976]) focuses his objective perspective on the act of interpretation itself, which he sees as a systematic cognitive process in which the author's intention can be recovered from the text.

Posing his theory of interpretation against modern relativistic theories that have their sources in Kant, Coleridge, and Heidegger, Hirsch argues that critics can escape the hermeneutic circle by consciously controlling their responses to the patterns of signs in a text. This control, Hirsch contends, depends on the critic's understanding of *will* and *type*. An author wills meaning into a text by controlling those signs that represent the generic and linguistic knowledge shared by experienced writers and readers. A reader reconceives that meaning by systematically drawing inferences from the configuration of signs in the text, deemphasizing his or her personality and background in the process. Writers and readers can, then, join together in the mutual conception and reconception of the meaning of a text, but they can accomplish this joint creation only by being careful to separate the construction of textual meaning from the making of statements of significance. Meaning, to Hirsch, resides *in* the text and can be recovered by readers who use hermeneutic methods to recover it; significance is the relating of that meaning to some aspect of social or cultural life.

For writing teachers, Hirsch's argument provides a conservative perspective on the claims made by extreme relativists. Hirsch enables teachers to explain how playing by the rules of the interpretive game can and often does result in the communication of stable meanings. His work can reinstill in the teaching of writing and reading a respect for the function of shared knowledge and skill in the creation and communication of meaning. Without agreeing with Hirsch's extreme anti-relativism, at least as it is expressed in these earlier books, composition teachers will find in his theory of interpretation a flexible and sensible counter to the "anything goes" relativism of some students.

Jonathan Culler's work provides an objective perspective on the knowledge that writers and readers share as they read and interpret. He complements Hirsch's focus on the act of interpretation with a focus on "literary competence." Using the structuralist's concept of binary opposites (*Structuralist Poetics* [Ithaca: Cornell University Press, 1975]), Culler explains how the abilities of readers to perceive patterns of structures as they read create a system within which writer and reader carry on stable communication. This system creates the literary competence that underlies every literary performance: ". . . a poem presupposes conventions of reading which the author may work against, which he can transform, but which are the conditions of his discourse" (p. 30). Culler suggests that critics begin to deemphasize the importance of interpretation of meaning in order to explain in much greater detail the competences that make reading and writing possible in the first place.

In *The Pursuit of Signs* (Ithaca: Cornell University Press, 1981), Culler explains the challenges that deconstructive theory poses for the concept of literary competence. Deconstructionists, Culler suggests, emphasize the state of mind within which experienced readers of literature operate; literary competence, however, enables readers to carry on traditional literary interpretation of meaning *and* deconstructive play with that meaning—often simultaneously. This is possible, Culler suggests, because readers are capable, with training and experience, of working recursively through the four stages of realizing a text (*Structuralist Poetics*, pp. 113–60)—the *realistic*, the *cultural*, the *generic*, the *ironic*. These stages of realization are made possible by the sharing of a literary competence that enables readers to recognize literary structures on these four levels of perception in a rapid and cyclical process. Meaning can, for example, be built on the mimetic or realistic level, be questioned almost simultaneously on the cultural level, be constructed once again when combined with ideas of literary type or genre, and then be deconstructed a second time by exposing itself to an ironic rereading or double-take.

Culler shows how shared, structural competences control the literary writer and reader's composing process. This competence works, Culler suggests, in tandem with what deconstructionists call "metaphoricity" to create a constant tension between constructive and deconstructive acts in the process of reading. With this balancing of critical perspectives, Culler provides the writing teacher with a means of explaining the friction all writers feel between the pressures of conventions and the need to express new forms and ideas.

Hirsch and Culler emphasize two different kinds of objective perspective, the first on the interpretive process as readers and writers work together to reconstruct the meaning of a work, the second on the literary competence that serves as the base for interpretation. We can close this discussion of objective perspectives with a summary of the work of two representative, traditional rhetorical critics, both of whom have become well known for their objective analyses of the rhetorical techniques and effects embodied in literary texts. Wayne Booth's *The Rhetoric of Fiction* (2nd ed., Chicago: University of Chicago Press, 1983, first published in 1961) provides an encyclopedia of fictional rhetorical techniques and many specific discussions of their effects in particular literary works. The general value of *The Rhetoric of Fiction* is its emphasis on the rhetorical layering of the communication process in the reading of fiction; Booth's specific discussion of how authors project narrative voices into texts that, in turn, enable them to develop a complex array of responses in readers considerably expanded our understanding of how writers can control the context of a literary work to criticize, ridicule, or applaud the actions of fictional characters. Booth extended his analysis of technique into a moral criticism of the unreliability and moral evasiveness of modern and post-modern fictions, where he feels that the signals writers send to readers are often inextricably mixed and confused.

Booth carries his rhetoric of fiction a step further in *A Rhetoric of Irony* (Chicago: University of Chicago Press, 1974), where he explains a system of cues that he believes writers use to signal ironic intent. Booth, like Hirsch, consistently strives to stabilize the literary communication process by showing how underlying strategies of composition can control reader responses, and by arguing for what he believes is a morally responsible attitude toward fictional experimentation. Experimental writers, Booth contends, should strive to alert readers to new forms through the sending of signals that are implied by textual cues.[9] Without such clear signals to readers, new forms are often misconstrued and responded to in unethical if not immoral ways.

Booth's emphasis on craft and effect is always focused on textual evidence, seldom if ever on biographical information, historical scholarship, or descriptive models of reading. His eye is consistently on the words on the page. Such is also the case in what remains the best example of traditional, stylistically oriented, rhetorical criticism: Edward P. J. Corbett's anthology of critical essays, *Rhetorical Analyses of Literary Works* (New York: Oxford University Press, 1969). The critics represented in Corbett's book are all engaged in analyzing text in order to discover potential effects on readers. Corbett's introduction to this book also provides an excellent account of the history of traditional, objective rhetorical criticism and its relationship to the then-prevalent New Criticism. Often using the figures and tropes of classical rhetoric, objective rhetorical critics explore texts to explain how these figures and tropes affect particular audiences, actual or implied.

In our attempt to bring the subjective, transactional, and objective perspectives together under a single, descriptive model of interpretation, we need to look at how the literary theories that are represented by these perspectives match up with current *discourse processing* models in the general field of communications. Robert deBeaugrande, "Writer, Reader, Critic: Comparing Critical Theories as Discourse," *CE,* 46 (1984), 533–59, undertakes just such a comparison. In this essay, deBeaugrande describes the

319

strengths and weaknesses of the theories of Hirsch, Fish, and J. Hillis Miller.

Hirsch, to deBeaugrande, ignores the complexity of the act of reading itself, but provides a fuller account of the traditional process of interpretation and its reliance on generic and psycholinguistic expectations as they are shared by readers and writers than do most recent literary theorists. Fish, in contrast to Hirsch, effectively demonstrates the complexities of the act of reading without addressing the ways in which parts of literary texts are "chunked" into whole meanings, and he fails to connect his concept of communal interpretive strategies to his close analysis of the reading process. Miller, representing American deconstructionist criticism, shows us how normative readings are always in the process of intersubjective deconstruction in which "stable meaning is to be displaced by 'metaphoricity itself'" (p. 555), but he fails to give due credit to the operation of what Culler calls "literary competence" in the reading-interpretation process.

In fact, deBeaugrande argues, psycholinguists assert that all discourse processing entails a "successive restarting of alternatives" in reader responses to texts (p. 554). These restartings, or pursuits of different avenues of meaning as they are suggested by previous avenues, could not exist without the sharing by readers and writers of a stable system of competences.

Each critical perspective, then, provides a valuable insight into one or more of the stages in the acts of reading, writing, and interpretation, but no one perspective explains the whole process. Teachers of composition would do well to fit these various perspectives into one expanded and descriptive model of interpretation, which might then help them develop and control the kind of writing-reading exercises that will encourage students to re-create the complex process of producing and consuming discourse.

III. USING LITERARY THEORY TO CREATE A FUNCTIONAL MODEL OF WRITING AND READING AS INTERPRETATION

We need, at this point, to turn away from the job of defining critical perspectives to a review of literary theorists who have argued for and begun to construct models of the interpretive process out of these perspectives. Robert Scholes, *Semiotics and Interpretation* (New Haven: Yale University Press, 1982), argues that "Interpretation—'reading' in the large sense—is one of the great goals of humanistic study, and the reading of literary texts is one of the best methods—perhaps *the* best—of developing interpretive skills in students" (p. xii). Much in the vein of Jonathan Culler, Scholes tells teachers to treat reading itself as interpretation, to refuse to separate criticism from reading, and to involve themselves in the study of how linguistic signs operate in literary contexts (semiotics) to produce strategies of interpretation that control both writers and readers. Subjectivity to Scholes is always subsumed by codes that are shared by communities of interpreters. Students must be taught to make conscious use of these codes "so that they can appreciate those texts that re-shape accepted ideas and at the same time defend themselves against the manipulative exploitation of received opinion" (p. 14). For Scholes texts are "open, incomplete, insufficient" (p. 15), but they are so constructed in order to be filled out by the codes that preexist the text in the minds of writers and readers.

Literary competence, Scholes argues, is activated whenever readers perceive "a difference between maker and speaker" in a text (p. 21). This quality of "literateness" characteristic of fiction becomes the writer's signal to the reader to look for literary effects—irony, role-playing, allusion, ambiguity—and to read with the intensified attention to the interaction of semiotic codes that literary interpretation demands. Interpretation, in this context, assures that readers will not simply read "through" a text for information, but will compare the "real" context behind the literary text with the fictional context in the text.

Scholes provides a general frame for interpretation that explains both why reading and interpretation must be combined in one process and why teaching writing through literature can produce more complex interpretive skills than most other forms of discourse. (Readers can, of course, apply literary interpretation to all kinds of discourse.)

Stephen Mailloux, *Interpretive Conventions: The Reader in the Study of American Fiction* (Ithaca: Cornell University Press, 1982), uses different terminology to accomplish the same purpose as Scholes. Mailloux argues that three different kinds of conventions—the *traditional,* the *regulative,* and the *constitutive*—combine to control both the temporal (phenomenological) and social aspects of interpretation. Traditional (culturally derived) and regulative (rule-governed) conventions control writers' illocutionary acts, providing them with a group of systematic codes from which to choose in constructing texts. Constitutive conventions result when particular readers and writers use combinations or permutations of traditional and regulative conventions "to create . . . new forms of behavior" (p. 129). Applied to interpretive reading, these types of conventions work together both to control and enable the creation of original interpretations. Writing teachers, Mailloux implies, need to look closely at particular stages in the process of interpretation—some governed by subjective, others by transactional and objective perspectives—in order to understand the balance among conventions and its effects on interpretive response. How are readers' subjective responses shaped by particular traditional conventions, how do the rules of language constrain personal responses during transactional phases of developing an interpretation, how are both regulative and traditional conventions combined into more complete interpretations during objective phases of interpretation, and how are regulative and traditional perspectives made constitutive during the acts of reading and writing about a reading experience? These are the types of questions Mailloux's book suggests for composition teachers who use literature.

Mailloux's essential questions direct our attention to relations among the temporal phases and overall structure of interpretation, and to the constructive acts of reading and writing that produce meaning as we read. But no account of the process of interpretation is complete without some attention to relationships between deep and surface structure in the processing of literary texts. Contemporary stylistics provides the needed perspective here.

Much current stylistic theory focuses on the question of whether or not readers read directly to meaning or by attending consciously to the linguistic structures on the page. At this point in the development of contemporary stylistics neither an extreme positivism nor an extreme mentalism is being supported by those who study reading from the perspective of style. George Dillon, relying a good deal on the work of Stanley Fish and Seymour Chatman,[10] presents a model of reading that balances the reader's attention to surface structure and holistic meanings. Dillon divides reading into stages of perception, comprehension, and interpretation (*Language Processing and the Reading of Literature* [Bloomington: Indiana University Press, 1978]), but he explains in much greater detail than most stylistic critics how readers work through these stages. Literary texts are not processed linearly, from perception through interpretation. Rather, readers begin very early in the processing of a text to posit whole meanings, to create what Wolfgang Iser would call the "horizon" of the reading experience, which they then use to contextualize the text's linguistic structures as they continue reading. Working very closely with clausal boundaries, appositional structures, sliding modifying units, semantic compatibility, and proleptic devices, Dillon demonstrates that readers of Spenser, Milton, James, Stevens, and Faulkner see the actual text as a pattern of cues that come progressively to link up with general structures of interpretation: ". . . we may find the relevance of a piece of information by altering our conception of what the passage as a whole is about . . . we do not comprehend by adding each completed sentence to the pile of ones previously processed; rather, we view each new sentence in relation to the set of expectations and possibilities arising from the previous ones" (p. 14).

Dillon provides a perspective on style in which the processing of texts connects perception of technical clues with the general processing of meaning. Readers, to Dillon, read for meaning and to the page in one interdependent process. In *Constructing Texts: Elements of a Theory of Composition and Style* (Bloomington: Indiana University Press, 1981), Dillon carries the implications of his approach more directly into the field of composition. He argues that approaches to reading that depend on efficiency models of text processing—which he calls "the intake-of-content" mode of reading (p. 163)—are limited by empirically derived concepts of the channel limitations of readers.

Real readers, however, are able to transcend these physiological limitations of short-term memory by learning to use the conventions of genres—in the composition classroom, the conventions of the expository essay serve as examples—to create a model of reading in which extremely economical packages or chunks of verbal clues and generic themes combine to direct their actions. Like Stephen Mailloux and Robert Scholes, George Dillon suggests that writing and reading courses be based on holistic, integrated models of interpretation, rather than on reductive models based on text structures alone, personal responses in isolation, or the experience of reading separate from either text or reader. These integrated models, Dillon argues, are more apt, today, to be found in literary and semiotic theory than they are in models drawn from positivistic linguistics or social science.

Michael Riffaterre, *Semiotics of Poetry* (Bloomington: Indiana University Press, 1978), provides a perspective on the processing of literary texts through stylistics that is similar to Dillon's. Riffaterre uses Charles Sanders Pierce's idea of *interpretants* to explain how readers connect the surface signs and evolving themes of a text (p. 81). Interpretants are literary signs that accomplish two functions for readers: they call attention to particularly significant passages in a text by synthesizing sets of cues that had previously appeared only in isolation; once they have been perceived, they create in the reader's mind patterns of cues which, in turn, clarify evolving thematic patterns. Riffaterre's system, although it has been criticized by Stanley Fish as too dependent on an artificial separation of literary and ordinary language, provides a technically specific account of the process through which generic and linguistic cues are put into gestalts or patterns by readers *as* they read literary texts.

A final word on developing a model of the reading process that is based on interpretive theory. A good deal of the literary theory that has been written since the 1950s has added more specific categories of readers to the critic's vocabulary. (See the articles by Walker Gibson, Gerald Prince, and Staney Fish in *Reader Response Criticism,* ed. Jane Tompkins [Baltimore: Johns Hopkins University Press, 1980] and articles by Tzvetan Todorov, Robert Crosman, Jacques Leenhardt, Gerald Prince, and Vicki Mistacco in *The Reader in the Text,* ed. by Susan Suleiman and Inge Crosman [Princeton: Princeton University Press, 1980]. These two anthologies also provide excellent review essays and complete annotated bibliographies on reader response criticism.) These new reader–oriented terms complement Wayne Booth and other objective critics' taxonomies of terms defining the various ways that writers project themselves (e.g., assumed author, reliable and unreliable narrators, authorial voices, shifting viewpoints) into texts. Prince and Todorov's concept of *narratee,* the image of the reader that is inscribed in a text by the author's use of and the reader's response to literary narrative conventions, is perhaps the most prominent and currently useful of these new terms describing readers. The concept of narratee enables critics to define tensions and relationships between the narrator and narratee, between the narratee and actual or implied readers, and between assumed author and narratee. The concept could enable teachers of interpretation to construct new types of writing-reading exercises in which students would take on the roles of different types of readers in the act of reading: narratees, informed readers, ideal readers, subjective, objective, and transactional readers.

What has this model of reading as interpretation produced in the way of pedagogy for composition and literature courses? Several clusters of recent articles in composition journals suggest particular classroom implications and strategies.

Two recent essays review recent literary theory in order to point out general pedagogical implications. Edward M. White, "Post-Structural Literary Criticism and Response to Student Writing," CCC, 35 (May 1984), 186–95, argues that reader-oriented theories will encourage composition teachers to give even more careful attention than they traditionally have to the processes that produce student texts. Now that a whole body of recent literary theory supports the idea that meanings do not reside in texts, but are the result of a transaction among readers, texts, the tacit knowledge of an interpretive community, and writers, writing teachers have substantial support from literary criticism for their recently developed emphasis on the entire process of composing. Taking cues from this more dynamic view of reading, writing teachers must spend more time teaching writers to figure out, as they write, what experienced readers would know and do as they respond to developing drafts of their texts.

Susan Miller, "What Does It Mean to Be Able to Write? The Question of Writing in the Discourses of Literature and Composition," CE, 45 (March 1983), 219–35, complements White's essay by suggesting that writing teachers must begin to see student texts in ways similar to the way literary critics evaluate literary texts. Rather than focusing on texts as a potentially endless series of drafts or subtexts, composition teachers must come to know when, Miller suggests, student texts should be given a unique status, where the teacher as implied reader reads beyond surface conventions and ideas developing to structures that depend on strategies of intertextuality and community. This valorization of particular drafts of student texts would combine with the currently emphasized developmental method of responding to student drafts to provide a balanced process and product approach to student texts. The key to the success of this combined approach, though, would reside in the teachers' understanding of their students' classroom communities, on their ability to become part of the negotiative process for every essay that a student writes. In summing up Miller's suggestion, we might say that writing teachers must develop a keener eye for those drafts that suggest closure.

A second cluster of two essays provides specific discussions of current literary theory's emphasis on writer-reader interactions in the classroom. Mariolina Salvatori, "Reading and Writing a Text: Correlations between Reading-Writing Patterns," *CE*, 45 (Nov. 1983), 657–66, uses Wolfgang Iser's work to counter the idea that students should always know exactly what they are going to say as they write. This pedagogical attitude, Salvatori says, causes students prematurely to close off the development of meaning during the production of a text, to produce facile and contrived thesis-ridden essays in which no sign of discovery is evident. Salvatori then illustrates her point by rendering the experience of a hypothetical student who uses Iser's idea of wandering viewpoints to explore and clarify the meanings of three personal experiences. This student is able to synthesize her text by first exploring and then pulling together her shifting perspectives on these experiences: "through the activity of a more dynamic 'wandering viewpoint' [this student writer] reorganizes and modifies minimal acts of comprehension . . . into larger patterns [of meaning]" (p. 666).

Bruce T. Peterson, "Writing About Responses: A Unified Model of Reading, Interpretation, and Composition," *CE*, 44 (Sept. 1982), 459–68, supplements Salvatori's suggestions with a pedagogical philosophy based on current learning theory and developmental psychology. Peterson describes three stages of response-writing that could be used by teachers to amplify and expand student readings of literary texts. Within this series of responses, students would use different aims of writing (particularly the expressive and transactional) to enhance their consciousness of how both personal reactions and public conventions combine to control and enrich the process of interpretation.

Finally, a third cluster of two essays discusses ways teachers might intervene directly into the cognitive processes of students as they write and read. Russell A. Hunt, "Toward a Process Intervention Model in Literature Teaching," *CE,* 44 (April 1982), 345–57, suggests a variety of very specific ways in which teachers can slow down the reading process in order to make students more aware of how they can use conventions combined with personal responses to enrich and control the act of reading. Hunt concludes by arguing that most of what readers do is directed by tacit knowledge. Making some of that knowledge conscious produces more directed and active readers.

Peter Parisi, "Close Reading, Creative Writing, and Cognitive Development," *CE,* 41 (Sept. 1979), 57–67, relates reader-response theory to cognitive development theory, particularly Piaget's concepts of egocentricity and decentration, in order to argue that effective readers must learn to relate form and content and part and whole as they read in ways that are not encouraged by ordinary reading: the student's "speculations swallow up the text, while mature, critical readers maintain a distanced, potentially ironic contemplation of any given skein of reasoning" (p. 60). Parisi argues that this special kind of literary attention can be learned by students when they are asked to write imaginatively and critically on common themes. By listening to peer responses to their own work, by reading others' writing, by writing their own versions of the fictional/poetic techniques they will read, and by reading professional writers of stories and poems, Parisi's students gradually learn to de-center, to stand back from their own and others' texts in order to construct meanings that are both personally expressive and publicly negotiable.

Because of lack of space, I have not mentioned numerous theoretical and practical essays that provide useful ideas for relating current literary theory and composition. What I have reviewed simply suggests the general direction in which future developments in both fields might go. But I cannot close this essay without at least mentioning a very particular and important application of literary theory to the composition curriculum.

In recent years, many writing programs have moved across the curriculum. The question of how these programs should incorporate the inquiry and communication paradigms of different academic and professional fields combines with the question of what is basic in all fields of writing to create a particularly problematic stage in the development of these programs. The theory I have reviewed suggests a simple but far-reaching solution: the reinstallation of a curriculum in which the process of interpretation provides the base from which writers in any field work. All writers and readers construct meanings from a shared set of linguistic and field-specific conventions; all writers must balance subjective and objective responses as they operate within these conventions; all writers, to some degree, construct the contexts within which they write. Perhaps literary texts as they are composed and de-composed by communities of readers and writers, using conventional strategies in often original ways, can create the kind of active, critical, and original writers a curriculum requires as it promotes writing across the disciplines. Effective readers and writers must learn to interpret before they learn to do the special jobs required by different academic disciplines and professional fields. Only when we in composition clearly define where writing programs must begin will we be able to avoid the superficial emphases on mechanical formats that often come to dominate writing across the curriculum programs.

NOTES

1. See *Validity in Interpretation* (New Haven: Yale University Press, 1967) and *The Aims of Interpretation* (Chicago: University of Chicago Press, 1976).

2. Iser's work relies most specifically on Ingarten's *The Literary*

Work of Art, transl. by George C. Grabowicz (Evanston: Northwestern University Press, 1973). Those who wish to read a sound, general introduction to earlier phenomenological criticism should consult Robert Magliola's *Phenomenology and Literature* (West Lafayette, Indiana: Purdue University Press, 1977). Magliola traces phenomenological criticism from Kant through Husserl, Heidegger, and Ingarten, to Sartre, Merleau-Ponty, Barthes, and beyond.

3. The second edition of Daiker, Kerek, and Morenberg's *The Writer's Options* (New York: Harper & Row, 1982) is probably the best of these rhetorically oriented sentence-combining texts.

4. Also see my "Burke's Dramatism as a Means of Using Literature to Teach Composition," *RSQ,* 9 (Summer 1979), 142–55.

5. Holland relies primarily on the *Collected Papers of Otto Fenichel: First Series* (New York: Norton, 1953) and Erikson's *Young Man Luther: A Study in Psychoanalysis and History* (New York: Norton, 1962) and *Childhood and Society* (New York: Norton, 1963) in his *Dynamics of Literary Response.*

6. For an earlier and briefer summary of Bleich's subjective epistemology see his "The Subjective Character of Critical Interpretation," *CE,* 36 (March 1975), 739–55.

7. More specific pedagogical applications of Rosenblatt's theory are described in *Literature as Exploration* (rev. ed., New York: Noble and Noble, 1968).

8. On speech-act theory and its origins see Searle's *Speech Acts: An Essay in the Philosophy of Language* (Cambridge: Cambridge University Press, 1969) and Austin's *How to Do Things with Words* (London: Oxford University Press, 1962). On speech-act theory and literary interpretation see Mary Louise Pratt, *Toward a Speech Act Theory of Literary Discourse* (Bloomington: Indiana University Press, 1977).

9. In *Critical Understanding* (Chicago: University of Chicago Press, 1979), Booth attempts to explain how "critical pluralism" can result in fuller readings of literary texts. In this book, Booth uses the criticism of Ronald S. Crane, Kenneth Burke, and Meyer H. Abrams to illustrate how different critical perspectives can be brought to bear on particular readings of literary texts without destroying the coherence of interpretation.

10. See, in particular, Fish's *Self-Consuming Artifacts,* cited earlier, and Chatman's *The Later Style of Henry James* (Oxford: Blackwell, 1972).

Studying Rhetoric and Literature

JIM W. CORDER, Texas Christian University

I'M SOMETIMES ASTONISHED TO LEARN HOW easily people get things fixed in their minds, fixed, right, by God, and forever. I'll cite four brief episodes that reveal the disjunction between rhetoric and literature that seems so firmly fixed in the minds of many.

In my freshman composition class last term, we tried to learn a little about argumentative discourse and to write a little along the way. One day I brought to class copies of "My Last Duchess" so that we could examine the argument in the poem. My students were not blunt about the matter, but they did gradually begin to reveal that they were puzzled that I should bring a *poem* to study as an *argument*. Arguments, by their reckoning, occur in political speeches, editorials, advertisements, and freshman essays.

The second episode comes from some years back, but I harbor grudges and nurse them to keep them warm. Noting that I had written some about rhetoric—he noted, but did not read what I had written—a young colleague asked me, "Why have you repudiated Literature?"

Third, at the end of last term, a student in my graduate rhetoric course told me, "I really enjoy learning about rhetoric, but I still come down on the side of literature."

Fourth, I was surprised to see that Robert J. Connors, reviewing Walter Minot's *Rhetoric: Theory and Practice for Composition* in the February 1985 issue of *College Composition and Communication,* said that rhetoric "is a tradition of instruction in persuasive public discourse extending back 2500 years. . . ." He was right, of course, but less than half so.

I'm not quick with responses, but I have now gathered myself to respond in each of these instances. To my freshmen, I'd say, "You'll just have to learn." To my young colleague, I'd say, "I didn't know I had repudiated literature." To my graduate student, I'd say, "Well, who the hell *doesn't* come down on the side of literature?" To Professor Connors, I'd say that his definition of rhetoric is tantamount to accepting a Ptolemaic cosmology, repudiating Newton's work on gravity, dodging quantum physics, mowing one's lawn with a scythe, and using ground-up-black-eyed peas for coffee. I understand Professor Connors's definition and appreciate its source and value, and I hope that I revere Aristotle, Cicero, and Quintilian according to my bond. They are generally right and for us not wholly adequate. Their eyes and thoughts went in certain directions and made wisdom, but they did not reach the end of wisdom. To paraphrase Dryden, I'd guess that were Aristotle put down live among us, he would not, could not write the same rhetoric.

If people want to believe that literature must have no traffic with rhetoric, if they want to believe that rhetoric is always and only "a tradition of instruction in persuasive public discourse," I'll be sorry, but I'll not be bound by them. Unlike that of many scientists, our work is cumulative, and we rightly keep, prize, and study all earlier texts. We do not, however, have to be stuck in any one of them. Though I'll suggest a closer congress later, I'll be content here to say that rhetoric can come to literature affording both particular and narrow avenues for entrance into literary study and a wider vision that embraces literature.

My assignment for this new edition of *Teaching Composition:* (now) *Twelve Bibliographical Essays* is to give some account of "what has been written in the last ten years about studying literature and thinking about, teaching, or doing rhetoric, with some special attention to what yet needs to be done." That seems a legitimate enterprise for a book that wants to focus on teaching composition, for many reasons. First, the works I am going to mention later provide information and insight about rhetoric, and that helps. Second, they provide information and insight about literature, and that helps. Third, they often show how rhetoric works as criticism, and I think that's an aid to composition teaching. Fourth, since many composition courses study and use literature, rhetoric is a place, some studies will show, to root around between literature and composition and sometimes discover that they aren't separate. I'm inclined to think that there is no reason to make a to-do about connecting rhetoric and literature in a book about teaching composition; they belong together, and they *are* together, even if we don't always realize it when we are pulled toward this or that presumably traditional definition of rhetoric. Even if some want to tug rhetoric toward persuasion (as if that were something separate from other discourse), we can remember that being in a poem, novel, essay, or play is being in an argument, the views, structures, and styles of each being the evidences of argument. As Richard Lanham says in a work I will cite shortly, "To conceive of literary texts as constituting a separate reality is also to conceive of a positivistic social reality just 'out there' and a self just 'in here,' halfway between the ears. Both concepts have been discarded by almost every other discipline that deals with human behavior. . . ."

In what follows, I want first to linger a little, nevertheless, over connections between rhetoric and literature. Second, I want to discuss briefly or sometimes just to record some recent publications that explore these connections and mutual illuminations. Finally, I want to say a little about some kinds of work that might yet be done. I am going to assume that what I say or record will also from time to time touch on the teaching of composition.

The various connections and identities between rhetoric and literature—and they do not, of course, have to be the same for everyone—still seem to escape us most of the time. Last year when I was young and foolish, I wanted the study of rhetoric and the study of literature to come together. Now that I am old and still not wise, I still do, but I'm less hopeful that the studies will come together. I think that students of rhetoric and students of literature can learn to listen to each other, but I am about ready to conclude that they won't *be* together. We've lived apart within the study of literature for generations, with our divisions among eras, centuries, groups, themes, and individual authors, and good work has been done. Rhetoricians will probably think about rhetoric, and students of literature will probably think about literature, and I suppose that we can sing a hymn in praise of diversity and hope that the two groups will once in a while sally forth to meet each other.

But there is peril of more than one kind in being apart. Administrators and other outlanders already look at us and think we don't know what our field is like and make noises about carrying composition off to some ill-founded conglomeration of communication studies. That may not yet seem to some an immediate risk, though I think it is. More immediately perilous is the risk that, as we are apart, the space between us comes to seem ever more real. Worse, where we have been divided with the literary studies on one side and the rhetorical studies on the other, there now appears to be developing a three-part division, with the teaching of composition, now increasingly acquiring methodology and research of its own, on point of becoming a third segment, no longer fully connected to the work of rhetoricians, who may be pursuing upper division and graduate level studies of their own with attendant special interests and research and study ambitions.

The division does disturb me, first because it's unnecessary. Any literary student can learn from a rhetoric student, just as any rhetoric student can learn from a literary student, and they are usually, at any rate, feeling of the same elephant. It disturbs me, second, because it almost invariably breeds a sense of hierarchy, the student of rhetoric and composition by definition pursuing what is at best an inferior art. The division disturbs me, third, because it is foolish, often because for no reason students of

334

rhetoric and compostion are regarded as inferior but often because students of rhetoric have allowed rhetoric to be defined as it
has formerly been defined.

For despite all, the connections and identities between rhetoric and literature still mostly evade us. But they are there.

Every human is a rhetoric, or a mixture of rhetoric. Every
discourse is a rhetoric, or a gathering of rhetorics. Each work of
literature is a rhetoric or a set of rhetorics; each novel, drama,
essay, poem is a rhetoric that may also be host to sets of rhetorics
swirling and whirling within the work. I haven't lost all sense of
distinction. I know that one can talk about rhetoric without talking about literature, as in analyses of political discourse, debates,
advertisements, and freshman English essays. I do not believe it is
possible, however, to talk about literature without talking about
rhetoric.

In an essay in the first edition of Gary Tate's book, I said that
all analysis of writing is rhetorical and added, "Anything that can
be said about writers, readers, and their coming together is rhetorical examination, though partial, and the sayer is a rhetorician,
though unaware." I'll go on now and say the obvious, that all
literary criticism is rhetorical criticism. Some students have long
since recognized that rhetorical criticism and literary study belong together. M. H. Abrams remarked in 1958 that "The perspectives, much of the basic vocabulary, and many of the characteristic topics of pragmatic criticism originated in the classical
theory of rhetoric" (*The Mirror and the Lamp* [New York: Oxford
University Press, 1958], p. 14). In 1969 E. P. J. Corbett observed
that "Contemporary writers are not less rhetorical than earlier
writers in the composition of their works, but because of the
disappearance of rhetorical training from schools, modern critics
have not been aware of how valuable rhetoric can be as a means of
explication" (introduction to *Rhetorical Analyses of Literary Works*
[New York: Oxford University Press, 1969], p. viii). Anyone
who has used Kinneavy's classification of discourse knows that
the author-subject-audience triangle he employs is a vehicle for

both rhetorical analysis of literary work and for instruction in the rhetoric/composition class. A recent study uses the Young, Becker, and Pike heuristic as a basis for the critical study of poems (B. Eugene McCarthy, "Heuristics in Composition and Literary Criticism," *Freshman English News,* Fall 1978, pp. 17–21). W. Ross Winterowd, while noting that literary criticism has traditionally been concerned with the text and how it operates and that rhetorical criticism has been concerned with the text and how it operates *on an audience,* argues that "the proper goal of *all* criticism is to find out how the text achieves its effects; that is, I would resist the separation of rhetorical and literary criticism" ("The Realm of Meaning: Text-Centered Criticism," *CCC,* 23 [December 1972], p. 399).

Whatever our current judgment, there need be no separation between literary study and rhetorical study. All human discourse comes from somewhere (is invented), takes some structure, manifests itself as a style, occurs in some context, and has some consequence. The divisions and sub-divisions of rhetorical study offer an almost endlessly varied set of entries into literary study. We want to know where texts come from, how their authors or their characters think, why they think as they do, and what there is in the world that allows texts to be generated or initiates their generation. These are inquiries proper not just to literary criticism, but also to rhetorical invention. We want to know the architecture of a literary work, the shape its parts take in making a whole, if they do, the relation of this structure to a literary genre, and, more importantly, the way structure makes meaning. These are inquiries proper not just to literary study, but also to rhetorical *dispositio.* We want to know how a style is generated and why, and what it does. These are inquiries proper not just to literary study, but also to the third canon of rhetoric. We want to know how a literary work exists in a context and what consequence it has; to learn, we may turn again, not just to literary study, but also to the canons of rhetoric and to the classical kinds of rhetoric—judicial, epideictic, and deliberative. And we are seldom limited to *a* rhetoric in studying a literary work; literary works are intersections where traffic crosses from many rhetorical universes—those of the authors, their ages, their contemporaries, their forebears, their created characters, and those of readers then and since. Pursuit of a single trope in its manifestations through ages and works will reveal philosophies.

When we take up literary study, I am suggesting, we *are* taking up rhetoric. We are called to move into and through literary works, always gladly bound by the works, to authors and their ways of thinking, through their ways of thinking into their views of the world, through their views of the world into their premises and needs. We are called to do the same thing for created characters, spokesmen, personae, exploring what Robert Browne calls the "internal rhetoric" of the work (see "Rhetorical Analysis and Poetic Structures," *Rhetoric: Theories for Application,* ed. Robert M. Gorrell [Champaign: National Council of Teachers of English, 1967]), and to do the same thing in formulating or understanding our own response to the work. We are obliged to examine authors' ways of taking their world in a particular way and stationing themselves in a particular place in regard to it, and to examine the relation between the authors and their various audiences, considering how and why they came together.

Literary criticism *is* rhetorical criticism, and rhetorical criticism is, at its best, non-reductionist, as Corbett suggests:

> If I were to make a plea for this system of practical criticism over others, I would say that it is not liable to the charge of "critical monism" that R. S. Crane once leveled against such critics as Cleanth Brooks, Allen Tate, John Crowe Ransom, Robert Penn Warren, and I. A. Richards. Allowing the critic to move back and forth between the work and the author and the audience, with glances, if need be, at external documents for supplementary or confirmatory evidence, rhetorical criticism enables him to discover a variety of the causes and con-

ditions for a literary work being what it is. (*Rhetorical Analyses of Literary Works*, p. xxviii)

I repeat myself: forms of literary criticism are forms of rhetorical criticism. Archetypal criticism, for example, may grow outward from its psychomythic base to striking insights about both a literary work and its genre, but rhetorical criticism contains archetypal criticism as a natural part of the study of invention, particularly a part of the study of how a literary work grows from, uses, alters, or transcends its sources. Stylistic criticism is a perpetually useful form that manifests itself in many ways, but all are contained in the third canon of rhetoric. The New Criticism was in most of its manifestations a form of studying the second and third canons of rhetoric. Structuralist criticism is an unsurprising extension of the study of rhetorical *dispositio*.

Rhetorical criticism is non-reductionist. It opens to literature, and opens to us. Nothing in the sacred texts requires now that rhetorical criticism study *only* public address, or *only* nonfiction, or *only* persuasive forms. Rhetorical criticism is connected to literature. Literature is rhetoric.

I was particularly glad to see Richard A. Lanham's "Composition, Literature, and the Lower-Division Gyroscope" in *Profession 84* (selected articles from the Bulletins of the Association of Departments of English and the Association of Departments of Foreign Languages, published by the Modern Language Association). Lanham suggests "a conceptual rather than a canonical solution" to the problem of general education and the core curriculum, focusing on the question, "How . . . do we refound the rhetorical paideia. . . ?"

The ideas Lanham strews about so richly here and in *Literacy and the Survival of Humanism* (New Haven: Yale University Press, 1983) might help us not only to unite rhetoric and literature, but also to work our way out of what so many regard as the general education mess. Patrick G. Scott, in "'Flowers in the Path of Science': Teaching Composition Through Traditional High Literature" (*College English*, September 1980), also wants to bring our various kinds of work together, I think, but winds up, as so many who talk about rhetoric and literature do, talking about how "the ideas of freshman rhetoric can help in designing useful reading and writing assignments in other undergraduate literature courses." James C. Raymond's "Rhetoric: The Methodology of the Humanities" (*College English*, December 1982) is an important account of the kinds of thinking rhetoric makes possible and of the humanists who are rhetoricians without knowing it. Susan Miller's article, "What Does It Mean to Be Able to Write? The Question of Writing in the Discourses of Literature and Composition" (*College English*, March 1983), looks for a common framework to hold composition and literary study so that we can think about the nature of writing.

As I expect everyone knows, several collections of essays have appeared in the last few years with a number of pieces that may be useful to us in bringing rhetoric and literature together. *The Rhetorical Tradition and Modern Writing*, edited by James J. Murphy and published in 1982 by the Modern Language Association, is an interesting and useful collection. I'm currently inclined to think that one of the selections, James Kinneavy's "Restoring the Humanities: The Return of Rhetoric from Exile," the Raymond article, and the Lanham article, both cited above, make a stout beginning for a new conception of ourselves, our divided field, and our hopes for rhetoric and literature. *Rhetorical Traditions and the Teaching of Writing*, by C. H. Knoblauch and Lil Brannon (Upper Montclair, New Jersey: Boynton/Cook, 1983) contains seven essays by the authors. While no one of them is specifically about rhetoric and literature, useful insights occur throughout, for as the authors say, "An important implication of modern rhetoric is that what is true of composing on the sublimest cultural heights has relevance down in the valleys as well. *All* human beings share in the creative ingenuity which is supremely articulated by Shakespeare, Kant, and Einstein" (p. 73). I'll not take time here to comment on individual articles in *Com-*

position and Literature: Bridging the Gap, edited by Winifred B. Horner (Chicago: University of Chicago Press, 1983), a collection of twelve essays by twelve leading figures in our field. While many issues engage the authors' attention, and while no one of the essays attempts to sketch out a conceptual framework for rhetoric and literature, each of the essays is busy with ideas that may set others to work. Any thoughtful teacher comes sometime to know, as Wayne Booth puts it in his essay, that "it is impossible to distinguish what one does as a teacher of writing and as a teacher of literature" (p. 67). *The Present State of Scholarship in Historical and Contemporary Rhetoric,* also edited by Horner (Columbia: University of Missouri Press, 1983), is indispensable as a guide to the field. A collection of seventeen articles by different hands, the book presented in honor of E. P. J. Corbett, *Essays on Classical Rhetoric and Modern Discourse,* edited by Robert J. Connors, Lisa S. Ede, and Andrea A. Lunsford (Carbondale: Southern Illinois University Press, 1984), is because of the richness of its rhetorical discussion invaluable to us all, though none of the essays directly addresses the connections between rhetoric and literature.

Recent work in reader-response theory may be ahead of that in other areas of rhetorical study; it is, at any rate, often provocative in its exploration of territories that I claim for rhetoric, given its primary concern with the audience for literature. I am thinking of such studies as Norman Holland's *Five Readers Reading* (New Haven: Yale University Press, 1975), Wolfgang Iser's *The Act of Reading: A Theory of Aesthetic Response* (Baltimore: The Johns Hopkins University Press, 1978), and Stanley Fish's *Is There a Text in This Class?* (Cambridge: Harvard University Press, 1980), and of the handsome collection of papers edited by Susan R. Suleiman and Inge Crosman, *The Reader in the Text: Essays on Audience and Interpretation* (Princeton: Princeton University Press, 1980). An extremely useful introduction to and extension of reader-response theory is Marshall W. Alcorn, Jr., and Mark Bracher, "Literature,Psychoanalysis, and the Re-Formation of the Self: A New Direction for Reader-Response Theory," *PMLA*, May 1985, pp. 343–54.

I can only suggest the range and type of literary studies that depend in one way or another upon rhetoric. I'll start with a lovely call, Winston Weathers's paper, "The Value of Rhetoric to the Creative Artist," in *A Symposium in Rhetoric,* edited by J. Dean Bishop, Turner S. Kobler, and William E. Tanner (Committee for the Federation Degree Program in English of the Federation of North Texas Area Universities, 1975). Richard Lanham's *The Motives of Eloquence: Literary Rhetoric in the Renaissance* (New Haven: Yale University Press, 1976) has been an influential study, and John Porter Houston's *The Rhetoric of Poetry in the Renaissance and Seventeenth Century* (Baton Rouge: Louisiana State University Press, 1983) is valuable. The collection of papers edited by David J. A. Clines, David M. Gunn, and Alan J. Hauser, *Art and Meaning: Rhetoric in Biblical Literature* (Journal for the Study of the Old Testament, Supplement Series 19, 1982) is valuable in its own right and offers a useful look into forms of rhetorical study that those of us in English Departments don't often see. George A. Kennedy's *New Testament Interpretation Through Rhetorical Criticism* (Chapel Hill: University of North Carolina Press, 1984) is, I think, an uncommonly important book, an analysis of New Testament texts through classical rhetoric. Zahava Karl McKeon's *Novels and Arguments: Inventing Rhetorical Criticism* (Chicago: University of Chicago Press, 1982) is an exciting book, and Shoshana Felman's *Writing and Madness* (Ithaca: Cornell University Press, 1985) in its first chapter sketches a rhetoric that will not be too familiar to those of us who come to rhetoric through composition studies. And these will suggest directions and possibilities: Walter J. Ong, "The Writer's Audience Is Always a Fiction," *PMLA*, January 1975, pp. 9–21; Paul D. McGlynn, "Rhetoric as Metaphor in *The Vanity of Human Wishes*," *Studies in English Literature,* Summer 1975, pp. 473–82; Norman N. Holland, "UNITY IDENTITY TEXT SELF," *PMLA*, October 1975, pp. 813–22; Robert Foulke and

Joan Hartman, "What Authorizes the Study of Literature?" *College English*, January 1976, pp. 468–77; C. W. Jentoff, "Surrey's Five Elegies: Rhetoric, Structure, and the Poetry of Praise," *PMLA*, January 1976, pp. 23–32; Arthur F. Kinney, "Rhetoric as Poetic: Humanist Fiction in the Renaissance," *English Literary History*, Winter 1976, pp. 413–43; Murray Cohen, "Versions of the Lock: Readers of 'The Rape of the Lock'," *English Literary History*, Spring 1976, pp. 53–73; Bruce Bashford, "The Rhetorical Method in Literary Criticism," *Philosophy and Rhetoric*, Summer 1976, pp. 133–46; Barrett J. Mandel, "What's at the Bottom of Literature?" *College English*, November 1976, pp. 250–262; Jim W. Corder, "Efficient Ethos in *Shane*, with a Proposal for Discriminating Among Kinds of Ethos," *Communication Quarterly*, Fall 1977, pp. 28–31; Thomas W. Benson, "The Senses of Rhetoric: A Topical System for Critics," *Central States Speech Journal*, Winter 1978, pp. 237–50; Jim W. Corder, "Varieties of Ethical Argument, with Some Account of the Significance of Ethos in the Teaching of Composition," *Freshman English News*, Winter 1978, pp. 1–23; Peter T. Koper, "Samuel Johnson's Rhetorical Stance in *The Rambler*," *Style*, Winter 1978, pp. 22–34; Merrill D. Whitburn, "The Rhetoric of Otherworldliness in *Night Thoughts*", *Essays in Literature*, Fall 1978, pp. 163–74; Timothy P. Martin, "The Art and Rhetoric of Chronology in Faulkner's *Light in August*," *College Literature*, Spring 1980, pp. 125–35; Michael C. Leff, guest editor, "Special Report—Rhetorical Criticism: The State of the Art," *Western Journal of Speech Communication*, Fall 1980, a special issue of seven papers on rhetorical criticism; Philip F. Gura, "Language and Meaning," *American Literature*, March 1981, pp. 1–21; Robert M. Coogan, "The Triumph of Reason: Sidney's *Defense* and Aristotle's *Rhetoric*," *Papers on Language and Literature*, Summer 1981, pp. 255–70; Charles S. Rutherford, "Troilus' Farewell to Criseyde: The Idealist as Clairvoyant and Rhetorician," *Papers on Language and Literature*, Summer 1981, pp. 245–54; Marshall Grossman, "The Subject of Narrative and the Rhetoric of the Self," *Papers on Language and Literature,* Winter 1982, pp. 398–415; Arlene N. Okerlund, "The Rhetoric of Love: Voice in the *Amoretti* and the *Songs and Sonets,*" *Quarterly Journal of Speech,* February 1982, pp. 37–46; G. Douglas Atkins, "Pope's Poetry and the Reader's Responsibilities," *College Literature,* Spring 1982, pp. 83–96; Fredric C. Bogel, "Dulness Unbound: Rhetoric and Pope's *Dunciad,*" *PMLA,* October 1982, pp. 844–55; Stephenie Yearwood, "The Rhetoric of Form in *The Temple,*" *Studies in English Literature,* Winter 1983, pp. 131–44; Judith W. Page, "Style and Rhetorical Intention in Wordsworth's *Lyrical Ballads,*" *Philological Quarterly,* Summer 1983, pp. 293–314; Thomas P. Joswick, "The Conversion Drama of 'Self-Reliance': A Logological Study," *American Literature,* December 1983, pp. 507–24; and James Van Oosting, "The Use of Imaginative Literature for Communication Theory Construction: Some Precautions," *Quarterly Journal of Speech,* May 1985, pp. 218–26.

From among the exciting and exasperating welter of recent work in literary theory, I'll cite only a few examples, contenting myself with the claim that all such studies are studies in rhetoric, though I certainly don't want to tell people what they are doing if they don't want to be doing it. Still, it seems to me that as books and essays in literary theory inquire how discourses exist, or how and when they generate and evolve and what becomes of them, or how they are situated with writers and readers, then they are exploring invention, structure, style, audience, and the other concerns of rhetoric. Patricia Bizzell's "On the Possibility of a Unified Theory of Composition and Literature" (forthcoming in *Rhetoric Review*) is a good account of the distance between literary theory/rhetoric and composition/rhetoric and of some hopeful signs of eventual cross-referencing. I have, however, made no effort to search out and to represent the work of literary theorists and will leave off with these specimens. A good place to start, as always I think, is with Wayne Booth; his *Critical Understanding: The Powers and Limits of Pluralism* (Chicago: University of Chicago Press, 1979) is a wise book, and the interesting Index of

Concepts aids one in tracking back and forth and sideways among ways of thinking in criticism and theory. I also find Robert de Beaugrande's "Writer, Reader, Critic: Comparing Critical Theories as Discourse," *College English,* October 1984, pp. 533–59, a very helpful guide to current theory. I'll also cite Mary Louise Pratt, *Toward a Speech Act Theory of Literary Discourse* (Bloomington: Indiana University Press, 1977); David Bleich, *Subjective Criticism* (Baltimore: The Johns Hopkins University Press, 1978); Louise Rosenblatt, *The Reader, the Text, the Poem: The Transactional Theory of the Literary Work* (Carbondale: Southern Illinois University Press, 1978); Stein Haugom Olsen, *The Structure of Literary Understanding* (Cambridge: Cambridge University Press, 1978); Barbara Herrnstein Smith, *On the Margins of Discourse: The Relation of Literature to Language* (Chicago: University of Chicago Press, 1978); Robert Young, editor, *Untying the Text: A Post-Structuralist Reader* (London: Routledge and Kegan Paul, 1981); and Ann Banfield, *Unspeakable Sentences: Narration and Representation in the Language of Fiction* (London: Routledge and Kegan Paul, 1982). Harold Bloom's "The Breaking of Form," in *Deconstruction and Criticism* (New York: Continuum, 1979) is a good, sometimes stunning, introduction to deconstructionism. Terry Eagleton's *Literary Theory: An Introduction* (Minneapolis: University of Minnesota Press, 1983) is a good opening to contemporary literary theory that calls for a reorganization of our work under a new rhetorical paradigm.

There's much to lean on and learn from, and exciting work is being done. But more needs to be done, for we have only begun to learn how rhetoric and literature are together. I think we must enter this waiting work more fully, chiefly because of the subject matters and their high promise, but also for ourselves so that we can learn more clearly about the nature and scope of the field of English, so that we can abandon hierarchies and assumed inferiorities within English Departments, so that we can once in a while be together instead of apart, and so that we can teach and write without dogma or arrogance or ignorance.

344

In the space left to me, I want to say a little about some of the work that I think still waits. We probably *don't* need a whole lot more papers that promise to be about rhetoric and literature or about composition and literature, but turn out to be talking about the use of literature in the freshman composition class, occasionally as a source for models, but more often as a source of subjects for writing. What work does need to be done, then? I can propose some lines of inquiry that I already know about (see "Rhetoric and Literary Study: Some Lines of Inquiry," *College Composition and Communication,* February 1981) and perhaps add a proposal or two.

The first is not *a* line of inquiry, but an invitation to pursue into literature diverse lines of inquiry offered by rhetoric. As I suggested earlier in talking about connections between the two, thinking through rhetoric is a way of learning about literary texts. It matters to the understanding of Dryden's *Religio Laici* to recognize that the poem is essentially judicial, not epideictic or deliberative, and we risk misunderstanding both the poem and Dryden if we don't attend to the structure of the poem's argument, so that we know when the speaker in the poem is making which argument against which antagonist. It matters to the understanding of Goldsmith's *The Deserted Village* to know when the speaker leaves off what begins as an ethical argument and begins, instead, to develop a full emotional argument. We can learn more about the speaker in Tennyson's "Ulysses"—and appreciate him a little more readily—if we understand why he makes the wrong kind of argument and what kind of argument it is. The young speaker in Pope's *An Essay on Criticism* is daring and successful; he takes on the literary establishment and wins. We would prize him the more, I think, and perhaps learn some things for our own uses, if we took pains to watch the way he argues, to learn how he manages—persuasively—to attack pride without becoming prideful himself. As the nineteenth century began, Wordsworth's early poetry sold slowly; it required several years for a few hundred volumes to be bought. At about the same time, readers bought some three thousand copies of Robert Bloomfield's *The Farmer's Boy* within the first month of its publication in 1802. If we learn to inquire about the relationships between texts and audiences, we can learn more about both texts and audiences, about the time and context in which they occur, about former times and times since. Any literary text, as I suggested earlier, is a crossroads where many rhetorical universes converge. We need to know how each works and how they consort with each other in a text.

Second, I hope more students will explore the modes of argument in both literary and other texts, particularly to learn how character emerges in language. I recommend this line of inquiry, I think, at least partly because of what Kenneth Burke has taught us. We are, after all, apart from each other, and it may be, as Burke said, that the only thing we have in common is our separateness. Distances open between us. We keep trying to tell ourselves to others across the way. We keep trying to enter their world or bring them into ours. Often we fail, but we keep trying. The trouble is that our speaking-forth—the primary need and issue of any age—is complex, confused, and messy, and often creates as many problems as it solves. Language is our way of composing our selves. It is our first and last line of defense, and we are vulnerable on each line.

Quite simply, nothing else seems so important right now as the questions generating and generated by such study. Can we learn how to say the truth? If we learn how to say the truth, can we say it to another? Whom will we listen to? Who will listen to us? Can we sing the Lord's song in a strange land? Will we recognize it if we hear another sing it? Somehow or other, everything depends on our speaking-forth. In a recent essay on the relation of rhetoric to poetic ("Chapter and Verse," *The American Poetry Review,* Jan.–Feb. 1978), Stanley Plumly remarks that, "Rhetoric, whatever the year, and whatever the aesthetic, establishes credentials, establishes voice" (p. 21). A little later, he adds, "What pulls us into the good book, the whole book, what keeps our attention, from poem to poem, part to part, is the accumulating strength and complexity and interest and full character of the speaking voice" (p. 28). We can learn from rhetoric, at least, where to look—to character as it emerges in language. But while rhetoric may tell us where to look, traditional forms of rhetorical study won't tell us all we need to know. S. M. Halloran, in "On the End of Rhetoric, Classical and Modern," *CE*, 36 (Feb. 1975), 621–31, has explained why the study of *ethos* has become so crucial and why traditional rhetorical wisdom won't suffice. He points out that while classical rhetoric rested on the assumption that wisdom is open and publicly available, in the modern world the speaker can scarcely know where to begin. No commonly accepted process of invention is available to us. There is no widely accepted set of common values that he or she can assume. There are no universally accepted *topoi* that he or she may use as places of argument. Modern man, Halloran suggests, has been denied the possibility of achieving knowledge on which to base his life. Assumptions about knowledge, Halloran goes on to say, are no longer tenable—external reality is paradoxical, and the effort to know something alters what we seek to know. Modern rhetoricians, Halloran says, face the fundamental problem of discovering why the gap between a speaker's world and a hearer's world is so broad and learning how one might bridge it successfully. When a speaker and a hearer inhabit the same world, it is enough, commonly, that both attend to the argument. But when a speaker and an audience inhabit different worlds, the audience may never be able to hear what the speaker is saying. (R. R. McGuire, in "Speech Acts, Communicative Competence, and the Paradox of Authority," *Philosophy and Rhetoric*, Winter 1977, pp. 30–45, makes an interesting distinction between communication, which occurs "against a background of mutually assumed validity claims," and discourse, which occurs when one or more of the claims is challenged.) Then, too often, that old ominous curse comes down again: "Let us go down and there confound their language, that they may not understand one another's speech." We are apart and cannot communicate, or, speaking, we risk the extraordinary extremes described by Georges Gusdorf in *Speaking* (Evanston: Northwestern University Press, 1965):

> It seems that the use of speech obliges us to choose between two opposite forms of alienation. On the one hand, like the madman or the mystic, we can speak as no one else speaks. On the other hand, like the practitioner of a "basic" language, we can speak as everyone else does. In both cases the very meaning of personality is done away with. The more I communicate, the less I express myself; the more I express myself, the less I communicate. It is necessary to choose between incomprehensibility and inauthenticity—between excommunication and self-denial. (p. 52)

And yet, that old curse both is and is not a curse. Great gaps open between us because we speak different tongues; yet because we speak different tongues we can be different and say different things. When speakers are deprived of a given or shared world, Halloran concludes, they are deprived, too, of a given rhetoric. They must create their own *topoi,* their own schemes and tropes, their own ways of inventing. They must constitute their own world and themselves by their language. They must create their own rhetoric, spacious enough to enfold another. Rhetoric, then, won't tell us all we need to know, but we can learn from rhetoric where to look—at the ways character emerges in language, at the ways worlds are constituted in individual discourse.

To be sure, no study will answer all the questions, or locate and solve all the problems, but surely there are reasons enough to study *ethos* and ethical argument.

The third line of inquiry I want to suggest is closely related to the second, though not identical. I hope we can begin to learn that reading a poem, getting to be *in* the poem, is pretty much the same as being *in* an argument, or several arguments. The same is true for novels, plays, and essays. Being *in* them as a literary reader is being *in* an argument, which is not the same thing as *making* an argument. In even the briefest lyric, if one enters the poem, one is present as a background is laid in, as a proposition is offered, as proofs are given, as sometimes refutations are made, as a conclusion is reached. In many poems and in nearly all novels and plays, a reader lives in a variety of such arguments. I don't want to talk about this line of inquiry any more, for two reasons: first, I don't know how; and second, I'm working on it elsewhere.

The fourth line of inquiry I want to suggest I will also mention and pass over quickly, though it is significant. If we learned to mingle our literary and our rhetorical interests more usefully, we might one day learn how to study great works of non-fiction prose as closely as we now study poems, novels, and plays.

Fifth, I hope we can learn more about how or whether the inventive universe out of which a speaker emerges generates a *rhetorical imperative* which the speaker serves as he or she works toward a structure and a style and responds to an audience and an occasion. Part of the universe of invention for any speaker is a set of information and premises acquired from birth (and perhaps before) onward that create, direct, or influence the speaker's vision of things. It seems likely that the universe of invention that a speaker occupies—which is always being created—presents imperatives for the speaker's utterances, and that these imperatives generate the specific ways in which the speaker can or will invent, dispose, and state, the ways in which the speaker will make discourse. I am supposing, in other words, that we learn (whether by overt or by silent instruction) from the beginning to expect language to behave in certain ways, to have certain kinds of potential, to accomplish certain things, to work in certain ways from the deep structure of the self. For example, if a speaker comes out of a world that is intensely Calvinistic, let us say, so that the speaker has it bred in his bones that humans are at best limited, fallible, or unfinished, at worst mischievous, and possibly depraved, then it seems likely that among the generating

forces that grow in such a speaker's inventive world is an imperative to recover from his own incompleteness or inadequacy. In
such a world, original sin is a rhetorical act: the first words
uttered and all subsequent words are incomplete renditions of experience. If imperfection or limitation is truly bred in the bone,
then the speaker must know that his utterances are going to be
inadequate and incomplete, and so he must always, at some level,
be seeking through language *to recover* from his own incompleteness. If, however, another speaker grows in another world
where he accepts at some deep level a knowledge that humankind
is good, or perfectible, though perhaps hemmed in by society's
restrictions, then the generating force might be stated as an imperative *to realize* his own fullness or potential. It may be, to put
the matter simply, that a short sentence or a quick imagistic poem
will serve the speaker who needs *to realize,* while the speaker
who needs *to recover* may have to build a long, cumulative sentence or a formally constructed poem. The one has to make a
sustained discourse in order to free himself from his own limitations; the other is already free to see himself in quick snapshots. It
may be, too, that speakers sometimes, for one reason or another,
serve or try to serve the wrong imperative.

I do not, of course, mean to suggest that these are consciously articulated imperatives, but rather that they silently
shape a speaker's conception of what language is for and how it
may work. If such imperatives exist, they lie somewhere down
below the deep structures of our statements. If the notion is tenable, I'd suppose that there are countless other imperatives. It
may be that each speaker responds to his own unique imperative;
it may be that ages or particular communities share imperatives.
That means, I think, that it would enlighten us to discover the
imperatives of discourse as they fail or succeed or shift. We can
only do so, of course, by accepting the text of the discourse
as symptomatic of the imperative and by pushing analytically
through the discourse back into the inventive world from which
it has emerged. Then, if we discover the imperatives that operate,

we would gain new understandings of the forms of invention used, the structural qualities of the discourse, and its style, for to the extent that the imperative generates the discourse, it plays, too, upon the choice and nature of every feature of the discourse. Certain kinds of structure and style, it may be, as I have already suggested, are more likely to develop from one imperative than from another. Indeed, it might be possible to write literary history as a sequence of shifting responses to shifting rhetorical imperatives. And there are other reasons to search out these imperatives and their consequences: the nature of the imperative may, for example, determine the rhetorical situation into which a discourse may be placed. A work built from the silent imperative *to recover* has the future implicit in it, as well as the past. It comes out of a past, as all discourses must, but is always aiming toward a future saved from past or present limitations. Such a work may, therefore, have epideictic, deliberative, and judicial possibilities not so easily won in a work built from the imperative *to realize,* which may in some instances confine the discourse to the epideictic moment.

Sixth and last, I hope we can learn to bring rhetoric and literature together for the further liberation of our studies and of ourselves, so that we can understand better how to look at literary texts as enabling capacities rather than as precious artifacts. The experience of recent years wants to tell me that literary studies are forms of exotic and spiritual exercise that tend to culminate in the production of critical and scholarly works substantively esoteric and stylistically inaccessible. In these exercises—so recent experience tells me—literary texts are treated as secrets, as holy tablets, the understanding of which is given only to a few priests, who explicate the sacred texts for each other, taking care to assure that the language of their explications is not understandable to the peasants sitting in the pews or tumbling in the fields nearby. Rhetoric and literature taken together, I believe, can take us farther than we have come toward what Wayne Booth once called "the knowledge most worth having": an understanding of Nature, including our own; the capacity to appropriate for ourselves the works of others, distinguishing as we do the trivial from the grand, the mean from the mighty; and the ability to make our intentions known clearly to others. Bringing rhetoric and literature together might also let us see that rhetoric can be an organizing agency for literary and other kinds of study and for curriculum design. *Invention* does not belong solely to the rhetorician or to the literary critic; style is meaning become voice, clutter become statement in all of the arts and sciences. The canons are a model for any study.

Whether through these lines of inquiry or through others, rhetoric and literary study, I'm inclined to think, do belong together. Perhaps, one day, we'll learn that we do not have to be either this or that, but can, with a little luck and a little work, be both this and that. Rhetoric is not far off from literature, or from any human endeavor. It is, after all, our major occupation. It is what we have instead of omniscience, our way of composing ourselves and the world, of constituting creation, of being ourselves.

Writing Across the Curriculum

JAMES L. KINNEAVY, *The University of Texas at Austin*

IT IS UNDOUBTEDLY SIGNIFICANT THAT THE first edition of this book did not have a chapter on writing across the curriculum. In the intervening ten years, there has literally been an explosion in the number of colleges in this country which have incorporated some version of this movement in their writing programs. A recent and as yet unpublished survey, by the Modern Language Association, reveals the rather astounding fact that 47% of the four-year colleges and universities surveyed have some program in writing across the curriculum (MLA Commission on Writing and Literature, "Survey of the Profession," May 2, 1985, p. 66). This is a growth from almost nothing ten years ago and may signal the most important change in teaching writing in America in the past decade as well as the shape of the future. Another recent survey supports this tremendous growth. C. W. Griffin, in "Programs for Writing Across the Curriculum: A Report," *CCC*, 36 (Dec. 1985), 398–403, gave the results of a 1984 survey of 404 institutions about the presence of such programs on their campuses; of the 194 respondents, 139 had programs and only 55 did not. This concern is reflected in the attention paid to this issue at the annual meetings of the Conference on College Composition and Communcation. In the past two years, over one-third of the panels addressed some aspects of this issue. Consequently, anyone involved in the teaching of writing ought to be aware of this dynamic movement.

Because it is so new, however, systematic knowledge about it is even more difficult to come by than is that about other areas of rhetoric and composition study. Frequently, bibliographies and indexes on rhetoric do not list writing across the curriculum as an entry. However, a few do; in addition there are some in-house publications which are useful. After a word about terminology and definitions, this survey will attempt to put together what these scattered sources offer in the following areas: bibliographies and collections of readings, textbooks, spread of the movement, types of programs, theory, and evaluations of programs.

I. TERMINOLOGY AND DEFINITIONS

The phrase "writing across the curriculum" seems first to have been used systematically in several reports put out by the Writing Research Unit and the Writing Across the Curriculum Project of the University of London Institute of Education in the early 1970s. A summary version of the third report of the project was entitled *Writing and Learning Across the Curriculum (11–18)*; much more widely known is the full report, *The Development of Writing Abilities (11–18)*, written by James Britton, Tony Burgess, Nancy Martin, Alex McLeod, and Harold Rosen (London: Macmillan Educational Ltd. for the Schools Council, 1975). The more general concern, not just with writing, but with reading, writing, and talking as tools of learning in all departments of the school is called "language across the curriculum" by this group (see Douglas Barnes, James Britton, and Harold Rosen, *Language, the Learner and the School* [Harmondsworth, England: Penguin Books, 1969]). A few years later these issues became the concerns of colleges and universities in this country with the initiation of writing programs in different disciplines at the University of Michigan and Beaver College. At the secondary level, at approximately the same time, scholars began to use the phrase "writing and reading in the content areas" or "writing and reading across the curriculum."

For this chapter, the phrase "Writing Across the Curriculum" will mean programs in schools and colleges in which there is a systematic attempt to have students write about the content of

354

the various major subjects studied in the curriculum. At the college level, this will normally apply to papers written by the students about their major field. Most of the time, this writing will be in the regular courses of the major, taught by subject matter specialists, as in chemistry, art, engineering, sociology, history, pharmacy, etc. But there has been a long tradition of having students write about their major field in courses in technical or business writing, even though these courses are not offered in the specialty field. This movement has been expanded in some institutions to include writing about all fields in courses offered in English departments. These latter courses and the technical writing and business writing courses will also be considered "writing across the curriculum" in this paper.

II. BIBLIOGRAPHIES AND COLLECTIONS

To date, to my knowledge, no comprehensive bibliography on writing across the curriculum has been published. There is "A Select Bibliography," by Bruce Petersen, at the end of the anthology of essays edited by Toby Fulwiler and Art Young, *Language Connections: Writing and Reading across the Curriculum* (Urbana, Ill.: NCTE, 1982), pp. 179–88, consisting of 77 entries. The bibliography is typical of most that follow. Over half of the entries (42) deal with general rhetorical and occasionally philosophical and literary principles, about one third (21) deal with issues specific to writing across the curriculum, and about one fifth (14) deal with psychological issues related to composition. Another bibliography, by Charles A. Bergman, "Writing Across the Curriculum: An Annotated Bibliography," *American Association of Higher Education Bulletin* (1983–1984), 33–38, has 41 entries and covers some of the general theories of writing which have been used as foundations for currently existing programs and then lists entries describing some of the programs—both of these concerns will be returned to later. This was followed in 1985 by an annotated "Bibliography," by Linda Clifton, at the end of a set of readings edited by Anne Ruggles Gere, *Roots in the Saw-*

355

dust: Writing to Learn Across the Disciplines (Urbana, Ill.: NCTE, 1985), pp. 229–35; the 37 entries reflect the concern of the subtitle of the book. Patricia Bizzell and Bruce Herzberg make a quick historical and theoretical sketch of some important figures and then examine eight current textbooks in "Writing-Across-the-Curriculum Textbooks: A Bibliographic Essay," *RR,* 3 (January 1985), 202–16. In a publication put out by the English Composition Board of the University of Michigan, with saturation circulation in the colleges and high schools of Michigan and considerable circulation elsewhere, a regular article by Robert Root gave bibliographic sources for writing across the curriculum. The *Fforum* usually had a thematic motif ("Everybody's Business," "The Development of Writers," etc.), and called on some of the best names in the profession to write on the subject. Unfortunately, this periodical is no longer published; but for the first half of the 1980s it was certainly the best voice in the country for writing across the curriculum.

A short, but more comprehensive, article by Robert Parker, "The 'Language Across the Curriculum' Movement: A Brief Overview and Bibliography," *CCC,* 36 (May 1985), 173–77, treats of reading, writing, and talking, and is addressed to college, high school, and elementary concerns. It is also more British in the number of its entries (63) than any of the other bibliographies cited.

A few bibliographic surveys appeared in ERIC in the seventies and early eighties, concerned with the necessity of writing across the curriculum programs, both in the college and in secondary school, but these are dated now. Finally, the author has been able to use two unpublished larger bibliographies on the subject, one by Robert McIlvaine and Joan C. Condravy of Slippery Rock State University, consisting of 217 entries, and one by Phillip Sipiora of the University of Texas, consisting of 263 entries.

More specific bibliographies exist for technical and business writing. Sarojini Balachandran, ed., in *Technical Writing: A Bibli-*

ography (Urbana, Ill., and Washington, D.C.: American Business Communication Association and Society for Technical Communication, 1977), surveys books and articles since 1965. The book is restricted to material about engineers and scientists; it is an excellent annotated bibliography about such topics as encouraging engineers to write, training engineers and scientists to write, manual writing, the impact of computers and word processors on writing, and other related topics. Gerald J. Alred, Diana C. Reep, Mohan R. Limaye, and Michael A. Mikolajczak, in *Business and Technical Writing: An Annotated Bibliography of Books, 1880–1980* (Metuchen, N.J.: Scarecrow Press, 1981) include both business and technical writing and take a much longer historical perspective. The most recent bibliographic survey of technical communications is that edited by Michael G. Moran and Debra Journet, *Research in Technical Communication: A Bibliographic Sourcebook* (Westport, Conn.: Greenwood Press, 1985). It has fifteen bibliographic chapters and three appendices; it treats theoretical and rhetorical concerns, types of communications, related issues and forms, texts on technical writing, etc.

In addition to bibliographies, a general view of writing across the curriculum programs can be obtained from several anthologies of articles. Fulwiler and Young's anthology, mentioned above, has twelve articles on the various purposes in courses in writing across the curriculum, on the history of the movement, and on the use of peer critiques and the writing lab, as well as the bibliography. Gere's anthology, also mentioned above, is more specific; it has articles addressing writing in art, German, social studies, special education, science, math, philosophy, and history, and some general articles applicable to all disciplines. Finally, C. Williams Griffin has edited a ten-essay collection which includes articles on the history of the movement, description of present programs, the process of writing, and writing as learning: *Teaching Writing in All Disciplines* (San Francisco, Calif: Jossey-Bass, 1982). The anthology edited by Patricia L. Stock, *FForum: Essays on Theory and Practice in the Teaching of Writing* (Montclair,

N.J.: Boynton/Cook, 1983), has fifty articles and a bibliography; some of the articles and the bibliographic entries are oriented to the practice of writing across the curriculum, especially as a way of learning.

III. TEXTBOOKS

There are only a few texts specifically written for courses in writing across the curriculum. One thorough review of them has already been cited, that by Bizzell and Herzberg, in the previous section. Also in the May 1984 edition of *CCC* there are reviews of five texts.

Elaine Maimon and her colleagues produced *Writing in the Arts and Sciences* (Cambridge, Mass.: Winthrop Publishers, 1981), based on the program at Beaver College, and followed it later with *Readings in the Arts and Sciences* (Boston: Little, Brown, 1984). The theoretical bases of the text derive, they say, from Mina Shaughnessy, Kenneth Bruffee, and James L. Kinneavy. Charles Bazerman, who bases his text partly on his excellent work in the rhetoric of science (see below) and on a theory explained in "A Relationship Between Writing and Reading: The Conventional Model," *CE*, 41 (1980), 656–61, has written *The Informed Writer* (Boston: Houghton Mifflin, 1981).

There are three books based on the case report method of writing, adopted from business and law. David Tedlock supplies a theoretical basis for this approach, as opposed to the genres of composition taught in English classes, in "The Case Approach to Composition," *CCC*, 32 (1981), 253–66. His textbook-reader, co-authored with Paul Jarvie, is *Casebook Rhetoric: A Problem Solving Approach to Composition* (New York: Holt, Rinehart and Winston, 1982). An earlier casebook is that of John Field and Robert Weiss, *Cases for Composition* (Boston: Little, Brown, 1979). Linda Woodson's *Cases for Composition* (Glenview, Ill.: Scott, Foresman, 1982) is the latest in this genre.

Laurence Behrens, as a result of a study criticizing composition readers for ignoring informative writing (see below), has edited a reader, in conjunction with Leonard Rosen, *Writing and Reading Across the Curriculum* (Boston: Little, Brown, 1982).

Three collections of readings in special areas merit mention. *Writing in the Social Sciences* (Glenview, Ill.: Scott, Foresman, 1984), edited by Joyce S. Steward and Marjorie Smelstor, has excellent editorial material, a workable theory, and a fine selection of readings to recommend it. *The Example of Science: An Anthology for College Composition* (Englewood Cliffs, N.J.: Prentice-Hall, 1981), edited by Robert E. Lynch and Thomas B. Swanzey, is based on the problem-solving approach and is intended for introductory writers, not for technical writers who already have mastered the material. *Writing About Science* (New York: Oxford University Press, 1979), edited by Mary Elizabeth Bowen and Joseph A. Mazzeo, has readings for professional audiences and for popular audiences.

A more ambitious anthology, edited by Nancy Comley, David Hamilton, Carl H. Klaus, Robert Scholes and Nancy Sommers, *Fields of Light: Readings Across the Curriculum* (New York: St. Martin's Press, 1984), uses a theoretical approach based on the functions of language and the modes of discourse to organize the selections.

IV. SPREAD OF THE MOVEMENT AND TYPICAL PROGRAMS

A fair proportion of the entries in the above-mentioned bibliographies is devoted to the spread of the writing across the curriculum movement and to a description of specific programs. Thus in Sipiora's and McIlvaine's two large bibliographies, between one-fifth and one-fourth of the entries are descriptions of specific programs.

Although there have been a few attempts to view writing across the curriculum as founded in antiquity, most of the movement is recent and largely a phenomenon of the English-speaking world. The heavy preponderance of writing activities in many of the disciplines in the French *lycée* and, possibly even more, in the Italian *lyceo,* and the rigorous final written examinations have maintained the importance of writing in the French and Italian schools. This is only slightly less true of the German *gymnasium*, which is also climaxed with a difficult writing examination, both in literary and political analysis. Some of the best comparative data for this can be seen in Alan Purves and S. Takala, eds., *An International Perspective on the Evaluation of Written Composition* (Oxford: The Pergamon Press, 1982) and Alan Purves, *Literature Education in Ten Countries* (Urbana, Ill.: NCTE, 1973). From the standpoint of writing across the curriculum, the tutorial practice of biweekly writing in nearly all areas at Oxford, Cambridge, and Dublin may still represent the ideal university program which others can only emulate.

By contrast, in the United States the assuming of the responsibility for writing by the departments of English since the nineteenth century has led to its neglect in many other departments of the university, the college, and the secondary and elementary schools. With the declining scores in standardized tests in reading, writing, and other areas since the early 1960s, one of the suggested solutions to counter this alleged literacy crisis has been to involve increasingly all the departments of a school in the teaching of literacy. This has most frequently taken the form of writing and reading across the curriculum programs in the schools in England, Canada, and Australia, and in the schools and in higher education in this country.

The British scene is possibly best seen in the classic research report by James Britton and his associates, mentioned earlier, *The Development of Writing Abilities (11–18)* (London: Macmillan Educational Ltd. for the Schools Council, 1975). This study of 2122 writing samples from 65 schools in England examined writing in 21 different curriculum subjects, especially English, history, geography, religious education, and science. The samples were analyzed for the purpose, the audience, and the age level of the writers. For purposes, the researchers used a variation of Roman Jakobson's functions of language—here called the transactional, the expressive, and the poetic. The transactional heavily dominated in all subjects except English, where the poetic was highest. The average for the transactional in the other subjects was 80%. The poetic was highest in English (39%) and religious education (12%) and non-existent in other subjects (except in history, 2%). The expressive also occurred only in English and religious education (11% in each). There were sprinklings of the persuasive in some fields. The dominating audience was the teacher, particularly the teacher as examiner (in the later years). The researchers were concerned about the rare occurrence of the expressive, using the language as a learning tool, and in later work tried to remedy this deficiency.

This report, undoubtedly the most influential study in writing across the curriculum in the last fifteen years, articulated some of the major motifs which currently preoccupy such programs in English-speaking countries—the concern with writing in all departments of a school, the attention given to the various purposes of writing, the distinguishing of different types of audiences in writing, and the care for some use of language as a learning device. It is not inaccurate to say that these concerns dominate nearly all of the programs which are described in the literature.

An early update of the Britton report can be seen in Suzanne Jacobs, "Writing Across the Curriculum: An Update," *EJ*, 67 (November 1978), 64–67, and in James Britton, *Prospect and Retrospect: Selected Essays of James Britton*, ed. Gordon Pradl (Montclair, N.J.: Boynton/Cook, 1982). The methodology of this London project was applied in the United States by Arthur N. Applebee, Fran Lehr, and Anne Auten, and their summary report can be seen in "Learning to Write in the Secondary School: How and Where," *EJ*, 70 (September 1981), 78–82.

The movement in this country had, in the meantime, accelerated considerably. In 1977, Beaver College in Glenside, Pennsylvania inaugurated a series of yearly seminars for the members of the faculty in all departments. In a short time, the Beaver program became a model and a prototype of many other programs across the country. In 1978, the faculty of the College of Literature, Science, and the Arts at the University of Michigan voted for a required writing course, preferably in the student's area of concentration, to be taken after the sophomore year. The program went into effect in 1981 and has also been widely imitated.

These two programs spearheaded others like them across the entire country. An MLA survey in May of 1985 found that 46% of all Ph.D.-granting institutions currently have some program of this sort, and 48% of BA/MA-granting institutions have such programs. The percentage at the two-year college level is lower, 28% (MLA Commission on Writing and Literature, "A Survey of the Profession," May 2, 1985, p. 66).

There has been some movement at the secondary level, but no statistics paralleling the MLA survey exist, to my knowledge. Particular states have been more influenced than others by the London project and by the colleges in the area. Every Michigan high school was visited by a representative from the English Composition Board, and programs were installed in many schools. Some of these are described in various issues of *Fforum*. A similar attempt can be seen for Wisconsin in Irene M. Diamond et al., eds., *Interdisciplinary Writing: A Guide to Writing Across the Curriculum* (Madison: The University of Wisconsin, 1980, ERIC ED 193655). For Virginia, see *An Inservice Model for an Urban/Suburban System, Arlington Public Schools, Virginia, Parts I, II, and III. Teacher Corps Reports: Inservice Development Processes* (Arlington, Va.: Arlington Public Schools, 1977, ERIC ED 143662).

For a view of writing across the curriculum in Northern Australia, Ilona Sparber's "Putting Language Across the Curriculum into Practice," *English in Australia,* 58 (1981), 62–66, can be consulted.

As was mentioned above, many of the articles on writing across the curriculum are descriptions of particular programs. These are quite useful because they depict the unique circumstances of the particular institutions involved and allow readers to make comparisons and contrasts to their own situations. A few useful generalizations can be made, however. Then it might be most practical to describe some quite different and influential programs in some detail, rather than to attempt to touch on thirty or forty.

Although some programs place writing across the curriculum in the junior or senior year in college, the prevalence of programs in the schools and in community colleges shows that this movement can be used in the first years of college also. There are some excellent articles on the use of writing across the curriculum with remedial students. Mike Rose argues against the use of strictly personal expressive writing in such courses and recommends using regular college readings and topics from the students' majors in "Remedial Writing Courses: A Critique and a Proposal," *CE,* 45 (1983), 109–23. Mary C. Grattan and Susan P. Robbins recommend the same strategies for use in writing centers in the two-year college in "Content Area Models: A Key to Student Writing Improvement in Writing Center Programs," *Teaching English in the Two-Year College,* 9 (Winter 1983), 117–21. In fact, some of the more serious writing done in community colleges is done in technical writing courses. For a description of such a program, see Marilyn B. Silver, "Technical Writing in the Community College: An Interdisciplinary Approach," *Technical Writing Teacher,* 9 (1982), 173–78.

Secondly, writing across the curriculum programs seem to work in nearly any type of subject at the university, college, or school level. The Michigan program mentioned above regularly offers about 150 courses per semester, and nearly every subject taught in the college is involved. The University of Texas catalog for Fall 1985 listed over 270 writing-intensive courses drawn from all of the twelve undergraduate colleges in the institution, from liberal arts to all of the professional schools. There are more articles in the literature describing successes and failures in particular subjects than on any other aspect of this topic. As mentioned above in Section I, the anthology by Ann Ruggles Gere is devoted primarily to this issue.

There are some useful summaries of institution-wide programs which can be consulted. The journal of the Association of American Colleges, *The Forum for Liberal Education,* devoted its October 1984 issue to describing twenty-four different programs, with articles by four guest authors and several staff authors. Robert P. Parker and Vera Goodkin describe programs in New Jersey in "Writing Across the Curriculum Programs in New Jersey's Public Colleges," *Community/Junior College Research Quarterly,* 5 (1981), 323–30.

The Michigan Program
There is no doubt that one of the largest and most influential programs in the country is that in the College of Literature, Science, and the Arts at the University of Michigan, the largest college at the university. The students write an essay for their entrance requirements; on the basis of it, they are required to pass either a remedial tutorial course or a regular freshman writing course taught in the English department (from which they may be exempted). They must also pass an upper-level writing-intensive course, usually in the major field. The course is taught by a regular faculty member, who gets help in the grading and conferencing from teaching assistants from the same field. The faculty members are assisted by seminars run by the executive agency which runs the program, an interdepartmental English Composition Board. The teaching assistants are given a full semester of training by teachers appointed by the board. The board also approves all course syllabuses before they are taught. In a regular semester, there are usually about 150 courses offered. There must be about 4000 words of writing, in several assignments, and the processes of writing are encouraged with drafts and conferences with teaching assistants or the teacher. The Michigan program was the inspiration for the volume of essays edited by Patricia L. Stock, *Fforum: Essays on Theory and Practice in the Teaching of Writing* (Montclair, N.J.: Boynton/Cook, 1983). About one-fifth of the fifty articles are by authors who worked with the Michigan program. Descriptions of one of the model

courses can be seen in John D. Reiff, "The In-Course Writing Workshop in a Program of Writing Across the Curriculum," *JBW,* 2 (Spring/Summer 1980), 53–61. This article is about a history course; in "Writing in the Disciplines at The University of Michigan," *Fforum,* 2 (Winter 1981), 75–77, 91–92, Reiff takes a more general view.

The Beaver College Program

The whole issue of *Fforum* mentioned in the previous sentence is about writing across the curriculum and contains an article about what may be the other most influential program in the country. The article, by Elaine Maimon, is "The Writing Program at Beaver College," *Fforum,* 2 (Winter 1981), 83, 95. She also described it in "Visions and Revisions Across the Curriculum," *ADE Bulletin,* 74 (Fall 1981), 39–40. All students take two regular freshman composition courses, each requiring approximately 1000 words of writing per week, although only four finished papers are graded. One of these four papers each semester is on a topic in another course, such as political science, biology, etc. Since nearly all of the faculty have taken NEH summer seminars, most of the upper-division courses are writing-intensive courses. The textbook and reading anthology used for the courses were analyzed above. They illustrate in a very practical way the type of course being offered. The Beaver program has been imitated in many liberal arts colleges.

The Program at Michigan Technological University

A third program which has also been quite influential, is that at a quite different type of institution from the large state university (Michigan) and the small liberal arts college (Beaver). The program at Michigan Technological University is thoroughly described from twelve different perspectives in the anthology mentioned above, Toby Fulwiler and Art Young, *Language Connections: Writing and Reading Across the Curriculum* (Urbana, Ill.:

NCTE, 1982). It would be difficult to improve upon the brief sketch they give of their program in the Introduction.

The cross-disciplinary writing program we developed at Michigan Technological University is teacher-centered. This framework assumes—computers and television aside—that the teacher is still the center of the educational experience. Other schools have taken different routes to improve writing proficiency for all students: junior-level competency examinations, for example, or senior-level writing courses required of all students. We believe that people soon forget knowledge acquired under an examination approach; we don't believe that one required course in our students' jam-packed curriculum will make them truly better writters. Our program attempts to achieve more fundamental changes than either of these solutions by addressing the students' total work across the school curriculum.

We conduct off-campus writing workshops to educate teachers from all disciplines in functions and processes of language and, at the same time, provide assistance with pedagogical strategies so that they, in turn, can teach their students to use language in a variety of meaningful ways. Through the format of these workshops we explore theoretical ideas and consider whether or not they may lead to useful classroom practices. . . . In addition to the summer workshops, our particular program involves academic-year seminars on writing for different university departments, follow-up activities for former workshop participants, a newsletter network, a university-wide language skills laboratory, and interdisciplinary research by writing and reading teachers. (pp. x–xi)

The Maryland Program

Finally, a fourth and again quite different program is that of the University of Maryland. It also has been imitated in different types of environments. Unlike the other three programs discussed above, it is a program centralized in a single department. The students take a regular freshman English course and then in the junior or senior year take a course from an English teacher in which they write themes in their field of concentration. This program extends to all of the undergraduate degree colleges or schools. The courses are offered in the three areas of arts and humanities, technical writing, and business writing. The arts and humanities courses emphasize argumentation, applied to the students' areas of concentration—except for pre-law students no differentiations are made in the class enrollments. The technical and business writing courses also incorporate argumentation in addition to the regular concerns of such courses. All of the courses also emphasize a humanities approach to the student's discipline, often by a research report of study concerned with a current ethical or political controversy in the field. About 120 sections each semester are offered. The program has been briefly described in published form in James L. Kinneavy, "Writing Across the Curriculum," *ADE Bulletin,* 76 (Winter 1983), 7–14. It has been imitated at Texas, Utah, Northeastern, Penn State, St. Mary's University (in San Antonio, Texas), and elsewhere. It is very similar to the current program at Brigham Young University, which antedated it.

Implementing Programs

For those institutions that do not have programs in writing across the curriculum, some of the experiences of those who have installed them may be useful. Elaine Maimon, who has consulted with many institutions, has written "Writing in All the Arts and Sciences: Getting Started and Gaining Momentum," *WPA: Writ-*

ing Program Administration, 4 (Spring 1981), 9–12. Mike Rose also has useful suggestions in "When Faculty Talk About Writing," *CE,* 41 (November 1979), 272–79, detailing the UCLA experience. Robert Weiss and Michael Peich discuss the faculty workshop and program at West Chester State College in "Faculty Attitude Change in a Cross-Disciplinary Writing Workshop," *CCC,* 31 (February 1980), 33–41.

V. THEORETICAL FOUNDATIONS

There have been few explicit, comprehensive and substantial statements on the theoretical foundations which have underpinned the many programs described in the preceding sections. On the other hand, there have been many brief and succinct statements accompanying various programs and there have been legions of articles and chapters of books written about writing as a way of learning. Two of the original foundation principles adopted by Britton and his associates were taken from Roman Jakobson and from James Moffett. Jakobson supplied the theory of six different functions of language in "Linguistics and Poetics," *Essays on the Language of Literature,* ed. Seymour Chatman and Samuel R. Levin (Boston: Houghton Mifflin, 1967), pp. 296–322). Britton simplified this system to four functions of language: transactional, persuasive, expressive, and poetic, as was pointed out above. Britton derived his theory of audiences from Moffett's orders of discourse (see the chapter on "Kinds and Orders of Discourse," *Teaching the Universe of Discourse* [Boston: Houghton Mifflin, 1968]). These two dimensions provided the main analytic tools for Britton's study. In a sense these two dimensions remain the major theoretical concerns of writing across the curriculum at the present time. But both dimensions have become considerably more complex. In the following analysis the first dimension to be considered will be that of audience, and the second will be that of functions of language. Under these two headings it is still possible to group the major theoretical issues of writing across the curriculum at the present time.

The Question of Audiences

One of the most critical (and divisive) issues having to do with the teaching of composition to students in different disciplines has to do with the audience to whom the student writes. Some theories tend to favor teaching the student to write to an expert audience. Others favor writing directed to a lay audience. A look at these theories and their practical programmatic corollaries should be of some use in explaining some of the existing programs.

The notion that different departments are made up of discourse communities with varying assumptions, logical criteria, senses of evidence, and stylistic conventions has come to dominate much thinking about the nature of academic (and professional) disciplines. Possibly one of the most important theorists in this area has been Stephen Toulmin, whose work, especially *Human Understanding* (Princeton: Princeton University Press, 1972), talked of the epistemic court and its criteria in each discipline. Some social scientists and rhetoricians have expanded and adapted his criteria to our discipline, especially Bryant Burleson, in "On the Foundations of Rationality: Toulmin, Habermas, and the *A Priori* of Reason," *Journal of the American Forensic Association,* 16 (Fall 1979), 112–27.

A second stream of thought converges with Toulmin's theory of discourse communities. Michel Foucault's analyses of disciplines and systems of discourse, both in "The Discourse on Language," *The Archaeology of Knowledge & the Discourse on Language,* translated by A. M. Sheridan Smith (New York: Pantheon Books, 1972, pp. 215–38) and in *The Order of Things: An Archaeology of the Human Sciences* (New York: Vintage Books, 1973), have emphasized the limitations, the arbitrariness, the discrete and discontinuous nature of many systems of thought and disciplines, and their frequent incompatibility.

From these two views of disciplines, some in rhetoric have drawn the conclusion that, especially in an era of more and more specialization and fragmentation, it is difficult to write or read the discourse of another scientific community. Different conclusions, however, have been drawn from these general principles. Some, like Lester Faigley, Kristine Hansen, David Joliffe, Richard Bailey, Lee Odell, and David Hamilton are concerned that these discourse communities are so self-contained that aliens in them will seriously misinterpret the discourses of the community. This corollary has, obviously, very serious consequences for writing across the curriculum. Howard Ranken makes this point with regard to composition in "Contributions of Cognitive Psychology to Composition Research," in *Multidisciplinary Studies in Composition,* ed. Janice Lauer (Lafayette, Ind.: Center for Multidisciplinary Studies in Composition, 1985), as do Lester Faigley and Kristine Hansen with two examples in "Learning to Write in the Social Sciences," *CCC,* 36 (May 1985), 140–49. The entire issue is devoted to writing across the curriculum, with twelve articles and three book reviews.

The extreme corollary of this position is that only the Michigan model for writing across the curriculum is a valid one. Courses in technical writing and business writing offered in English departments are not really seriously teaching writing. And the only advanced composition course which the ordinary English teacher with a background in literature can handle is a course in literary criticism or history—a position which some English departments have taken. Jay L. Robinson takes this position in a recent somber article, "Literacy in the Department of English," *CE,* 47 (September 1985), 482–99, and suggests that unless English departments rethink their discipline and its vocabulary, they will not be able to teach literacy.

The antithesis of this position is the traditional one in which English departments teach technical writing. In fact, the majority of English departments embrace this position—63% of the colleges surveyed in the MLA survey cited in the first paragraph of this essay offer technical writing and 46% even offer business writing (pp. 33 and 29, respectively). Technical writing for forty years has been a continuing and growing success story: in Ph.D. institutions it grew by 83% in the years 1981 to 1984 (same re-

WRITING ACROSS THE CURRICULUM

port, p. 103). Whatever the theoretical arguments against English teachers' not being able to teach people to write in other disciplines, the facts would seem to demolish such arguments, as far as writing for the lay audience is concerned.

The factual argument is aided by the theoretical support from several quarters. First, the concern about fragmentation and increasing isolation of disciplines has spawned a theoretical concern for interdisciplinarity. Robinson, in the article cited above, believes that the work of Clifford Geertz can serve as a theoretical base, especially "Blurred Genres: The Refiguration of Social Thought," and "The Way We Think Now: Toward an Ethnography of Modern Thought," both in *Local Knowledge: Further Essays in Interpretive Anthropology* (New York: Basic Books, 1983), pp. 19–35, 147–163. Toulmin, whose work helps to define and distinguish disciplines, is also concerned about fragmentation and argues that science must now be integrated into the total human endeavor: "the scientific history of the entire last three hundred years is littered with unredeemed social IOUs" (Stephen Toulmin, "The Twin Moralities of Science," *Science and Society: Past, Present, and Future,* ed. Nicholas H. Steneck [Ann Arbor: University of Michigan Press, 1975], p. 116). Two more general works in this field are Joseph Kockelmans, ed., *Interdisciplinarity and Higher Education* (University Park: Pennsylvania State University Press, 1979), and Raymond Williams, *Writing in Society* (Thetford, England: Thetford-Verso, 1983).

Some attempt to wed the two positions: students need to learn how to write for their own discourse communities, and they also need to be able to write to the lay audience of politicians and consumers. In other words, students need to learn to adjust to different audiences in their writings. Kinneavy makes this point strongly in "Writing Across the Curriculum," *ADE Bulletin,* 76 (Winter 1983), 18–19.

Different Functions of Language

The second major issue which Britton and his colleagues examined carefully in the London Project was the matter of functions of language. In particular, they were concerned that the students were writing too many informative pieces, and not using writing as a tool for thinking and for understanding. The issue of writing for learning probably accounts for more bibliographic concern than any other issue which has been considered in this chapter. There are also a few signficant articles on other aims of language, but the first attention must be given to writing across the curriculum as a tool for thinking.

In addition to Britton and his colleagues, many of the authors who write on this issue call attention to the importance of Janet Emig's article, "Writing as a Mode of Learning," *CCC,* 28 (May 1977), 122–28, reprinted in Gary Tate and Edward P. J. Corbett, eds., *The Writing Teacher's Sourcebook* (New York: Oxford University Press, 1981), pp. 69–78. Another frequently cited article is that by Anne J. Hetherington, "Writing to Learn: Writing Across the Disciplines," *CE,* 43 (April 1981), 379–87. (See also the reply to a criticism of the article, in *CE,* 47 [Jan. 1985], 85–88.) Another excellent article is David Hamilton's "Interdisciplinary Writing," *CE,* 41 (March 1980), 780–96. All four of the typical programs which were outlined above in the fourth section of this chapter are preoccupied with this topic, as both the Fulwiler and Stock anthologies demonstrate. The text used in the Maryland program is called *A Rhetoric of Argument* (New York: Random House, 1982), by Jeanne Fahnstock and Marie Secor; each of the major sections of the books is a question, not an answer. Writing as learning is also the major concern of the Gere anthology, also mentioned above.

There are different types of writing activities used in this approach to writing. Many of the articles talk about the journal as a medium of exploratory thought. Sometimes the journal is a record of the student's understanding of the material; sometimes it is a free writing experience for the student to react to the material or the course or the professor; sometimes it is an attempt to move the student's understanding of the material on to applications; etc. In addition to the anthologized selections already cited, the reader can also profitably look at Mike Rose, "Remedial Writing Courses: A Critique and a Proposal," *CE*, 45 (February 1983), 109–28. Like Hetherington, mentioned in the preceding paragraph, Rose recommends not limiting writing, even remedial, to expressive essays. Another intelligent approach to the journal is Ira Progoff's *At a Journal Workshop: The Basic Text and Guide for Using the Intensive Journal Process* (New York: Dialogue House Library, 1975). Finally, Anne Miller Wotring and Robert Tierney, in *Two Studies of Writing in High School Science* (Berkeley: Bay Area Writing Project, 1981), discuss in detail the use of expressive writing in teaching biology.

A few words ought to be said about the other functions of language in writing across the curriculum programs. Lynn Atherton Phillips's dissertation, *An Assessment of a College Course in Freshman Composition* (The University of Texas at Austin, 1978), attempted to survey the kinds of writing going on in different departments of the university to see if the freshman course actually prepared students for their future needs. She used the same theoretical framework of functions of language which Britton had used—in this case Kinneavy's adaptation of Jakobson. She found the following percentages of occurrence in 60 papers from six colleges: 40% informative, 33% scientific (proving), 24% exploratory; and the remaining 3% were expressive, persuasive, and poetic. Her findings seem to support the findings of Laurence Behrens in his study of texts, "Meditations, Reminiscences, Polemics: Composition Readers and the Service Course," *CE*, 41 (Jan. 1980), 561–70. He criticizes the texts for their ignoring of the informative paper. A good many of the papers being written in the writing-intensive courses at Michigan and at Texas, two of the largest institutions with such courses, are, in fact, informative. In addition, many of the papers are also demonstrative.

If there is lively discussion about use of the exploratory and some concern for the expressive and informative uses of language in writing across the curriculum, there is relatively little for either the literary or the persuasive—at least at the college level. The

London Project, of course, praised the heavy incidence of poetic writing in English deparments that it found in British schools. But this aspect of their project has not been given much prominence at the college level in the States, though Art Young has a fine piece in the Fulwiler anthology, "Considering Values: The Poetic Function of Language."

Nor has there been much said about the persuasive use of language. James L. Kinneavy, in "Writing Across the Curriculum," *ADE Bulletin,* 76 (Winter 1983), 18–19, and in "Restoring the Humanities: The Return of Rhetoric from Exile," *The Rhetorical Tradition and Modern Writing,* ed. James J. Murphy (New York: MLA, 1982), pp. 19–28, insists that all disciplines should teach students to write both expositorily and persuasively. S. Michael Halloran and Merrill Whitburn, in an essay in the same volume, "Ciceronian Rhetoric and the Rise of Science: The Plain Style Reconsidered," pp. 58–72, speak to the same issue.

A tangential aspect of the rhetorical emphasis in writing across the curriculum is a movement which might be called the rhetoric of science, which has begun to attract considerable attention at the present time. This is the attempt to analyze the persuasive aspects of the writing and of the marketing and the acceptance of scientific prose at the present time and in other periods. Both of Foucault's works cited earlier, *The Archaeology of Knowledge* and *The Order of Things,* examine these phenomena in great detail. So do some of the articles by Charles Bazerman, such as "Modern Evolution of the Experimental Report in Physics: Spectroscopic Articles in *Physical Review,* 1893–1980," *Social Studies of Science,* 14 (May 1984), 163–96, and "Scientific Writing as a Social Act: A Review of the Literature of the Sociology of Science," *New Essays in Technical Writing and Communication,* ed. Paul V. Anderson, John Brockmann, and Carolyn R. Miller (Farmingdale, N.Y.: Baywood, 1983), pp. 156–84. Another book analyzing many non-rational aspects of scientific persuasion is *Laboratory Life: The Social Construction of Scientific Facts* (Beverly Hills, Calif.: Sage Publications, 1979), by Bruno Latour and Steve

Woolgar. Finally, Herbert W. Simon's chapter, "Are Scientists Rhetors in Disguise? An Analysis of Discursive Processes Within Scientific Communities," in *Rhetoric in Transition: Studies in the Nature and Uses of Rhetoric,* ed. Eugene E. White (University Park: Pennsylvania State University Press, 1980), pp. 115–30, is an investigation in the same general direction.

This movement may, in the long run, be as important as any other aspect of writing across the curriculum. Our age, whether we like it or not, in many ways is controlled by scientists, and their political and ethical and academic rhetoric may determine what our futures are going to be or whether we are going to have any.

VI. EFFECTS OF WRITING ACROSS THE CURRICULUM

It is certainly too early to judge the effectiveness of the various programs which have been described in the preceding pages. The very perseverance of the programs for this length of time argues that administrators have seen some value in them. This is the opinion of Griffin, cited in the first page of this chapter. But it really is still too early, either at the high school or at the college level, to see whether writing across the curriculum is actually a serious attempt to integrate language fully into the entire curriculum, or whether it is a fad, or, even more cynically, whether it is merely a clever device of English departments to divest themselves of the onerous job of teaching writing, or whether there is enough motivation, especially in research institutions, for teachers to take the time to teach writing in content courses.

A few studies have been made which affirm the expectations of the initiators of programs. Let us take a quick look at some of them. The four typical programs which were described in the earlier part of this essay have all stood the test of some time. There is an excellent evaluation of the Michigan Tech program in an article by Toby Fulwiler, "How Well Does Writing Across the Curriculum Work?" *CE,* 46 (February 1984), 113–25. It is an honest attempt to assess the successes of the six-year-old program, the problems, and the unpredicted happy results of the program in bringing about a more collegial community of scholars, in producing better speakers and writers in the graduates, in improving scholarly writing in the faculty, and in bringing a more cohesive atmosphere to the environment at the university. Fulwiler summarizes his evaluation as follows:

> Suffice it to say that I believe the programs do work and that the interdisciplinary writing workshops are the very best way to introduce those programs to college and university faculties. (p. 113)

Young and Fulwiler have amassed considerable empirical data on the success or failure of the program, but it has not yet been published. The sponsors of the Beaver, Michigan, and Maryland programs are in a similar position. The reactions of students and of most of the faculty to the programs have been enthusiastic at all three institutions, but there have been no published systematic evaluations, whether empirical or not, to my knowledge. There is evidence for the enthusiasm of the Beaver faculty, as can be seen in the report of Elaine P. Maimon and Barbara F. Nodine, *Measuring Behavior and Attitude in the Teaching of Writing Among Faculties in Various Disciplines* (ERIC Ws 167999).

Some studies have made useful suggestions for future directions for the movement. Robert H. Weiss, in *Research in Writing and Learning: Some Effects of Learning-Centered Writing in Five Subject Areas* (ERIC ED 191073) finds that more subject-area writing increases the learning of the subject, the hypothesis of much of the writing-as-learning positions. A similar approval is given to a joint English and social studies program at the secondary level in a study by Anita Brostoff, *Thinking Through Writing: A Report on the Project, Its Evaluation, and Its Uses* (ERIC ED 214173). There are a few other similar studies. To these might be added the overview of Britton in his *Prospect and Retrospect: Selected Essays of James Britton,* ed. Gordon Pradl (Montclair, N.J.: Boynton/Cook, 1982).

But the fact remains that the jury is out on writing across the curriculum, both at the school level and at the college and university levels, in the United States and in England, Canada, and Australia. In fact, the current jury does not have enough facts to make a decision. Further cases must be brought to the courts to test the movement. At the present, the promise seems most favorable— writing across the curriculum may be the best academic response to the literacy crisis in English-speaking countries, though it cannot be a total social response.

Computers and Composition

HUGH BURNS, United States Air Force

WRITING IS DYNAMIC—THAT WE HAVE KNOWN—
but now we have a dynamic tool—one we do not know or trust
very well. Frankly, we have much to learn about how to use it.
Unfortunately, this education is complicated because the tool is
still emerging as a technology and because computers and software are in a developmental jet stream that few of us can comprehend. Our intuitions tell us that computer programs could allow
us more access to the interactive process itself—the human mind's
recursiveness, the rhetorical decisions, the visions and revisions.
But where exactly are we? As teachers of composition, we have
approximately twenty years of limited experience with computers, but much of that experience has been of the "underground"
kind. For example, we may write on word processors, but we
have not yet used them to supplement our teaching. The only
mention of computers in Gary Tate's *Teaching Composition: 10
Bibliographical Essays* (Ft Worth: TCU Press, 1976) was Edward
Corbett's mention of the computer as a tool for stylistic analysis.
Indeed, we are just beginning our efforts to integrate such tools
easily and effectively into our composition curricula. But that
does not mean there has been a lack of activity.

One central question before us is simply, "How do we get
there from where we are?" In other words, what scholarship, research, and practical computing approaches are showing us the
way in the composition setting? Is the tao of computational composition achievable? My bias will show, for I am certain that

computer–assisted technology will enable us to perceive new dimensions of our writing and teaching. From using computers, we are learning to clarify our expertise, to verify our insights about a writer's performance, to develop more robust and flexible instruction, and to humanize our machines and, consequently, ourselves. The computer will impact the teaching of composition—for better or worse. By being knowledgeable about this continually emerging technology, English educators should inevitably discover the better course.

In this essay, I examine the context surrounding computers in composition settings, trying to summarize most of the major historical issues of computer literacy as they have affected the composition instructor specifically and the English education profession in general. Next, I review word processing as a major tool for teaching composition, here trying to point out some of the most promising theories and practices. The third major section of the essay examines the theories and practices of computer-assisted instruction and points out how the evolution of computer-assisted instruction in composition is pushing beyond basic drill and practice. Overall, the literature is generally robust in what I will call the "advent of computer technology in the humanities." The word processing literature is uneven but plentiful even though this tool is not yet being truly exploited in many composition courses nationwide. Actual research in computer-assisted instruction for writing is relatively lean by comparison. However, there have been several different developmental pedagogies worth understanding despite the paucity of empirical studies which examine if writing effectiveness actually improved as a result of the computer-assisted instruction. What should become clear is that computers in the composition classroom have not created a revolution as many have claimed, but rather an evolution—and a sporadic one at that. Finally, many of my comments along the way illustrate one major fact: as teaching composition becomes more and more interdisciplinary, emerging technologies such as artificial intelligence, natural language understanding, and intelli-

379

gent computer-assisted instruction will challenge us to think even more about the nature of rhetorical expertise and the processes involved in performing well all four of the language arts: writing, reading, speaking, listening.

So, this essay provides more observations than you may need, enough scholarship for at least one independent study, and—by far—fewer resources than exist. I believe the work reviewed here as well as the "works within" should easily stimulate more than enough questions for writing teachers for the next decade. Each contribution has been a sounding because these authors trust we can get to effective computer-supplemented composition teaching from where we are today.

I. TOWARD A CONTEXT FOR COMPUTERS IN COMPOSITION

If you started teaching when I did, in the late sixties, you are part of a generation of teachers who hardly saw computer-assisted instruction or word processing in an English classroom. The curricula generally emphasized literature and basic writing skills. The available educational technologies were television, film, 35mm slides, and some "systems" curricula such as self-paced programmed textbooks. The computer wasn't there. Word processing systems such as IBM's Magnetic Tape Selectric Typewriter (MT/ST) were appearing in industry and business, but at that time they hardly foreshadowed systems for home and for classrooms. Nevertheless, there was early interest and some excitement as researchers, mostly at universities, speculated how an analytical engine could be employed to supplement English composition instruction.

Perhaps the first idea to catch on and truly provoke the profession was computer grading: computers which could be programmed to evaluate, mark, and grade compositions. A historical anecdote illustrates the general, prevailing context beautifully. Ellis B. Page sought and received funding from the Office of Education to investigate the feasibility of using computer programs for the automatic analysis and evaluation of student writing. His work is reported in "The Use of the Computer in Analyzing Student Essays," *International Review of Education*, 14 (1968), 210–25. Though relying on keypunch data entry and mainframe machines, a methodology was formed. English teachers articulated standards and notions of composition analysis such as content, organization, style, and mechanics, and the computer was programmed to recognize these standards. The reviews were mixed, for the computer was providing a view of English composition evaluation that was too analytical for many as we soon would see.

Ken Macrorie recounts in the first chapter of *Uptaught* (New York: Hayden, 1970) receiving a letter from the editor of *Research in the Teaching of English* asking him to review Ellis's original research called *The Analysis of Essays by Computer* (ERIC: ED 028 633). He was told that the purpose of the study was "to find out if computers could analyze and evaluate students' essays as well as teachers do." And, to his huge dismay, Macrorie admits that the computer did as well as an English teacher: "It could. It did." What the computer looked for were such characteristics as variety of sentence structures, frequent long sentences, a title, frequent paragraphing—lots of mechanical traits. Such a machine would need a name so Macrorie christened the computer "Percival," noting "After all, any machine that could write, 'Do you really think the past participle of "break" is "busted" or were you just being careless?' had to have a name." Macrorie concluded that "Percival incarnate is a monster who helps us see the English teacher incarnate—a cultivated, liberal, well-intentioned pusher of the life of the mind and feelings, dedicated to promoting moving and memorable expressions of the complexities of life" (pp. 6–7). That was the original dialectic, and it continues today with some gusto. Until artificial intelligence produces the Composition Teacher's Intelligent Associate, computers are either tormentors or mentors—a theme Helen J. Schwartz has made well ("Monsters and Mentors: Computer Applications for Humanistic Education," *CE*, 44 [Feb. 1982], 141–52).

If this portrayal illustrated what was occurring in the English profession, it was only part of a larger dialectic—the quest for national computer literacy to be nurtured by the schools, for the schools, and in the schools. Another major historical tome for establishing the sense of computer-assisted education in this country, though it does not address English composition singularly, is entitled *Computers and the Learning Society: Hearings Before the Subcommittee on Domestic and International Scientific Planning, Analysis and Cooperation of the Committee on Science and Technology* (Washington: U.S. Government Printing Office, 1978). The volume established the context of what had been happening in educational technology for over twenty years. The room was full of true pioneers. Among the witnesses were William Norris, Chief Executive of Control Data Corporation and a creator of the PLATO authoring tools; Seymore Papert, who was directing the Artificial Intelligence Laboratory at Massachusetts Institute of Technology; John Seely Brown, who was at Bolt, Beranek and Newman at the time; Arthur Melmed of the National Institute of Education; Patrick Suppes of Stanford; Sylvia Charp of the Philadelphia School System, and others. Many of these people have continued to lead the field of educational technology, but in 1977 they were forecasting the educational technology climate for the nation. At one point, when Raymond Kurzweil demonstrated his reading machine for the blind, Mr. Scheuer, the Chair of the Subcommittee, noted, "We've had a quantum jump forward in congressional hearings when the computer testifies" (p. 449). Indeed, the reading machine was a testimonial to the creativity that industry was showing for filling educational needs. The testimony is vital for understanding the important characteristics of educational technology's research, development, test, and engineering cycle, namely: slow progress, financial crises, courseware and software gaps, vast improvements in hardware, special education needs, products and materials developed outside of the classroom, poor evaluation methodologies, and, beneath it all, the public's perception of general dissatisfaction with the cost and the effectiveness of education. This volume allows English teachers to step back for a moment and establish their particular place on the dialectical continuum somewhere between Percival paralysis and electronic ecstasy.

Perhaps the best known book for helping one discover these intervening points for instructional computing literacy is Robert Taylor's (ed.) *The Computer in Education: Tutor, Tool, Tutee* (New York: Teachers College Press, 1980). Taylor and particularly Alfred Bork in "Computers and the Future: Education," pp. 15–52, make it clear that this machine can play at least these three roles in the classroom—a troika worth remembering because the other machines in education cannot capitalize on this interactive quality. An earlier book by Edmund J. Farrell entitled *English, Education, and the Electronic Revolution* (Urbana, Ill.: NCTE, 1967) offers ways to see what was coming and what roles the computer and other electronic media could serve in sustaining literacy in language arts education. Some of the principles may sound gospel-like to us today; nevertheless, Farrell reviews much of the 1960s futuristic literature (e.g., R. Buckminster Fuller's computer feeding game called "How to Make the World Work"), sorts through comprehensive implications for the teaching of English, and provides a useful, seven-page bibliography of early efforts. For example, Farrell's work points to Martin Greenberger's (ed.) *Computers and the World of the Future* (Cambridge, Mass.: MIT Press, 1962) which in turn contains essays by John Kemeny ("A Library for 2000 A.D.") and Alan J. Perlis ("The Computer in the University"). Rodney J. Barth in "ERIC/RCS Report: An Annotated Bibliography of Readings for the Computer Novice and the English Teacher," *EJ*, 68 (January 1979), 88–92, lists over twenty-five references for high school teachers which are available through the Education Research Information Center (ERIC). Barth selected for his classification the following seven subjects: general issues, computer literacy, grading and computers, English language arts, writing, software, and miscellaneous research. The coverage is good through 1977—and most of the pre-micro concerns are well articulated in the pieces that Barth has selected. In fact, the research in the mainframe heyday sometimes seems more systematic and more carefully designed than research which has been done to date on the micro-computers. *Computers and Composing: How Technologies are Changing Writing* by Jeanne W. Halpern and Sarah Liggett (Carbondale: Southern Illinois University Press, 1984) recently examined how computers are part and parcel of the social fabric, outside of the schools for the most part. They stress the computer's importance in the business writing courses, explicitly arguing that composition professionals must attend to the world student writers will work in and, as a certain consequence, write for. The impetus for the book was in research conducted on the connections between dictation and processing.

While such scholarship has helped increase our profession's general acceptance of computers, poor computer programs and user-nasty interfaces often keep our skepticism intact. A few comments on this theme may be appropriate. H. Dominic Covey and Neil Harding McAlister in *Computer Consciousness: Surviving the Automated 80s* (Reading, Mass.: Addison-Wesley, 1980) captured the essence of the major problem noting that the computer is an agent of change with the "potential to become a giant freezer that can solidify procedures and perceptions, [and] imperceptibly overtake those functions to which we apply automation" (p. 7). Joseph Weizenbaum, the creator of ELIZA—the most famous psychoanalytic computer program—still speaks to many of the same themes he annunciated in *Computer Power and Human Reason: From Judgment to Calculation* (San Francisco: W. H. Freeman, 1976). Generally, Weizenbaum would argue that we should treat computers as uncomfortable allies in most intellectual endeavors.

So the computer provides a power to magnify what we do well and what we do poorly. That phenomenon has provided a platform for a series of articles which have tried to encourage us to forsake the irrational paranoia about the technology. One of the best pieces was Ellen W. Nold's "Fear and Trembling: The

> Allan Collins +
> Dedre Gentner
>
> "A Framework for
> a Cog. The. of Writing"
> * IN →
> LW Gregg & ER Steinbag, eds.
> Cog Processes in writing
> (1980

26 (Oct. 1975), :viewed English speculate about Improving Edu-. The best point t their peril the ning profession, us. . . . Already for emphasizing r discipline. Un-d to encompass schools' money, arning" (pp. 12– known. Dorothy ⟩gy to Teach En-g ...position, ... 1981), 18–22, blames many of these fears on three misconceptions: (1) that understanding complicated mathematical relationships is neces-sary to operate and program computers; (2) that using micro-computers mechanizes and depersonalizes instruction; and (3) that computers are devices of the future, not the present. The fear issue will not go away, and perhaps it should not. The argument that always convinces me that we ought to be active in using the technology as well as we humanly can is simply this: since the machine is already in our garden, let's not be afraid to use it to help us do our jobs more efficiently and, perhaps, effectively.

Of the major essay collections on computers and comput-ing, some are worth noting even though I will cover some of the scholarship separately. Joseph Lawlor edited *Computers and Com-position Instruction* (Los Alamitos, Calif.: SWRL Educational Re-search and Development, 1982); this volume has been updated and reprinted by the International Conference on Computers in Education (University of Oregon, Eugene, 1983), with Robert Shostak as editor. Essays appear here on prewriting, grammar instruction, and the beginnings of what was to be the integrated word processing research. William Wresch edited *The Computer in Composition Instruction: A Writer's Tool* (Urbana, Ill.: NCTE, 1984)—a collection of thirteen pieces which cover prewriting, editing and grammar programs, word processing research and applications, and programs for the writing process, as well as an annotated bibliography. A special issue of *Computers and Composition* guest-edited by Lillian Bridwell and Donald Ross is entitled "Selected Papers from the Conference on Computers in Writing: New Directions in Teaching and Research" (1985). Essentially, the twenty-one papers represent the proceedings of a major conference on writing and computing. Kathleen E. Kiefer and Cynthia L. Selfe, the editors of *Computers and Composition,* describe the following six categories of articles: "research design, software evaluation, responses to word processing, descriptions of composition programs, descriptions of software for basic writers, and descriptions of software for first-year composition and beyond" (p. iii). *Computer-Aided Instruction in the Humanities,* edited by Solveig Olsen (New York: Modern Language Association, 1985), promises to be a most useful resource. The first half of the volume contains twelve articles discussing applications and challenges of computer-assisted instruction in the humanities. Two articles discuss composition in particular: Kathleen E. Kiefer, "Writing: Using the Computer as a Tool," pp. 90–102; Donald Ross, Jr., and Lillian S. Bridwell, "Computer-Aided Composing: Gaps in the Software," pp. 103–115. The second half details people, resources, and research in computer-related education in the humanities with the caveat that "even a humanist with experience in CAI finds it nearly impossible to keep up with the developments." (See Hugh Burns, Glyn Holmes, and Solveig Olsen, "People and Programs," pp. 176–98; Solveig Olsen, "Print Sources," pp. 199–253.) This volume also has a glossary should you have a need for better understanding of the jargon and language of the computer scientist, e.g. *a* as in algorithm, *b* as in byte, *c* as in CPU. It is complete enough for the average humanist.

Computers should always be judged guilty until they are proved innocent—that is probably the safest and most popular notion for English educators to use as they confront computers in the teaching of composition. By degrees and as time goes on, composition instructors will grasp how to use this maturing technology in the classroom. In 1985, however, many composition teachers see word processing as the most promising and the most applicable computer technology for an immediate impact. Where are we in that regard?

II. TOWARD A WORD PROCESSING PEDAGOGY

Did your interest in teaching composition with computers develop because of your experiences as a writer working with a word processor? It is not surprising that a writer's tool could easily be viewed by an open-minded teacher as a first-rate candidate for enriching composition instruction. Word processing was the technological gateway for many teachers of composition. Bestsellers such as William Zinsser's *Writing with a Word Processor* (New York: Harper and Row, 1982) or Peter A. McWilliams's *The Word Processing Book* (Los Angeles: Prelude Press, 1982) are lively, humorous, informative expositions about encounters of the word processing kind and their effects. Zinsser writes, "The word processor will help you achieve three cardinal goals of writing—clarity, simplicity and humanity—if you make it your servant and not your master" (p. 112). I would add fluency as a fourth goal, but not all of us can be as fluent as Issac Asimov. Asimov argues that speed really has little to do with the writing process in "The Word Processor and I—A Question of Speed," *Popular Computing* (June 1982), 24–25. Such books and popular articles are icebreakers for individuals who are approaching the task of writing themselves. Nevertheless, a composition teacher can infer many appropriate instructional strategies from reading how writers are actually using such tools.

Theoretically, however, the interactive quality of writing on a word processor should parallel any process-oriented cognitive theory of writing. Cognitive modelling is, of course, of great interest to many researchers, but making a cognitive model computationally explicit is a difficult proposition to say the least. It remains to be done, but provocative and substantial research has been done in this area, and more will have to be undertaken.

An excellent place to start searching for an assessment of the word processing state of the art is in the most comprehensive annotated bibliography available. Under a grant from the University of Minnesota's Educational Development Program, *Word Processors and the Writing Process* was compiled by Paula Reed Nancarrow, Donald Ross, and Lillian Bridwell (Westport, Conn.: Greenwood Press, 1983). It is an indispensable tool listing most of the open literature as well as attending to specific computer-related journals such as *Educational Technology, Journal of Computer-Based Instruction,* and *Journal of Information Science.*

Perhaps the most valuable book published thus far for composition teachers on cognition, computers, and writing is Colette Daiute's *Writing and Computers* (Reading, Mass.: Addison-Wesley, 1985). She examines four main considerations: the writing processes—social, physical, and cognitive; computer tools and the writing process—prewriting, composing, revising, and editing; composing strategies of writers of all ages as they encounter the computer—an especially strong section; and practical advice about setting up computer writing environments. Allan Collins and Dedre Gentner of Bolt, Beranek and Newman in "A Framework for a Cognitive Theory of Writing" (in L. W. Gregg and E. R. Steinberg, eds., *Cognitive Processes in Writing* [Hillsdale, N.J.: Lawrence Erlbaum, 1980]) also describe ways to investigate and exploit links between composing and computing. They postulate a dynamic, computer-assisted 'Writing Land' in which the cognitive theories can be constructed and examined as the procedural skills are taught and performed.

Over the past ten years, the composition textbook industry has been generally reluctant to address using computers as writing tools. But the latest texts may have a chapter devoted to word processing. From the marketing point of view, publishers believe computers are not as pervasive in the schools, so publishing a book for which writers must have hardware and software is highly risky. In addition, to have enough savvy to know what specific hardware and software products are the most effective is no simple task. At this time, I know of only one college rhetoric centered on computers and composition: Helen J. Schwartz, *Interactive Writing: Composing with a Word Processor* (New York: Holt, Rinehart and Winston, 1985). Schwartz's idea of a "Fast-Track Guide to Your Word Processing Program" is one way to provide an interactive apparatus for her interactive premise. Another strategy which seems to accommodate the uncertain marketplace is Schwartz's activities "With Word Processing." Here is an example: "When you try a new phrasing, *do not* delete the original version. Instead, mark the passage you are revising (for example, with an @ at the beginning and an = at the end), and then insert the new version (with a third marker + at the end?). When you are through, check back and *choose* the version of each passage which you like best" (p. 252). Other texts will follow, and, of course, on-line textbooks will eventually be marketed for teaching composition—the nature of which would certainly spark a lively staff interchange. Needless to say, future authors of interactive composition texts will have to be blessed with extra portions of imagination and of patience.

Those English composition researchers who are actually deriving data through empirical methodologies, as I have indicated, are few and far between. One such researcher is Richard M. Collier. In "The Effect of Computer-Based Text Editors on the Revision Strategies of Inexperienced Writers," a paper presented at the Northeast Regional Conference on the Teaching of English in the Two Year College, 1982 (ERIC: ED 211 998) and in "The Word Processor and Revision Strategies," *CCC,* 34 (May 1983), Collier delivers some good news and some bad. Yes, student writers will indeed revise more with a word processor, but those revisions will not necessarily affect the overall quality of their compositions. He found that his students generally made surface-level changes rather than text-level changes: seeing trees—bark, needles, and moss—and significantly missing the forest of discourse. Richard H. Bullock is another instructor paying careful attention to word processing responses in the classroom. In "The

Lure of the Cursor, the Fear of the Byte: Affective Responses to Word Processors," *Computers and Composition* (1985 Special Issue), Bullock describes how a small study showed that remedial students were "very reluctant to abandon their usual writing strategies" until he was willing to rethink his own "instructional strategy" (pp. 49–50). Glenn Fisher, "Word Processing—Will It Make All Kids Love to Write?" in *Instructor,* 92 (February 1983), 87–88, reports that teachers "think their students' writing is better when it is done on a word processor" (p. 88). Is it really? The profession will need to test this hypothesis soon. Glenn describes three major stumbling blocks for having students work regularly with word processing systems: limited access to computers, poor typing skills, and faculty resistance. Mimi Schwartz argues in "Computers and the Teaching of Writing," *Educational Technology,* 22 (November 1982), 27–29, that the quality of research and of writing was improved by two interrelated factors: "the use of computers to write and then to revise drafts in progress; and the use of weekly group sessions to discuss the case studies as they evolved into writing" (p. 29). Among the benefits Schwartz sees are (1) careful manuscript preparation, (2) more audience interaction, (3) fewer defensive writers, (4) revision ease, (5) more objective rereading, (6) self-confidence improvements, and (7) better planning. What summarizes much of this work is that English composition teachers have had to adapt as well to the power of the word processor, but many have been alert to forming research hypotheses. Most of the studies are still descriptive; the next step will be in producing research designs which will allow for more inferential techniques.

Some of these same points are made and elaborated upon in Lillian Bridwell, Paula Reed Nancarrow and Donald Ross's "The Writing Process and The Writing Machine: Current Research on Word Processors Relevant to the Teaching of Composition" in Beach and Bridwell, *New Directions in Composition Research* (New York: Guilford Press, 1984). Colette Daiute's "Word Processing: Can It Make Good Writers Better?" in *Electronic Learning*

(March/April 1982), 29–31, is another piece that defines the territory so that teachers can approach the problem asking the right questions about the nature of the larger process.

Such findings are disturbing to those who would hype the "computer on every desk" theory of higher education. What such initial findings suggest is that word processing pedagogies are still ill formed and that composition instruction should attend to addressing the meta-skills—purpose, coherence, rhetorical stance, audience, surprise value, voice, sustained exposition, and so forth.

One of the ways English composition researchers are solving this problem is by designing integrated prewriting, writing, and revising software. There are four noble starts: WANDAH (a.k.a. HBJ Writer), Wordsworth II (of late, Wordswork), DRAFT, and WARRANT. More are either under development or in the process of being released, e.g., Deborah Holdstein's HoltWriter, D. C. Heath's QUILL Planner and Publisher (BBN), Xerox PARC's Notecards, but some of these integrated packages have a more detailed legacy in the literature.

Ruth Von Blum and Michael E. Cohen in "WANDAH: Writing-Aid AND Author's Helper," in William Wresch, ed., *The Computer in Composition Instruction: A Writer's Tool* (Urbana, Ill.: NCTE, 1984), pp. 154–173, review the steps they took in order to design, develop, and evaluate an integrated software package. WANDAH has three major components: a word processor, a set of prewriting aids, and a set of editing, reviewing, and revising tools at the thematic, stylistic, and grammatical levels. The insights Von Blum and Cohen have about the development process are quite good. They discovered early a central paradox of software development in English composition, namely, "We learned that all of our proposed writing aids had analogues in actual classroom practice and that none of them had unanimous support" (p. 169). They also admit their tactical errors and give us a refreshingly honest assessment of the state of WANDAH as an evolving system.

Wordsworth II was a cooperative venture of English teachers and computer scientists at Michigan Technological University. Cynthia L. Selfe in "Wordsworth II: Process-Based CAI for College Composition Teachers" (Wresch, pp. 174–190) tells us that this integrated software package consists of eight modules that supplement composition assignments in description, narration, classification, evaluation, persuasion, writing, in personal journals, comparison and contrast, and writing about literature. Selfe's comments on formative evaluation of software are accurate in that the original student experimental groups "found ways to sabotage the programs." Selfe also describes how their integrated software supplements regular composition instruction when neophyte writers venture into the university's Language Laboratory. Writers can work on different modules such as PLANNING, POLISHING, EARLY, MIDDLE, or LATE. The teachers also can access Wordsworth II's files to monitor a writer's progress on particular modules.

DRAFT is another computer-based writing environment which has been designed and developed at Carnegie-Mellon University. Christine M. Neuwirth in "Toward the Design of a Flexible, Computer-Based Writing Environment" (Wresch, pp. 191–205) iterates the goals of their software development project. She writes, "The goals of the computer program are to provide writers, teachers, and researchers with a flexible, integrated, and easily used system that can (1) guide writers during the process of composing, (2) aid teachers in diagnosing problems and fostering change in students' composing strategies, (3) allow researchers to record the evolving processes and products of writers as they perform under natural or experimental conditions, and (4) provide all these users with a screen–oriented text editor to help them carry out their activities." (191) Neuwirth's discussion of feedback is excellent as is the discussion regarding how composition researchers may use DRAFT as a data collection instrument.

Such research has continued at Carnegie-Mellon with the

development of WARRANT, another integrated system which capitalizes on the latest computer interfaces, i.e., multiple windows, high resolution bit-map display graphics (as in the MacIntosh), and large-screen computer workstations. In other words, areas of the computer screen are reserved for different writing activities such as a text window, a plan window, a note card window, and a comment window. David S. Kaufer, Cheryl Geisler, Christine Neuwirth, and Preston Covey in "WARRANT: A Flexible Computer Environment for Critical Reading, Reasoning, and Writing" (First-Year Report to the Fund for the Improvement of Postsecondary Education, March 1, 1985) report their progress, most of the accomplishments thus far being tied to the organization and collection of protocols from expert writers, novice writers, and a single composition class.

The real measure of merit for determining the worth of word processing as a pedagogy is some years away, I would assert. It will occur when a notable writer somewhere in our future (who at this moment may be only sixteen years old) writes an autobiographical testimonial to the joy of discovering language and the power of written ideas while at a computer terminal in a public high school. All of the good work with word processors now being done is merely preparation.

III. TOWARD EFFECTIVE COMPUTER–ASSISTED INSTRUCTION IN COMPOSITION

Whence cometh CAI in English composition? Marian Beard's "Computer-Assisted Instruction: The Best of ERIC, 1973–May 1976" is a good place to trace the roots of computer-assisted instruction in the pre-microcomputer age. Among the references are specific applications including the PLATO materials as well as some indicators for training teachers to discover and use computers in their classrooms. But the world of CAI then was largely a world of drill and practice, a land of true-false and multiple choice. Paul L. Briand's "Technology in the Teaching of Composition," Paper for the Conference of College Composition and

Communication, 1978 (ERIC: ED 162 324) points out the context for computer-assisted instruction and enumerates the kinds of computer-assisted instruction which were prevalent, namely matters mechanical. Thus the English teacher is freed to discuss matters of content, organization, and style—an argument which I still find most persuasive.

Among the programs devoted to helping writers master the mechanics of writing, one of the first and also one of the most thorough was Susan Wittig's DIALOGUE, which was developed at the University of Texas at Austin under a grant from the National Science Foundation. Wittig gives an overview of the forty-two lesson modules in "DIALOGUE: Computer-Based English Drill and Practice," *Pipeline,* 4 (1978), 20–22; she also reasons about the sentence-combining with grammar pedagogy which formed the basic design notion for these programs. Michael G. Southwell in "The COMP-LAB Writing Modules: Computer-Assisted Grammar Instruction" (Wresch, pp. 91–104) presents a strong argument for requiring computer-assisted instruction for "students whose writing exhibits severe problems of correctness and clarity" (p. 91). Southwell along with his colleagues, Mary Epes and Carolyn Kirkpatrick, has emphasized focused practice on common problems for basic writing students, e.g., noun plural forms, verbs and subjects, verb agreement, past-tense verb forms, and *to be* verbs.

Eventually, researchers wanted to supplement drill and practice programs with more "open-ended" computer-assisted instruction. Hugh Burns's "Stimulating Invention in English Composition Through Computer-Assisted Instruction" (dissertation, University of Texas, 1979) helped break the notion that all CAI in English composition had to be drill and practice. Three computer programs in the INVENT series were written to help writers learn and use three popular prewriting strategies: Aristotle's enthymeme topics, Burke's dramatistic pentad, and the Young-Becker-Pike tagmemic matrix. The primary findings were (1) CAI could be programmed that would encourage growth both in number and sophistication of ideas; (2) questioning dialogues could help students articulate, refine, and preserve their ideas; (3) these dialogues could ignore content in favor of perspective and still help students begin writing; and (4) theories of creativity based on intersecting content and perspective were programmable. With George Culp, Burns summarizes the study in "Stimulating Invention in English Composition Through Computer-Assisted Instruction," *Educational Technology,* 20 (August 1980), 5–10; also "The Writer's Tool: Computing as a Way of Brainstorming," in Janice Hays et al., eds., *The Writer's Mind* (Urbana, Ill.: NCTE, 1983). What second thoughts he has had are revealed in "Recollections of First Generation Computer-Assisted Prewriting." There, he lists five goals for the development of second-generation computer-assisted instruction in rhetorical invention: "better rhetorical connections, better accounting for content and audience, better instructional and elaboration routines, better color, graphic, and sound integration, and better intuitive models of inquiry (Wresch, ed., *The Computer in Composition Instruction,* p. 32).

Helen J. Schwartz's SEEN and ORGANIZE programs extended this research and subjected invention to peer review ("SEEN: A Tutorial and User Network for Hypothesis Testing" [Wresch, pp. 47–62]). She writes, "The name SEEN, an acronym for Seeing-Eye Elephant Network, refers to the program's three parts, each providing in the learning environment an element widely advocated in composition theory" (p. 48). Valarie Arms at Drexel University extended this open-ended approach to the technical writing context in a program called CREATE with promising results, and she describes her approach in "The Computer Kids and Composition," 1982 (ERIC: ED 217 489).

Dawn Rodrigues and Raymond J. Rodrigues are among those teachers looking at the computer's potential and complete integration in the composition classroom. In "The Computer-Based Writing Program from Load to Print," *EJ,* 73 (January 1984), 27–30, Raymond J. Rodrigues reviews and examines what a computer-based composition course using microcomputers would be for the total course—breaking down the composition curriculum into prewriting, word processing, and editing. One of the major ideas Rodrigues presents is a way for the teacher to be actively involved in the computer-based evaluation and editing. He recommends (1) using the split screen options to present student text alongside teacher comments and (2) keying the comments to other exercise programs, e.g., "In evaluating a student's writing on a computer screen we might hit one key and automatically type SUBJ-VERB AGR or TOPIC SENT? or whatever other comments we most commonly make. If a student needs exercises to improve specific weaknesses, we can direct that student toward electronic workbook-style exercises to work on grammar, mechanics. . ." (p. 30). One of the important research issues is determining a way to coach particular students on particular mechanical matters in themes they are actually writing. In "Computer-Based Creative Problem Solving" (Wresch, pp. 34–46), the Rodrigueses provide variations on the theme of computer-assisted prewriting and organizing. They write, "It seems a logical procedure for an instructor to provide as many invention techniques as possible for students, as well as to make it relatively simple for the student to use those techniques" (p. 42).

To genuinely spark creativity is an often unarticulated goal of some who are English teachers by day and computer hackers by night. Most teachers want to nurture more than an appreciation of language and its correct use. They want to nurture discovery and other creative instincts through language, so they leave the drill-and-practice mentality far behind and look at the computer as a creative machine slouching toward Silicon Valley. Stephen Marcus's "COMPUPOEM: A Computer Writing Activity," *EJ*, 71 (February 1982), 96–99, describes such a computer-assisted activity in which syntactic cues prompt a young student, probably in elementary school or junior high, to compose a short poem. The activities surrounding the program, such as "Martian Rain," keep the writer's on-line motivation generally high.

More recently, a special double issue of *Computers and the*

Humanities, 18, (Nos. 3–4, 1984) was devoted to computer-assisted instruction. While only a few articles are related directly to teaching language arts, the several articles represent the state of the art in the humanities and social sciences. Among the pieces, Hugh Burns's "The Challenge for Computer-Assisted Rhetoric" outlines what intelligent strategies the computer program will have to emulate in order to assist a writer with invention, arrangement, and style.

Despite Macrorie's polemic against Percival, the research and development of text analysis software, feedback systems, and automated composition evaluation is alive and well. Allan J. Moe in "Analyzing Texts with Computers," *Educational Technology,* 20 (July 1980), 29–31, reviews these capabilities in the areas of recognizing vocabulary, word strings, syntax, and readability.

In the area of feedback systems, there have been a few attempts to provide a mixed initiative system in which the instructor uses the computer to manage many of the instructional materials. The Exxon Educational Foundation funded one such program called RSVP (Response System with Variable Prescriptions). Kamala Anandam, the principal investigator, describes the system in "Effectiveness of a Computer-Based Feedback System for Writing," *Journal of Computer-Based Instruction,* 6 (May 1980), 125–33. The Exxon research report is also available: Kamala Anandam, et. al., *RSVP: Feedback Program for Individualized Analysis of Writing* (New York: Exxon Education Foundation; ERIC: ED 191 511). Generally, the study itself is inconclusive as to whether writing improved. The RSVP process involved having each instructor read the student's essays, then mark computer cards which would deliver a hard copy of prescriptive remarks to the student. In other words, the system sought to maximize the generic feedback available through the programmed handbook, yet insure that a human instructor was still in control of the instructional process. Lorne Kotler reported on the trends of this elaborate feedback system in "Some Trends in RSVP Feedback to English Students," *TIES* (*Technological Innovations in Educational Settings*), 6 (January 1982), 5. RSVP is indeed an after-the-fact feedback system and basically content and context-free. Where it is strong, it is strong because of these features. Ironically, where it is weak, it is also because of these features. Nevertheless, the project was ambitious and exploratory—and one which English professionals ought to know more about; see *RSVP: Feedback Program for Individualized Analysis of Writing. Manual for Faculty Users, Part I: Analyzing Students' Writing* (New York: Exxon Educational Foundation, 1979; ERIC: ED 1901 67). Work is continuing at Miami-Dade Community College on CAMELOT, a feedback system spinoff which would capitalize on RSVP's strengths as a manager of instructional technology with increased portability.

More press has been devoted to Bell Laboratories' "Writer's Workbench" than any of the other automated text analysis and feedback systems. Kathleen Kiefer and Charles R. Smith of Colorado State University in "Improving Student's Revising and Editing: The Writer's Workbench System" (Wresch, pp. 65–82) write an excellent overview of how an automated tool for business writing came to be converted into a tool for the composition classroom. In their research, Kiefer and Smith have been careful to quantify where possible, not only citing results and descriptions of the various programs, (e.g. ORGANIZATION, DEVELOPMENT, FINDBE, DICTION, SUGGEST, SPELL, PASSIVE, and STYLE) but also attending to the teacher's grading. Interestingly, teachers have not saved time in their evaluations of essays, but many of them admit to looking beyond the mechanics of the essay. Work will continue at Colorado State to tailor the responses more precisely and to offer appropriate explanations of *how* to interpret what the workbench programs point out. Among the articles which describe these efforts are Kiefer and Smith, "Textual Analysis with Computers: Tests of Bell Laboratories' Computer Software," *Research in the Teaching of English,* 17 (1983), 201–14; Lorinda L. Cherry, "Writing Tools," *IEEE Transactions on Communications,* 30 (January 1982), 100–105; Nina MacDonald et al., "The Writer's Workbench: Computer Aids for Text Analysis," *IEEE Transactions on Communication,* 30 (January 1982), 105–10; and Lawrence T. Frase et al.,

"Computer Aids for Text Assessment and Writing Instruction," *NSPI Journal* (November 1981), 21–24.

At IBM, the counterpart to Workbench has been EPISTLE. Again, the impetus for the research and its associated implementations has been to provide the business world with a tool for assisting the business writer. Lance A. Miller describes the project's goals and the natural language premises which underpin the software in "Project EPISTLE: A System for the Automatic Analysis of Business Correspondence," *Proceedings of the American Association for Artificial Intelligence Conference* (August 1980), 280–82. Miller, G. E. Heidorn, and K. Jensen also chronicle the evolving development of this parsing tool in "Text-Critiquing with the EPISTLE System: An Author's Aid to Better Syntax" (National Computer Conference Paper, May 1981). EPISTLE and Writer's Workbench are tools which will be more and more effective, especially when the suggestions they make to an author can be incorporated immediately into the text and when writers thoroughly understand the controls they now have over the revising and editing process.

What would be particularly impressive would be taking the information which such text evaluation programs provide and deriving "on the fly" individualized lessons for the student. Philip D. Gillis in "Refining Computer-Based Invention Through Computer-Aided Evaluation and 'State-of-the-Art' Tutorial Design," *Journal of Educational Technology Systems,* 13 (1984–85), 315–23, investigates instructional strategies which could produce beneficial prewriting experiences, thus modelling what expert tutors would do if giving individual writing instruction. Look for more such studies to illustrate how well these prewriting, organizing, editing, and revising skills are integrated with text evaluation programs.

IV. EPILOGUE: TOWARD INTELLIGENT "TEACHING COMPOSITION" SYSTEMS

Computers did not just appear in the English classroom; they represent a synthesis of technologies, experiments, trials, and investments. It is fun today to read old soundings, especially those few bold predictions for the English classroom of the future. In such pieces as Joseph Auciello's "On Using Computers in English," *EJ*, 57 (May 1968), 650–51, English classrooms take on "Tomorrow Land" characteristics. Margot Critchfield's "Beyond CAI: Computers as Personal Intellectual Tools," *Educational Technology*, 19 (October 1979) is another piece which sounds fanfares of evolutionary hope. In fact, it will be interesting (if not fun or too embarrassing) to read this "sounding" essay in ten years. So much is happening as networks of scholars and teachers experiment with the computer in the composition classroom. Indeed, so much is happening as the computing machine becomes a "learning" machine. The entire research area of intelligent human-machine communications, whether written, spoken, or graphic, is such an intriguing idea that inquisitive researchers in linguistics, speech, and written communication will be unable to resist eventual classroom applications. English composition practitioners should become a foremost beneficiary. Also, as more and more research is completed in intelligent computer-assisted instruction (ICAI), the English composition teacher must do more than note it. English educators will have to incorporate "smart" algorithms for representing writing expertise, for capturing writing performance, and intelligently providing the appropriate feedback. These issues were always there, and a motivated, intelligent teacher succeeded. Likewise, an intelligent computer program will be more likely to succeed than one which cannot understand a writer's typographical errors, strategies, blunders, and goals. But all of that is another essay. So many algorithms, so little time.

Index

Names

Subjects

Titles

40 72